AF411671

SURFACE ENGINEERING GEOMETRY FOR COMPUTER-AIDED DESIGN AND MANUFACTURE

SURFACE ENGINEERING GEOMETRY FOR COMPUTER-AIDED DESIGN AND MANUFACTURE

DING QIULIN
Associate Professor, Nanjing Aeronautical Institute
People's Republic of China

and

B. J. DAVIES
Professor of Manufacturing Technology and
Head of Manufacturing and Machine Tools Division
Department of Mechanical Engineering
University of Manchester Institute of Science and Technology

ELLIS HORWOOD LIMITED
Publishers · Chichester

Halsted Press: a division of
JOHN WILEY & SONS
New York · Chichester · Brisbane · Toronto

First published in 1987 by
ELLIS HORWOOD LIMITED
Market Cross House, Cooper Street,
Chichester, West Sussex, PO19 1EB, England
The publisher's colophon is reproduced from James Gillison's drawing of the ancient Market Cross, Chichester.

Distributors:

Australia and New Zealand:
JACARANDA WILEY LIMITED
GPO Box 859, Brisbane, Queensland 4001, Australia

Canada:
JOHN WILEY & SONS CANADA LIMITED
22 Worcester Road, Rexdale, Ontario, Canada

Europe and Africa:
JOHN WILEY & SONS LIMITED
Baffins Lane, Chichester, West Sussex, England

North and South America and the rest of the world:
Halsted Press: a division of
JOHN WILEY & SONS
605 Third Avenue, New York, NY 10158, USA

British Library Cataloguing in Publication Data
Ding, Qiulin
Surface engineering geometry for computer-aided design and manufacture. —
(Ellis Horwood series in mechanical engineering).
1. Engineering design — Data processing
I. Title   II. Davies, B. J. (Beaumont John)
620.'.00425'0285   TA174

Library of Congress CIP data available

ISBN 0–7458–0181–1 (Ellis Horwood Limited)
ISBN 0–470–20997–6 (Halsted Press)

Typeset in Times by Heather FitzGibbon of Fleet
Printed in Great Britain by Unwin Bros., Woking

Table of Contents

Foreword   13

Preface   15

Acknowledgements   17

1   Curve and Surface Geometry
    1.1   Curve Vector Equation   19
        1.1.1   Vector function   19
        1.1.2   Curve vector equation   20
    1.2   Tangent Vectors   23
        1.2.1   Differentiation of a vector function   23
        1.2.2   Applications of tangent vectors   25
    1.3   Curve Nature Parameter Equation   26
    1.4   The Local Coordinate System and the Frenet–Serret Formulae   29
        1.4.1   The local coordinate system   29
        1.4.2   The Frenet–Serret formulae   30
    1.5   Curvature and Torsion   32
        1.5.1   Curvature   32
        1.5.2   Torsion   34
    1.6   Surface Vector Equation   36
    1.7   Partial Derivative Vectors   40

1.8 Tangent Plane and Unit Normal Vector 42

1.9 Curvature of a Surface 43

   1.9.1 Normal curvatures 43

   1.9.2 Principal curvatures 45

   1.9.3 Gaussian curvature 46

1.10 Advantages of Parametric Description 46

   References 48

2 Geometric Transformations and Projections

2.1 Introduction 49

2.2 Two-dimensional Transformations 50

   2.2.1 Two-dimensional transformation formulae 50

   2.2.2 Homogeneous coordinates 54

   2.2.3 Homogeneous transformations 55

   2.2.4 Concatenated transformation 59

2.3 Three-dimensional Transformations 61

   2.3.1 Three-dimensional transformation formulae 61

   2.3.2 Concatenated transformation 63

2.4 Projections 64

   2.4.1 Orthogonal projections 64

   2.4.2 Perspective projections 65

   References 67

3 Ruled Surfaces

3.1 Introduction 69

3.2 Ruled Surfaces 69

3.3 Tabulated Cylinders 72

3.4 Developable Surfaces 72

3.5 Surfaces of Revolution 74

3.6 Bi-cubic Expressions of Ruled Surfaces 75

   References 76

4 Spline Curves and Surfaces

4.1 Physical Splines and Mathematical Splines 78

   4.1.1 Physical splines 78

   4.1.2 Mechanical background 78

   4.1.3 Mathematical splines 79

4.2 Cubic Splines 80

   4.2.1 The first-derivative form 80

   4.2.2 The second-derivative form 86

   4.2.3 Oscillation problems 89

4.3 Parametric Cubic Splines 90

   4.3.1 The accumulated chord length parameter for cubic splines 91

   4.3.2 Polar angle parametric cubic splines 94

4.4 Bi-cubic Surface Patch 97

4.5   Bi-cubic Spline Surfaces   102
         4.5.1   Bi-cubic patch with irregular boundaries   102
         4.5.2   Bi-cubic spline surfaces   104
         4.5.3   Parametrization of bi-cubic spline surfaces   108
4.6   Example   108
         References   110

5   Bezier Curves and Surfaces
5.1   Introduction   112
5.2   Bezier Curves   113
         5.2.1   Bezier cubic curves   113
         5.2.2   Bezier curves of degree n 117
5.3   Bezier Curve Algorithms   123
         5.3.1   The de Casteljau algorithm   123
         5.3.2   Subdivision algorithm   126
         5.3.3   Degree elevation   126
         5.3.4   The inverse algorithm   127
5.4   Composite Bezier Curves   128
5.5   Bezier Surfaces   131
         5.5.1   Bezier bi-cubic surfaces   131
         5.5.2   The relationship between Bezier form and Ferguson form   133
         5.5.3   Bezier surfaces   135
5.6   Composite Bezier Surfaces   136
5.7   Three Forms of Bezier Curve (Appendix)   138
         References   140

6   B-spline Curves and Surfaces
6.1   Introduction   141
6.2   B-splines (1)   141
         6.2.1   Cubic B-splines   142
         6.2.2   The cubic B-spline curve span   142
         6.2.3   Continuity conditions between spans   144
         6.2.4   From continuity conditions to B-splines   145
6.3   B-spline Curves   147
         6.3.1   Geometric properties of a B-spline curve   147
         6.3.2   Algorithms of B-spline curves   148
         6.3.3   The fitting and design procedure   150
6.4   B-splines (2)   151
6.5   Non-uniform B-spline Curves   158
         6.5.1   Non-uniform B-spline curves with degree 1   158
         6.5.2   Non-uniform B-spline curves with degree 2   159
         6.5.3   Non-uniform B-spline curves with degree 3   160
         6.5.4   Non-uniform B-spline curves with degree $(m-1)$ 162
6.6   B-spline Curves with Multiple Vertices   162
6.7   B-spline Curves with Multiple Knots   166

6.8	Bi-cubic B-spline Surfaces	168
	6.8.1 The patch of a bi-cubic B-spline surface	168
	6.8.2 Bi-cubic B-spline surfaces	170
	6.8.3 Algorithms of bi-cubic B-spline surfaces	170
6.9	Non-uniform Bi-cubic B-spline Surfaces	174
6.10	Further Aspects of B-splines	174
	References	175

7   Rational Curves and Surfaces

7.1	Ball Curves	176
7.2	Rational Ball Curves	178
7.3	Rational Extension of Other Curves	182
	7.3.1 Rational Bezier curves	182
	7.3.2 Rational B-spline curves	184
7.4	Degenerate Rational Curves	186
7.5	Special Rational Curves	191
	7.5.1 The generalized conic segment	191
	7.5.2 The linear parameter segment	192
7.6	Rational Splines	193
	7.6.1 Rational splines	193
	7.6.2 The rational fitting of circular arcs and straight lines	195
7.7	Rational Surfaces	197
	7.7.1 Rational surface patch with sixteen weights	197
	7.7.2 Rational surface patch with eight weights	199
	7.7.3 Rational surface patch with four weights	201
	7.7.4 Rational surface patch with two weights	201
	7.7.5 Applications	202
7.8	Family of rational curves in CAGD (Appendix)	205
	References	209

8   Fairing of Curves and Surfaces

8.1	Concepts of Fairing	210
	8.1.1 Design and fairing	210
	8.1.2 Mathematical fairing	210
	8.1.3 Fairing criteria	211
8.2	The Local Spring-back Method	211
	8.2.1 Generating a spline	212
	8.2.2 Indicators of the fairing	212
	8.2.3 Adjusting the poor data points	213
	8.2.4 Application	215
8.3	The Circle Rate Method	215
	8.3.1 Calculating circle rates	215
	8.3.2 Indicators of the fairing	216
	8.3.3 Adjusting the position of data points	216

8.4	Energy Method	218
	8.4.1 Indicator of the fairing	218
	8.4.2 Equations of the fairing	218
	8.4.3 Fairing with weights	224
8.5	Surface Mesh Fairing	225
8.6	Surface Fairing	226
	8.6.1 Energy method	226
	8.6.2 Interactive fairing	227
	References	228

9 Tool Paths for Surface Machining
9.1	Introduction	229
9.2	Two-dimensional Tool Paths	230
	9.2.1 Offset curves	231
	9.2.2 Linear approximation	233
	9.2.3 Circular arc approximation	235
9.3	Two- and-a-half-dimensional Tool Paths	236
9.4	Three-dimensional Tool Paths	239
	9.4.1 Offset surfaces	239
	9.4.2 Tool paths along parameter curves on surfaces	242
	9.4.3 Tool paths along intersection curves between a surface and a plane	246
	9.4.4 Tool paths along curves between two surfaces	247
	9.4.5 Part surface, drive surface and check surface	251
	9.4.6 Three-axis, four-axis and five-axis operations	252
9.5	Tool-path Simulation and Verification	253
9.6	Tool-path Software	253
	9.6.1 APT	254
	9.6.2 CADDS 4 of Computervision	254
	9.6.3 MEDUSA of Cambridge	255
	9.6.4 NC programming of Intergraph	255
	References	256

10 The Surface Intersection Problem
10.1	Introduction	257
10.2	Principle of Solution	258
	10.2.1 Parameter equations	258
	10.2.2 Implicit equations	259
	10.2.3 Mixed form equations	260
10.3	Methods of Solution	260
10.4	Intersections between Surfaces and a Plane	263
10.5	Intersection between Surfaces (1)	268
	10.5.1 The hunting phase	269
	10.5.2 The tracing phase	271
	10.5.3 The ordering phase	272

10.6   Intersection between Surfaces (2)   272
        10.6.1   The de Casteljau subdivision algorithm   272
        10.6.2   Detecting boxes   274
        10.6.3   Computing the intersection   274
                 References   276

11   Hidden Surface Removal
11.1   Introduction   277
11.2   Depth Comparisons   278
        11.2.1   Visibility between two points   278
        11.2.2   Visibility between a point and a line   280
        11.2.3   Visibility between a point and a planar polygon   281
        11.2.4   Visibility between a point and a surface patch   282
11.3   Coherence Principles   284
11.4   Sorting Algorithms   288
11.5   Silhouette Curves   290
11.6   Hidden Surface Removal   292
        References   293

12   Implementation of Surface Modelling
12.1   Choosing a Surface Modelling System   295
12.2   Implementing a Surface Modelling System   297
12.3   Using a Surface Modelling System   299
        References   309

13   Environment of Surface Modelling (B. J. Davies)
13.1   Introduction   311
13.2   The Three Generations of CAD/CAM Systems   311
        13.2.1   First-generation CAD/CAM systems   311
        13.2.2   Second-generation CAD/CAM systems   312
        13.2.3   Third-generation CAD/CAM systems   312
13.3   The Typical Workstation for a Third-generation CAD/CAM System   313
13.4   Micro CAD/CAM Hardware   313
        13.4.1   The microprocessor   313
        13.4.2   Main memory and mass storage   315
        13.4.3   Input devices   316
        13.4.4   Output devices   318
        13.4.5   Communications interfaces   318
13.5   The Software   319
        13.5.1   Operating systems   319
        13.5.2   High-level languages   319
        13.5.3   Database management software   320
        13.5.4   Micro CAD application software   321
        13.5.5   Microcomputer CAM application software   322

13.6   A Typical Turnkey Microcomputer CAD/CAM System   323

    13.6.1   Computervision's Personal Designer   323

    13.6.2   Intergraph's Micro II system   324

    13.6.3   List of microcomputer CAD/CAM systems   325

13.7   Choosing a Microcomputer CAD/CAM System   326

    13.7.1   Turnkey systems   326

    13.7.2   Key facilities   326

    13.7.3   Key capabilities   327

13.8   The Future of Microcomputer CAD/CAM Systems   327

    13.8.1   Future hardware development   327

    13.8.2   Future software development   328

    References   328

14   Recent Developments of Surface Modelling (B. J. Davies)

14.1   The Capabilities of Advanced Surface Modelling   329

    14.1.1   Surface definition model   329

    14.1.2   Surface definition procedure   330

    14.1.3   Surface generation   330

    14.1.4   Surface editing   331

    14.1.5   Surface data extraction   331

    14.1.6   Surface display   331

    14.1.7   Surface software compatibility   332

14.2   Recent Developments of Advanced Surface Modelling   332

    14.2.1   Method development   332

    14.2.2   Unified surface and solid modelling   335

    14.2.3   Adding artificial intelligence in surface modelling systems   335

    14.2.4   Surface modelling in a microcomputer environment   336

    References   337

Index   338

Foreword

The advent of the computer resulted, a decade or so later, in the development of CAD/CAM, which may be considered to be one of the most vital transformations that has taken place in industry for a very long time.

Until the advent of CAD/CAM, accurate parts were defined by straight lines and circles, with the exception of threads and gear flanks. Other forms could be obtained only by copy-machines, either lathes, or grinders or milling machines. Models were hand-made templates or 3-D masters, which gave only an approximate definition of the required shape, hence a lack of accuracy and reliability.

It was immediately obvious that, if properly developed, CAD could bring the important advantages of shorter delays, better accuracy, improved data transmission and reduced cost.

The problem so raised has different aspects since the objects to be designed and manufactured belong to three major categories:

- objects playing a fundamental role in the functioning and the efficiency of the assembly in which they are included; a good example is the blade of a turbine, the hull of a boat, or the body of a racing car. The shape arrived at by successive experiments and modifications must be reproduced with the best accuracy available;

- objects which have purely or mainly an aesthetic purpose; the model, which is generally hand-made, must be correctly reproduced, but the accuracy is not as important as in the preceding case, but attention should be paid to shape continuity, and sometimes curvature, in order to obtain a 'smooth', or 'fair', or 'sweet' shape;

- objects without aesthetical requirements and which do not need great accuracy, except in zones related to assembly with other parts of welding, gluing, crimping, etc. An example is the inner panels of a car body.

The first development of CAD was to express with numbers the shape of an existing object, e.g. aircraft, boat hull, turbine blade or car body. The traditional sequence for manufacturing such products included several different steps, e.g. measuring offsets, tracing cross-sections, adjusting templates, carving cross-sections in a model, interpolating the intervals by hand, copy milling, and finishing and polishing the model. CAD could bypass most of these steps, including the design of the original shape, but was used for translating an existing shape, and the Coons' method is perfectly adapated to this process.

For the design of aesthetic objects, some systems can be used by non-mathematicians, hence avoiding the risk of distortion or drift by the operator in his interpretation of the stylist's work.

There is a large field for mathematicians in CAD/CAM, and the solutions are many; most, if not all, of them take advantage of the properties of parametric spaces. Professor Ding's book describes the solutions most commonly used in industry.

To be truly valid, a solution must offer the following features:

- be applicable to a great variety and flexibility of curves and surfaces: lines, circles, conics, cubics and, in case of need, curves of a higher degree;
- be easy to compute; hence the advantage of polynomials over harmonics;
- have a shape which is independent of the system of coordinates;
- be easily understood by non-mathematicians: stylists, designers, method technicians, operators, and others who know geometry rather well but have had no training in analysis.

CAD software now has a great variety of operations available: windowing, scaling, zooming, rotating, hidden line removal, perspective, colour, reflection lines, etc.

The cost of powerful CAD hardware and software has been reduced to the point when now it is no longer available only to large and wealthy companies. Small companies can now afford CAD systems.

The CAD-office is now equipped with CAD stations, drawing machines and plotters. Some companies have found it useful to include milling machines that can manufacture 3-D objects rapidly either in soft material or in ferrous alloys to check the programs, because seeing and touching an object are better than looking at the most beautiful drawing.

Mathematics has clearly play a major role in the development of CAD, but there is still much to be discovered and invented in this field, and this book provides plenty of food for thought for CAD users and developers.

Paris, February 1987   Pierre E. Bezier

Preface

Surface modelling for CAD/CAM (computer-aided design and computer-aided manufacture) is used to design the curved surfaces of products such as aircraft, ships and automobiles, and is rapidly increasing in many fields. Not so long ago, all surface modelling systems required mainframe computers, because only they were powerful enough to run three-dimensional surface modelling software whose application in CAD/CAM can improve the performance even of companies of small size. Surface modelling is now a very important part of CAD/CAM systems with wide and increasing use in manufacturing industry.

Microcomputer systems are now also powerful enough to create cutter centre path NC data for ball-ended cutters to machine the surfaces defined by the surface modelling techniques described. Machined, sculptured surfaces can be produced by this means, requiring very little hand-finishing. This opens up a whole new application area for surface modelling in CAD/CAM, for example, designing and manufacturing moulds for injection of blow moulding. In the past such products were produced by manual means, which requires great skill and much time, and produces only a very approximate result.

At the other end of the technological scale, developments in surface modelling in the manufacture of surfaces in aircraft and missiles enable manufacture to be closely integrated with design. They also offer a route for speeding up and automating tooling for forming sheet or carbon fibre composites or machining from solid billets of AL Alloy or titanium.

The ability of microcomputer CAD systems to display surface models as colour-shaded images or surface nets greatly enhances the designer's appreciation of the shape of the surface, enables him to identify problems in shape and blend areas, and helps to make surface manufacture via surface modelling a rapid, user-friendly, and economical technique which will be much more used in the future.

The purpose of this book is to enable readers to understand, apply and develop many aspects of surface modelling, bridging the substantial gap between the mathematics and the engineering applications. It will enable the reader to progress logically from the fundamental basis of solutions through the mathematical method to the computer solutions, systems implementation, environment and new developments.

The book can be divided into five parts:

BASIS: Chapters 1, 2

METHOD: Chapters 3, 4, 5, 6, 7

COMPUTING: Chapters 8, 9, 10, 11

SURFACE MODELLING SYSTEM IMPLEMENTATION AND ENVIRONMENT:
   Chapters 12, 13

NEW DEVELOPMENTS: Chapter 14

There is significant discussion on the major mathematical methods for defining and computing surface models in engineering, with descriptions of practical applications of the methods, reinforced with instances of new developments. The book reflects the author's extensive experience in surface modelling software design, industrial applications (including aviation, motor cars, ships, etc.) and teaching, and also that of professional colleagues referred to in the references.

The book provides a comprehensive treatment of the subject for engineers. It has a firm, but simply explained, mathematical basis and is aimed at design and production engineers and research workers and students involved with CAD/CAM surface modelling.

Ding Qiu-Lin
Address: Nanjing Aeronautical Institute,
The People's Republic of China

B. J. Davies
UMIST, Manchester, UK
30th December, 1986

Acknowledgements

Thanks are due to:

Professor P. Bezier (ex-Director of Renault and Honorary Professor of C.N.A.M.), H. Nowacki (Technical University of Berlin), Professor Cheng Bao-Qu, Zhu Jian-Ying (Nanjing Aeronautical Institute) and Professor H. Wiele (Technical University of Magdeburg, German Democratic Republic), for their suggestions and encouragement.

The British Council, the Consulate General of the P.R. of China (in Manchester, U.K.), the State Education Commission and the Aeronautical Industry Department of the P.R. of China, the University of Manchester Institute of Science and Technology, and Nanjing Aeronautical Institute, for their support.

Dr. E.M. Trent (Birmingham University), Dr. S. Hinduja and Mr. W.A. Smith (UMIST), Stephen Lee Siang-Guan, Senior Lecturer (Nanyang Technological Institute, Singapore), Mr. Y.S. Sun (Technical University of Berlin), Mr. Z.L. Lie (Taiwan University), and Mr. L.Y. Ho, for their encouragement, and my friends and colleagues in Chinese universities, institutes and companies in this field for their co-operation.

The publisher, Ellis Horwood Ltd. (Chichester) and Series Editor, Professor J. M. Alexander, for publishing the book.

Alexander, Stocker visiting Professor of Engineering & Technology, for Ohio University, U.S.A.

Very special thanks are due to Mrs. A. Clapham for her continued help and support, and to Mrs. P. Murray for patiently typing the manuscript. Her hard work and excellent typing technique have enabled the manuscript to be completed before Professor Ding's return to China.

Finally, not to be forgotten are many anonymous workers in this field whose valuable contributions are included in surface modelling technology.

Ding Q.-L.

Davies B. J.

1

Curve and Surface Geometry

Curve and surface geometry is the underlying theory for surface modelling techniques. In this chapter, we will introduce curve and surface representation and discuss their geometric properties. We always apply vector equations for representation, analysis and synthesis of curves and surfaces because vector equations are very concise and offer a considerable economy in writing. The vector equations are a powerful tool. Vector symbols will be denoted by boldface letters and graphically with an arrow in this text.

1.1 CURVE VECTOR EQUATION

1.1.1 Vector function

Vectors, as we know from vector algebra, are quantities that depend on both magnitude and direction. Vector calculus obeys certain laws described in vector algebra.

A vector function $\mathbf{r}(t)$ means that its magnitude or direction, or both, is a function of parametric variable t. The components of the vector function $\mathbf{r}(t)$ are scalar functions $x(t)$, $y(t)$ and $z(t)$. The vector function $\mathbf{r}(t)$ may be expressed by

$$\mathbf{r}(t) = x(t)\mathbf{i} + y(t)\mathbf{j} + z(t)\mathbf{k} \tag{1.1}$$

$$(t_1 \leqslant t \leqslant t_2)$$

in which the $\mathbf{i}$, $\mathbf{j}$, $\mathbf{k}$ are unit vectors in the directions of the coordinate axes x, y, z respectively (see Fig. 1.1).

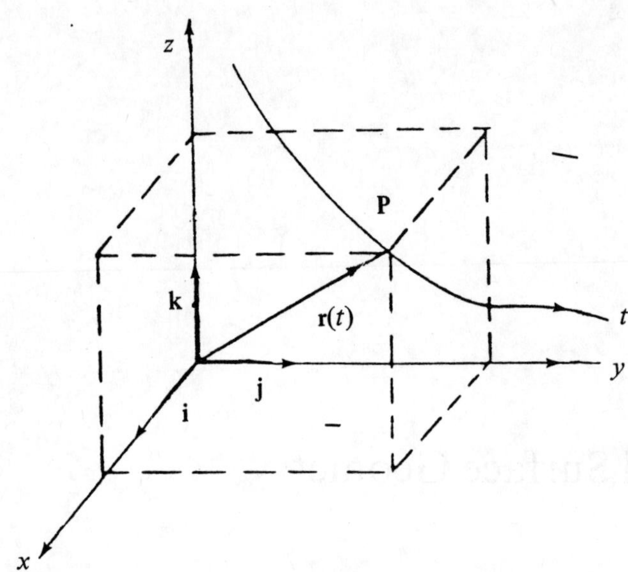

Fig. 1.1 Vector function

The vector function can be written in matrix form

$$\mathbf{r}(t) = [x(t)\, y(t)\, z(t)] \tag{1.2}$$

since the multiplying matrix $[\mathbf{i}\,\mathbf{j}\,\mathbf{k}]^{\mathrm{T}}$ is omitted for convenience.

The concepts, such as limitation, continuity, differentiation and integration, for scalar functions may be directly applied to vector functions, since the vector function can be expressed by three scalar functions. For example, the differentiation of $\mathbf{r}(t)$ can be described by

$$d\mathbf{r} = \mathbf{r}'(t)\,dt = x'(t)\,dt\,\mathbf{i} + y'(t)\,dt\,\mathbf{j} + z'(t)\,dt\,\mathbf{k}$$

and its integration by

$$\int \mathbf{r}(t)\,dt = \left[\int x(t)\,dt\right]\mathbf{i} + \left[\int y(t)\,dt\right]\mathbf{j} + \left[\int z(t)\,dt\right]\mathbf{k}$$

There is no space to prove the above results for vector functions. However, this should not prevent the reader understanding and applying the above results.

1.1.2 Curve vector equation

A point $\mathbf{P}(x,\,y,\,z)$ in 3-D space can be described by a vector $\mathbf{r}$ which positions the point $\mathbf{P}$ in relation to the origin O (see Fig. 1.1). The terms '**point**' and '**vector**' are interchangeable. A point moving in 3-D space forms a curve which may be described by a vector function

$$\mathbf{r} = \mathbf{r}(t) \tag{1.3}$$

in which t is a variable and is called a *parameter*.

(1.3) is called a vector equation of a curve. Its three component equations are as follows:

$$x = x(t)$$

$$y = y(t)$$

$$z = z(t) \tag{1.4}$$

This is a parametric representation of a curve.

In order to understand better what a parametric curve is, let us consider the case of a straight line. A straight line may be defined in the traditional manner,

$$y = mx + c$$

in which m is the slope, and c the intercept on the y-axis. Equally a straight line may also be defined parametrically; let us set the value of segment $|\mathbf{P_0P_1}| = 1$, and the value of $|\mathbf{P_0P}| = t$. It can be seen that $|\mathbf{PP_1}| = 1 - t$ (see Fig. 1.2). Then

$$\frac{\mathbf{r}(t) - \mathbf{r}(0)}{\mathbf{r}(1) - \mathbf{r}(0)} = \frac{t}{1}$$

Thus

$$\mathbf{r}(t) = (1 - t)\,\mathbf{r}(0) + t\mathbf{r}(1) \tag{1.5}$$

t is a real number which varies from 0 to 1.

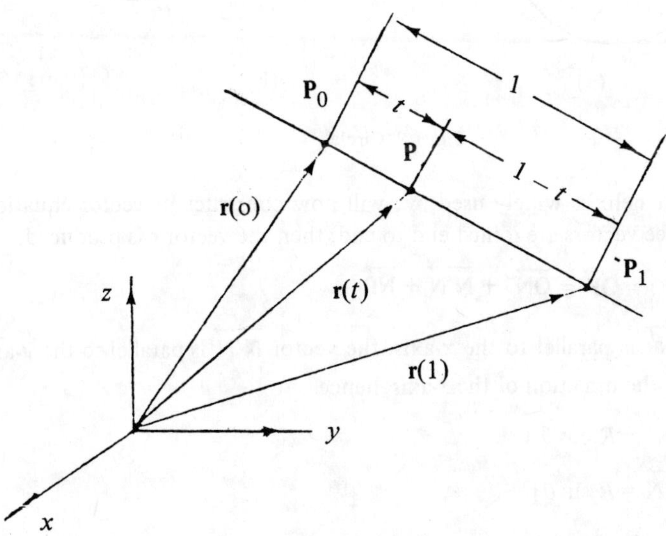

Fig. 1.2 Straight line

We will now consider a circle as another example. The equation of a circle with centre at the origin ($x = 0$, $y = 0$) is $x^2 + y^2 = R^2$. The projection of $\overrightarrow{OP}$ onto the x-axis yields the component $R \cos \theta \, \mathbf{i}$ and the projection of $\overrightarrow{OP}$ onto the y-axis yields the component $R \sin \theta \, \mathbf{j}$; thus the vector equation of the circle is

$$\mathbf{r}(\theta) = R \cos \theta \, \mathbf{i} + R \sin \theta \, \mathbf{j}$$

$$= [R \cos \theta \quad R \sin \theta]$$

Its component forms are

$$x = R \cos \theta$$

$$y = R \sin \theta$$

If the centre of the circle is not at the origin (see Fig. 1.3(b)), the vector equation is

$$\mathbf{r}(\theta) = [x_c + R \cos \theta \quad y_c + R \sin \theta] \tag{1.6}$$

in which x_c, y_c are the coordinates of the centre of the circle.

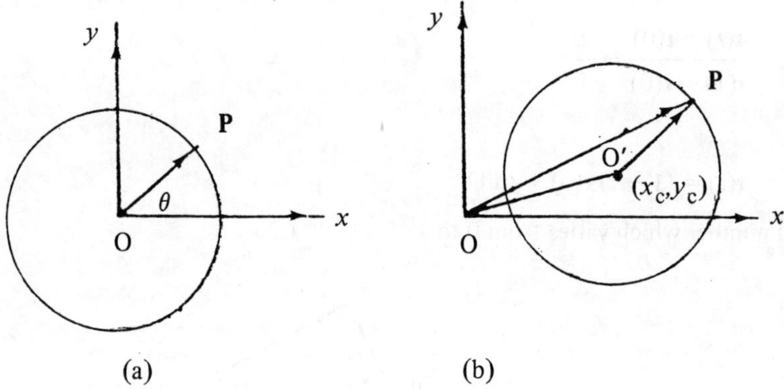

(a)　　　　　　　　　　　　　　　　　(b)

Fig. 1.3 Circle

The circular helix is widely used; we will now construct its vector equation. Fig. 1.4 shows that three vectors are joined end to end; then the vector $\mathbf{r}$ is produced.

$$\mathbf{r}(\theta) = \overrightarrow{OP} = \overrightarrow{ON'} + \overrightarrow{N'N} + \overrightarrow{NP}$$

The vector $\overrightarrow{ON'}$ is parallel to the x-axis, the vector $\overrightarrow{N'N}$ is parallel to the y-axis, and the vector $\overrightarrow{NP}$ is in the direction of the z-axis; hence

$$\overrightarrow{ON'} = R \cos \theta \, \mathbf{i}$$

$$\overrightarrow{N'N} = R \sin \theta \, \mathbf{j}$$

$$\overrightarrow{NP} = \frac{L}{2\pi} \theta \mathbf{k}$$

since the helix advances one pitch lead L in the z direction, a rotation θ produces an axial advance of $(L/2\pi)\theta$.

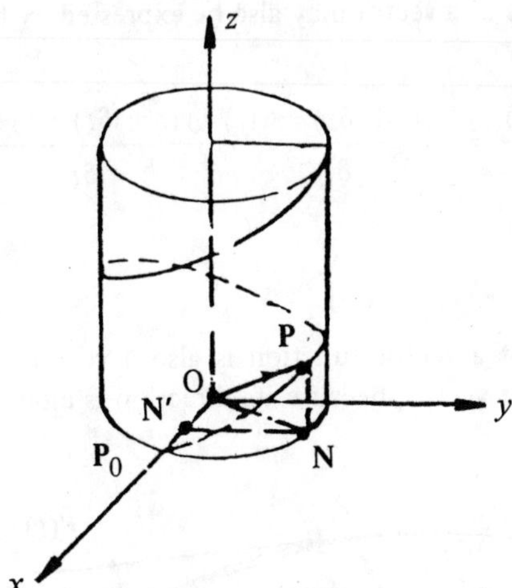

Fig. 1.4 Circular Helix

Finally, the vector equation of the helix is

$$\mathbf{r}(\theta) = R \cos \theta \, \mathbf{i} + R \sin \theta \, \mathbf{j} + \frac{L}{2\pi} \theta \mathbf{k}$$

$$= \left[R \cos \theta \quad R \sin \theta \quad \frac{L}{2\pi} \theta \right] \tag{1.7}$$

1.2 TANGENT VECTORS

1.2.1 Differentiation of a vector function

If a parameter t increases by δt, the increase in the vector function may be expressed by

$$\delta \mathbf{r}(t) = \mathbf{r}(t + \delta t) - \mathbf{r}(t)$$

Its rate of change is

$$\frac{\delta \mathbf{r}(t)}{\delta t} = \frac{\mathbf{r}(t + \delta t) - \mathbf{r}(t)}{\delta t}$$

Vector $\delta \mathbf{r}(t)$ is parallel to the chord vector $\overrightarrow{\mathbf{PP}_1}$ (see Fig. 1.5). If $\delta t > 0$, $\delta \mathbf{r}/\delta t$ and the chord vector $\overrightarrow{\mathbf{PP}_1}$ are in the same direction; if $\delta t < 0$, the vectors are in opposite directions.

If $\delta t \to 0$, the limit of $\delta \mathbf{r}/\delta t$ is called the derivative vector, and is denoted by $\mathbf{r}'(t)$:

$$\mathbf{r}'(t) = \lim_{\delta t \to 0} \frac{\delta \mathbf{r}(t)}{\delta t} = \frac{d\mathbf{r}(t)}{dt}$$

Since the rate of change of a vector may also be expressed by the rate of change of the component of the vector

$$\frac{\mathbf{r}(t+\delta t)-\mathbf{r}(t)}{\delta t}=\left[\frac{x(t+\delta t)-x(t)}{\delta t}\quad\frac{y(t+\delta t)-(y(t))}{\delta t}\quad\frac{z(t+\delta t)-z(t)}{\delta t}\right]$$

we obtain

$$\mathbf{r}'(t)=[x'(t)\quad y'(t)\quad z'(t)] \tag{1.8}$$

The derivative vector of a vector function is also a vector function. The derivative vector is called the tangent vector, because its direction is along the line of the tangent (see Fig. 1.5).

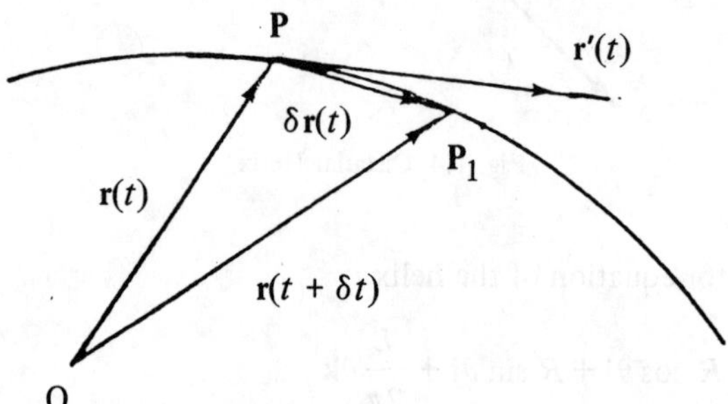

Fig. 1.5 Derivative vector

The modulus of the tangent vector may be calculated by

$$|\mathbf{r}'(t)|=\sqrt{[x'(t)]^2+[y'(t)]^2+[z'(t)]^2} \tag{1.9}$$

The following laws apply for deriving a tengent vector, and are consequences of its definition:

. $\mathbf{C}'=\mathbf{0}$ ($\mathbf{C}$ is a constant vector)

. $[\mathbf{r}_1(t)\pm\mathbf{r}_2(t)]'=\mathbf{r}_1'(t)\pm\mathbf{r}_2'(t)$

. $[K\mathbf{r}(t)]'=K\mathbf{r}'(t)$ (K is a constant)

. $[f(t)\cdot\mathbf{r}(t)]'=f'(t)\cdot\mathbf{r}(t)+f(t)\cdot\mathbf{r}'(t)$ ($f(t)$ is a scalar function)

. $[\mathbf{r}_1(t)\cdot\mathbf{r}_2(t)]'=\mathbf{r}_1'(t)\cdot\mathbf{r}_2(t)+\mathbf{r}_1(t)\cdot\mathbf{r}_2'(t)$

. $[\mathbf{r}_1(t)\times\mathbf{r}_2(t)]'=\mathbf{r}_1'(t)\times\mathbf{r}_2(t)+\mathbf{r}_1(t)\times\mathbf{r}_2'(t)$

Similarly, the higher degree derivative vectors of a vector function may be defined by

$$\mathbf{r}''(t)=[x''(t)\quad y''(t)\quad z''(t)] \tag{1.10}$$

$$\cdots\cdots$$

$$\mathbf{r}^n(t)=[x^n(t)\quad y^n(t)\quad z^n(t)] \tag{1.11}$$

1.2.2 Applications of tangent vectors

The tangent vector at an arbitrary point on a curve is given by $d\mathbf{r}(t)/dt$.

Fig. 1.6 shows that there is a point $\mathbf{r}(t_0)$ on a curve, and a corresponding tangent vector $\mathbf{r}'(t_0)$ at the point $\mathbf{r}(t_0)$. We will now construct the tangent line equation. If $\mathbf{P}^*(x^*, y^*, z^*)$ is an arbitrary point on the tangent line, the tangent line equation may be defined by

$$\mathbf{R} = \mathbf{r}(t_0) + \lambda \mathbf{r}'(t_0)$$

in which λ is a real number. Its component equations are

$$x^* = x(t_0) + \lambda x'(t_0)$$

$$y^* = y(t_0) + \lambda y'(t_0)$$

$$z^* = z(t_0) + \lambda z'(t_0)$$

Eliminating λ from the above component equations we obtain

$$\frac{x^* - x(t_0)}{x'(t_0)} = \frac{y^* - y(t_0)}{y'(t_0)} = \frac{z^* - z(t_0)}{z'(t_0)}$$

which is the well-known straight line equation. Then the tangent line equation of an arbitrary point on the curve may be described by

$$\mathbf{R} = \mathbf{r}(t) + \lambda \mathbf{r}'(t) \tag{1.12}$$

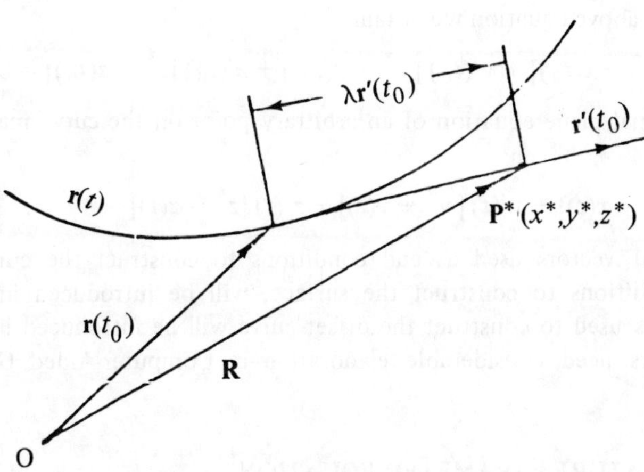

Fig. 1.6 Tangent line vector equation

Fig. 1.7 shows that $\mathbf{P}^*(x^*, y^*, z^*)$ is an arbitrary point in the normal plane which is perpendicular to the tangent vector $\mathbf{r}'(t_0)$ at the point $\mathbf{r}(t_0)$ on the curve $\mathbf{r}(t)$. It is simple to write the normal plane vector equation as

$$\mathbf{r}'(t_0) \cdot [\mathbf{R} - \mathbf{r}(t_0)] = 0 \tag{1.13}$$

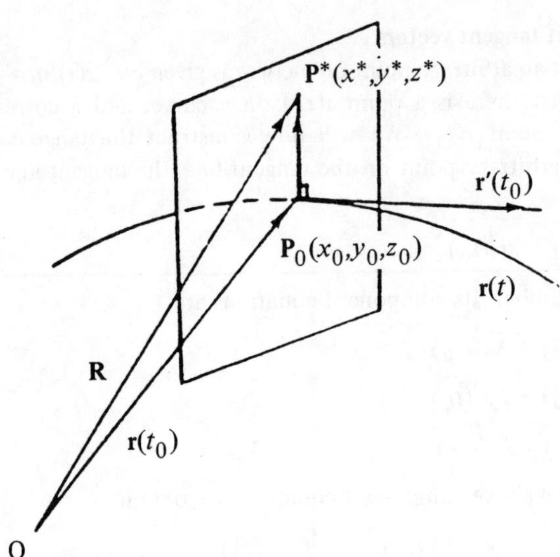

Fig. 1.7 Normal plane vector equation

Since the scalar product of two vectors perpendicular to each other is equal to zero, (1.13) may be represented by their components

$$[x'(t_0) \quad y'(t_0) \quad z'(t_0)] \cdot [[x^* - x(t_0)] \quad [y^* - y(t_0)] \quad [z^* - z(t_0)]] = 0$$

Expanding the above equation we obtain

$$x'(t_0)[x^* - x(t_0)] + y'(t_0)[y^* - y(t_0)] + z'(t_0)[z^* - z(t_0)] = 0$$

Then the normal plane equation of an arbitrary point on the curve may be represented by

$$x'(t)[x^* - x(t)] + y'(t)[y^* - y(t)] + z'(t)[z^* - z(t)] = 0$$

The tangent vectors used as end conditions to construct the curve, and used as boundary conditions to construct the surface, will be introduced in Chapter 4. The tangent vectors used to construct the offset curve will be introduced in Chapter 9. The tangent vectors need considerable elaboration in Computer-Aided Geometric Design (CAGD).

1.3 CURVE NATURE PARAMETER EQUATION

In engineering, most modelling applications require that the choice of a coordinate system does not affect the model shape; in other words, the shapes of most products which we want to model should be independent of any coordinate system.

We choose the curve arc length s as the parametric variable, since arc length is an intrinsic geometric variable of a curve, which is independent of any coordinate system (see Fig. 1.8). This provides some advantages both in theoretical research and in practical applications.

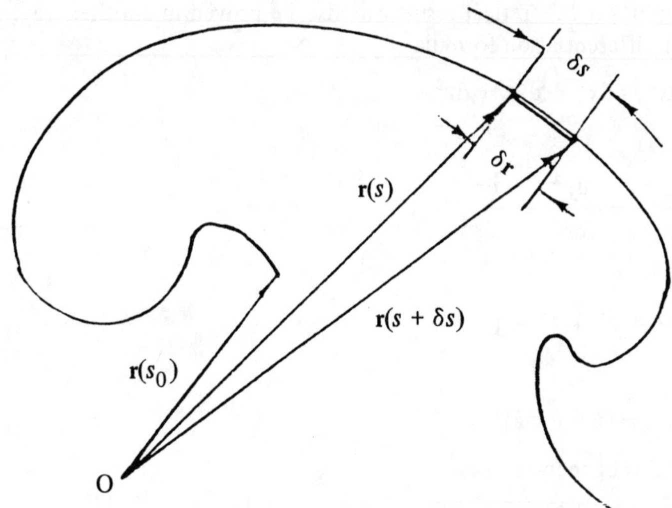

Fig. 1.8 Arc length as parameter

Given the initial point $\mathbf{r}(s_0)$ of a curve, then the variation of arc length s will completely define the curve $\mathbf{r}(s)$ by

$$\mathbf{r} = \mathbf{r}(s) = [x(s) \quad y(s) \quad z(s)] \tag{1.14}$$

This is called the curve nature parameter equation; its component equations are

$$x = x(s)$$

$$y = y(s)$$

$$z = z(s) \tag{1.15}$$

If this increase in the arc length s is δs, the corresponding increase in the vector function is

$$\delta\mathbf{r}(s) = \mathbf{r}(s + \delta s) - \mathbf{r}(s)$$

Its rate of change is

$$\frac{\delta\mathbf{r}(s)}{\delta s} = \frac{\mathbf{r}(s + \delta s) - \mathbf{r}(s)}{\delta s}$$

and the chord length $|\delta\mathbf{r}|$ and the arc length δs become equal in the limit; thus

$$\frac{d\mathbf{r}(s)}{ds} = \lim_{\delta s \to 0} \frac{\delta\mathbf{r}(s)}{\delta s} = 1 \tag{1.16}$$

We denote differentiation with respect to arc length s by a dot to distinguish $\dot{\mathbf{r}}(s)$ and $\mathbf{r}'(t)$. Equation (1.16) illustrates that $\dot{\mathbf{r}}(s)$ is a vector with unit length and in the direction of the tangent to the curve, so $\dot{\mathbf{r}}(s)$ is called the unit tangent vector and is denoted by

$\mathbf{T}(s)$. This important theoretical result can also be proved in another way. According to the arc length differentiation formula

$$ds^2 = dx^2 + dy^2 + dz^2$$

we obtain

$$\frac{dx^2}{ds^2} + \frac{dy^2}{ds^2} + \frac{dz^2}{ds^2} = 1$$

that is

$$\dot{x}^2 + \dot{y}^2 + \dot{z}^2 = 1$$

Since

$$\dot{\mathbf{r}}(s) = [\dot{x} \quad \dot{y} \quad \dot{z}]$$

then the modulus of the vector is

$$|\dot{\mathbf{r}}(s)| = \sqrt{\dot{x}^2 + \dot{y}^2 + \dot{z}^2} = 1$$

and $\dot{\mathbf{r}}(s)$ is a unit tangent vector

$$\mathbf{T} = \dot{\mathbf{r}}(s) \tag{1.17}$$

The following helix example shows how to obtain the arc length parameter equation from (1.7). Denoting $L/2\pi$ by b to simplify the formula, we obtain

$$\mathbf{r}(\theta) = [R \cos \theta \quad R \sin \theta \quad b\theta] \tag{1.18}$$

then

$$\mathbf{r}'(\theta) = [-R \sin \theta \quad R \cos \theta \quad b]$$

and

$$|\mathbf{r}(\theta)| = \sqrt{(-R \sin \theta)^2 + (R \cos \theta)^2 + b^2}$$
$$= \sqrt{R^2 + b^2}$$

The arc length s is given by the integral

$$s = \int_0^\theta |\mathbf{r}'(\theta)| \, d\theta \tag{1.19}$$

Substituting the above result into (1.19), we obtain

$$s = \sqrt{R^2 + b^2} \, \theta$$

The parameter θ may now be expressed by the arc length parameter s

$$\theta = s/\sqrt{R^2 + b^2}$$

The arc length parameter equation may be obtained by substituting θ into (1.18)

$$\mathbf{r}(s) = [R \cos (s/\sqrt{R^2 + b^2}) \quad R \sin (s/\sqrt{R^2 + b^2}) \quad bs/\sqrt{R^2 + b^2}] \tag{1.20}$$

In fact, the arc length will be replaced by the accumulated chord length discussed in Chapter 4.

1.4 THE LOCAL COORDINATE SYSTEM AND THE FRENET–SERRET FORMULAE

1.4.1 The local coordinate system

The origin of a local coordinate system is a point which moves along the curve; the directions of the three axes are not fixed. We now examine how to choose the three axes (see Fig. 1.9).

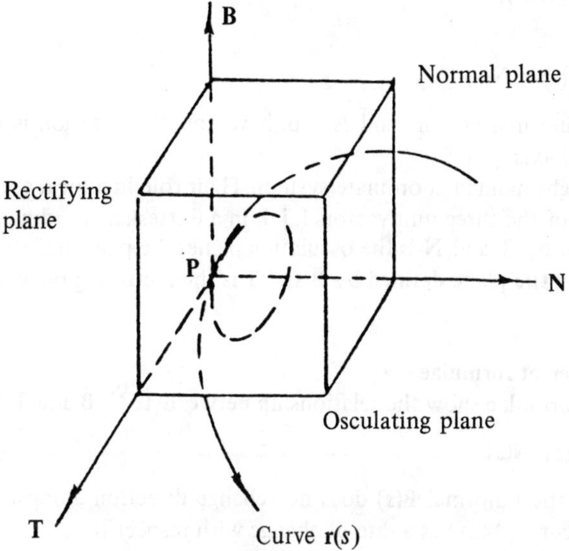

Fig. 1.9 Local coordinate system

The unit tangent vector **T**

$\mathbf{T} = \dot{\mathbf{r}} = d\mathbf{r}/ds$ is a unit vector, which is tangent to the curve. Its direction will be chosen as the direction of the first axis of the local coordinate system.

The unit normal vector **N**

The normal plane mentioned in subsection 1.2.2 is perpendicular to the tangent vector **T**; thus there are any number of lines in the normal plane which are perpendicular to **T**. In other words, any vector perpendicular to **T** is a normal vector.

Since **T** is a unit vector (see section 1.3), the scalar product $\mathbf{T} \cdot \mathbf{T} = 1$ and its differential $2\mathbf{T} \cdot \dot{\mathbf{T}} = 0$. This shows that the vector $\dot{\mathbf{T}}$ is perpendicular to the vector **T**.

The unit normal vector **N** in the direction of $\dot{\mathbf{T}}$ is known as the principal normal vector. $\dot{\mathbf{T}}$ is not a unit vector; we express the relationship by

$$\dot{\mathbf{T}}(s) = \kappa(s)\,\mathbf{N}(s) \tag{1.21}$$

where $\kappa(s)$ is a positive scalar of magnitude, and is known as the curvature of the curve

$$\kappa(s) = |\dot{\mathbf{T}}(s)| = |\ddot{\mathbf{r}}(s)| \tag{1.22}$$

We denote

$$1/\kappa(s) = \rho(s) \tag{1.23}$$

where $\rho(s)$ is the reciprocal of the curvature and is called the curvature radius of the curve.

We choose the direction of the unit normal vector $\mathbf{N}$ as the direction of the second axis of the local coordinate system.

The unit binormal vector $\mathbf{B}$

Setting

$$\mathbf{B}(s) = \mathbf{T}(s) \times \mathbf{N}(s) \tag{1.24}$$

$\mathbf{B}(s)$ is called the binormal vector, and is a unit vector. Its direction is regarded as the direction of the third axis.

$\mathbf{T}$, $\mathbf{N}$, $\mathbf{B}$ form a right-handed coordinate system. Their role in a local coordinate system is similar to the role of the three unit vectors $\mathbf{i}, \mathbf{j}, \mathbf{k}$ in a Cartesian coordinate system.

The plane defined by $\mathbf{T}$ and $\mathbf{N}$ is the osculating plane; the plane defined by $\mathbf{N}$ and $\mathbf{B}$ is the normal plane; and the plane defined by $\mathbf{B}$ and $\mathbf{T}$ is the rectifying plane (see Fig. 1.9).

1.4.2 The Frenet–Serret formulae

The Frenet–Serret formulae show the relationship between $\dot{\mathbf{T}}, \dot{\mathbf{N}}, \dot{\mathbf{B}}$ and $\mathbf{T}, \mathbf{N}, \mathbf{B}$.

$$\dot{\mathbf{T}}(s) = \kappa(s)\ \mathbf{N}(s)$$

In a plane curve, the binormal $\mathbf{B}(s)$ does not change direction along arc length s; thus $\dot{\mathbf{B}}(s) = 0$. In a space curve, $\mathbf{B}(s)$ has a rate of change with respect to s.

Since $\mathbf{B}(s) \cdot \mathbf{T}(s) = 0$, the differential of $\mathbf{B}(s) \cdot \mathbf{T}(s)$ equals zero, that is

$$\dot{\mathbf{B}}(s) \cdot \mathbf{T}(s) + \mathbf{B}(s) \cdot \dot{\mathbf{T}}(s) = 0$$

Since

$$\mathbf{B}(s) \cdot \dot{\mathbf{T}}(s) = \mathbf{B}(s) \cdot \kappa(s)\,\mathbf{N}(s)$$

$$= \kappa(s)\,\mathbf{B}(s) \cdot \mathbf{N}(s)$$

$$= 0$$

we obtain

$$\dot{\mathbf{B}}(s) \cdot \mathbf{T}(s) = 0$$

Since

$$\mathbf{B}(s) \cdot \mathbf{B}(s) = 1$$

the differential equals zero, that is

$$\dot{\mathbf{B}}(s) \cdot \mathbf{B}(s) = 0$$

It follows therefore that $\dot{\mathbf{B}}(s)$ is perpendicular to both $\mathbf{T}(s)$ and $\mathbf{B}(s)$ and is parallel to $\mathbf{N}(s)$.

We set

$$\dot{\mathbf{B}}(s) = -\tau(s)\,\mathbf{N}(s) \tag{1.25}$$

$\tau(s)$ is known as the torsion of the curve.

We now examine the rate of change of $\mathbf{N}$ with respect to s. Since

$$\mathbf{N}(s) = \mathbf{B}(s) \times \mathbf{T}(s)$$

its differential is

$$\begin{aligned}
\dot{\mathbf{N}}(s) &= \dot{\mathbf{B}}(s) \times \mathbf{T}(s) + \mathbf{B}(s) \times \dot{\mathbf{T}}(s) \\
&= [-\tau(s)\,\mathbf{N}(s)] \times \mathbf{T}(s) + \mathbf{B}(s) \times [\kappa(s)\,\mathbf{N}(s)] \\
&= \tau(s)\,\mathbf{B}(s) - \kappa(s)\,\mathbf{T}(s)
\end{aligned} \tag{1.26}$$

The four equations (1.17), (1.21), (1.25) and (1.26) are the principal equations of the differential geometry of space curves, and are known as the Frenet–Serret formulae: they can be written as

$$\begin{aligned}
\dot{\mathbf{r}}(s) &= \mathbf{T}(s) \\
\dot{\mathbf{T}}(s) &= \kappa(s)\,\mathbf{N}(s) \\
\dot{\mathbf{N}}(s) &= \tau(s)\,\mathbf{B}(s) - \kappa(s)\,\mathbf{T}(s) \\
\dot{\mathbf{B}}(s) &= -\tau(s)\,\mathbf{N}(s)
\end{aligned} \tag{1.27}$$

The Frenet–Serret formulae illustrate the rate of change of $\mathbf{r}, \mathbf{T}, \mathbf{N}$ and $\mathbf{B}$ with respect to arc length s. Curvature $\kappa(s)$ and torsion $\tau(s)$ are two important concepts of space curves.

Example

For the circle with centre (x_c, y_c) and radius R, the arc length parametric equation may be described by

$$\mathbf{r}(s) = \left[\left(x_c + R\cos\frac{s}{R}\right) \quad \left(y_c + R\sin\frac{s}{R}\right) \quad 0 \right]$$

Since

$$\mathbf{T}(s) = \dot{\mathbf{r}}(s) = \left[-\sin\frac{s}{R} \quad \cos\frac{s}{R} \quad 0 \right]$$

then

$$\dot{\mathbf{T}}(s) = \frac{-1}{R}\left[\cos\frac{s}{R} \quad \sin\frac{s}{R} \quad 0 \right]$$

thus

$$\kappa(s) = |\dot{\mathbf{T}}(s)| = \frac{1}{R}$$

This show that the curvature of a circle is constant. Since

$$\mathbf{N}(s) = \frac{\dot{\mathbf{T}}(s)}{\kappa(s)} = \left[-\cos\frac{s}{R} \quad -\sin\frac{s}{R} \quad 0 \right]$$

then

$$\mathbf{B}(s) = \mathbf{T}(s) \times \mathbf{N}(s) = \left[-\sin\frac{s}{R} \quad \cos\frac{s}{R} \quad 0 \right] \times \left[-\cos\frac{s}{R} \quad -\sin\frac{s}{R} \quad 0 \right]$$

$$= \begin{bmatrix} \mathbf{i} & \mathbf{j} & \mathbf{k} \\ -\sin\dfrac{s}{R} & \cos\dfrac{s}{R} & 0 \\ -\cos\dfrac{s}{R} & -\sin\dfrac{s}{R} & 0 \end{bmatrix} = [0 \quad 0 \quad 1]$$

thus

$$\dot{\mathbf{B}}(s) = [0 \quad 0 \quad 0]$$

This shows that $\tau(s) = 0$; the torsion of the circle equals zero.

1.5 CURVATURE AND TORSION

Curvature and torsion are intrinsic properties depending on the curve itself and are not related to the reference system.

1.5.1 Curvature

The rate of change of the direction of the tangent vector of the curve with respect to arc length s is called the curvature.

$$\kappa(s) = \left| \frac{d\mathbf{T}(s)}{ds} \right| = |\dot{\mathbf{T}}(s)| = |\ddot{\mathbf{r}}(s)| \tag{1.28}$$

$\kappa = 0$ means that the curve is a straight line.

The above formula defines the curvature. However, there are many different ways of calculating the curvature, the choice of which depends on the forms of the curve equations themselves.

If the curve is described by the arc length parameter equation

$$\mathbf{r}(s) = [x(s) \quad y(s) \quad z(s)]$$

differentiating

$$\dot{\mathbf{r}}(s) = [\dot{x}(s) \quad \dot{y}(s) \quad \dot{z}(s)]$$

and differentiating again

$$\ddot{\mathbf{r}}(s) = [\ddot{x}(s) \quad \ddot{y}(s) \quad \ddot{z}(s)]$$

so that we compute the curvature by

$$\kappa(s) = |\ddot{\mathbf{r}}(s)| = [\ddot{x}(s)^2 + \ddot{y}(s)^2 + \ddot{z}(s)^2]^{1/2} \tag{1.29}$$

In a plane curve, $x = x(s)$, $y = y(s)$, since $\ddot{z}(s) = 0$; thus

$$\kappa(s) = [\ddot{x}(s)^2 + \ddot{y}(s)^2]^{1/2} \tag{1.30}$$

If the curve is described by general parameter equations

$$\mathbf{r}(t) = [x(t) \quad y(t) \quad z(t)]$$

$$\mathbf{r}'(t) = [x'(t) \quad y'(t) \quad z'(t)]$$

$$\mathbf{r}''(t) = [x''(t) \quad y''(t) \quad z''(t)]$$

The curvature can be derived from

$$\kappa = \frac{|\mathbf{r}' \times \mathbf{r}''|}{|\mathbf{r}'|^3} \tag{1.31}$$

Proof

$$\dot{\mathbf{r}} = \frac{d\mathbf{r}}{ds} = \frac{d\mathbf{r}}{dt} \cdot \frac{dt}{ds} = \mathbf{r}' \frac{dt}{ds} = \mathbf{r}'/s'$$

and since $\dot{\mathbf{r}}^2 = 1$, so that $\mathbf{r}'^2 = (s')^2$, $s' = (\mathbf{r}'^2)^{1/2}$. Hence we have

$$\dot{\mathbf{r}} = \mathbf{r}'/(\mathbf{r}'^2)^{1/2}$$

Differentiating the above formula with respect to parameter t

$$\ddot{\mathbf{r}} s' = \frac{\mathbf{r}''}{(\mathbf{r}'^2)^{1/2}} - \frac{(\mathbf{r}' \cdot \mathbf{r}'')\mathbf{r}'}{(\mathbf{r}'^2)^{3/2}} = \frac{\mathbf{r}'' \mathbf{r}'^2 - (\mathbf{r}' \cdot \mathbf{r}'')\mathbf{r}'}{(\mathbf{r}'^2)^{3/2}}$$

Squaring the above formula and letting $(s')^2 = \mathbf{r}'^2$, we obtain

$$\ddot{\mathbf{r}}^2 = \frac{\mathbf{r}''^2 \mathbf{r}'^2 - (\mathbf{r}' \cdot \mathbf{r}'')^2}{(\mathbf{r}'^2)^3}$$

$$\ddot{\mathbf{r}}^2 = \frac{|\mathbf{r}' \times \mathbf{r}''|^2}{(\mathbf{r}'^2)^3}$$

thus

$$\kappa = \frac{|\mathbf{r}' \times \mathbf{r}''|}{|\mathbf{r}'|^3}$$

The formula is expressed by components

$$\kappa = \frac{[(y'z'' - y''z')^2 + (z'x'' - z''x')^2 + (x'y'' - x''y')^2]^{1/2}}{(x'^2 + y'^2 + z'^2)^{3/2}} \tag{1.32}$$

In a plane curve, since $z' = z'' = 0$, the formula for curvature is reduced to

$$\kappa = \frac{x'y'' - x''y'}{(x'^2 + y'^2)^{3/2}} \tag{1.33}$$

In a plane curve $y = y(x)$, since $x' = 1$, $x'' = 0$, the formula for curvature is further reduced to

$$\kappa = \frac{y''}{(1 + y'^2)^{3/2}} \tag{1.34}$$

In a plane curve $y = y(x)$ with a small deflection, since $y' \ll 1$, the curvature can be expressed approximately by the second derivative.

$$\kappa \simeq y'' \tag{1.35}$$

In a plane curve $x = x(s)$ and $y = y(s)$, the curvature may be computed by another formula

$$\kappa = \dot{x}(s)\,\ddot{y}(s) - \ddot{x}(s)\,\dot{y}(s) \tag{1.36}$$

Proof
Since

$$y'(x) = \dot{y}(s)/\dot{x}(s)$$

differentiating with respect to arc length s yields

$$y''(x) = [\ddot{y}(s)\,\dot{x}(s) - \dot{y}(s)\,\ddot{x}(s)]/[\dot{x}(s)]^3$$

Substituting $y'(x)$ and $y''(x)$ into (1.34), we obtain

$$\kappa = \frac{\dot{x}(s)\,\ddot{y}(s) - \ddot{x}(s)\,\dot{y}(s)}{[\dot{x}(s)^2 + \dot{y}(s)^2]^{3/2}}$$

Since $\dot{x}(s)^2 + \dot{y}(s)^2 = 1$, the above formula becomes

$$\kappa = \dot{x}(s)\,\ddot{y}(s) - \ddot{x}(s)\,\dot{y}(s).$$

1.5.2 Torsion

The rate of turning of the direction of the binormal vector of the curve with respect to arc length s is called the torsion.

$$\tau(s) = \left| \frac{d\mathbf{B}(s)}{ds} \right| = |\dot{\mathbf{B}}(s)| \tag{1.37}$$

Torsion is a measure of how much a space curve twists out of the osculating plane. In a plane curve, the osculating plane has no variance, $\mathbf{B}$ is fixed, then $\dot{\mathbf{B}} = 0$, thus $\tau = 0$.

In arc length parametric form
According to the Frenet–Serret formulae

$$\dot{\mathbf{B}} = -\tau\mathbf{N}$$

The scalar product obtained by multiplying both sides of the above equation by $\mathbf{N}$ produces

$$\tau = -\dot{\mathbf{B}} \cdot \mathbf{N}$$

Since

$$\dot{\mathbf{N}} = -\kappa\mathbf{T} + \tau\mathbf{B}$$

The scalar product of two sides of the above equation by $\mathbf{B}$ yields

$$\tau = \dot{\mathbf{N}} \cdot \mathbf{B} + \kappa\mathbf{T} \cdot \mathbf{B} = \dot{\mathbf{N}} \cdot \mathbf{B} \tag{1.38}$$

Since

$$\mathbf{B} = \mathbf{T} \times \mathbf{N} = \dot{\mathbf{r}} \times \mathbf{N} = \dot{\mathbf{r}} \times \ddot{\mathbf{r}}/\kappa$$

and

$$\dot{\mathbf{N}} = \frac{\dddot{\mathbf{r}}}{\kappa} + \ddot{\mathbf{r}}\,\frac{d(1/\kappa)}{ds}$$

Substituting $\mathbf{B}$ and $\dot{\mathbf{N}}$ into (1.38) yields

$$\tau = \left[\frac{\dddot{\mathbf{r}}}{\kappa} + \ddot{\mathbf{r}}\,\frac{d(1/\kappa)}{ds}\right] \cdot [\dot{\mathbf{r}} \times \ddot{\mathbf{r}}/\kappa]$$

$$= \frac{1}{\kappa^2}\dddot{\mathbf{r}} \cdot (\dot{\mathbf{r}} \times \ddot{\mathbf{r}})$$

$$= \dddot{\mathbf{r}} \cdot (\dot{\mathbf{r}} \times \ddot{\mathbf{r}})/(\ddot{\mathbf{r}})^2 \tag{1.39}$$

In general parametric form
Since

$$\dot{\mathbf{r}} = \mathbf{r}'\,\frac{dt}{ds}$$

$$\ddot{\mathbf{r}} = \mathbf{r}''\left(\frac{dt}{ds}\right)^2 + \mathbf{r}'\,\frac{d^2t}{ds^2}$$

$$\dddot{\mathbf{r}} = \mathbf{r}'''\left(\frac{dt}{ds}\right)^3 + 3\mathbf{r}''\,\frac{dt}{ds}\frac{d^2t}{ds^2} + \mathbf{r}'\,\frac{d^3t}{ds^3}$$

then

$$(\dot{\mathbf{r}} \times \ddot{\mathbf{r}}) \cdot \dddot{\mathbf{r}} = (\mathbf{r}' \times \mathbf{r}') \cdot \mathbf{r}''' \left(\frac{dt}{ds}\right)^6$$

Since $\dot{\mathbf{r}} = \mathbf{r}'(dt/ds)$ and $|\dot{\mathbf{r}}| = 1$, thus $(dt/ds) = 1/|\mathbf{r}'|$. According to (1.31), we obtain

$$\ddot{\mathbf{r}}^2 = \kappa^2 = \frac{(\mathbf{r}' \times \mathbf{r}'')^2}{|\mathbf{r}'|^6}$$

Substituting the above equations into (1.39) yields

$$\tau = \frac{(\mathbf{r}' \times \mathbf{r}'') \cdot \mathbf{r}'''}{(\mathbf{r}' \times \mathbf{r}'')^2} \tag{1.40}$$

1.6 SURFACE VECTOR EQUATION

As we know, the explicit equation of a surface may be described by

$$z = f(x, y)$$

and the implicit equation of a surface may be described by

$$F(x, y, z) = 0$$

This is not a convenient way of controlling the shape of a surface. In surface modelling, the most convenient way is to use a parametric description of the surface.

As we saw for curves, a curve may be described by a vector equation with a parameter t

$$\mathbf{r} = \mathbf{r}(t)$$

A surface may be expressed by vector equation with two parameters, u and w (see Fig. 1.10).

$$\mathbf{r} = \mathbf{r}(u, w) \tag{1.41}$$

The vector equation may be expressed by its component functions

$$\mathbf{r}(u, w) = x(u, w)\mathbf{i} + y(u, w)\mathbf{j} + z(u, w)\mathbf{k}$$

The vector function can be written in matrix form

$$\mathbf{r}(u, w) = [x(u, w) \quad y(u, w) \quad z(u, w)] \tag{1.42}$$

The multiplying matrix $[\mathbf{i} \ \mathbf{j} \ \mathbf{k}]^{\mathrm{T}}$ is omitted for convenience. Its component equations are

$$x = x(u, w)$$

$$y = y(u, w)$$

$$z = z(u, w) \tag{1.43}$$

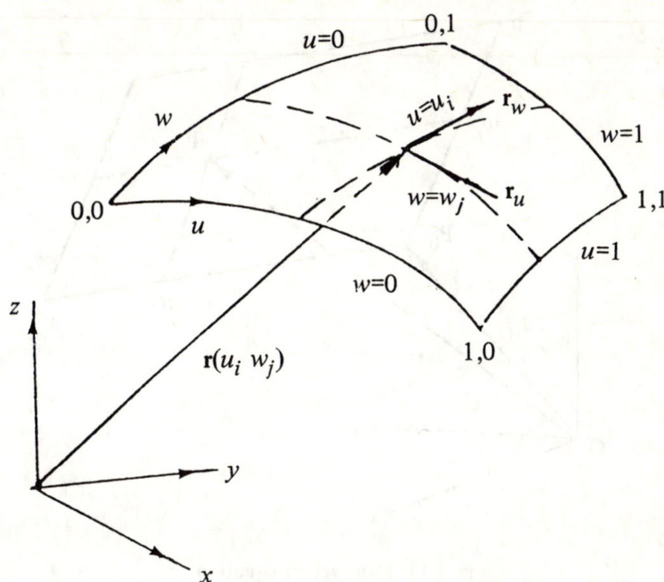

Fig. 1.10 Parametric description of a surface patch

The parametric variables u and w are constrained to the intervals $0 \leqslant u,\ w \leqslant 1$. Fixing the value of one of the parameters results in a curve which is called a parametric curve on the surface. Fixing the value of two parameters results in a point on the surface.

The following examples will help to understand better the parametric description of a surface.

Example 1   Plane vector equation
The simplest example is a plane vector equation. Fig. 1.11 shows a plane defined by two non-parallel vectors **a** and **b**; the plane passes through a given point $P_0(x_0,\ y_0,\ z_0)$.

If **P** is any point on the plane, using simple vector addition

$$\overrightarrow{OP} = \overrightarrow{OP_0} + u\mathbf{a} + w\mathbf{b}$$

that is

$$\mathbf{r}(u,\ w) = \mathbf{r}_0 + u\mathbf{a} + w\mathbf{b} \qquad (0 \leqslant u,\ w \leqslant 1) \tag{1.44}$$

where u and w are independent parameters which fix the position of the general point **P**. This is a parametric description of a plane; (1.44) is called a plane vector equation. Fixing the value of one of the parameters results in a straight line parallel to vector **a** or vector **b**. Its component functions are

$$x(u,\ w) = x_0 + u\mathbf{a}_x + w\,\mathbf{b}_x$$

$$y(u,\ w) = y_0 + u\mathbf{a}_y + w\,\mathbf{b}_y$$

$$z(u,\ w) = z_0 + u\mathbf{a}_z + w\,\mathbf{b}_z \tag{1.45}$$

Eliminating parameters u and w yields the general plane equation.

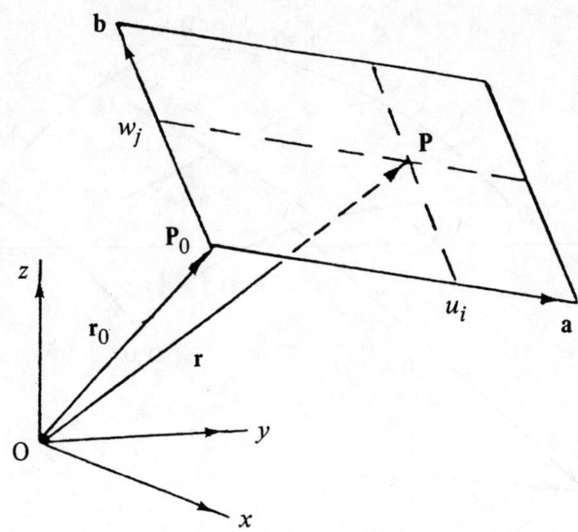

Fig. 1.11 Plane vector equation

Example 2 The vector equation of surface of revolution
A surface of revolution can be generated by revolving a plane curve around an axis line
in its plane (see Fig. 1.12). The plane curve $y = f(x)$ is called the profile curve. Setting
$x = u$, then $y = f(u)$.

If **P** is any point on the surface of revolution, using simple vector addition, we obtain

$$\overrightarrow{OP} = \overrightarrow{OO'} + \overrightarrow{O'P}$$

$$= u\,\mathbf{i} + f(u)\cos w\,\mathbf{j} + f(u)\sin w\,\mathbf{k}$$

that is

$$\mathbf{r}(u, w) = [u \quad f(u)\cos w \quad f(u)\sin w] \qquad (1.46)$$

where u and w are independent parameters which fix the position of the general point **P**.
This is parametric description of a surface of revolution. Its component equations are

$$x = u$$

$$y = f(u)\cos w$$

$$z = f(u)\sin w \qquad (0 \leqslant w \leqslant 2\pi, \quad u_0 \leqslant u \leqslant u_n) \qquad (1.47)$$

Fixing the value of parameter w in (1.47) creates a profile curve, but fixing the value
of parameter u results in a cross-section which is a circle.

Fig. 1.12 shows a mathematical model of the head of a missile.

Example 3 The sphere surface vector equation
The curve of intersection between a sphere and a plane is always a circle, and the curve of
intersection passing through the north/south polar points is a great circle.

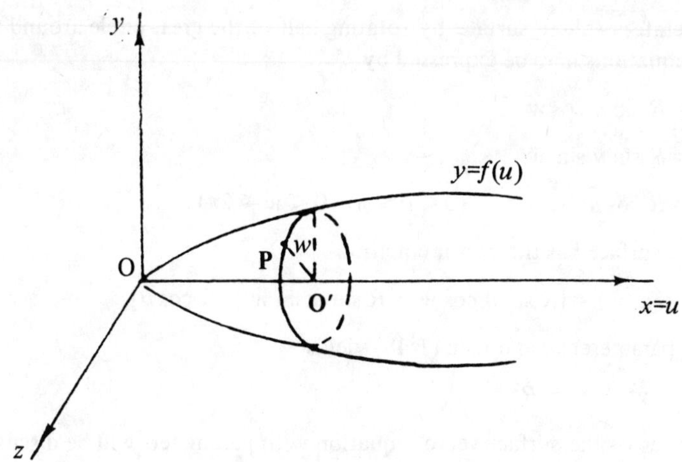

Fig. 1.12 Surface of revolution

Let us express one half of a great circle in the xOz plane by

$$x = R \sin u$$

$$z = R \cos u \qquad\qquad (0 \leqslant u \leqslant \pi)$$

where R is the radius of the great circle, u is an angle between $\overrightarrow{OP}$ and the z-axis (see Fig. 1.13).

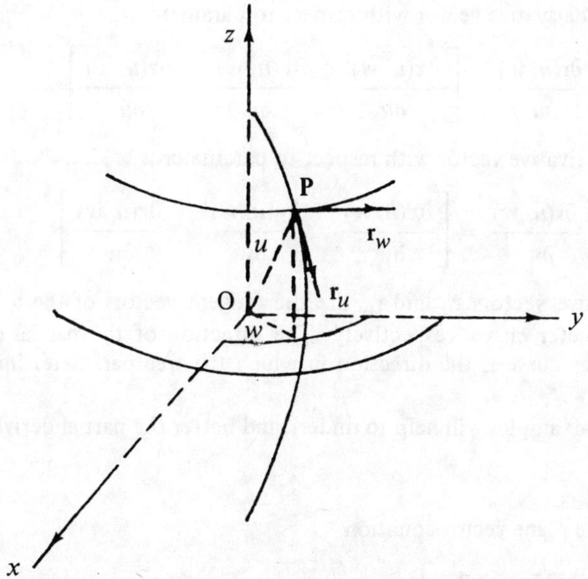

Fig. 1.13 Sphere surface vector equation

We can generate a sphere surface by rotating half of the great circle around the z-axis; its parametric equations may be expressed by

$$x = R \sin u \cos w$$

$$y = R \sin u \sin w$$

$$z = R \cos u \qquad (0 \leqslant u \leqslant \pi, \ \ 0 \leqslant w \leqslant 2\pi) \qquad (1.48)$$

Then the sphere surface has the vector equation

$$\mathbf{r} = \mathbf{r}(u, w) = [R \sin u \cos w \quad R \sin u \sin w \quad R \cos u] \qquad (1.49)$$

Eliminating parameters u and w in (1.48) yields

$$x^2 + y^2 + z^2 = R^2$$

The advantages of the surface vector equation with parameters will be discussed in the last section of this chapter.

1.7 PARTIAL DERIVATIVE VECTORS

Let us quickly review the bi-variable function $z = f(x, y)$ and its partial derivatives

$$\frac{\partial z}{\partial x} = \frac{\partial f(x, y)}{\partial x}, \qquad \frac{\partial z}{\partial y} = \frac{\partial f(x, y)}{\partial y}$$

Similarly, differentiating the surface vector equation

$$\mathbf{r} = \mathbf{r}(u, w) = [x(u, w) \quad y(u, w) \quad z(u, w)]$$

yields the partial derivative vector with respect to parameter u

$$\mathbf{r}_u = \frac{\partial \mathbf{r}(u, w)}{\partial u} = \left[\frac{\partial x(u, w)}{\partial u} \quad \frac{\partial y(u, w)}{\partial u} \quad \frac{\partial z(u, w)}{\partial u} \right] \qquad (1.50)$$

and the partial derivative vector with respect to parameter w

$$\mathbf{r}_w = \frac{\partial \mathbf{r}(u, w)}{\partial w} = \left[\frac{\partial x(u, w)}{\partial w} \quad \frac{\partial y(u, w)}{\partial w} \quad \frac{\partial z(u, w)}{\partial w} \right] \qquad (1.51)$$

Partial derivative vectors $\mathbf{r}_u$ and $\mathbf{r}_w$ are the tangent vectors of the u parameter curve and the w parameter curve, respectively. The direction of the partial derivative vector for any parameter curve is the direction in which the free parameter increases (see Fig. 1.10).

The following examples will help to understand better the partial derivative vectors.

Example 1

Differentiating the plane vector equation

$$\mathbf{r}(u, w) = \mathbf{r}_0 + u\,\mathbf{a} + w\,\mathbf{b}$$

with respective parameters u and w yields the partial derivative vectors

$$\mathbf{r}_u = \mathbf{a}$$

and

$$\mathbf{r}_w = \mathbf{b}$$

This shows that the partial derivative vectors of the parameter curves are vectors $\mathbf{a}$ and $\mathbf{b}$ defining the plane.

Example 2

Differentiating the sphere surface vector equation (1.49) with respect to parameter u yields

$$\mathbf{r}_u = [R \cos u \cos w \quad R \cos u \sin w \quad -R \sin u]$$

The partial derivative vector $\mathbf{r}_u$ is the tangent vector of the longitude curve.

Differentiating the sphere surface vector equation (1.49) with respective to parameter w yields

$$\mathbf{r}_w = [-R \sin u \sin w \quad R \sin u \cos w \quad 0]$$

The partial derivative vector $\mathbf{r}_w$ is the tangent vector of the latitude curve.

If $w = 0$, the tangent vector of the longitude curve on the coordinate plane xOz is

$$\mathbf{r}_u = [R \cos u \quad 0 \quad -R \sin u]$$

and at

$$u = 0 \qquad \mathbf{r}_u = [R \quad 0 \quad 0]$$
$$u = \pi/2 \quad \mathbf{r}_u = [0 \quad 0 \quad -R]$$
$$u = \pi \qquad \mathbf{r}_u = [-R \quad 0 \quad 0]$$

At $u = \pi/3, w = \pi/3$, the partial derivative vectors are

$$\mathbf{r}_u = [R/4 \quad \sqrt{3}R/4 \quad -\sqrt{3}R/2]$$
$$\mathbf{r}_w = [-3R/4 \quad \sqrt{3}R/4 \quad 0]$$

Example 3

A classical explicit surface equation $z = f(x, y)$ may be rewritten as the parametric description

$$x = u$$

$$y = w$$

$$z = f(u, w)$$

Its vector equation is

$$\mathbf{r}(u, w) = [u \quad w \quad f(u, w)]$$

Setting $w = w_j$ yields the equation of the u parameter curve

$$\mathbf{r}(u, w_j) = [u \quad w_j \quad f(u, w_j)]$$

Its tangent vector equation is

$$\mathbf{r}_u = [1 \quad 0 \quad f_u]$$

Similarly, setting $u = u_i$ yields the equation of the w parameter curve

$$\mathbf{r}(u_i, w) = [u_i \quad w \quad f(u_i, w)]$$

Its tangent vector equation is

$$\mathbf{r}_w = [0 \quad 1 \quad f_w]$$

1.8 TANGENT PLANE AND UNIT NORMAL VECTOR

There are two partial derivative vectors $\mathbf{r}_u$ and $\mathbf{r}_w$ at any point $\mathbf{r}(u, w)$ on a surface patch. The vectors $\mathbf{r}_u$ and $\mathbf{r}_w$ may define a plane, which is called the tangent plane at the point on the surface patch. The vectors $\mathbf{r}_u$ and $\mathbf{r}_w$ also define a vector, which is perpendicular to the tangent plane at the point on the patch, and is called the normal vector (see Fig. 1.14).

We may find a unit normal vector $\mathbf{n}(u, w)$ by computing the vector product of the partial derivative vectors $\mathbf{r}_u$ and $\mathbf{r}_w$ at the point.

$$\mathbf{n}(u, w) = \frac{\mathbf{r}_u \times \mathbf{r}_w}{|\mathbf{r}_u \times \mathbf{r}_w|} \tag{1.52}$$

The order in which we take the vector product determines the direction of $\mathbf{n}(u, w)$.

At any point $\mathbf{r}(u, w)$ on a surface patch, the two partial derivative vectors may be expressed by

$$\mathbf{r}_u = [x_u \quad y_u \quad z_u]$$
$$\mathbf{r}_w = [x_w \quad y_w \quad z_w]$$

Their vector product is

$$\begin{aligned}
\mathbf{r}_u \times \mathbf{r}_w &= [x_u \quad y_u \quad z_u] \times [x_w \quad y_w \quad z_w] \\
&= [(y_u z_w - z_u y_w) \quad (z_u x_w - x_u z_w) \quad (x_u y_w - y_u x_w)] \\
&= [A \quad B \quad C]
\end{aligned}$$

and the magnitude of the vector product is

$$|\mathbf{r}_u \times \mathbf{r}_w| = (A^2 + B^2 + C^2)^{1/2}$$

Thus the unit normal vector may be expressed by

$$\mathbf{n}(u, w) = \left[\frac{A}{(A^2 + B + C^2)^{1/2}} \quad \frac{B}{(A^2 + B^2 + C^2)^{1/2}} \quad \frac{C}{(A^2 + B^2 + C^2)^{1/2}} \right]$$

$$\tag{1.53}$$

The concept of the unit normal vector of a surface at any point is very important in surface modelling techniques; for example, we apply it to compute hidden surface removal in CAD and to determine tool paths in CAM, etc.

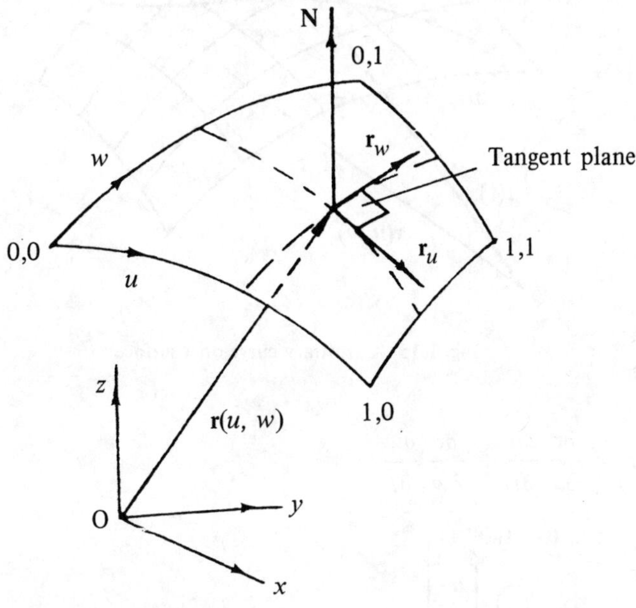

Fig. 1.14 Tangent plane and normal vector

1.9 CURVATURE OF A SURFACE

1.9.1 Normal curvatures

For a surface expressed by $\mathbf{r} = \mathbf{r}(u, w)$, $\mathbf{r}(u, w_j)$ stands for a u parameter curve, $\mathbf{r}(u_i, w)$ stands for a w parameter curve. The two curve families form orthogonal curve nets.

We will now discuss another type of curve on a surface. Denote the arbitrary curve on a surface by $\mathbf{r}(t)$ (see Fig. 1.15). The arbitrary curve equation $\mathbf{r}(t)$ may be written as

$$\mathbf{r} = \mathbf{r}(t) = \mathbf{r}(u(t), w(t)) \tag{1.54}$$

since the curve is on the surface.

Note that u and w are surface parameters; t is a general parameter of the curve on the surface. In this subsection, we will also use the curve arc length parameter s.

A tangent vector to this curve is given by $\mathbf{r}'$, which we may expand by the chain rule to give

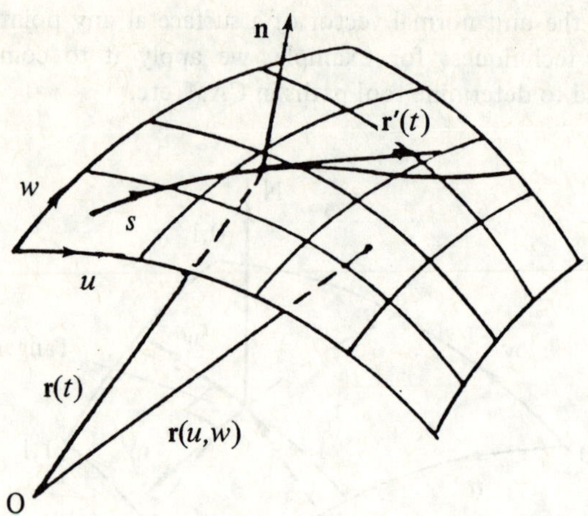

Fig. 1.15 A arbitrary curve on a surface

$$\mathbf{r}' = \frac{\partial \mathbf{r}}{\partial u}\frac{\partial u}{\partial t} + \frac{\partial \mathbf{r}}{\partial w}\frac{\partial w}{\partial t}$$

$$= \mathbf{r}_u u' + \mathbf{r}_w w'$$

$$= [\mathbf{r}_u \quad \mathbf{r}_w]\begin{bmatrix} u' \\ w' \end{bmatrix} \tag{1.55}$$

The length of the tangent vector $\mathbf{r}'$ is given by

$$|\mathbf{r}'| = [(x_u u' + x_w w')^2 + (y_u u' + y_w w')^2 + (z_u u' + z_w w')^2]^{1/2}$$

thus

$$|\mathbf{r}'|^2 = (x_u u' + x_w w')^2 + (y_u u' + y_w w')^2 + (z_u u' + z_w w')^2$$

$$= [u' \quad w']\begin{bmatrix} \mathbf{r}_u \cdot \mathbf{r}_u & \mathbf{r}_u \cdot \mathbf{r}_w \\ \mathbf{r}_u \cdot \mathbf{r}_w & \mathbf{r}_w \cdot \mathbf{r}_w \end{bmatrix}\begin{bmatrix} u' \\ w' \end{bmatrix}$$

$$= [u' \quad w']\,\mathbf{G}\begin{bmatrix} u' \\ w' \end{bmatrix} \tag{1.56}$$

Differentiating (1.55) with respect to parameter t by the chain rule yields

$$\mathbf{r}'' = \mathbf{r}_{uu}u'^2 + 2\mathbf{r}_{uw}u'w' + \mathbf{r}_{ww}w'^2 + \mathbf{r}_u u'' + \mathbf{r}_w w'' \tag{1.57}$$

The curve equation $\mathbf{r}(t)$ can also be written as

$$\mathbf{r} = \mathbf{r}(t) = \mathbf{r}(s(t))$$

thus

$$r' = \frac{dr}{ds} \cdot \frac{ds}{dt} = \dot{r}s' = Ts'$$ (1.58)

and

$$r'' = \dot{T}s'^2 + Ts''$$

$$= \kappa N s' + Ts''$$ (1.59)

Comparing (1.57) and (1.59), we obtain after scalar product by the surface unit normal vector **n**

$$\kappa N s'^2 \cdot n = n \cdot r_{uu}u'^2 + 2n \cdot r_{uw}u'w' + n \cdot r_{ww}w'^2$$

$$= [u' \quad w'] \begin{bmatrix} n \cdot r_{uu} & n \cdot r_{uw} \\ n \cdot r_{uw} & n \cdot r_{ww} \end{bmatrix} \begin{bmatrix} u' \\ w' \end{bmatrix}$$

$$= [u' \quad w'] D \begin{bmatrix} u' \\ w' \end{bmatrix}$$ (1.60)

Since **n** is perpendicular to T, r_u and r_w.

We know that for such a curve, its unit normal vector **N** is parallel to the surface unit normal vector **n**, so

$$N \cdot n = 1$$ (1.61)

and according to (1.58)

$$s'^2 = |r'|^2$$ (1.62)

Using (1.60), (1.61), (1.62) and (1.56), we obtain the curvature of the curve

$$\kappa = [u' \quad w'] D \begin{bmatrix} u' \\ w' \end{bmatrix} \Big/ [u' \quad w'] G \begin{bmatrix} u' \\ w' \end{bmatrix}$$ (1.63)

in which the matrix **G** is the first fundamental matrix of the surface, and the matrix **D** is the second fundamental matrix of the surface. The matrices **G** and **D** are determined by the surface itself.

The curvature κ of the curve on the surface is defined as the normal curvature κ_n of the surface in the direction of the curve $r(t)$.

1.9.2 Principal curvatures

Formulae (1.56) and (1.60) show that the matrices **G** and **D** are determined by surface $r(u, w)$ itself. Formula (1.63) show that $[u' \quad w']$ is determined by the curve $r(t)$ on the surface; in other words, different $r(t)$ determine different normal curvatures κ_n of the surface.

We will now examine the maximum and minimum normal curvatures, which are called the *principal* curvatures of the surface.

From (1.63), we have

$$\kappa_n \begin{bmatrix} u' & w' \end{bmatrix} \mathbf{G} \begin{bmatrix} u' \\ w' \end{bmatrix} = \begin{bmatrix} u' & w' \end{bmatrix} \mathbf{D} \begin{bmatrix} u' \\ w' \end{bmatrix}$$

then

$$(\mathbf{D} - \kappa_n \mathbf{G}) \begin{bmatrix} u' \\ w' \end{bmatrix} = 0$$

that is

$$\left(\begin{bmatrix} d_{11} & d_{12} \\ d_{21} & d_{22} \end{bmatrix} - \kappa_n \begin{bmatrix} g_{11} & g_{12} \\ g_{21} & g_{22} \end{bmatrix} \right) \begin{bmatrix} u' \\ w' \end{bmatrix} = 0$$

or

$$(d_{11} - \kappa_n g_{11})u' + (d_{12} - \kappa_n g_{12})w' = 0$$

$$(d_{21} - \kappa_n g_{21})u' + (d_{22} - \kappa_n g_{22})w' = 0$$

Eliminating u' and w', we obtain

$$|\mathbf{G}|\kappa_n^2 - (g_{11}d_{22} + d_{11}g_{22} - 2g_{12}d_{12})\kappa_n + |\mathbf{D}| = 0 \qquad (1.64)$$

According to (1.64), the maximum and minimum curvatures may be obtained, since they are two roots of the quadratic equations.

(1.64) shows that the maximum and minimum curvatures are determined by the surface $\mathbf{r}(u, w)$ itself. The principal curvatures are important geometric properties of the surface.

1.9.3 Gaussian curvature

The product of the maximum and minimum curvatures is called the Gaussian curvature κ of the surface

$$\kappa = \kappa_{n,max} \cdot \kappa_{n,min}$$

Let us review the product of two roots of equation $ax^2 + bx + c = 0$:

$$x_1 \cdot x_2 = c/a$$

Similarly we obtain from (1.64)

$$\kappa = \kappa_{n,max} \cdot \kappa_{n,min} = |\mathbf{D}|/|\mathbf{G}| \qquad (1.65)$$

1.10 ADVANTAGES OF PARAMETRIC DESCRIPTION

Parametric description is a powerful mathematical tool for defining curves and surfaces in surface modelling techniques. Parametric equations have many advantages over other non-parametric forms, for example classical algebraic formulation.

1. Modeller aspect
A curve is expressed by the vector function with a single parameter

$$\mathbf{r} = \mathbf{r}(u) = [x(u) \quad y(u) \quad z(u)]$$

A surface is described by the vector function with two parameters

$$\mathbf{r} = \mathbf{r}(u, w) = [x(u, w) \quad y(u, w) \quad z(u, w)]$$

A solid is represented by the vector function with three parameters

$$\mathbf{r} = \mathbf{r}(u, v, w) = [x(u, v, w) \quad y(u, v, w) \quad z(u, v, w)]$$

The roles of the parametric variables are clear. The geometric form is much more convenient to use to define, analyse and control the shape of a curve, a surface and a solid. The common form for all curves and common form for all surfaces offer many advantages in computing the curves and surfaces. For example, the common parametric format for describing the curve and surface greatly reduces the number and complexity of the subroutines of computer programs.

2. Mathematical aspect

- Vector tool. The parametric description is easy to express in the form of vectors. The vector equations are very concise and offer a considerable economy in terms of writing and computation.
- Matrix tool. The parametric description is also easy to express in the form of matrices. The use of matrix multiplication allows the use of standard subroutines.
- The parametric description makes the curves and surfaces independent of any co-ordinate system. We always require that the choice of a coordinate system does not affect the shape of curves and surfaces. Furthermore, the computation of the three components may employ the same subroutines; this drastically reduces the number of subroutines in a computer program.
- Normalization of the parametric variables. It is convenient to normalize the parameter value between 0 and 1. This means that curves and surfaces are bounded. In fact, the shape of products is always bounded; however, the classical mathematical methods describing the shape do not offer a boundary. Furthermore, the parametric description leads to the piecewise way of curves and surfaces; this means that we may compose complex curves and surfaces.
- The parametric description may express infinite slopes, since $dy/dx = (dy/du)/(dx/du)$; $dx/du = 0$ means that dy/dx is infinite. In fact, the profiles of products often have vertical tangent lines.

3. Engineering aspect

Parametric description is convenient for plotters and graphics display terminals, since the two time functions $x(t)$ and $y(t)$ can be chosen as a driving function for the servo systems of a plotter or the electron beam deflection system of a cathode ray tube.

Transformations can easily be performed on parametric equations; this is very useful for plotting and display.

Parametric description also offers a convenient way to produce tool paths, since the computation of cutter offset curves and surfaces can be simplified.

The following chapters will help to understand better the advantages of the parametric description of curves and surfaces.

REFERENCES

[1]　Faux, I. D. and Pratt, M. J., *Computational Geometry for Design and Manufacture*, Ellis Horwood Chichester, 1985.

[2]　Mortensen, M. E., *Geometric Modelling*, John Wiley & Sons, New York, 1985.

[3]　Gasson, P. C., *Geometry of Spatial Forms*, Ellis Horwood, Chichester, 1983.

[4]　Clar, L. M. and Hart, J. A., *Calculus with Analytic Geometry for the Technologies*, Prentice-Hall, Englewood Cliffs, N.J., 1980.

[5]　Spivak, M., *A Comprehensive Introduction to Differential Geometry*, Publish, INC, Berkeley, 1979.

[6]　Spain, B., *Vector Analysis*, Van Nostrand, London, 1967.

2

Geometric Transformations and Projections

2.1 INTRODUCTION

The purpose of this chapter is to introduce the geometrical transformations and projections used widely in CAD/CAM.

The geometrical transformations and projections that we discuss here include translation, rotation, scaling, symmetry, reflection, parallel projection, central projection and concatenated transformations.

When designing we often encounter the need to translate and rotate axes from a global to a local position. For example, an aircraft has a global Cartesian coordinate system, but wing, tailplane and engine have their local Cartesian coordinate systems, and complex parts within these units may also have sub-local Cartesian coordinate systems.

In drafting and computer graphics display, perspective is one of the most valuable features for visualizing objects. Dynamic display will also improve the recognition of displayed objects and will become increasingly important for simulation techniques in CAD.

In manufacture, when we select tools and calculate tool paths, many interesting and useful geometrical coordinate transformations are employed.

Modern CAD/CAM systems include powerful geometrical transformation packages. Three-dimensional and two-dimensional displays are matched by introducing projections.

Such transformations as those from Cartesian to polar, spherical, or cylindrical systems are generally of little use in geometric modelling, since it is awkward and difficult to support parametric representations in these systems. In this chapter we will apply homogeneous coordinates and matrix representations in order to facilitate design, manufacture and programming.

The simplest mathematical element we use to express a curve or a surface is a point vector $\mathbf{r}(u)$ or $\mathbf{r}(u, w)$. We treat the transformations of any point on a curve or surface as the transformations of the curve or surface, since the curve or surface may be regarded as a so-called rigid body.

We will start with two-dimensional transformations, and then discuss three-dimensional transformations and projections.

2.2 TWO-DIMENSIONAL TRANSFORMATIONS

2.2.1 Two-dimensional transformation formulae

Translation
Fig. 2.1(a) shows an initial point $\mathbf{P}(x, y)$ translated by a vector $\mathbf{T}(m, n)$, so that a translated point $\mathbf{P}^*(x^*, y^*)$ is given by

$$x^* = x + m$$

$$y^* = y + n \tag{2.1}$$

Fig. 2.1(b) shows an initial curve $\mathbf{r}(u)$ translated by a vector $\mathbf{T}(m, n)$, so that the translated curve $\mathbf{r}^*(u)$ is given by

$$x^*(u) = x(u) + m$$

$$y^*(u) = y(u) + n \tag{2.2}$$

Since the curve may be regarded as a rigid body, its translation implies that every point on the curve is translated by an equal distance in a given direction.

We will denote a transformed point, curve or surface by an asterisk in this chapter.

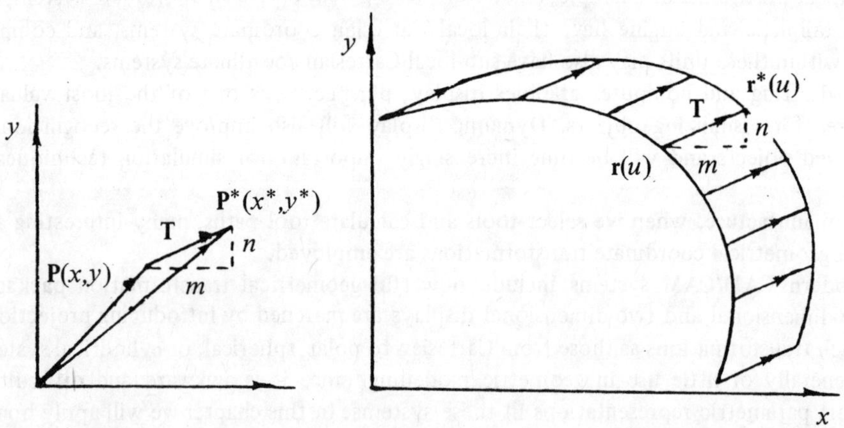

Fig. 2.1 Translation

Rotation

Fig. 2.2 shows an initial point $\mathbf{P}(x, y)$ rotated around the origin through the angle ψ in the counterclockwise direction, so that the rotated point $\mathbf{P}^*(x^*, y^*)$ is given by

$$x^* = x \cos \psi - y \sin \psi$$

$$y^* = x \sin \psi + y \cos \psi \tag{2.3}$$

Note that we are using right-hand convention, in which angle ψ is a counterclockwise direction.

Conversely, if the coordinate axes are rotated around the origin through an angle $-\psi$ in the clockwise direction, the effect is the same.

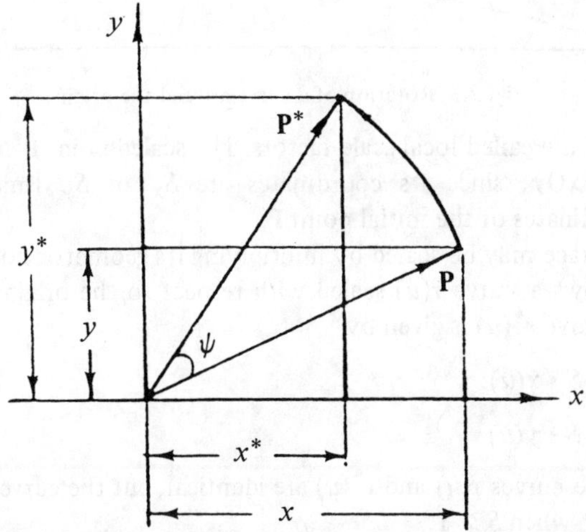

Fig. 2.2 Rotation of a point

Fig. 2.3 shows an initial curve $\mathbf{r}(u)$ rotated around the origin through an angle θ in the counterclockwise direction, so that the rotated curve $\mathbf{r}^*(u)$ is given by

$$x^*(u) = x(u) \cos \theta - y(u) \sin \theta$$

$$y^*(u) = x(u) \sin \theta + y(u) \cos \theta \tag{2.4}$$

Since the curve may be regarded as a rigid body, its rotation implies that every point on the curve is rotated through the same angle.

Scaling (zoom)

A point $\mathbf{P}(x, y)$ may be scaled with respect to the origin by multiplying its coordinates by a scale factor. The scaled point $\mathbf{P}^*(x^*, y^*)$ can be given by

$$x^* = S_x \cdot x$$

$$y^* = S_y \cdot y \tag{2.5}$$

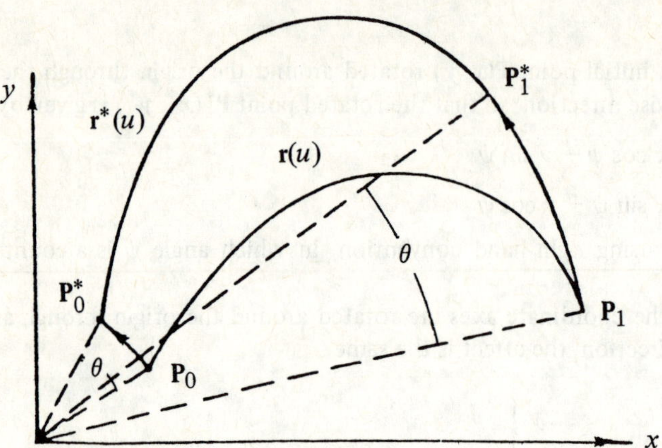

Fig. 2.3 Rotation of a curve around the origin

in which S_x and S_y are called local scale factors. The scaled point $\mathbf{P}^*$ occupies a different position in plane xOy, since its coordinates are S_x or S_y times larger than the corresponding coordinates of the initial point $\mathbf{P}$.

A curve or a surface may be scaled by multiplying its geometric coefficients by a scale factor. Fig. 2.4 shows a curve $\mathbf{r}(u)$ scaled with respect to the origin by an overall scale factor S. The new curve $\mathbf{r}^*(u)$ is given by

$$x^*(u) = S \cdot x(u)$$

$$y^*(u) = S \cdot y(u) \tag{2.6}$$

The shapes of the curves $\mathbf{r}(u)$ and $\mathbf{r}^*(u)$ are identical, but the curve $\mathbf{r}^*(u)$ is larger than the initial curve $\mathbf{r}(u)$, when $S > 1$.

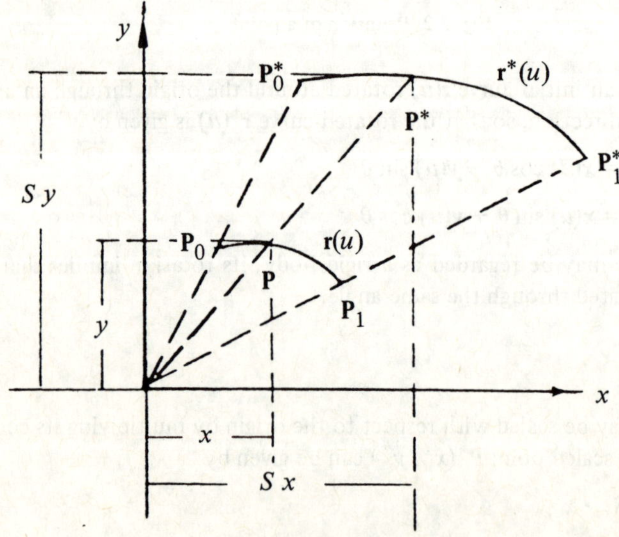

Fig. 2.4 Overall scaling of a curve

Fig. 2.5 shows that the tangent vector $\mathbf{r}'^*(u)$ is also larger than the corresponding $\mathbf{r}'(u)$. The $\mathbf{r}'^*$ may be computed as

$$\mathbf{r}'^*(u) = S \cdot \mathbf{r}'(u) \tag{2.7}$$

The scaling of a curve leads to an expansion or contraction of the curve with respect to the origin.

We will now examine the local scaling of a curve (see Fig. 2.6). Each component of the curve is scaled by a local scale factor S_x or S_y. The effect of the local scaling of a curve is to stretch or shrink the shape of the curve.

Translation, rotation and scaling are widely applied in surface modelling systems.

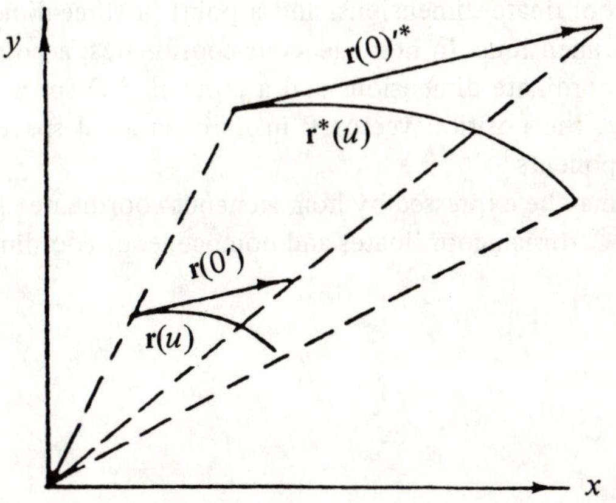

Fig. 2.5 Scaling of tangent vector

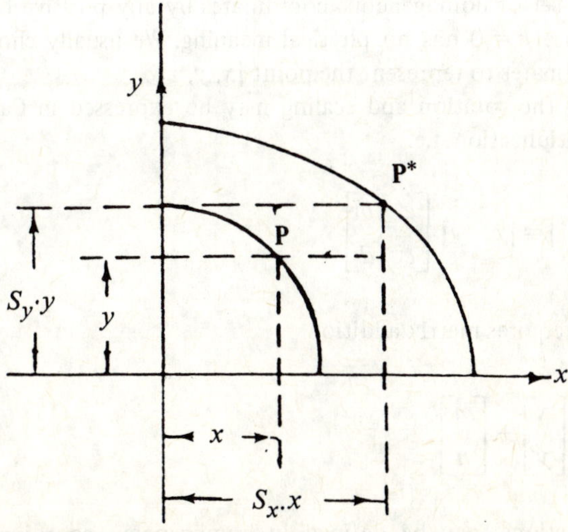

Fig. 2.6 Local scaling of a curve

2.2.2 Homogeneous coordinates

Homogeneous coordinates provide facilities for geometric transformations. One of the reasons for this is that any type of geometric transformation may be expressed in unity form by homogeneous coordinates. Another advantage is that they allow the concatenation of any number of individual transformations into a single transformation matrix. In CAD/CAM the calculation of transformations can be time-consuming and can prove to be a bottleneck in the performance of a display system; the concatenation of transformations will overcome this problem. However, the concatenation of transformations is impossible in the conventional form, since transformation requires matrix addition.

In a certain coordinate system we define the position of a point in two-dimensional (2-D) space by two coordinate dimensions, and a point in three-dimensional(3-D) space by three coordinate dimensions. In homogeneous coordinates, a point in 2-D space can be defined by three coordinate dimensions and a point in 3-D space by four coordinate dimensions. Generally, the position vector $\mathbf{P}$ in n-dimensional space is expressed by a vector of $(n + 1)$ components.

A point $\mathbf{P}(x, y, z)$ may be expressed by homogeneous coordinates $[hx, hy, hz, h]$. The relationships between Cartesian coordinates and homogeneous coordinates are given by

$$x = hx/h$$

$$y = hy/h$$

$$z = hz/h \tag{2.8}$$

For example, a point may have coordinates $[3, 2, 1]$, but the same point may be expressed in homogeneous coordinates by $[3, 2, 1, 1]$, $[6, 4, 2, 2]$, $[9, 6, 3, 3]$, $[900, 600, 300, 300]\ldots$, so there is no unique homogeneous coordinate representation. We may multiply a set of homogeneous coordinates by any positive or negative number except 0, as the case $h = 0$ has no physical meaning. We usually choose $[x, y, z, 1]$ in homogeneous coordinates to represent the point $[x, y, z]$.

In the 2-D case, the rotation and scaling may be expressed in Cartesian coordinate form by matrix multiplication, i.e.

$$[x^* \quad y^*] = [x \quad y] \begin{bmatrix} a & b \\ c & d \end{bmatrix} \tag{2.9}$$

but the translation requires matrix addition

$$\begin{bmatrix} x^* \\ y^* \end{bmatrix} = \begin{bmatrix} x \\ y \end{bmatrix} + \begin{bmatrix} m \\ n \end{bmatrix} \tag{2.10}$$

These transformations may be defined in homogeneous coordinate form by unity matrix multiplication, i.e.

$$[hx^* \quad hy^* \quad h] = [x \quad y \quad 1] \begin{bmatrix} a & b & 0 \\ c & d & 0 \\ m & n & 1 \end{bmatrix} \tag{2.11}$$

If $a = 1$, $b = 0$, $c = 0$, $d = 1$, (2.11) reduces to (2.10). The uniform form of the geometric transformation (2.11) has a crucial importance in any geometric modelling system.

2.2.3 Homogeneous transformations
We will now discuss geometric transformations by homogeneous coordinates.

Translation
Translate points with the following matrix product:

$$[x^* \quad y^* \quad 1] = [x \quad y \quad 1] \begin{bmatrix} 1 & 0 & 0 \\ 0 & 1 & 0 \\ m & n & 1 \end{bmatrix} \tag{2.12}$$

It is evident from (2.12) that $x^* = x + m$, $y^* = y + n$. And when $x = 0$, $y = 0$, $x^* = m$, $y^* = n$, that is, the point $\mathbf{P}(0, 0)$ can also be translated to $\mathbf{P}^*(m, n)$. However, it is not possible for the point $\mathbf{P}(0, 0)$ to be translated by the method shown in (2.9).

Rotation
Rotate points around the origin with the following matrix product:

$$[x^* \quad y^* \quad 1] = [x \quad y \quad 1] \begin{bmatrix} \cos \psi & \sin \psi & 0 \\ -\sin \psi & \cos \psi & 0 \\ 0 & 0 & 1 \end{bmatrix} \tag{2.13}$$

Scaling
Scale points around the origin with the following matrix product:

$$[x^* \quad y^* \quad 1] = [x \quad y \quad 1] \begin{bmatrix} S_x & 0 & 0 \\ 0 & S_y & 0 \\ 0 & 0 & 1 \end{bmatrix} \tag{2.14}$$

where S_x and S_y are called local scale factors, since $x^* = S_x \cdot x$, $y^* = S_y \cdot y$.

$$[hx^* \quad hy^* \quad h] = [x \quad y \quad 1] \begin{bmatrix} 1 & 0 & 0 \\ 0 & 1 & 0 \\ 0 & 0 & S \end{bmatrix} \tag{2.15}$$

where S is called the overall scale factor, since $x^* = x/h$, $y^* = y/h$. If the overall factor scale factor S is greater than unity, a reduction in scale is effected, but if S is less than unity, an increase in scale is effected.

Reflection

Reflection of points around the y-axis may be defined by

$$[x^*\ \ y^*\ \ 1] = [x\ \ y\ \ 1]\begin{bmatrix} -1 & 0 & 0 \\ 0 & 1 & 0 \\ 0 & 0 & 1 \end{bmatrix} \tag{2.16}$$

It is evident that $x^* = -x$, $y^* = y$.

Reflection of points around the origin may be expressed by

$$[x^*\ \ y^*\ \ 1] = [x\ \ y\ \ 1]\begin{bmatrix} -1 & 0 & 0 \\ 0 & -1 & 0 \\ 0 & 0 & 1 \end{bmatrix} \tag{2.17}$$

It is clear that $x^* = -x$, $y^* = -y$.

Reflection of points around the x-axis may be calculated by

$$[x^*\ \ y^*\ \ 1] = [x\ \ y\ \ 1]\begin{bmatrix} 1 & 0 & 0 \\ 0 & -1 & 0 \\ 0 & 0 & 1 \end{bmatrix} \tag{2.18}$$

The results are $x^* = x$, $y^* = -y$.

Fig. 2.7 shows the effects of these reflections.

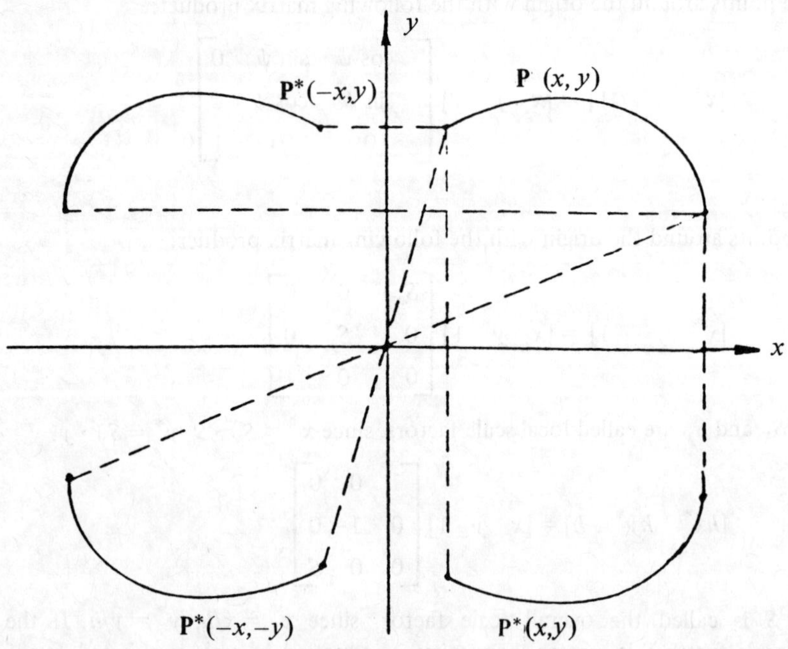

Fig. 2.7 Reflection

Shearing

Points may be moved in the x direction by

$$[x^* \quad y^* \quad 1] = [x \quad y \quad 1] \begin{bmatrix} 1 & 0 & 0 \\ c & 1 & 0 \\ 0 & 0 & 1 \end{bmatrix} \qquad (2.19)$$

We obtain from the above equation

$$x^* = x + cy$$

$$y^* = y$$

This means that the point moves in a direction parallel to the x-axis.

Points may be moved in the y direction by

$$[x^* \quad y^* \quad 1] = [x \quad y \quad 1] \begin{bmatrix} 1 & b & 0 \\ 0 & 1 & 0 \\ 1 & 0 & 1 \end{bmatrix} \qquad (2.20)$$

The results of the movements are

$$x^* = x$$

$$y^* = bx + y$$

This means that the point moves in a direction parallel to the y-axis. Fig. 2.8 shows the movement of the points.

Fig. 2.9 shows the effect of the shearing of a rectangle, which is transformed into a rhomboid.

Projection

Projection points may be obtained by

$$[hx^* \quad hy^* \quad h] = [x \quad y \quad 1] \begin{bmatrix} 1 & 0 & p \\ 0 & 1 & q \\ 0 & 0 & 1 \end{bmatrix}$$

$$= [x \quad y \quad (px + qy + 1)] \qquad (2.21)$$

The results of projection are as follows:

$$x^* = \frac{x}{px + qy + 1}, \quad y^* = \frac{y}{px + qy + 1}$$

For example, an initial point $\mathbf{P}(1, 2)$ is projected by the transformation matrix

$$\begin{bmatrix} 1 & 0 & 2 \\ 0 & 1 & 1 \\ 0 & 0 & 0 \end{bmatrix}$$

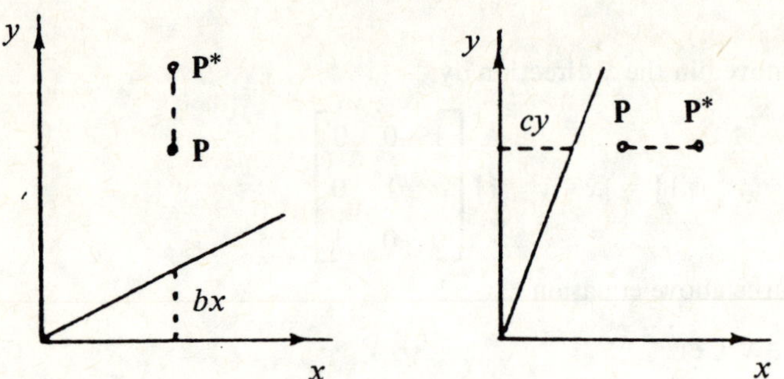

Fig. 2.8 Movement of points

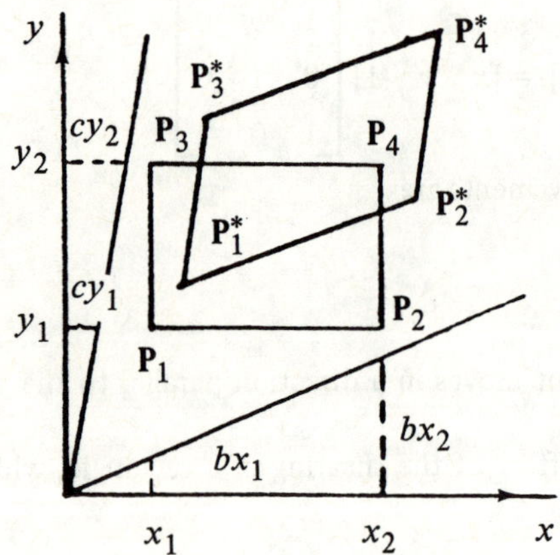

Fig. 2.9 Shearing of a rectangle

The projection $\mathbf{P}^*$ may be calculated as

$$x^* = \frac{1}{2 \times 1 + 1 \times 2 + 1} = \frac{1}{5}, \quad y^* = \frac{2}{5}$$

We will investigate the effect of projection in more detail in the next section.

The geometric transformation matrix may be summarized by

$$T = \begin{bmatrix} a & b & \vdots & p \\ c & d & \vdots & q \\ \cdots & \cdots & \vdots & \cdots \\ m & n & \vdots & S \end{bmatrix} \tag{2.22}$$

The matrix may be divided into four partitions whose function is as follows:

- The 2 × 2 square matrix

$$\begin{bmatrix} a & b \\ c & d \end{bmatrix}$$

  induces rotation, local scaling, reflection and shearing.
- The 2 × 1 row matrix $[m \quad n]$ induces translation.
- The 1 × 2 column matrix

$$\begin{bmatrix} p \\ q \end{bmatrix}$$

  induces projection.
- The 1 × 1 matrix $[S]$ induces overall scaling.

2.2.4 Concatenated transformation

We sometimes encounter the need to rotate a point or a plane curve around an arbitrary point in the plane, or scaling a point or a plane curve around an arbitrary point in the plane.

The rotation of a curve $r(u)$ around an arbitrary point $P(m, n)$ can be handled in the following way (see Fig. 2.10).

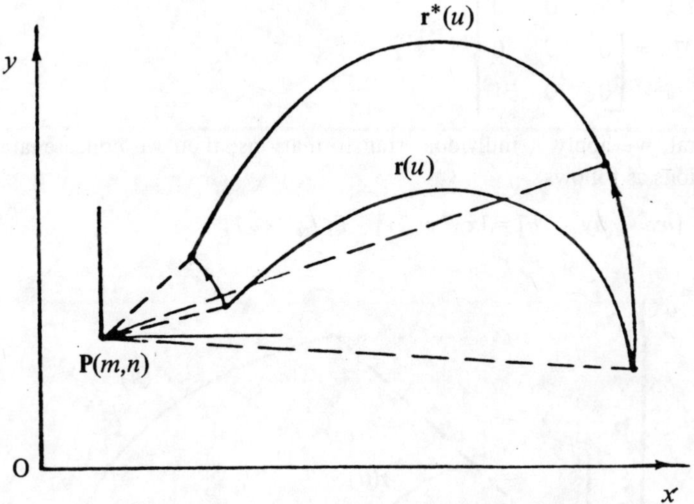

Fig. 2.10 Rotation of a curve around an arbitrary point

- First step: Translate the point $P(m, n)$ and the curve $r(u)$, so that the point P and the origin of the coordinate system are coincident. The translation matrix should be

$$T_1 = \begin{bmatrix} 1 & 0 & 0 \\ 0 & 1 & 0 \\ -m & -n & 1 \end{bmatrix}$$

- Second step: Rotate the curve $\mathbf{r}(u)$ around the point $\mathbf{P}$, since it coincides with the origin. The rotation matrix should be

$$T_2 = \begin{bmatrix} \cos\theta & \sin\theta & 0 \\ -\sin\theta & \cos\theta & 0 \\ 0 & 0 & 1 \end{bmatrix}$$

- Third step: The opposite translation matrix should be

$$T_3 = \begin{bmatrix} 1 & 0 & 0 \\ 0 & 1 & 0 \\ m & n & 1 \end{bmatrix}$$

The concatenated transformation matrix may be obtained from the product of the above three individual matrices:

$$T = T_1 T_2 T_3$$

The scaling of a curve $\mathbf{r}(u)$ around an arbitrary point $\mathbf{P}(m, n)$ can be handled in a similar way; T_2 is the scaling matrix (see Fig. 2.11).

$$T_2 = \begin{bmatrix} S_x & 0 & 0 \\ 0 & S_y & 0 \\ 0 & 0 & 1 \end{bmatrix}$$

In general, we apply n individual transformations; then we concatenate the matrix multiplications as follows:

$$[hx^* \quad hy^* \quad h] = [x \quad y \quad 1] \ T_1 T_2 \cdots T_n \tag{2.23}$$

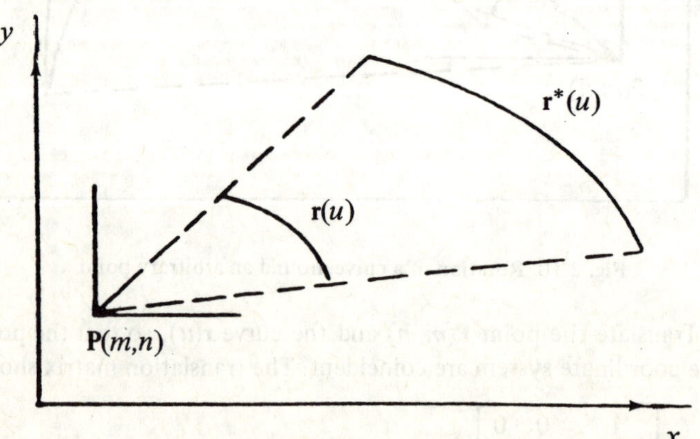

Fig. 2.11 Scaling of a curve around an arbitrary point

The order in which the n transformations are handled is important, since matrix multiplication is non-commutative. Concatenated transformation will be investigated in more detail in the 3-D case.

2.3 THREE-DIMENSIONAL TRANSFORMATIONS

The concepts of geometric transformations, including translation, rotation, scaling, reflection, shearing and projection, may be extended from the 2-D to the 3-D case.

2.3.1 Three-dimensional transformation formulae

An initial point $\mathbf{P}(x, y, z)$ in 3-D space may be represented by $\mathbf{P}_h(x, y, z, 1)$ in homogeneous coordinates. The transformed point is denoted by $\mathbf{P}_h^*(x^*, y^*, z^*, 1)$. Thus the three-dimensional transformation may be defined in unity form as

$$[x^* \quad y^* \quad z^* \quad 1] = [x \quad y \quad z \quad 1] \begin{bmatrix} a & b & c & \vdots & p \\ d & e & f & \vdots & q \\ g & i & j & \vdots & r \\ \cdots & \cdots & \cdots & \vdots & \cdots \\ l & m & n & \vdots & S \end{bmatrix} \tag{2.24}$$

Translation

$$[x^* \quad y^* \quad z^* \quad 1] = [x \quad y \quad z \quad 1] \begin{bmatrix} 1 & 0 & 0 & 0 \\ 0 & 1 & 0 & 0 \\ 0 & 0 & 1 & 0 \\ l & m & n & 1 \end{bmatrix}$$

$$= [x + l \quad y + m \quad z + n \quad 1] \tag{2.25}$$

where l, m, n are values of translation in the directions of the three coordinate axes, respectively.

Rotation

If a point is rotated around the origin, we denote the angle of rotation around the x, y, z axes by θ, ϕ, ψ, respectively. According to the right-hand convention, ψ is positive in a counterclockwise direction when viewed from a point on the $+z$-axis and toward the origin, ϕ is positive in a counterclockwise direction when viewed from a point on the $+y$-axis and toward the origin, and θ is positive in a counterclockwise direction when viewed from a point on the $+x$-axis and toward the origin (see Fig. 2.12).

Rotation around the z-axis may be expressed by

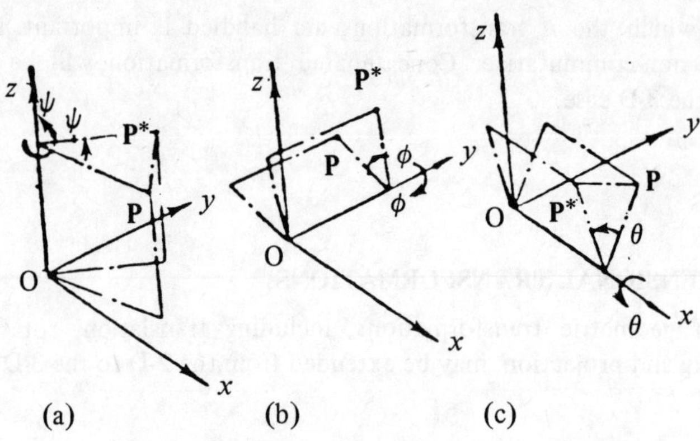

Fig. 2.12 Right-hand convention for rotational angles

$$[x^* \quad y^* \quad z^* \quad 1] = [x \quad y \quad z \quad 1] \begin{bmatrix} \cos\psi & \sin\psi & 0 & 0 \\ -\sin\psi & \cos\psi & 0 & 0 \\ 0 & 0 & 1 & 0 \\ 0 & 0 & 0 & 1 \end{bmatrix}$$

$$= [(x\cos\psi - y\sin\psi) \quad (x\sin\psi + y\cos\psi) \quad z \quad 1]$$

$$(2.26)$$

Rotation around the y-axis may be expressed by

$$[x^* \quad y^* \quad z^* \quad 1] = [x \quad y \quad z \quad 1] \begin{bmatrix} \cos\phi & 0 & -\sin\phi & 0 \\ 0 & 1 & 0 & 0 \\ \sin\phi & 0 & \cos\phi & 0 \\ 0 & 0 & 0 & 1 \end{bmatrix}$$

$$= [(x\cos\psi + z\sin\phi) \quad y \quad (z\cos\phi - x\sin\phi) \quad 1] \quad (2.27)$$

Rotation around the x-axis may be expressed by

$$[x^* \quad y^* \quad z^* \quad 1] = [x \quad y \quad z \quad 1] \begin{bmatrix} 1 & 0 & 0 & 0 \\ 0 & \cos\theta & \sin\theta & 0 \\ 0 & -\sin\theta & \cos\theta & 0 \\ 0 & 0 & 0 & 1 \end{bmatrix}$$

$$= [x \quad (y\cos\theta - z\sin\theta) \quad (y\sin\theta + z\cos\theta) \quad 1]$$

$$(2.28)$$

Scaling

Local scaling around the origin is given by

$$[x^* \quad y^* \quad z^* \quad 1] = [x \quad y \quad z \quad 1] \begin{bmatrix} S_x & 0 & 0 & 0 \\ 0 & S_y & 0 & 0 \\ 0 & 0 & S_z & 0 \\ 0 & 0 & 0 & 1 \end{bmatrix}$$

$$= [S_x x \quad S_y y \quad S_z z \quad 1] \tag{2.29}$$

Overall scaling around the origin is given by

$$[hx^* \quad hy^* \quad hz^* \quad h] = [x \quad y \quad z \quad 1] \begin{bmatrix} 1 & 0 & 0 & 0 \\ 0 & 1 & 0 & 0 \\ 0 & 0 & 1 & 0 \\ 0 & 0 & 0 & S \end{bmatrix}$$

$$= [x \quad y \quad z \quad S]$$

Thus

$$[x^* \quad y^* \quad z^* \quad 1] = [x/S \quad y/S \quad z/S \quad 1] \tag{2.30}$$

Note that $S > 1$ produces a reduction, and $S < 1$ an increase in scale.

2.3.2 Concatenated transformation

Concatenation is a chain transformation; it represents the product of n separate transformations. The n separately imposed transformations may be concatenated into a single transformation matrix. The following examples will illustrate how to construct concatenated transformation.

Example 1

Rotation of a point $\mathbf{P}(x, y, z)$ [or a curve $\mathbf{r}(x(u), y(u), z(u))$, or a surface $\mathbf{r}(x(u, w), y(u, w), z(u, w))$] around the x, y, z coordinate axes by the corresponding angles θ, ϕ, ψ may be obtained as follows. The total effect of three rotation transformations may be calculated by applying the matrix multiplications:

$$[x^* \quad y^* \quad z^* \quad 1] = [x \quad y \quad z \quad 1] \begin{bmatrix} 1 & 0 & 0 & 0 \\ 0 & \cos\theta & \sin\theta & 0 \\ 0 & -\sin\theta & \cos\theta & 0 \\ 0 & 0 & 0 & 1 \end{bmatrix}$$

$$\begin{bmatrix} \cos\phi & 0 & -\sin\phi & 0 \\ 1 & 1 & 0 & 0 \\ \sin\phi & 0 & \cos\phi & 0 \\ 0 & 0 & 0 & 1 \end{bmatrix} \begin{bmatrix} \cos\psi & \sin\psi & 0 & 0 \\ -\sin\psi & \cos\psi & 0 & 0 \\ 0 & 0 & 1 & 0 \\ 0 & 0 & 0 & 1 \end{bmatrix} \tag{2.31}$$

Similar dual transformations may be written for other rotation sequences in different cases.

Example 2

Scaling of a point $\mathbf{P}(x, y, z)$ [or a curve $\mathbf{r}(x(u), y(u), z(u))$, or a surface $\mathbf{r}(x(u, w), y(u, w), z(u, w))$] around an arbitrary point (x_p, y_p, z_p) may be obtained by

$$[x^* \quad y^* \quad z^* \quad 1] = [x \quad y \quad z \quad 1] \begin{bmatrix} 1 & 0 & 0 & 0 \\ 0 & 1 & 0 & 0 \\ 0 & 0 & 1 & 0 \\ -x_p & -y_p & -z_p & 1 \end{bmatrix}$$

$$\begin{bmatrix} S_x & 0 & 0 & 0 \\ 0 & S_y & 0 & 0 \\ 0 & 0 & S_z & 0 \\ 0 & 0 & 0 & 1 \end{bmatrix} \begin{bmatrix} 1 & 0 & 0 & 0 \\ 0 & 1 & 0 & 0 \\ 0 & 0 & 1 & 0 \\ x_p & y_p & z_p & 1 \end{bmatrix}$$

$$(2.32)$$

If $S_x = S_y = S_z$, its effect is equal to the overall scaling.

The concatenated transformation is very different in different cases; however the concept is simple. Note that the order of matrix multiplications is very important, because using the wrong order will lead to the wrong result.

The concatenated transformation is often used in design; for example, a high-speed aircraft has a swept-back wing with a twist angle and an inverted dihedral angle, and the equation of the swept-back wing may be defined by the concatenated transformation form.

2.4 PROJECTIONS

Projections are most valuable geometric transformations, which generate two-dimensional representations of three-dimensional curves and surfaces. Projections may be classified into orthogonal (or isometric, or parallel) projection and perspective (or central) projection.

2.4.1 Orthogonal projections

Orthogonal projections are widely used in engineering drawings because measurements can be related easily to the orthogonal projections.

We will examine the most used method of orthogonal projection in engineering. If an object is rotated (point, curve or surface) around the y-axis by angle ϕ, then around the x-axis by angle θ, and finally projected onto the coordinate plane $z = 0$, we obtain the so-called orthogonal projection.

The rotation matrix of the orthogonal projection may be calculated by

$$T = \begin{bmatrix} \cos\phi & 0 & -\sin\phi & 0 \\ 0 & 1 & 0 & 0 \\ \sin\phi & 0 & \cos\phi & 0 \\ 0 & 0 & 0 & 1 \end{bmatrix} \begin{bmatrix} 1 & 0 & 0 & 0 \\ 0 & \cos\theta & \sin\theta & 0 \\ 0 & -\sin\theta & \cos\theta & 0 \\ 0 & 0 & 0 & 1 \end{bmatrix}$$

$$= \begin{bmatrix} \cos\phi & \sin\phi\cdot\sin\theta & -\sin\phi\cdot\cos\theta & 0 \\ 0 & \cos\theta & \sin\theta & 0 \\ \sin\phi & -\cos\phi\cdot\sin\theta & \cos\phi\cdot\cos\theta & 0 \\ 0 & 0 & 0 & 1 \end{bmatrix} \tag{2.33}$$

If $\phi = 45°$ and $\theta = 35°12'$, then

$$T = \begin{bmatrix} 0.707 & 0.408 & -0.578 & 0 \\ 0 & 0.817 & 0.577 & 0 \\ 0.707 & -0.408 & 0.578 & 0 \\ 0 & 0 & 0 & 1 \end{bmatrix} \tag{2.34}$$

The effect of the projection onto the plane $z = 0$ is that all three principal axes are equally foreshortened, allowing measurements along the axes to be made with the same scale (0.82) and the angles between principal axes are $120°$. These are useful properties to draw manually. This is called isometric projection.

In order to project an object onto the plane $z = 0$, the z coordinates of all the points are set to zero. Similarly, for the projection on plane $x = 0$ and $y = 0$, we may set the x coordinates and y coordinates of all the points to zero. These are the most simple parallel projections.

2.4.2 Perspective projections

Perspective projection is one of the most valuable methods for visualizing objects. Orthogonal projection is used in engineering; however, from aesthetics the perspective view looks realistic and its use has greatly increased, because it is very easy to generate perspective transformations.

Fig. 2.13 shows a perspective projection system which consists of a viewpoint (x_e, y_e, z_e), and object $\mathbf{P}(x, y, z)$ and a projection plane. We denote the projection point by $\mathbf{P}^*(x^*, y^*, z^*)$ which is the intersection point between the plane xOy and the straight line joining the viewpoint and the object point.

Using similar triangles, we can obtain the following equation:

$$\frac{x^* - x_e}{x - x_e} = \frac{y^* - y_e}{y - y_e} = \frac{z^* - z_e}{z - z_e}$$

$$z^* = 0 \tag{2.35}$$

since the projection point $\mathbf{P}^*$ lies on the plane xOy, solving (2.35), we obtain

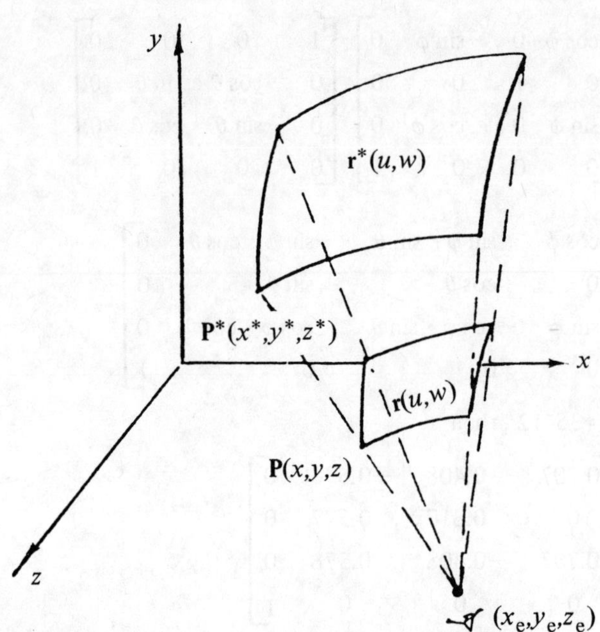

Fig. 2.13 Perspective projection

$$x^* = \frac{z \cdot x_e - x \cdot z_e}{z - z_e}$$

$$y^* = \frac{z \cdot y_e - y \cdot z_e}{z - z_e}$$

$$z^* = 0 \qquad\qquad (2.36)$$

(2.36) may be written in homogeneous coordinate form

$$[hx^* \quad hy^* \quad hz^* \quad h] = [x \quad y \quad z \quad 1] \begin{bmatrix} z_e & 0 & 0 & 0 \\ 0 & z_e & 0 & 0 \\ -x_e & -y_e & 0 & -1 \\ 0 & 0 & 0 & z_e \end{bmatrix} \qquad (2.37)$$

If the viewpoint, that is the observer's eye, is situated at the point $(0, 0, -k)$, then (2.36) may be simplified to

$$x^* = \frac{x}{z/k + 1}$$

$$y^* = \frac{y}{z/k + 1}$$

$$z^* = 0 \qquad\qquad (2.38)$$

(2.38) may also be written in homogeneous coordinate form

$$[hx^* \quad hy^* \quad hz^* \quad h] = [x \quad y \quad z \quad 1] \begin{bmatrix} 1 & 0 & 0 & 0 \\ 0 & 1 & 0 & 0 \\ 0 & 0 & 0 & 1/k \\ 0 & 0 & 0 & 1 \end{bmatrix} \qquad (2.39)$$

In (2.39), when $k \to \infty$, $1/k \to 0$; this is just parallel projection as discussed in sub-section 2.4.1. In fact, the element in the 3rd row and the 3rd column of the projection transformation matrix may be set to 1, since the third coordinate is useful to compare the depth of an object in hidden line removal and to control the brightness of an object.

In the 4×4 transformation matrix, where the elements of the last 3×1 column submatrix are not zero, a perspective projection is generated. We will not develop the perspective projection in more detail here.

Note again that the geometric transformation matrix in 3-D space may be summarized by

$$T = \left[\begin{array}{ccc:c} a & b & c & p \\ d & e & f & q \\ g & i & j & r \\ \hdashline l & m & n & S \end{array} \right]$$

The matrix may be divided into four partitions whose function is as follows:

- The 3×3 square matrix

$$\begin{bmatrix} a & b & c \\ d & e & f \\ g & i & j \end{bmatrix}$$

generates rotation, local scaling, reflection, shearing.
- The 3×1 row matrix $[l \quad m \quad n]$ induces translation.
- The 1×3 column matrix

$$\begin{bmatrix} p \\ q \\ r \end{bmatrix}$$

handles projection effects.
- The 1×1 matrix $[S]$ induces overall scaling.

REFERENCES

[1] Besant, C. B. and Lui, C. W. K., *Computer-aided Design and Manufacture*, Ellis Horwood, Chichester, 1986.

[2] Mortenson, M. E., *Geometric Modelling*, John Wiley & Sons, New York, 1985.

[3] Gasson, P. C., *Geometry of Spatial Forms*, Ellis Horwood, Chichester, 1983.

[4] Foley, J. D. and Dam, A. V., *Fundamentals of Interactive Computer Graphics*, Addison-Wesley, Reading, MA, 1982.

[5] Newman, W. M. and Sproull, R. F., *Principles of Interactive Computer Graphics*, McGraw-Hill, Maidenhead, 1978.

[6] Forrest, A. R., *Coordinates and Transformations*, Memo OGP77/10, University of East Anglia (1977).

[7] Gourand, H., Computer display of curved surfaces, PhD thesis, Department of Electrical Engineering, University of Utah, 1971.

[8] Watkins, G. S., A real time visible surface algorithm, PhD thesis, Department of Electrical Engineering, University of Utah, 1970.

[9] Roberts, L. C., Homogeneous matrix representation and manipulation of N-dimensional constructs, *Computer Display Review*, **5** (1965), 1–16.

3

Ruled Surfaces

3.1 INTRODUCTION

Ruled surfaces have been widely applied in designing cars, ships, aeroplanes, etc. After 1960–1970, Coons, Ferguson, Gordon, Sabin, Bezier, Riesenfeld, Forrest and others developed new surface definitions which will be examined in Chapters 4, 5, 6 and 7, and which now form the theoretical basis of surface models in CAD/CAM systems. However, modern surface modelling systems still include ruled surfaces. Ruled surfaces are still widely used for three reasons.

Firstly, ruled surfaces can meet functional and aesthetic requirements of simple geometric shapes in some cases.

Secondly, the ruled surfaces themselves are still developed by using complex directrices, e.g. spline curves, Bezier curves, B-spline curves and rational curves which are discussed in the following chapters.

Thirdly, the ruled surfaces may be expressed by the bi-cubic parameter form introduced in the last section of this chapter. This simple mathematical form possesses the advantage of simplifying the programs.

In this chapter, we will investigate ruled surfaces and special ruled surfaces including tabulated cylinders, conic surfaces and developable surfaces. We will also discuss the surface of revolution. Finally, the bi-cubic expression of ruled surfaces will be introduced in section 3.6 which should be tackled after Chapter 4, which establishes the concept.

3.2 RULED SURFACES

A ruled surface is a three-dimensional surface entity defined by two curves that can be thought of as consisting of a number of straight lines, each going through a separate point on one curve to a separate or corresponding point on the other curve.

As seen in Chapter 1, the locus of a moving point with one degree of freedom is a curve. The locus of a straight line moving with one degree of freedom is a ruled surface.

A ruled surface based on straight lines joining corresponding points on two space curves $\mathbf{r}_0(u)$ and $\mathbf{r}_1(u)$ is given by vector addition:

$$\mathbf{r}(u, w) = \mathbf{r}_0(u) + w[\mathbf{r}_1(u) - \mathbf{r}_0(u)] \tag{3.1a}$$

It may be rewritten as

$$\mathbf{r}(u, w) = (1 - w)\,\mathbf{r}_0(u) + w\,\mathbf{r}_1(u) \tag{3.1b}$$

It may be also expressed in matrix form:

$$\mathbf{r}(u, w) = \begin{bmatrix} 1 & w \end{bmatrix} \begin{bmatrix} 1 & 0 \\ -1 & 1 \end{bmatrix} \begin{bmatrix} \mathbf{r}_0(u) \\ \mathbf{r}_1(u) \end{bmatrix} \tag{3.1c}$$

In this case, the curves $\mathbf{r}_0(u)$ and $\mathbf{r}_1(u)$ are directrices (see Fig. 3.1). A wing of an aeroplane is a typical ruled surface.

The following entities can be selected as directrices in surface modelling systems: straight lines, arcs, circles, conics (parabola, ellipse, hyperbola), spline curves, Bezier curves, B-spline curves and rational curves, etc.

Any two curves can be joined by straight lines in two different ways: from the start of $\mathbf{r}_0(u)$ to the start of $\mathbf{r}_1(u)$ (see Fig. 3.1), or from the start of $\mathbf{r}_0(u)$ to the end of $\mathbf{r}_1(u)$ (see Fig. 3.2). In interactive design systems, the location of the digitized points selecting the directrices is used to determine how the curves are joined.

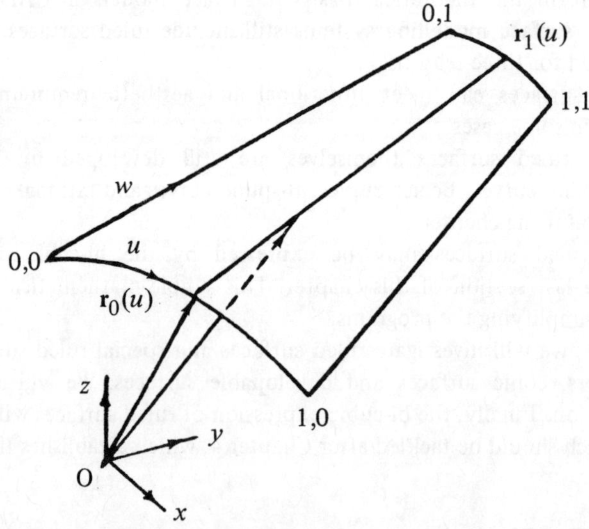

Fig. 3.1 Ruled surface defined by two directrices

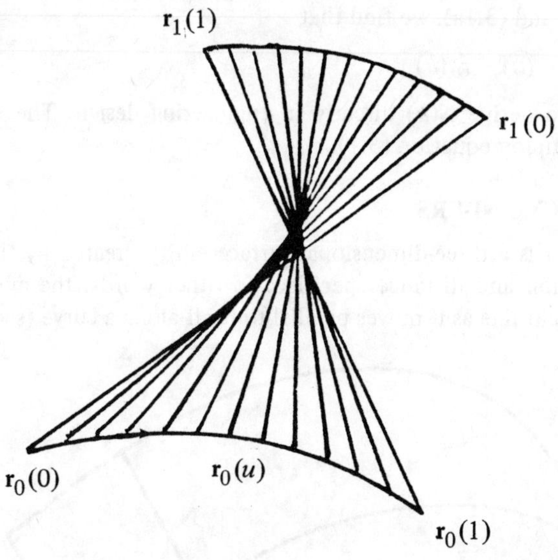

Fig. 3.2

As we know, a ruled surface is a surface generated by a family of straight lines; it may be expressed by

$$\mathbf{r}(u, w) = \mathbf{r}_0(u) + w\,\mathbf{N}(u) \qquad (0 \leqslant u, \quad w \leqslant 1) \tag{3.2}$$

where $\mathbf{r}_0(u)$ is a directrix and $\mathbf{N}(u)$ is a ruling vector. The parameter w gives the distance ratio of the point $\mathbf{r}(u, w)$ from $\mathbf{r}_0(u)$ (see Fig. 3.3).

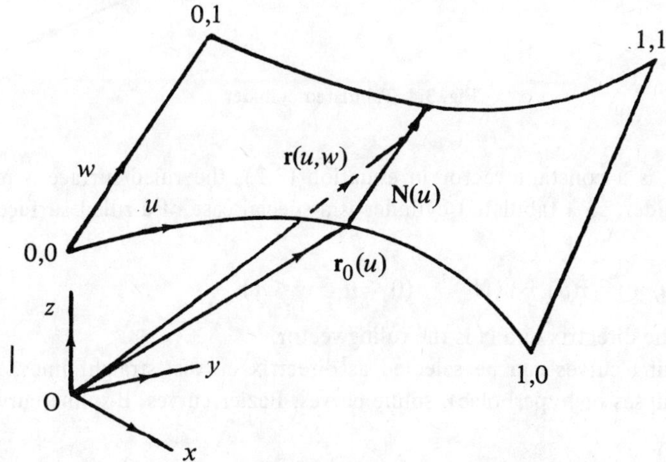

Fig. 3.3 Ruled surface defined by a directrix and a ruling vector

Comparing (3.2) and (3.1a), we find that

$$\mathbf{N}(u) = \mathbf{r}_1(u) - \mathbf{r}_0(u)$$

It is not easy to define $\mathbf{N}(u)$ directly in engineering design. The surface modelling systems prefer to employ equation (3.1).

3.3 TABULATED CYLINDERS

A tabulated cylinder is a three-dimensional surface entity created by the translation of a curve in the direction and distance specified. In other words, the cylinder is a surface generated by a straight line as it moves parallel to itself along a curve (see Fig. 3.4).

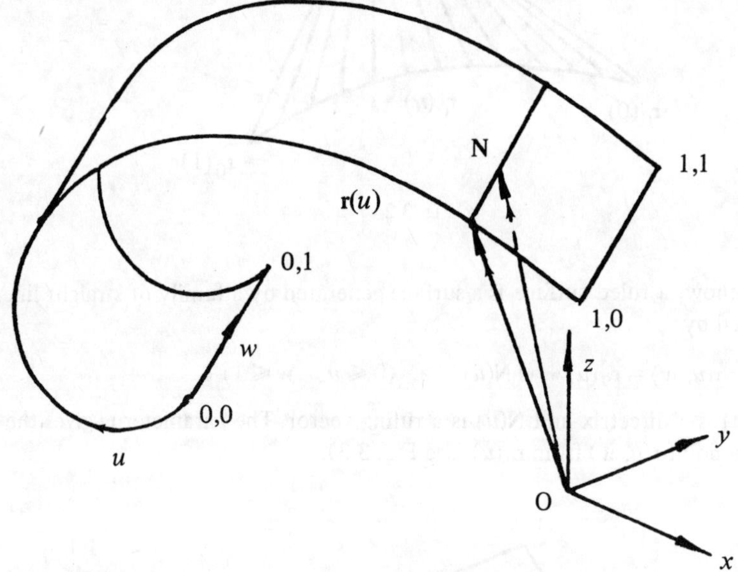

Fig. 3.4 Tabulated cylinder

When $\mathbf{N}(u)$ is a constant vector in equation (3.2), the ruled surface is reduced to a tabulated cylinder, so a tabulated cylinder is a special case of a ruled surface. It may be defined by

$$\mathbf{r}(u, w) = \mathbf{r}(u) + w\,\mathbf{N} \qquad (0 \leqslant u, \quad w \leqslant 1) \tag{3.3}$$

where $\mathbf{r}(u)$ is the directrix and $\mathbf{N}$ is the ruling vector.

The following curves can be selected as directrix curves, straight lines, arcs, conics (parabolae, ellipses or hyperbolae), spline curves, Bezier curves, B-spline curves, rational curves, etc.

3.4 DEVELOPABLE SURFACES

Three aspects of developable surfaces will be discussed in this section: definition of developable surfaces; how to judge a surface to be developable, and the development of developable surfaces.

A developable surface is one which may be generated by rolling or bending on a flat plane into the form required. Conversely, a developable surface is one which may be unrolled or unbent onto a plane without stretching or distorting it. It is common knowledge that cones and cylinders are developable surfaces.

A developable surface possesses an intrinsic geometric property that all corresponding geodesic distances on both the curved and the flat forms are invariant.

Note that every developable surface is ruled, but every ruled surface is not developable. For example, a hyperbolic paraboloid is a ruled surface, but not a developable one, since it is a twisted surface.

How is a surface to be judged developable or not? If the Gaussian curvature κ is equal to zero everywhere, the surface is developable.

As we know, the product of the principal curvatures is known as the Gaussian curvature κ of the surface. We now examine some examples to understand the following sufficient condition for a surface to be developable:

$$\kappa = \kappa_1 \times \kappa_2 = 0 \tag{3.4}$$

Example 1   Circular cylinder

The principal curvature along the direction of ruling is equal to zero, since the ruling is a straight line. The other principal curvature along the direction of the directrix is constant, since the directrix is a circle, then the Gaussian curvature

$$\kappa = \kappa_1 \times \kappa_2 = 0 \times \frac{1}{\rho} = 0$$

where ρ is the radius of the circle, so a circular cylinder is a developable surface.

Example 2   Tabulated cylinder

The principal curvature along the direction of ruling is equal to zero. Although the other principal curvature along the direction of the directrix is a function of the parameter u, then the Gaussian curvature

$$\kappa = \kappa_1 \times \kappa_2 = 0 \times \kappa_2(u) = 0$$

so a tabulated cylinder is also a developable surface.

Example 3   The cone

A cone is a developable surface defined by rulings (straight lines) and two directrices: one is a curve, the other an apex (see Fig. 3.5).

In engineering, it is necessary to calculate the plane developments of developable surfaces which define the shape of objects, such as aircraft wings, roofs, conical filters, and so on.

If the equations of the directrices are known, the plane developments of the developable surface are easily expressed mathematically.

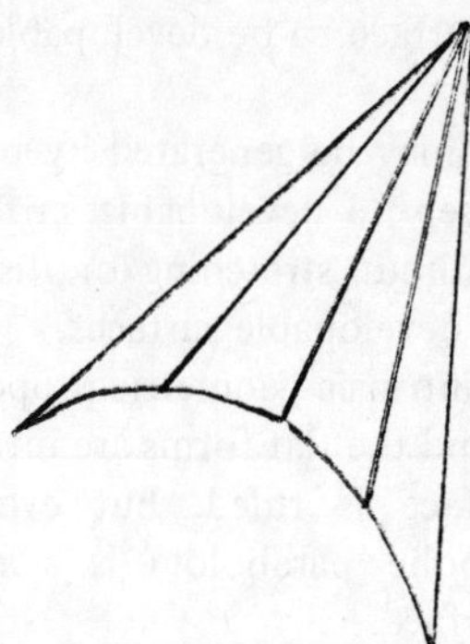

Fig. 3.5 A cone

3.5 SURFACES OF REVOLUTION

A surface of revolution is a three-dimensional surface entity generated by the revolution
of a plane curve about an axis through a given angle.

We will take this axis to be the z-axis, and let the surface intersect the xOz plane in
the curve $\mathbf{r}(u)$ (see Fig. 3.6), which may be expressed by

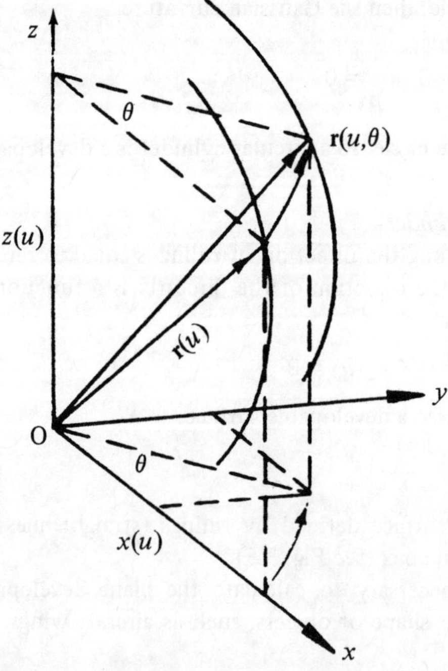

Fig. 3.6 Surface of revolution

$$\mathbf{r}(u) = x(u)\,\mathbf{i} + z(u)\,\mathbf{k}$$

$$= [x(u) \quad 0 \quad z(u)]$$

where $x(u), z(u)$ are the component functions of the plane curve.

Then the surface of revolution has the equation

$$\mathbf{r}(u, \theta) = x(u)\cos\theta\,\mathbf{i} + x(u)\sin\theta\,\mathbf{j} + z(u)\,\mathbf{k}$$

$$= [x(u)\cos\theta \quad x(u)\sin\theta \quad z(u)] \tag{3.5}$$

Since the plane curve is revolved around the z-axis, its z coordinates are not changed.

In a surface modelling system, the following geometric entities can be selected as generator curves: straight lines, arcs, circles, conics (parabolae, ellipses or hyperbolae), spline curves, Bezier curves, B-spline curves, rational curves, etc.

3.6 BI-CUBIC EXPRESSIONS OF RULED SURFACES

As we will see, rulings are straight lines, and the directrices may be any curves for ruled surfaces. We also know that one of the parameter curves may be of any type while the other must be a straight line. The vector equation $\mathbf{r}(u, w)$ of the ruled surface is simple, e.g. equations (3.1), (3.2) and (3.3).

However, in surface modelling systems, to reduce the number and complexity of subroutines designed to solve ruled surfaces, one common mathematical format (see equation (4.54) in Chapter 4) is used which is a coefficient matrix of the bi-cubic polynomial function capable of describing a surface patch. We may regard the ruled surface as a special case of the bi-cubic surface patch.

Example 1   Ruled surfaces
Fig. 3.7(a) shows two directrix curves $\mathbf{r}_0(u)$ and $\mathbf{r}_1(u)$. We construct a ruled surface by joining each point on $\mathbf{r}_0(u)$ with a straight line to a point on $\mathbf{r}_1(u)$ having an equivalent u value. The geometric coefficient matrix of the ruled surface may be expressed by

$$\begin{bmatrix} \mathbf{r}_0(0) & \mathbf{r}_1(0) & \mathbf{r}_1(0)-\mathbf{r}_0(0) & \mathbf{r}_1(0)-\mathbf{r}_0(0) \\ \mathbf{r}_0(1) & \mathbf{r}_1(1) & \mathbf{r}_1(1)-\mathbf{r}_0(1) & \mathbf{r}_1(1)-\mathbf{r}_0(1) \\ \mathbf{r}_0'(0) & \mathbf{r}_1'(0) & 0 & 0 \\ \mathbf{r}_0'(1) & \mathbf{r}_1'(1) & 0 & 0 \end{bmatrix} \tag{3.6}$$

Each w parameter curve is a straight line.

Example 2   Tabulated cylinder
Fig. 3.7(b) shows a directrix curve $\mathbf{r}(u)$ and a ruling vector $\mathbf{N}$. We construct a tabulated cylinder by moving the vector $\mathbf{N}$ in a parallel mode along the directrix curve $\mathbf{r}(u)$. The geometric coefficient matrix of the tabulated cylinder may be described as

$$\begin{bmatrix} \mathbf{r}(0) & \mathbf{r}(0)+\mathbf{N} & \mathbf{N} & \mathbf{N} \\ \mathbf{r}(1) & \mathbf{r}(1)+\mathbf{N} & \mathbf{N} & \mathbf{N} \\ \mathbf{r}'(0) & \mathbf{r}'(0) & 0 & 0 \\ \mathbf{r}'(1) & \mathbf{r}'(1) & 0 & 0 \end{bmatrix} \qquad (3.7)$$

The direction vector $\mathbf{N}$ stands for the w parameter curve.

Example 3   Cone
Fig. 3.7(c) shows a directrix curve $\mathbf{r}_0(u)$ and a point $\mathbf{r}_1$. We construct a cone by joining each point on $\mathbf{r}_0(u)$ with a straight line to the point $\mathbf{r}_1$. The geometric coefficient matrix of the cone may be written as

$$\begin{bmatrix} \mathbf{r}_0(0) & \mathbf{r}_1 & \mathbf{r}_1-\mathbf{r}_0(0) & \mathbf{r}_1-\mathbf{r}_0(0) \\ \mathbf{r}_0(1) & \mathbf{r}_1 & \mathbf{r}_1-\mathbf{r}_0(1) & \mathbf{r}_1-\mathbf{r}_0(1) \\ \mathbf{r}_0'(0) & 0 & 0 & 0 \\ \mathbf{r}_0'(1) & 0 & 0 & 0 \end{bmatrix} \qquad (3.8)$$

One of two directrices is reduced to a point.

REFERENCES

[1]   Mortenson, M. E., *Geometric Modelling*, John Wiley & Sons, New York, 1985.
[2]   Faux, Z. D. and Pratt, M. J., *Computational Geometry for Design and Manufacture*, Ellis Horwood, Chichester, 1985.
[3]   Gasson, P. C., *Geometry of Spatial Forms*, Ellis Horwood, Chichester, 1983.

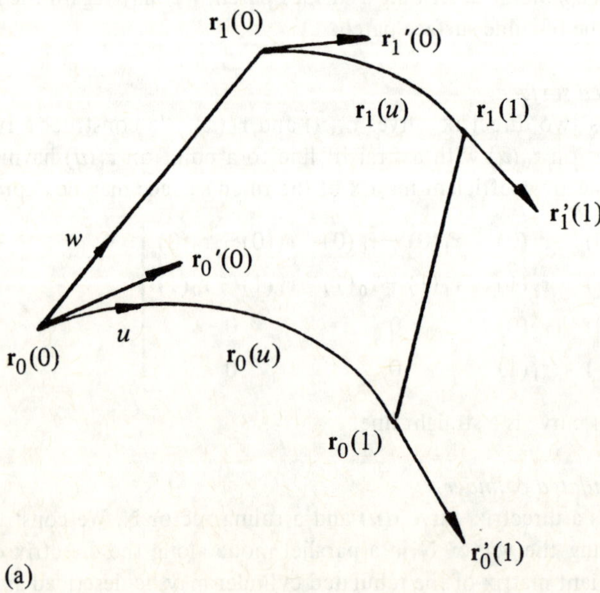

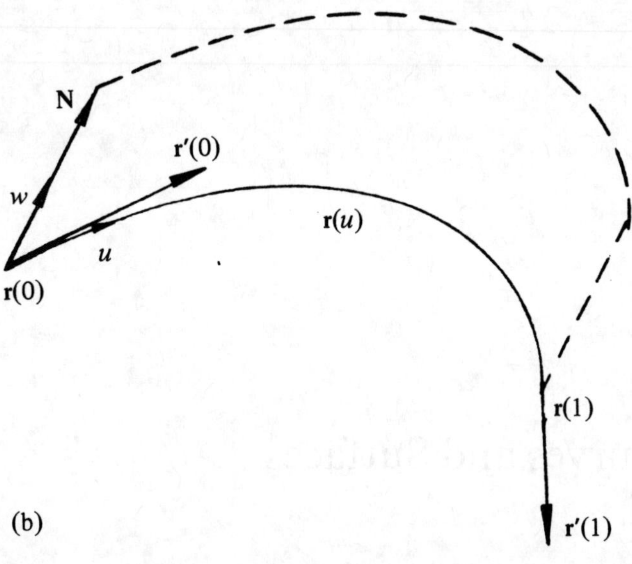

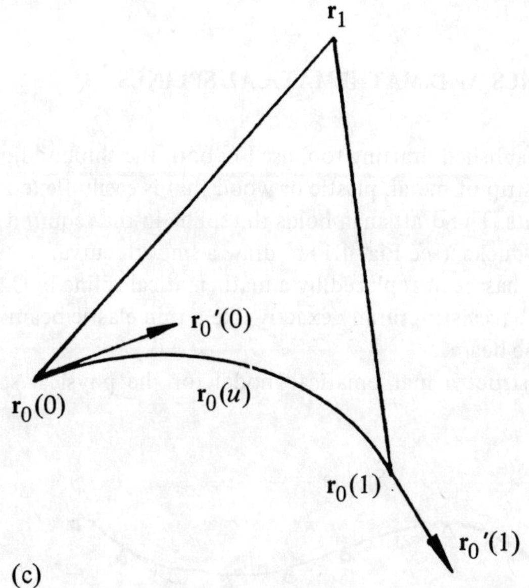

Fig. 3.7 Bi-cubic expressions of ruled surfaces

4

Spline Curves and Surfaces

4.1 PHYSICAL SPLINES AND MATHEMATICAL SPLINES

4.1.1 Physical Splines

The spline is a long-established drafting tool used in both the shipbuilding and the aircraft industries. It is a thin strip of metal, plastic or wood that is easily flexed to pass through a set of design data points. The draftsman holds the spline in the required position with the help of weights called 'ducks' (see Fig. 4.1) to draw a smooth curve.

The physical spline has been replaced by a mathematical spline in CAD/CAM systems. The physical spline behaves structurally exactly like a thin elastic beam; the ducks can be regarded as loads on the beam.

We can easily construct a mathematical model for the physical spline, using beam theory.

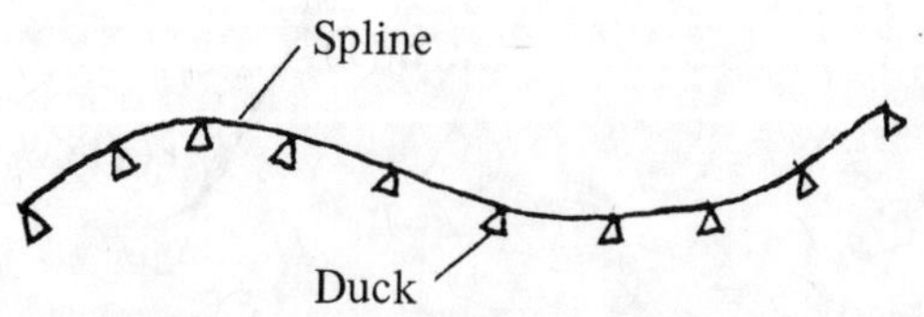

Fig. 4.1 Spline: a drafting tool

4.1.2 Mechanical background

Let us review elastic beam theory. Let us examine a span of an elastic beam between two point loads, in which the bending moment $M(x)$ is a linear function (see Fig. 4.2).

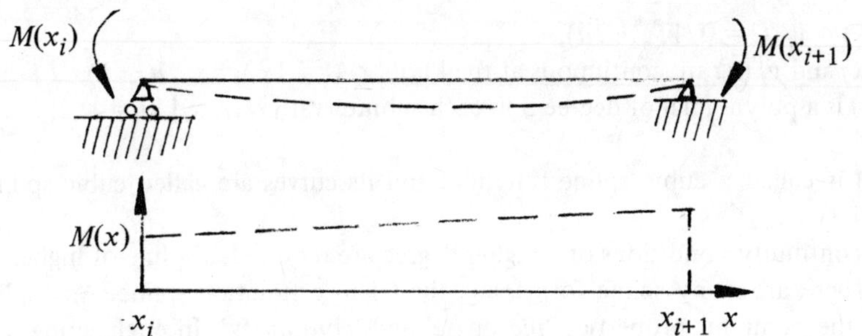

Fig. 4.2 A span of an elastic beam

The Euler formula for bending can be expressed as

$$\frac{1}{\rho(x)} = \frac{M(x)}{EJ} \tag{4.1}$$

where

$M(x)$ is the bending moment

$\rho(x)$ is the beam curvature radius

EJ is the bending constant.

Since the plane curve curvature is

$$\frac{1}{\rho(x)} = \frac{y''(x)}{(1 + y'(x)^2)^{3/2}} \tag{4.2}$$

we obtain from (4.1) and (4.2)

$$\frac{y''}{(1 + y'(x)^2)^{3/2}} = \frac{M(x)}{EJ} \tag{4.3}$$

And since $y'(x) \ll 1$ in this case of an elastic deflected beam, the above equation can be simplified to become

$$y''(x) = M(x)/EJ \tag{4.4}$$

This shows that function $y(x)$ is a cubic polynomial, since bending moment $M(x)$ in a span is a linear function. The y coordinate is the span deflection; the first derivative is the span slope; and the second derivative is the span curvature.

A beam deflection curve can be described by a piecewise and continuous cubic polynomial, since the bending moment $M(x)$ is a piecewise and continuous linear function. We can use piecewise and continuous cubic curves as a mathematical model of a physical spline.

4.1.3 Mathematical splines

We will now consider the definition of the cubic spline function $y(x)$ which fits the given data (x_i, y_i) $(i = 0, 1, \ldots, n)$. If the function $y(x)$ conforms to the following conditions:

- $y(x_i) = y_i$ $(i = 0, 1, \ldots, n)$,
- $y'(x)$ and $y''(x)$ are continuous at the knots x_i $(i = 1, 2, \ldots, n-1)$,
- $y(x)$ is a polynomial of degree 3 in each subinterval $[x_{i-1}, x_i]$ $(i = 1, 2, \ldots, n)$,

then $y(x)$ is called a cubic spline function, and its curves are called cubic spline curves (see Fig. 4.3).

When continuity conditions of a higher degree are required, a spline of higher degree is needed. There are many spline forms, e.g. the triangle function spline. Any spline form possesses the common properties *'piecewise'* and *'continuity'*. In engineering, the cubic polynomial spline is widely used. We will concentrate our attention on the cubic polynomial spline.

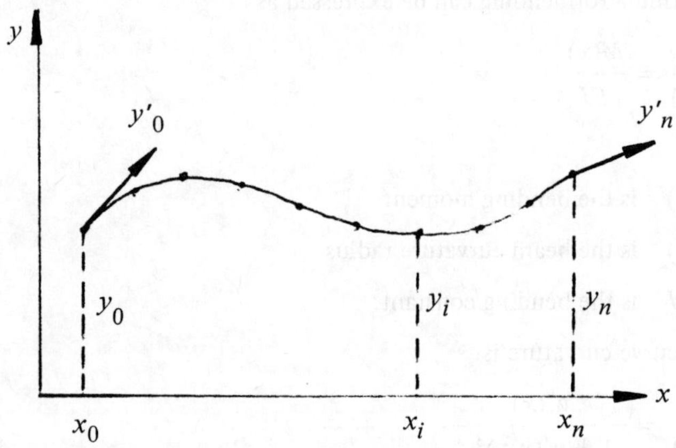

Fig. 4.3 Mathematical spline

4.2 CUBIC SPLINES

The most commonly used spline curve is a plane curve. We will discuss the plane spline curve in this section, then introduce 3-D spline curves in the next section and, finally, consider spline surfaces and their applications.

4.2.1 The first-derivative form

We first develop the first-derivative form of a cubic curve equation in the interval $0 \leqslant u \leqslant 1$. This is a mathematically convenient way of delimiting the values of the parametric variable, because

$$u = (x - x_{i-1})/(x_i - x_{i-1})$$

when x changes from x_{i-1} to x_i, u changes correspondingly from zero to one.

For Hermite interpolation, the four conditions defining a cubic curve segment are function values y_0 and y_1, and the first-derivative values y_0' and y_1' with respect to u at the two end points (see Fig. 4.4).

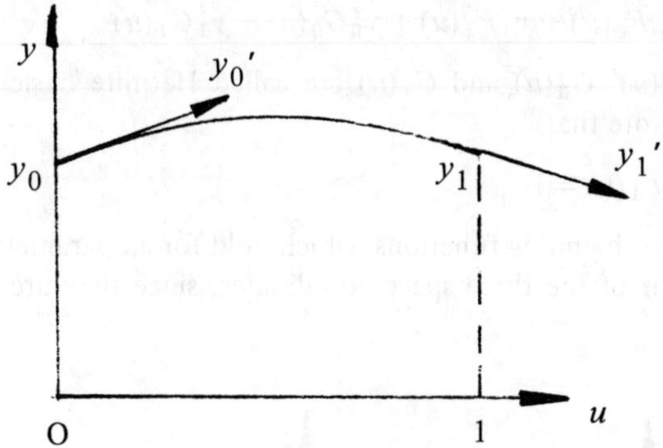

Fig. 4.4 Hermite interpolation for a cubic curve segment

We assume the equation for the cubic curve segment is

$$y(u) = a_0 + a_1 u + a_2 u^2 + a_3 u^3 \tag{4.5}$$

Differentiating the above equation we obtain

$$y'(u) = a_1 + 2a_2 u + 3a_3 u^2 \tag{4.6}$$

Then, substituting the four given conditions into the above two equations, we obtain

$$a_0 = y_0$$
$$a_1 = y_0'$$
$$a_2 = (3y_1 - 3y_0 - 2y_0' - y_1')$$
$$a_3 = (2y_0 - 2y_1 + y_0' + y_1')$$

Thus

$$y(u) = y_0 + y_0' u + (3y_1 - 3y_0 - 2y_0' - y_1')u^2 + (2y_0 - 2y_1 + y_0' + y_1')u^3$$

which can be rewritten as

$$y(u) = y_0(2u^3 - 3u^2 + 1) + y_1(-2u^3 + 3u^2)$$
$$+ y_0'(u^3 - 2u^2 + u) + y_1'(u^3 - u^2)$$

Denoting

$$F_0(u) = 2u^3 - 3u^2 + 1$$
$$F_1(u) = -2u^3 + 3u^2$$
$$G_0(u) = u(u-1)^2$$
$$G_1(u) = u^2(u-1) \tag{4.7}$$

the cubic segment equation can be expressed by

$$y(u) = y_0 F_0(u) + y_1 F_1(u) + y_0' G_0(u) + y_1' G_1(u) \tag{4.8}$$

in which $F_0(u)$, $F_1(u)$, $G_0(u)$ and $G_1(u)$ are called Hermite basic functions or cubic blending functions. Note that

$$F_0(u) + F_1(u) \equiv 1 \tag{4.9}$$

Fig 4.5 shows the four blending functions, which hold for all parametric cubic curves and are identical for each of the three space coordinates, since they are dependent only on parameter u.

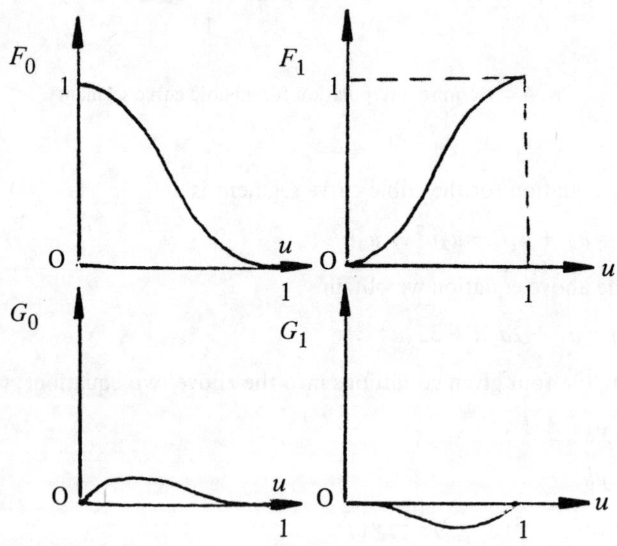

Fig. 4.5 Blending functions for parametric cubic curves

We find that at $u = 0$ only $F_0(u)$ determines the value of $y(u)$, since here $F_0(0) = 1$ and $F_1(0) = G_0(0) = G_1(0) = 0$, and that the influence of $F_0(u)$ gradually diminishes to zero as the value of u gradually increases to one. At $u = 1$ only $F_1(u)$ determines the value of $y(u)$, since here $F_1(1) = 1$ and $F_0(1) = G_0(1) = G_1(1) = 0$, and the influence of $F_1(u)$ gradually increaces to one as the value of u gradually increases to one.

Differentiating (4.7) we obtain

$$F_0'(u) = 6u(u - 1)$$

$$F_1'(u) = 6u(1 - u)$$

$$G_0'(u) = 3u^2 - 4u + 1$$

$$G_1'(u) = 3u^2 - 2u \tag{4.10}$$

Fig. 4.6 shows the corresponding first-derivative functions of blending functions. We see that at $u = 0$, only $G_0'(u)$ determines the value of $y'(u)$, since here

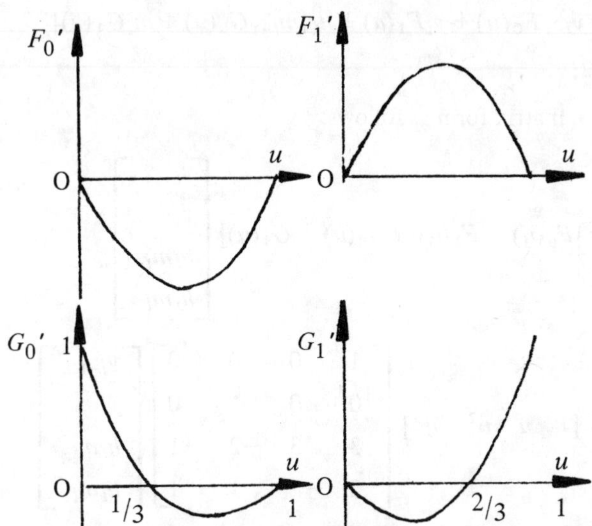

Fig. 4.6 First-derivative functions of blending functions

$F'_0(0) = F'_1(0) = G'_1(0) = 0$, and $G'_0(0) = 1$, and that at $u = 1$, only $G'_1(u)$ determines the value of $y'(u)$, since here $F'_0(1) = F'_1(1) = G'_0(1) = 0$, and $G'_1(1) = 1$.

It is evident that the second-derivative functions of blending functions are a set of linear functions.

Using the four blending functions and corresponding derivative functions, we can calculate the coordinates and first and second derivatives of any point on any parametric cubic curve. Using them, we can modify the end conditions to alter the interior shape of a curve. The set of blending functions is widely used in CAD/CAM applications.

We will now construct a cubic curve segment on the interval $[x_{i-1}, x_i]$. The given end conditions are function values y_{i-1} and y_i, and first derivatives with respect to x, y'_{i-1} and y'_i. Note that there is a relationship between y'_u and y'_x as follows:

$$y'_u = \frac{dy}{du} = \frac{dy}{dx}\frac{dx}{du} = y'_x\frac{dx}{du}$$

Since

$$u = (x - x_{i-1})/(x_i - x_{i-1}) = (x - x_{i-1})/h_i$$

and differentiating yields

$$du/dx = 1/h_i$$

Let m denote the first derivatives y' with respect to x; the above relationship can then be represented by

$$y'_u = y'_x h_i = m h_i \tag{4.11}$$

According to (4.8), the ith curve segment can be described as

$$y_i(x) = y_{i-1}F_0(u) + y_iF_1(u) + h_i[m_{i-1}G_0(u) + m_iG_1(u)] \qquad (4.12)$$

$$(i = 1, 2, \ldots, n)$$

It can be rewritten in matrix form as follows:

$$y_i(x) = [F_0(u) \quad F_1(u) \quad G_0(u) \quad G_1(u)] \begin{bmatrix} y_{i-1} \\ y_i \\ h_i m_{i-1} \\ h_i m_i \end{bmatrix}$$

$$= [1 \quad u \quad u^2 \quad u^3] \begin{bmatrix} 1 & 0 & 0 & 0 \\ 0 & 0 & 1 & 0 \\ -3 & 3 & -2 & -1 \\ 2 & -2 & 1 & 1 \end{bmatrix} \begin{bmatrix} y_{i-1} \\ y_i \\ h_i m_{i-1} \\ h_i m_i \end{bmatrix} \qquad (4.13)$$

$$(i = 1, 2, \ldots, n)$$

This expresses the cubic curve segment on the interal $[x_{i-1}, x_i]$ in terms of two known values y_{i-1} and y_i, and two unknown values m_{i-1} and m_i.

Differentiating (4.12) twice with respect to x yields

$$y_i''(x) = y_{i-1}F_0''(u)/h_i^2 + y_iF_1''(u)/h_i^2$$
$$+ m_{i-1}G_0''(u)/h_i + m_iG_1''(u)/h_i \qquad (4.14)$$

where

$$F_0''(u) = 12u - 6$$

$$F_1''(u) = -12u + 6$$

$$G_0''(u) = 6u - 4$$

$$G_1''(u) = 6u - 2$$

The second derivative at $u = 1$, that is $x = x_i$ for the ith segment, can be calculated from (4.14):

$$y_i''(x_i) = 6y_{i-1}/h_i^2 - 6y_i/h_i^2 + 2m_{i-1}/h_i + 4m_i/h_i \qquad (4.15)$$

Similarly at $u = 0$ for the $(i + 1)$th segment:

$$y_{i+1}''(x_i) = -6y_i/h_{i+1}^2 + 6y_{i+1}/h_{i+1}^2 - 4m_i/h_{i+1} - 2m_{i+1}/h_{i+1} \qquad (4.16)$$

To ensure C^2 continuity at (x_i, y_i) the following condition must exist:

$$y_i''(x_i) = y_{i+1}''(x_i)$$

In other words, the right-hand sides of (4.15) and (4.16) must be equal; we obtain after some simplification

$$\lambda_i m_{i-1} + 2m_i + \mu_i m_{i+1} = C_i \qquad (i = 1, 2, \ldots, n-1) \qquad (4.17)$$

in which

$$\lambda_i = h_{i+1}/(h_i + h_{i+1})$$

$$\mu_i = 1 - \lambda_i$$

$$C_i = 3[\lambda_i(y_i - y_{i-1})/h_i + \mu_i(y_{i+1} - y_i)/h_{i+1}]$$

The first-derivative relationship equations (4.17) guarantee C^2 continuity at (x_i, y_i) $(i = 1, 2, \ldots, n - 1)$ (see Fig. 4.7).

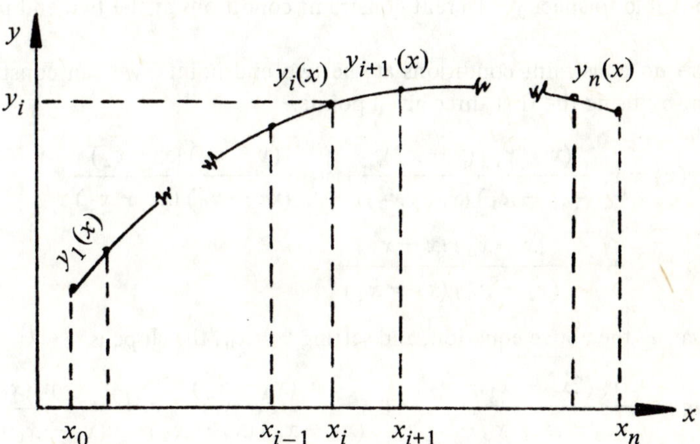

Fig. 4.7 Plane cubic spline curve

We see that (4.17) is linear in the three unknowns m_{i-1}, m_i and m_{i+1}. (4.17) provides only $(n - 1)$ equations for internal knots x_i $(i = 1, 2, \ldots, n - 1)$, but there are $(n + 1)$ unknowns m_i $(i = 0, 1, \ldots, n)$; we therefore need two additional equations to resolve the linear equation system. The two additional conditions are called end conditions and must be provided by the designer in any specific application.

The most widely used end conditions are first derivatives m_0 and m_n at two end points; then only $n - 1$ remains unknown in (4.17). The first equation can be replaced by

$$2m_1 + \mu_1 m_2 = C_1 - \lambda_1 m_0$$

the $(n - 1)$th equation can be replaced by

$$\lambda_{n-1} m_{n-2} + 2m_{n-1} = C_{n-1} - \mu_{n-1} m_n$$

This enables us to resolve the system unambiguously.

By specifying the second derivatives y_0'' and y_n'' at two end points, and setting $i = 0$ in (4.16) we obtain

$$2m_0 + m_1 = C_0$$

where

$$C_0 = [3(y_1 - y_0)/h_1] - [h_1 y_0''/2]$$

and setting $i = n$ in (4.15), we obtain

$$m_{n-1} + 2m_n = C_n$$

where

$$C_n = [3(y_n - y_{n-1})/h_n] + [h_n y_n''/2]$$

If $y_0'' = y_n'' = 0$, implying zero curvature of the spline at the two end points, then the end conditions are called free ends.

But it is possible to specify different constraint conditions at the two end points of the spline.

If there are no constraint conditions at the two end points, we can construct a conic curve segment by using the first three given points.

$$y(x) = y_0 \frac{(x - x_1)(x - x_2)}{(x_0 - x_1)(x_0 - x_2)} + y_1 \frac{(x - x_0)(x - x_2)}{(x_1 - x_0)(x_1 - x_2)}$$

$$+ y_2 \frac{(x - x_0)(x - x_1)}{(x_2 - x_0)(x_2 - x_1)}$$

By differentiating the above equation, and setting $x = x_0$, the slope is

$$m_0 = \frac{y_0(2x_0 - x_1 - x_2)}{(x_0 - x_1)(x_0 - x_2)} + \frac{y_1(x_0 - x_2)}{(x_1 - x_0)(x_1 - x_2)} + \frac{y_2(x_0 - x_1)}{(x_2 - x_0)(x_2 - x_1)}$$

Similarly for the slope of the last point by using the last three given points

$$m_n = \frac{y_{n-2}(x_n - x_{n-1})}{(x_{n-2} - x_{n-1})(x_{n-2} - x_n)} + \frac{y_{n-1}(x_n - x_{n-2})}{(x_{n-1} - x_{n-2})(x_{n-1} - x_n)}$$

$$+ \frac{y_n(2x_n - x_{n-1} - x_{n-2})}{(x_n - x_{n-2})(x_n - x_{n-1})}$$

m_0, m_n can be regarded as the approximate end conditions.

After calculating the m_i, the piecewise cubic curve $y_i(x)$ can be determined by (4.12) or (4.13), and the C^2 continuous spline can be defined by

$$y(x) = y_i(x) \quad (i = 1, 2, \ldots, n)$$

We emphasize again that the spline is piecewise, but is continuous; this is probably the most important concept for any form of splines.

4.2.2 The second-derivative form

The cubic curve segment described by (4.8) can also be defined by two function values y_0 and y_1, and two second-derivative values y_0'' and y_1'' with respect to u at the two end points.

Differentiating (4.6)

$$y''(u) = 2a_2 + 6a_3 u \tag{4.18}$$

and substituting four conditions into (4.15) and (4.18), we resolve four coefficient equations to obtain four coefficients

$$a_0 = y_0$$

$$a_1 = (y_1 - y_0 - \tfrac{1}{6} y_1'' - \tfrac{1}{3} y_0'')$$

$$a_2 = y_0''/2$$

$$a_3 = (y_1'' - y_0'')/6$$

Substituting the four coefficients into (4.5) yields after some reformatting

$$y(u) = y_0 \bar{F}_0(u) + y_1 \bar{F}_1(u) + y_0'' \bar{G}_0(u) + y_1'' \bar{G}_1(u) \quad (0 \leqslant u \leqslant 1) \qquad (4.19)$$

where

$$\bar{F}_0(u) = 1 - u$$

$$\bar{F}_1(u) = u$$

$$\bar{G}_0(u) = -u(u-1)(u-2)/6$$

$$\bar{G}_1(u) = u(u-1)(u+1)/6 \qquad (4.20)$$

These form another set of blending functions for the cubic curve. Note that

$$\bar{F}_0(u) + \bar{F}_1(u) \equiv 1$$

We now construct a cubic curve segment on the interval $[x_{i-1}, x_i]$ with four end conditions including two function values y_{i-1}, y_i and two second derivatives with respect to x denoted by M_{i-1} and M_i.

There is a relationship similar to (4.11)

$$y_u'' = y_x'' \frac{\mathrm{d}^2 x}{\mathrm{d}u^2} = y_x'' h_i^2 = M h_i^2 \qquad (4.21)$$

According to (4.19) the ith cubic curve segment can be expressed

$$y_i(x) = y_{i-1} \bar{F}_0(u) + y_i \bar{F}_1(u) + h_i^2 [M_{i-1} \bar{G}_0(u) + M_i \bar{G}_1(u)] \qquad (4.22)$$

It can be rewritten in matrix form ($i = 1, 2, \ldots, n$)

$$y_i(x) = [\bar{F}_0(u) \quad \bar{F}_1(u) \quad \bar{G}_0(u) \quad \bar{G}_1(u)] \begin{bmatrix} y_{i-1} \\ y_i \\ h_i^2 M_{i-1} \\ h_i^2 M_i \end{bmatrix} \qquad (4.23)$$

This shows the cubic curve segment on the interval $[x_{i-1}, x_i]$ in terms of two known values y_{i-1}, y_i and two unknown values M_{i-1}, M_i.

Differentiating (4.23) with respect to x yields

$$y_i'(x) = y_{i-1} \bar{F}_0'(u)/h_i + y_i \bar{F}_1'(u)/h_i + M_{i-1} \bar{G}_0'(u) h_i + M_i \bar{G}_1'(u) h_i \qquad (4.24)$$

$$(i = 1, 2, \ldots, n)$$

in which

$$\bar{F}_0'(u) = -1$$

$$\bar{F}_1'(u) = 1$$

$$\bar{G}_0'(u) = -(3u^2 - 6u + 2)/6$$

$$\bar{G}_1'(u) = (3u^2 - 1)/6$$

The first derivative at $u = 1$, that is $x = x_i$, for the ith segment can be calculated from (4.24):

$$y_i'(x_i) = (y_i - y_{i-1})/h_i + h_i(M_{i-1} + 2M_i)/6 \qquad (4.25)$$

Similarly, at $u = 0$, that is $x = x_i$, for the $(i + 1)$th segment

$$y_{i+1}'(x_i) = (y_{i+1} - y_i)/h_{i+1} - h_{i+1}(2M_i + M_{i+1})/6 \qquad (4.26)$$

To guarantee C^1 continuity at (x_i, y_i), the following condition must exist:

$$y_i'(x_i) = y_{i+1}'(x_i)$$

In other words, the right-hand sides of (4.25) and (4.26) must be equal, and we obtain

$$\mu_i M_{i-1} + 2M_i + \lambda_i M_{i+1} = d_i \qquad (i = 1, 2, \ldots, n-1) \qquad (4.27)$$

in which

$$\lambda_i = h_{i+1}/(h_i + h_{i+1})$$

$$\mu_i = 1 - \lambda_i$$

$$d_i = 6[\lambda_i(y_{i+1} - y_i)/h_{i+1}^2 - \mu_i(y_i - y_{i-1})/h_i^2]$$

The second-derivative relationship, equations (4.27), ensures C^1 continuity at (x_i, y_i) $(i = 1, 2, \ldots, n-1)$.

It is evident that (4.27) is linear in the three unknown M_{i-1}, M_i and M_{i+1}. (4.27) provides only $(n - 1)$ equations for internal knots x_i $(i = 1, 2, \ldots, n-1)$, but there are $(n + 1)$ unknowns M_i $(i = 0, 1, \ldots, n)$. We therefore need two additional equations.

Specifying the second derivatives M_0 and M_n at the two end points eliminates two unknowns; thus the system (4.27) can be resolved unambiguously.

By providing first derivatives m_0 and m_n at the two end points, we can obtain from the first and last equations (4.24)

$$2M_0 + M_1 = d_0 \qquad (4.28)$$

in which

$$d_0 = 6[(y_1 - y_0)/h_1 - m_0]/h_1$$

and

$$M_{n-1} + 2M_n = d_n \qquad (4.29)$$

in which

$$d_n = 6[m_n - (y_n - y_{n-1})/h_n]/h_n$$

(4.28), (4.27) and (4.29) include $(n+1)$ linear equations; we may compute the unknown M_i ($i = 0, 1, \ldots, n$), then the piecewise cubic curve $y_i(x)$ can be determined by (4.22) or (4.23), which guarantees C^0, C^1 and C^2 continuity.

Note that the first-derivative relationship equations (4.17) and the second-derivative relationship equations (4.27) are all tridiagonal linear equation systems, and can be calculated from the standard algorithm.

4.2.3 Oscillation problems

Plane cubic splines may be constructed in the two ways described in subsections 4.2.1 and 4.2.2. The splines are widely used, since they are probably the simplest spline form. They do have some limitations, as pointed out by Faux and Pratt [1].

- A local modification involves the recomputation of the entire splines.
- A spline, as treated here, will not cope with a vertical tangent.
- Oscillation problems may arise in the approximation of a curve with a discontinuity in its second derivative, e.g. the continuation of a straight line by a circular arc, or the insertion of a straight line between two curves.

The first limitation can be avoided by the use of B-splines mentioned in Chapter 6; the second can be overcome by the use of parametric splines explained in the next section; the third can be alleviated by the use of parametric splines.

We will now introduce a method to overcome oscillation problems (see Fig. 4.8). In a practical application, the profile of a product may include curved segments and straight lines, as shown in Fig. 4.8(a). The use of given data points and the construction of plane cubic splines for the profiles always lead to oscillations in the straight line segment and in its vicinity.

The curve segments and straight lines will usually be treated separately in order to avoid oscillations. However, this is not always convenient. The following method treats the profile as a spline curve, but holds the straight line property in the required regions without the oscillation problems mentioned above.

(4.17) and two additional equations can be expressed in matrix form,

$$
\begin{bmatrix}
2 & \mu_0 & & & & & & \\
\lambda_1 & 2 & \mu_1 & & & & & \\
& \ddots & \ddots & \ddots & & & 0 & \\
& & \lambda_{i-1} & 2 & \mu_{i-1} & & & \\
& & & \lambda_i & 2 & \mu_i & & \\
& & & & \ddots & \ddots & \ddots & \\
& & & & & \lambda_{n-1} & 2 & \mu_{n-1} \\
0 & & & & & & \lambda_n & 2
\end{bmatrix}
\begin{bmatrix}
m_0 \\ m_1 \\ \vdots \\ m_{i-1} \\ m_i \\ \vdots \\ m_{n-1} \\ m_n
\end{bmatrix}
=
\begin{bmatrix}
C_0 \\ C_1 \\ \vdots \\ C_{i-1} \\ C_i \\ \vdots \\ C_{n-1} \\ C_n
\end{bmatrix}
\tag{4.30}
$$

in which $\mu_0 = 0$, $C_0 = 2m_0$, $\lambda_n = 0$, $C_n = 2m_n$.

To ensure the straight line property between (x_{i-1}, y_{i-1}) and (x_i, y_i), we need to set in (4.30)

$$\lambda_{i-1} = \mu_{i-1} = \lambda_i = \mu_i = 0$$

$$C_{i-1} = C_i = 2(y_i - y_{i-1})/(x_i - x_{i-1})$$

and obtain

$$
\begin{bmatrix}
2 & \mu_0 & & & & & & \\
\lambda_1 & 2 & \mu_1 & & & & 0 & \\
 & \ddots & \ddots & \ddots & & & & \\
 & 0 & 2 & 0 & & & & \\
 & & 0 & 2 & 0 & & & \\
 & & & \ddots & \ddots & \ddots & & \\
 & & & & \lambda_{n-1} & 2 & \mu_{n-1} & \\
 0 & & & & & \lambda_n & 2 &
\end{bmatrix}
\begin{bmatrix}
m_0 \\ m_1 \\ \vdots \\ m_{i-1} \\ m_i \\ \vdots \\ m_{n-1} \\ m_n
\end{bmatrix}
=
\begin{bmatrix}
C_0 \\ C_1 \\ 2\left(\dfrac{y_i - y_{i-1}}{x_i - x_{i-1}}\right) \\ 2\left(\dfrac{y_i - y_{i-1}}{x_i - x_{i-1}}\right) \\ \vdots \\ C_{n-1} \\ C_n
\end{bmatrix}
$$

$$\tag{4.31}$$

It is evident that the line between (x_{i-1}, y_{i-1}) and (x_i, y_i) is a straight line, because its slope is

$$m_{i-1} = m_i = (y_i - y_{i-1})/(x_i - x_{i-1})$$

and its equation is

$$y = y_{i-1} + \frac{y_i - y_{i-1}}{x_i - x_{i-1}}(x - x_{i-1}) \qquad (x_{i-1} \leqslant x \leqslant x_i) \tag{4.32}$$

(4.31) can be extended to the case in which the profile includes many curved segments and straight lines.

For the profile consisting of a cubic curve segment, a straight line and a circle arc are as shown in Fig. 4.8(b); the curvature of the straight line is zero, but the curvature of the circle arc is $1/R$ (where R is the radius of curvature), so the curvature is discontinuous at the tangent point between the circle arc and the straight line. The spline technique will produce oscillations in the vicinity of the tangent line: the smaller the radius, the more serious the oscillations. We can also treat this case as an entire spline, without causing oscillations, by using the method as described above.

4.3 PARAMETRIC CUBIC SPLINES

The cubic splines introduced in section 4.2 are used in 2-D space, and are valid only in

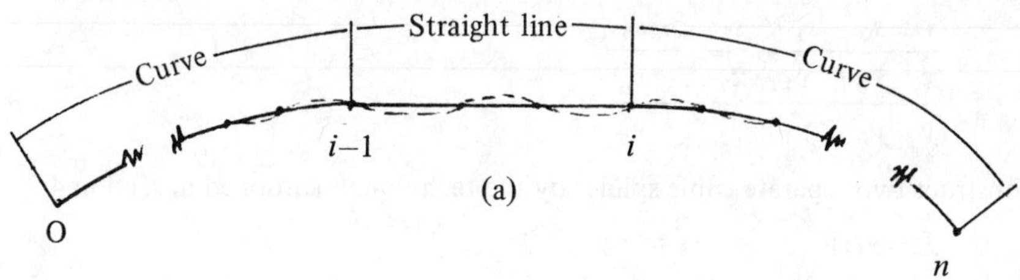

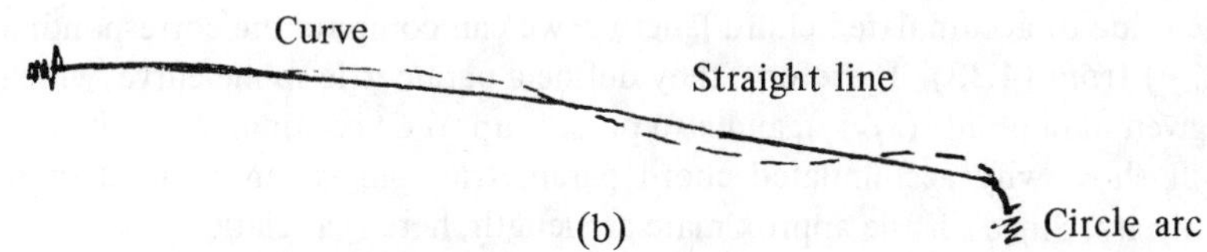

Fig. 4.8 Oscillation problems

the case of 'minor deflections'. We need to eliminate these limitations to enable us to use the spline technique in 3-D space and in the case of 'large deflections'.

The parametric spline is an efficient tool to eliminate the above limitations. A 3-D parametric spline can be defined by three components so that space vector equations can be expressed by three scale equations.

The accumulated arc length of a curve is a natural parameter, and possesses obvious geometric significance. However, we cannot know the arc length between data points until we have constructed the spline curve. An approximate alternative is to use the accumulated chord length.

4.3.1 The accumulated chord length parameter for cubic splines

Using the accumulated chord length s, as a parameter, we construct two cubic splines passing through $(s_i, x_i), (s_i, y_i)$ for a plane curve, and construct three cubic splines passing through $(s_i, x_i), (s_i, y_i)$ and (s_i, z_i) for a space curve; these are called plane or space parametric splines respectively.

Given a set of data points (x_i, y_i) $(i = 0, 1, \ldots, n)$, we may calculate the accumulated chord length, setting $s_0 = 0$, and

$$s_k = \sum_{i=1}^{k} \sqrt{(x_i - x_{i-1})^2 + (y_i - y_{i-1})^2} \qquad (k = 1, 2, \ldots, n)$$

We can then obtain the following data:

s	s_0	s_1	s_2	...	s_n
x	x_0	x_1	x_2	...	x_n
y	y_0	y_1	y_2	...	y_n

and construct two separate cubic splines by the technique mentioned in section 4.2.

$$x = x(s)$$

$$y = y(s) \tag{4.33}$$

These splines are all piecewise cubic polynomials and possess up to C^2 continuity. Given the value of accumulated chord length s, we can compute the corresponding pair of values (x, y) from (4.33). Therefore, they define a parametric spline curve, which possess through given data points (x_i, y_i), and also possess up to C^2 continuity.

We will show why accumulated chord parametric splines can be used in the 'large deflection' case. Since s is the approximate arc length, here is a relation:

$$ds^2 = [dx(s)]^2 + [dy(s)]^2$$

that is

$$\left[\frac{dx(s)}{ds}\right]^2 + \left[\frac{dy(s)}{ds}\right]^2 = 1$$

This produces two inequalities:

$$\frac{dx}{ds} \leqslant 1, \quad \frac{dy}{ds} \leqslant 1$$

which are valid for all values of s. So we can say that parametric splines translate the 'large deflection' curve $y = y(x)$ into two 'minor deflection' curves $x = x(s)$, $y = y(s)$.

When $dy/dx = \infty$, that is a vertical tangent, normal splines cannot be treated in this way, but parametric splines can be so treated, since a vertical tangent can be expressed by $dy/ds = 1$ and $dx/ds = 0$.

The end conditions should be correspondingly treated to suit the parametric splines. Three cases are given as examples:

1. Slope value y' at end point
Since

$$y' = \frac{dy}{dx} = \frac{dy}{ds}\bigg/\frac{dx}{ds} = \frac{\dot{y}}{\dot{x}}$$

$$1 + y'^2 = 1 + \frac{\dot{y}^2}{\dot{x}^2} = \frac{\dot{x}^2 + \dot{y}^2}{\dot{x}^2} = \frac{1}{\dot{x}^2}$$

we obtain

$$\dot{x} = \pm \frac{1}{\sqrt{1 + y'^2}}$$

$$\dot{y} = \pm \frac{y'}{\sqrt{1 + y'^2}} \qquad (4.34)$$

And since $y' = \mathrm{tg}\,\alpha = \sin\alpha/\cos\alpha$, the end point conditions can be expressed by

$$\dot{x} = \pm \cos\alpha$$

$$\dot{y} = \pm \sin\alpha \qquad (4.35)$$

For the end point condition with a vertical tangent, since

$$y' = \dot{y}/\dot{x} = \infty$$

so we set

$$\dot{x} = 0$$

$$\dot{y} = \pm 1 \qquad (4.36)$$

For the end point condition with a horizontal tangent, since

$$y' = 0$$

so we set

$$\dot{x} = \pm 1$$

$$\dot{y} = 0 \qquad (4.37)$$

2. Free end

Since

$$[\kappa(s)]^2 = \ddot{\mathbf{r}}(s)^2 = \ddot{x}^2 + \ddot{y}^2 = 0$$

we should set

$$\ddot{x} = 0$$

$$\ddot{y} = 0 \qquad (4.38)$$

3. Centre of curvature at end point (see Fig. 4.9)

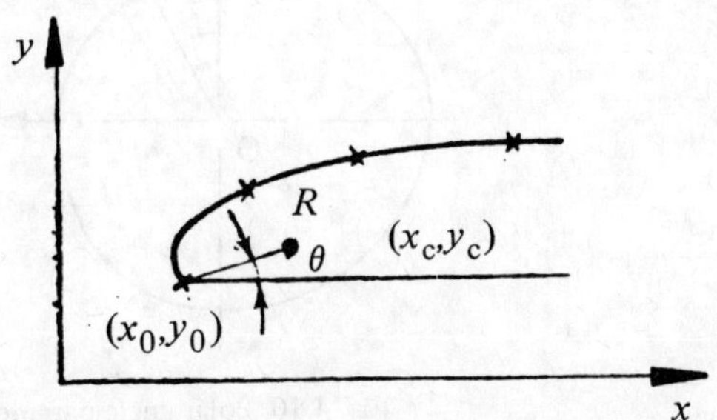

Fig. 4.9

Since $\ddot{\mathbf{r}}(s) = [\ddot{x}(s) \quad \ddot{y}(s)] = \dot{\mathbf{T}}(s) = \kappa\mathbf{N} = \kappa\,[\cos\theta \quad \sin\theta]$ in which

    T   is the unit tangent vector

    N   is the unit normal vector

    κ is the curvature of the end point and $\kappa = 1/R$

    $\cos\theta = (x_c - x_0)/R$

    $\sin\theta \ = (y_c - y_0)/R$

$$R = \sqrt{(x_c - x_0)^2 + (y_c - y_0)^2}$$

The end point conditions are

$$\ddot{x}(s) = \frac{x_c - x_0}{(x_c - x_0)^2 + (y_c - y_0)^2}$$

$$\ddot{y}(s) = \frac{y_c - y_0}{(x_c - x_0)^2 + (y_c - y_0)^2} \tag{4.39}$$

In 3-D space, we construct $x = x(s)$, $y = y(s)$ and $z = z(s)$, which form a space parametric spline. The tangent vector at the end point is usually chosen as the end point condition. In practical applications, the direction of the tangent vector is easily estimated, but the magnitude of the tangent vector is not. We suggest setting the chord length between the first two points as the magnitude of the tangent vector at the end point.

4.3.2 Polar angle parametric cubic splines

Some closed curves, such as the cross-section of an aircraft fuselage, can be fitted by using parametric splines with accumulated chord length parameter. They can also be fitted by using parametric splines with polar angle parameter (see Fig. 4.10).

    The polar coordinate equation of the curve can be described by

$$\rho = \rho(\theta) \quad (0 \leqslant \theta \leqslant 2\pi) \tag{4.40}$$

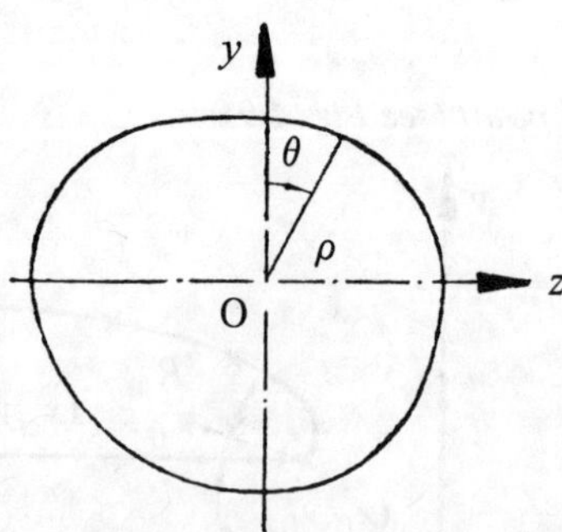

Fig. 4.10 Polar angle parameter

Given a set of data points (θ_i, ρ_i) $(i = 0, 1, \ldots, n)$, the spline $\rho = \rho(\theta)$ may be constructed. Then the curve parametric equations can be directly written:

$$y = \rho(\theta) \cos \theta$$
$$z = \rho(\theta) \sin \theta \qquad (0 \leqslant \theta \leqslant 2\pi) \tag{4.41}$$

Fig. 4.10 shows that $y = y(z)$ is a 'large deflection' curve in the yOz coordinate plane, but Fig 4.11 shows that $\rho = \rho(\theta)$ is a 'minor deflection' curve. This illustrates that the underlying idea of using a polar angle parameter is the translation of a 'large deflection' curve into a 'minor deflection' curve.

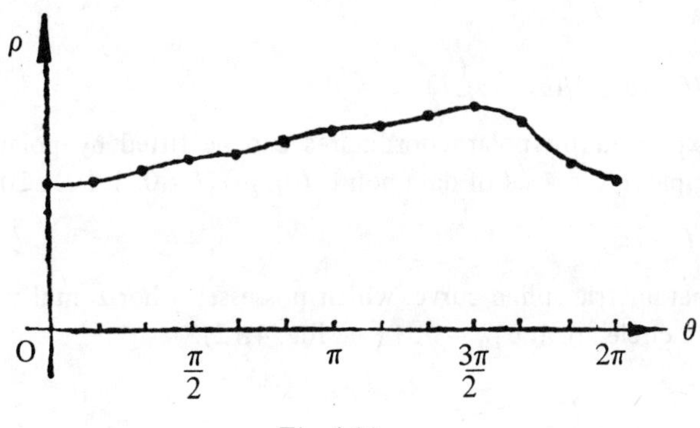

Fig. 4.11

Using the first-derivative form of cubic splines, we construct splines with polar angle parameter

$$\lambda_i m_{i-1} + 2m_i + \mu_i m_{i+1} = C_i \qquad (i = 1, 2, \ldots, n-1) \tag{4.42}$$

in which

$$m = d\rho/d\theta$$
$$h_i = \theta_i - \theta_{i-1}$$
$$\lambda_i = h_{i+1}/(h_i + h_{i+1})$$
$$\mu_i = 1 - \lambda_i$$
$$C_i = 3[\lambda_i(\rho_i - \rho_{i-1})/h_i + \mu_i(\rho_{i+1} - \rho_i)/h_{i+1}]$$

Two additional equations can be chosen using the closed curve property

$$m_0 = m_n \tag{4.43}$$

and

$$\lambda_n m_{n-1} + 2m_n + \mu_n m_1 = C_n \tag{4.44}$$

where

$$\lambda_n = h_1/(h_n + h_1)$$

$$\mu_n = 1 - \lambda_n$$

$$C_n = 3\left[\lambda_n(\rho_n - \rho_{n-1})/h_n + \mu_n(\rho_1 - \rho_0)/h_1\right]$$

since we can set $i-1 = n-1, i = n, i+1 = 1$ in (4.42).

(4.42), (4.43) and (4.44) form a linear system, which may be computed using a standard aglorithm. After calculating m_i, the parametric spline $\rho = \rho(\theta)$ can be directly written.

$$\rho_i(\theta) = \rho_{i-1}F_0(u) + \rho_i F_1(u) + h_i\left[m_{i-1}G_0(u) + m_i G_1(u)\right] \tag{4.45}$$

$$(i = 1, 2, \ldots, n)$$

in which

$$u = (\theta - \theta_{i-1})/(\theta_i - \theta_{i-1})$$

Any curve expressed by polar coordinates can be fitted by polar angle parameter splines. For example: given a set of data points (θ_i, ρ_i) $(i = 0, 1, \ldots, 10)$

$$\theta_i = i \times 7.5°$$

we construct a parametric spline curve, which possesses a horizontal tangent at $\theta_0 = 0°$, and a tangent to a circle arc at $\theta_{10} = 75°$ (see Fig. 4.12).

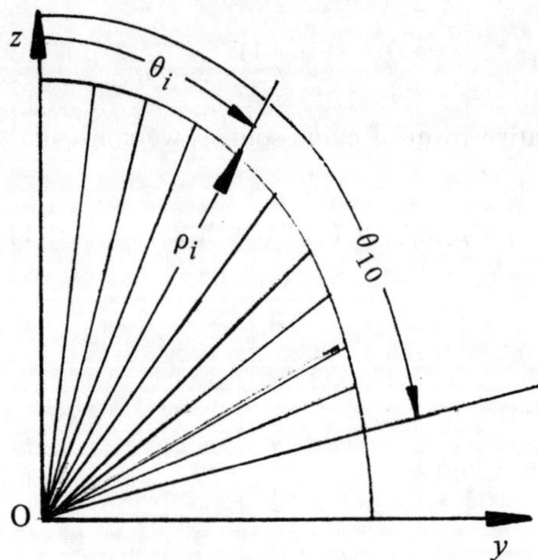

Fig. 4.12

The most important thing is to analyse the end point conditions correctly. Since there is a horizontal tangent at $\theta = 0°$

$$\left.\frac{dy}{dz}\right|_{z=0} = \left.\left(\frac{dy}{d\theta}\bigg/\frac{dz}{d\theta}\right)\right|_{\theta=0} = 0$$

then

$$\left. \frac{dy}{d\theta} \right|_{\theta=0} = 0$$

Differentiating $y = \rho(\theta) \cos \theta$, we obtain

$$\frac{dy}{d\theta} = \rho'(\theta) \cos \theta - \rho(\theta) \sin \theta$$

Substituting $\theta_0 = 0$ into the above formula, and using the result

$$\left. \frac{dy}{d\theta} \right|_{\theta=0} = 0$$

we obtain the end point condition at the first point

$$m_0 = \rho'(\theta_0) = 0$$

Since the curve tangent to a circle arc at θ_{10}, ρ is constant for a circle, then $d\rho/d\theta = 0$. Another end point condition is

$$m_{10} = \rho'(\theta_{10}) = 0$$

We see that the $\Delta\theta_i$ are equal.

$$\Delta\theta_i = h_i = \theta_i - \theta_{i-1} = 7.5° = 0.1309 \text{ arc} \qquad (i = 1, 2, \ldots, 10)$$

$$\lambda_i = \mu_i = \tfrac{1}{2}$$

Thus the linear system may be rewritten in matrix form

$$\begin{bmatrix} 2 & \tfrac{1}{2} & & & & \\ \tfrac{1}{2} & 2 & \tfrac{1}{2} & & & 0 \\ & \tfrac{1}{2} & 2 & \tfrac{1}{2} & & \\ & & \cdot & \cdot & \cdot & \\ & & & \cdot & \cdot & \cdot \\ & & \tfrac{1}{2} & 2 & \tfrac{1}{2} \\ 0 & & & \tfrac{1}{2} & 2 \end{bmatrix} \begin{bmatrix} m_1 \\ m_2 \\ m_3 \\ \vdots \\ m_8 \\ m_9 \end{bmatrix} = \begin{bmatrix} C_1 \\ C_2 \\ C_3 \\ \vdots \\ C_8 \\ C_9 \end{bmatrix}$$

in which

$$m_i = \rho'(\theta_i)$$

$$C_i = \frac{3}{0.2618} (\rho_{i+1} - \rho_{i-1}) \qquad (i = 1, 2, \ldots, 9)$$

Resolving the system, we obtain m_i. Then substituting them into (4.45), we obtain the polar coordinate equation for the curve. Finally, using (4.41), we obtain the curve.

4.4 BI-CUBIC SURFACE PATCH

The algebraic form of a bi-cubic patch may be expressed as

$$r(u, w) = a_{00}u^0 w^0 + a_{01}u^0 w + a_{02}u^0 w^2 + a_{03}u^0 w^3 +$$

$$a_{10}uw^0 + a_{11}uw + a_{12}uw^2 + a_{13}uw^3 +$$

$$a_{20}u^2 w^0 + a_{21}u^2 w + a_{22}u^2 w^2 + a_{23}u^2 w^3 +$$

$$a_{30}u^3 w^0 + a_{31}u^3 w + a_{32}u^3 w^2 + a_{33}u^3 w^3 \qquad (4.46)$$

$$(0 \leqslant u, w \leqslant 1)$$

Its compact form is given by

$$r(u, w) = \sum_{i=0}^{3} \sum_{j=0}^{3} a_{ij} u^i w^j \qquad (4.47)$$

The a_{ij} ($i = 0, 1, 2, 3; j = 0, 1, 2, 3$), which are called the algebraic coefficients, determine the patch shape and its position in space. They have no obvious geometric significance in understanding and controlling the patch shape. We prefer to use the geometric form definition for bi-cubic patches.

Fig. 4.13 shows that there is a unique pair of u_i, w_j values associated with each point on the surface patch.

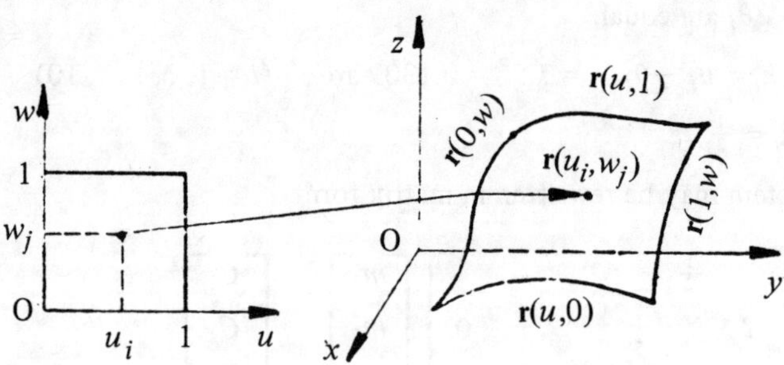

Fig. 4.13 Surface patch and its parameter plane

Fig. 4.14 shows that a bi-cubic patch is bounded by four boundary curves, $r(u, 0)$, $r(u, 1)$, $r(0, w)$, $r(1, w)$. Each boundary curve is a cubic parametric curve, e.g.

$$r(u, 0) = a_{00} + a_{10}u + a_{20}u^2 + a_{30}u^3$$

There are also four unique corner points, $r(0, 0)$, $r(0, 1)$, $r(1, 0)$, $r(1, 1)$, e.g. $r(0, 0) = a_{00}$.

We will use the partial derivative vector of the function $r(u, w)$:

$$r_u(u, w) = \partial r(u, w)/\partial u$$

$$r_w(u, w) = \partial r(u, w)/\partial w$$

and we will use the mixed partial derivative vector of the function $r(u, w)$:

$$r_{uw}(u, w) = \partial^2 r(u, w)/\partial u \partial w$$

It is the so-called 'twist vector'.

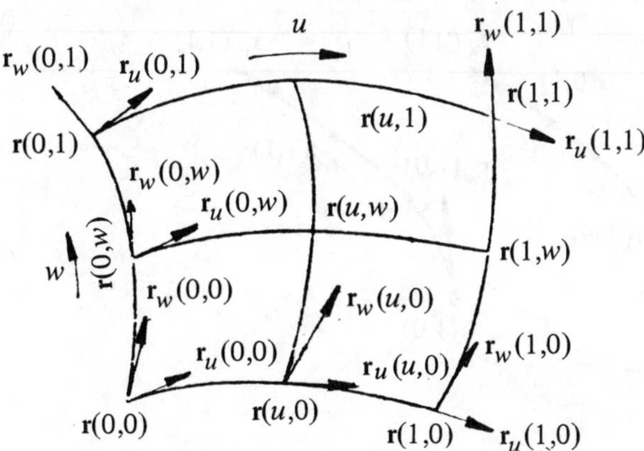

Fig. 4.14 Nomenclature for a bi-cubic surface

For any corner point of a patch, such as $u = 0$, $w = 0$, there are four geometric vectors: position vector $\mathbf{r}(0, 0)$, u-direction partial derivative vector $\mathbf{r}_u(0,0)$, w-direction partial derivative vector $\mathbf{r}_w(0, 0)$, and twist vector $\mathbf{r}_{uw}(0,0)$.

Fig. 4.15 shows how to form a bi-cubic patch.

First step
We construct the boundary curves $\mathbf{r}(0, w)$ and $\mathbf{r}(1, w)$.

$$\mathbf{r}(0, w) = F_0(w)\,\mathbf{r}(0, 0) + F_1(w)\,\mathbf{r}(0, 1)$$

$$+ G_0(w)\,\mathbf{r}_w(0, 0) + G_1(w)\,\mathbf{r}_w(0, 1) \tag{4.48}$$

$$\mathbf{r}(1, w) = F_0(w)\,\mathbf{r}(1, 0) + F_1(w)\,\mathbf{r}(1, 1)$$

$$+ G_0(w)\,\mathbf{r}_w(1, 0) + G_1(w)\,\mathbf{r}_w(1, 1) \tag{4.49}$$

Second step
We construct two tangent vector functions $\mathbf{r}_u(0, w)$ and $\mathbf{r}_u(1, w)$. There is an analogy between the way we construct a cubic curve segment defined by two position vectors and two tangent vectors at two end points, and the way we construct tangent vector functions defined by two tangent vectors and two twist vectors at two corner points. The tangent vector functions can be expressed as

$$\mathbf{r}_u(0, w) = F_0(w)\,\mathbf{r}_u(0, 0) + F_1(w)\,\mathbf{r}_u(0, 1)$$

$$+ G_0(w)\,\mathbf{r}_{uw}(0, 0) + G_1(w)\,\mathbf{r}_{uw}(0, 1) \tag{4.50}$$

$$\mathbf{r}_u(1, w) = F_0(w)\,\mathbf{r}_u(1, 0) + F_1(w)\,\mathbf{r}_u(1, 1)$$

$$+ G_0(w)\,\mathbf{r}_{uw}(1, 0) + G_1(w)\,\mathbf{r}_{uw}(1, 1) \tag{4.51}$$

$\mathbf{r}_w(0,1)$
$\mathbf{r}_w(1,1)$
$\mathbf{r}(0,1)$
$\mathbf{r}(1,1)$
$\mathbf{r}_w(1,0)$
$\mathbf{r}(1,w)$
w
$\mathbf{r}_w(0,0)$
$\mathbf{r}(0,w)$
$\mathbf{r}(1,0)$
$\mathbf{r}(0,0)$
1
$\mathbf{r}_u(0,1)$
$\mathbf{r}_{uw}(0,1)$
$\mathbf{r}_u(1,1)$
$\mathbf{r}_{uw}(1,1)$
$\mathbf{r}_u(0,w)$
$\mathbf{r}_u(1,w)$
$\mathbf{r}_{uw}(0,0)$
$\mathbf{r}_u(1,0)$
$\mathbf{r}_{uw}(1,0)$
$\mathbf{r}_u(0,0)$
2
$\mathbf{r}_u(0,w)$
$\mathbf{r}(0,w)$
$\mathbf{r}(1,w)$
$\mathbf{r}_u(1,w)$
3
$\mathbf{r}(0,1)$
$\mathbf{r}(u,1)$
$\mathbf{r}(1,1)$
$\mathbf{r}(u,w)$
$\mathbf{r}(1,w)$
w
$\mathbf{r}(0,w)$
$\mathbf{r}(u,0)$
$\mathbf{r}(1,0)$
u
$\mathbf{r}(0,0)$
4

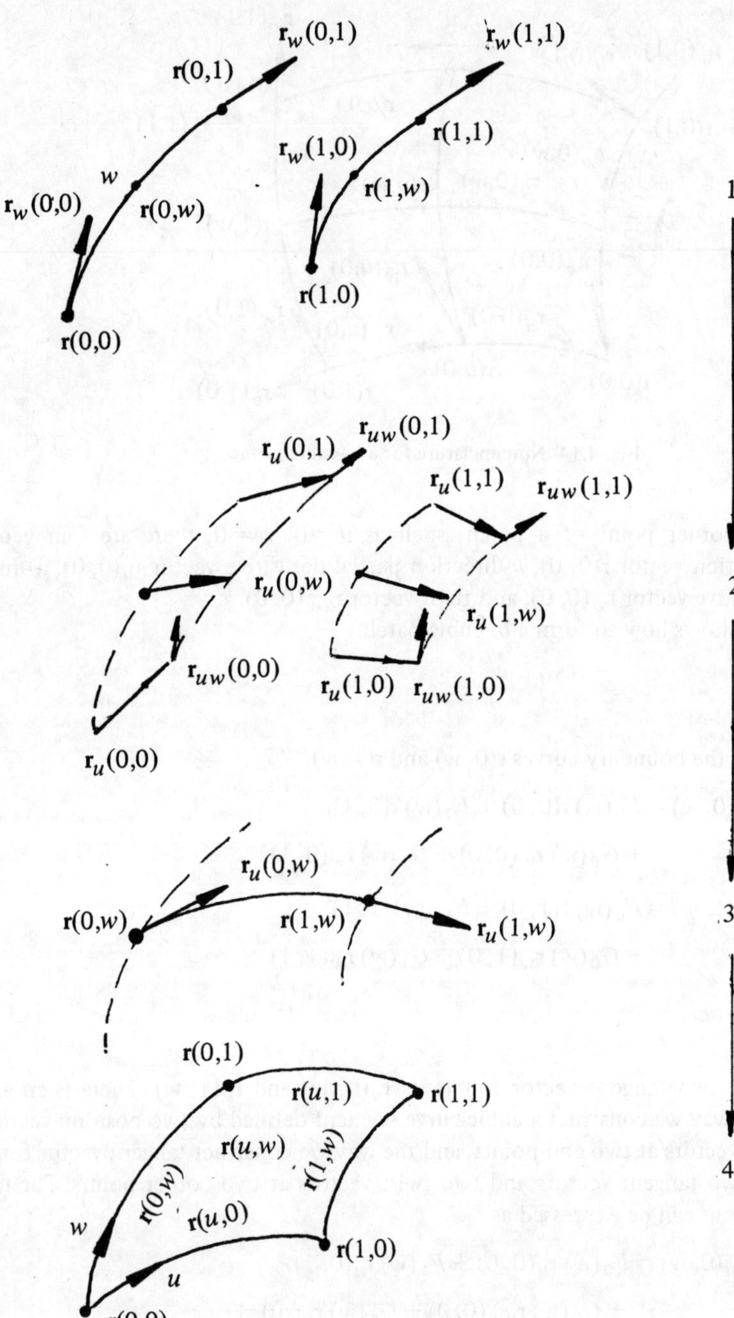

Fig. 4.15

Third step

Setting $w = $ constant in (4.48)–(4.51), we obtain two position vectors $\mathbf{r}(0, w)$ and $\mathbf{r}(1, w)$ and two tangent vectors $\mathbf{r}_u(0, w)$ and $\mathbf{r}_u(1, w)$. Using them, we may construct a cubic curve segment with respect to parameter u:

$$\mathbf{r}(u, w) = [F_0(u) \quad F_1(u) \quad G_0(u) \quad G_1(u)] \begin{bmatrix} \mathbf{r}(0, w) \\ \mathbf{r}(1, w) \\ \mathbf{r}_u(0, w) \\ \mathbf{r}_u(1, w) \end{bmatrix} \tag{4.52}$$

Fourth step

Substituting (4.48)–(4.51) into (4.52), and letting $0 \leqslant u, w \leqslant 1$, we obtain the bi-cubic patch

$$\mathbf{r}(u, w) = [F_0(u) \quad F_1(u) \quad G_0(u) \quad G_1(u)] \; B \begin{bmatrix} F_0(w) \\ F_1(w) \\ G_0(w) \\ G_1(w) \end{bmatrix} \tag{4.53}$$

in which

$$B = \begin{bmatrix} \mathbf{r}(0,0) & \mathbf{r}(1,0) & \mathbf{r}_w(0,0) & \mathbf{r}_w(1,0) \\ \mathbf{r}(0,1) & \mathbf{r}(1,1) & \mathbf{r}_w(0,1) & \mathbf{r}_w(1,1) \\ \mathbf{r}_u(0,0) & \mathbf{r}_u(1,0) & \mathbf{r}_{uw}(0,0) & \mathbf{r}_{uw}(1,0) \\ \mathbf{r}_u(0,1) & \mathbf{r}_u(1,1) & \mathbf{r}_{uw}(0,1) & \mathbf{r}_{uw}(1,1) \end{bmatrix} \tag{4.54}$$

Since

$$[F_0(u) \quad F_1(u) \quad G_0(u) \quad G_1(u)] = [1 \quad u \quad u^2 \quad u^3]M_c$$
$$= UM_c$$

in which

$$M_c = \begin{bmatrix} 1 & 0 & 0 & 0 \\ 0 & 0 & 1 & 0 \\ -3 & 3 & -2 & -1 \\ 2 & -2 & 1 & 1 \end{bmatrix}$$

$$U = [1 \quad u \quad u^2 \quad u^3]$$

(4.53) may be rewritten in compact form:

$$\mathbf{r}(u, w) = UM_c BM_c^T W^T \tag{4.55}$$

in which B is the corner information matrix; each element of the matrix consists of three components. So the B matrix is a $4 \times 4 \times 3$ array. Denoting the three components of B by B_x, B_y and B_z, then the parameter equations of the bi-cubic patch are

$$x(u, w) = U M_c B_x M_c^T W^T$$

$$y(u, w) = U M_c B_y M_c^T W^T$$

$$z(u, w) = U M_c B_z M_c^T W^T \tag{4.56}$$

The same results can be obtained, if we first construct u parameter curves then w parameter curves. This means that u and w are completely interchangeable, and the order of constructing the patch is unimportant.

When the B matrix is divided into quadrants, we find that the four position vectors in the upper-left quadrant define the four corner points. The upper-right quadrant contains the tangent vectors with respect to parameter w at the corner points, and the lower-left quadrant contains those with respect to u. The lower-right quadrant contains the twist vectors at the corner points. Thus the B matrix is called the corner point information matrix; it includes 16 vectors defining the bi-cubic patch. Substituting these 16 conditions into equation (4.46) and its differentiating equations, we can resolve 16 unknowns a_{ij} defining the bi-cubic patch. This is an algebraic derivation procedure.

From this B matrix, we also find that the geometric coefficients of the four boundary curves and the four partial derivative vector curves can be easily extracted:

$$
\begin{array}{c c c c c}
 & \mathbf{r}(u,0) & \mathbf{r}(u,1) & \mathbf{r}_w(u,0) & \mathbf{r}_w(u,1) \\
 & \downarrow & \downarrow & \downarrow & \downarrow \\
\mathbf{r}(0,w) \rightarrow & \mathbf{r}(0,0) & \mathbf{r}(0,1) & \mathbf{r}_w(0,0) & \mathbf{r}_w(0,1) \\
\mathbf{r}(1,w) \rightarrow & \mathbf{r}(1,0) & \mathbf{r}(1,1) & \mathbf{r}_w(1,0) & \mathbf{r}_w(1,1) \\
\mathbf{r}_u(0,w) \rightarrow & \mathbf{r}_u(0,0) & \mathbf{r}_u(0,1) & \mathbf{r}_{uw}(0,0) & \mathbf{r}_{ww}(0,1) \\
\mathbf{r}_u(1,w) \rightarrow & \mathbf{r}_u(1,0) & \mathbf{r}_u(1,1) & \mathbf{r}_{uw}(1,0) & \mathbf{r}_{uw}(1,1)
\end{array}
$$

Bi-cubic patches defined by the corner point information are often called *Hermite patches*. Ferguson defined a bi-cubic patch with four corner twist vectors equal to zero; this type of patch is called a *Ferguson patch*. It is simple and adequate for applications with C^1 continuity across the adjacent boundaries.

4.5 BI-CUBIC SPLINE SURFACES

A bi-cubic spline surface is a composite surface, which is a collection of individual surface patches joined to form a continuous, more complex surface. Fig. 4.16 shows a bi-cubic spline surface including $n \times m$ bi-cubic patches.

4.5.1 Bi-cubic patch with irregular boundaries

In the last section, we explained the bi-cubic surface patch. Its restriction on the

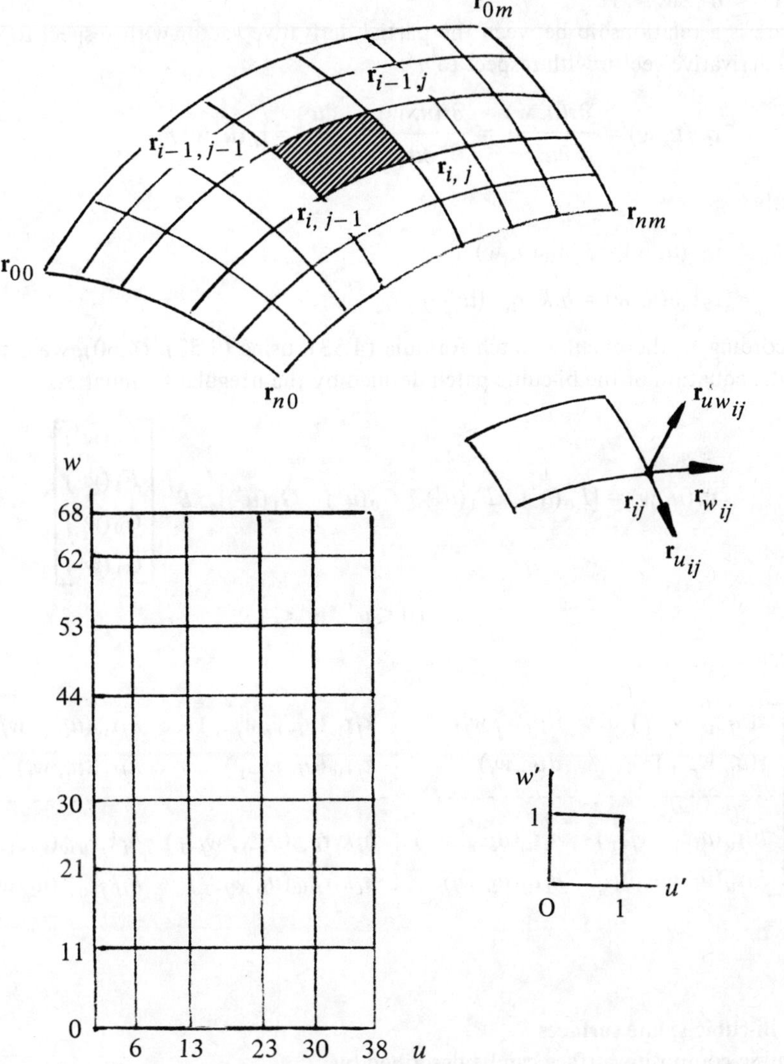

Fig. 4.16 Bi-cubic spline surface and its parametric plane

parametric variables is $0 \leqslant u,\ w \leqslant 1$. We will now discuss the use of irregular boundaries, that is

$$u_{i-1} \leqslant u \leqslant u_i, \qquad w_{j-1} \leqslant w \leqslant w_j$$

Using parameter transformation, we set

$$u' = (u - u_{i-1})/(u_i - u_{i-1}) = (u - u_{i-1})/h_i$$

$$w' = (w - w_{j-1})/(w_j - w_{j-1}) = (w - w_{j-1})/k_j \tag{4.57}$$

so that $0 \leqslant u', \; w' \leqslant 1$.

There is a relationship between the partial derivative vector with respect to u and the partial derivative vector with respect to u':

$$\mathbf{r}_{u'}(u, w) = \frac{\partial \mathbf{r}(u, w)}{\partial u'} = \frac{\partial \mathbf{r}(u, w)}{\partial u} \cdot \frac{du}{du'} = \mathbf{r}_u(u, w)\, h_i \qquad (4.58)$$

Similarly

$$\mathbf{r}_{w'}(u, w) = k_j\, \mathbf{r}_w(u, w) \qquad (4.59)$$

$$\mathbf{r}_{u'w'}(u, w) = h_i k_j\, r_{uw}(u, w) \qquad (4.60)$$

According to the bi-cubic patch formula (4.53), using (4.57)–(4.60), we can directly write the equation of the bi-cubic patch defined by the irregular boundaries.

$$\mathbf{r}_{ij}(u, w) = [F_0(u') \quad F_1(u') \quad G_0(u') \quad G_1(u')] \; B' \begin{bmatrix} F_0(w') \\ F_1(w') \\ G_0(w') \\ G_1(w') \end{bmatrix} \qquad (4.61)$$

$$(0 \leqslant u', \; w' \leqslant 1)$$

in which

$$B' = \left[\begin{array}{cc:cc} \mathbf{r}(u_{i-1}, w_{j-1}) & \mathbf{r}(u_{i-1}, w_j) & k_j \mathbf{r}_w(u_{i-1}, w_{j-1}) & k_j \mathbf{r}_w(u_{i-1}, w_j) \\ \mathbf{r}(u_i, w_{j-1}) & \mathbf{r}(u_i, w_j) & k_j \mathbf{r}_w(u_i, w_{j-1}) & k_j \mathbf{r}_w(u_i, w_j) \\ \hdashline h_i \mathbf{r}_u(u_{i-1}, w_{j-1}) & h_i \mathbf{r}_u(u_{i-1}, w_j) & h_i k_j \mathbf{r}_{uw}(u_{i-1}, w_{j-1}) & h_i k_j \mathbf{r}_{uw}(u_{i-1}, w_j) \\ h_i \mathbf{r}_u(u_i, w_{j-1}) & h_i \mathbf{r}_u(u_i, w_j) & h_i k_j \mathbf{r}_{uw}(u_i, w_{j-1}) & h_i k_j \mathbf{r}_{uw}(u_i, w_j) \end{array}\right]$$

$$(4.62)$$

4.5.2 Bi-cubic spline surfaces

A bi-cubic composite surface can be described by

$$\mathbf{r}(u, w) = [x(u, w) \quad y(u, w) \quad z(u, w)] \qquad (4.63)$$

$$(u_0 \leqslant u \leqslant u_n; \; w_0 < w \leqslant w_m)$$

It may be divided into $n \times m$ patches defined by (4.61), each with $u_{i-1} \leqslant u \leqslant u_i$ along both its u boundaries and $w_{j-1} \leqslant w \leqslant w_j$ along both its w boundaries.

The key problem now is how to obtain the partial derivative vectors $\mathbf{r}_u$, $\mathbf{r}_w$ and the twist vector $\mathbf{r}_{uw}$ at points $\mathbf{r}_{ij}$ $(i = 0, 1, \ldots, n; j = 0, 1, \ldots, m)$, since $\mathbf{r}_{ij}$ and boundary conditions are usually provided by the designer.

An efficient algorithm called the bi-cubic spline interpolation may provide the necessary information about the net points $\mathbf{r}_u$, $\mathbf{r}_w$ and $\mathbf{r}_{uw}$. Cubic spline interpolation mentioned in section 4.2 can be directly extended to bi-cubic spline interpolation. Cubic spline interpolation is an efficient tool for fitting curves; bi-cubic spline interpolation is an efficient tool for fitting surfaces.

A bi-cubic composite surface described by (4.63) is calculated in terms of each component, that is, $x(u, w)$, $y(u, w)$ and $z(u, w)$. We shall discuss only the scalar function $x(u, w)$; the same procedure holds for scalar functions $y(u, w)$ and $z(u, w)$.

To simplify formulae, let

$$
\begin{aligned}
x_{i,j} &= x(u_i, w_j) \\
x_{u_{i,j}} &= x_u(u_i, w_j) \\
x_{w_{i,j}} &= x_w(u_i, w_j) \\
x_{uw_{i,j}} &= x_{uw}(u_i, w_j)
\end{aligned}
$$

we may rewrite the x-component function for (4.61) and (4.62)

$$
x_{i,j}(u, w) = [F_0(u') \quad F_1(u') \quad G_0(u') \quad G_1(u')] \; B_x' \begin{bmatrix} F_0(w') \\ F_1(w') \\ G_0(w') \\ G_1(w') \end{bmatrix} \tag{4.64}
$$

$$
(u_{i-1} \leqslant u \leqslant u_i; \; w_{j-1} \leqslant w \leqslant w_j)
$$

in which

$$
B_x' = \left[\begin{array}{cc:cc}
x_{i-1,j-1} & x_{i-1,j} & k_j x_{w_{i-1,j-1}} & k_j x_{w_{i-1,j}} \\
x_{i,j-1} & x_{i,j} & k_j x_{w_{i,j-1}} & k_j x_{w_{i,j}} \\ \hdashline
h_i x_{u_{i-1,j-1}} & h_i x_{u_{i-1,j}} & h_i k_j x_{uw_{i-1,j-1}} & h_i k_j x_{uw_{i-1,j}} \\
h_i x_{u_{i,j-1}} & h_i x_{u_{i,j}} & h_i k_j x_{uw_{i,j-1}} & h_i k_j x_{uw_{i,j}}
\end{array} \right] \tag{4.65}
$$

Known interpolation conditions are

$$
x_{i,j} \; (i = 0, 1, \ldots, n; \; j = 0, 1, \ldots, m) \tag{4.66}
$$

And known boundary conditions are

$$
x_{u_{i,j}} \quad (i = 0, n; \; j = 0, 1, \ldots, m) \tag{4.67}
$$

$$
x_{w_{i,j}} \quad (i = 0, 1, \ldots, n; \; j = 0, m) \tag{4.68}
$$

$$
x_{uw_{i,j}} \quad (i = 0, n; \; j = 0, m) \tag{4.69}
$$

According to the above known conditions we construct a bi-cubic spline interpolation for the scalar function $x(u, w)$.

1. Calculating the partial derivatives in the u direction at the internal net points

$$x_{u_{i,j}} \quad (i = 1, 2, \ldots, n-1; \ j = 0, 1, \ldots, m)$$

The spline curves are computed in the u direction by setting $w = w_j \ (j = 0, 1, \ldots, m)$. Each curve will require the function values $x_{i,j} \ (i = 0, 1, \ldots, n)$, which may be provided by (4.66), and two partial derivatives $x_{u_{i,j}} \ (i = 0, n)$ provided by (4.67). Their partial derivative relationship equations are similar to (4.17).

$$\lambda_i x_{u_{i-1,j}} + 2x_{u_{i,j}} + \mu_i x_{u_{i+1,j}} = C_{i,j} \tag{4.70}$$

$$(i = 1, 2, \ldots, n-1; \ j = 0, 1, \ldots, m)$$

in which

$$\lambda_i = h_{i+1}/(h_i + h_{i+1})$$

$$\mu_i = 1 - \lambda_i$$

$$C_{i,j} = 3[\lambda_i(x_{i,j} - x_{i-1,j})/h_i + \mu_i(x_{i+1,j} - x_{i,j})/h_{i+1}]$$

This means that all of $x_{u_{i,j}}$ may now be regarded as known.

2. Calculating the partial derivatives in the w direction at the internal net points

$$x_{w_{i,j}} \quad (i = 0, 1, \ldots, n; \ j = 1, 2, \ldots, m-1)$$

Spline curves are computed in the w direction by setting $u = u_i \ (i = 0, 1, \ldots, n)$. Each curve will require the function values $x_{i,j} \ (j = 0, 1, \ldots, m)$ provided by (4.66) and two partial derivatives $x_{w_{i,j}} \ (j = 0, m)$ provided by (4.68). Their partial derivative relation equations are

$$\lambda_j x_{w_{i,j-1}} + 2x_{w_{i,j}} + \mu_j x_{w_{i,j+1}} = C_{i,j} \tag{4.71}$$

in which

$$\lambda_j = k_{j+1}/(k_j + k_{j+1})$$

$$\mu_j = 1 - \lambda_j$$

$$C_{i,j} = 3[\lambda_j(x_{i,j} - x_{i,j-1})/k_j + \mu_j(x_{i,j+1} - x_{i,j})/k_{j+1}]$$

This means that all of $x_{w_{i,j}}$ may now be regarded as known.

3. Calculating the mixed partial derivatives at internal knot points of two u boundaries of the composite surface

$$x_{uw_{i,j}} \quad (i = 1, 2, \ldots, n-1; \ j = 0, m)$$

Two spline curves are computed in the u direction by setting $w = w_j \ (j = 0, m)$. If we consider $x_{w_{i,j}} \ (i = 0, 1, \ldots, n; j = 0, m)$ provided by (4.68) as the function values and $x_{uw_{i,j}} \ (i = 0, n; j = 0, m)$ provided by (4.69) as the derivatives, we may construct two partial derivative curves $x_w(u, w_j)$ $(j = 0, m)$, whose mixed partial derivative relation equations are also similar to (4.17)

$$\lambda_i x_{uw_{i-1,j}} + 2x_{uw_{i,j}} + \mu_i x_{uw_{i+1,j}} = C_{i,j} \tag{4.72}$$

$$(i = 1, 2, \ldots, n-1; j = 0, m)$$

in which λ_i, μ_i have the same definitions as in (4.70)

$$C_{i,j} = 3 \left(\lambda_i \frac{x_{w_{i,j}} - x_{w_{i-1,j}}}{h_i} + \mu_i \frac{x_{w_{i+1,j}} - x_{w_{i,j}}}{h_{i+1}} \right)$$

Then $x_{uw_{i,j}}$ $(i = 1, 2, \ldots, n-1; j = 0, m)$ may now be considered as known.

4. Calculating all of the mixed partial derivatives at net points

$$x_{uw_{i,j}} \quad (i = 0, 1, \ldots, n; j = 1, 2, \ldots, m-1)$$

$(n + 1)$ spline curves are computed in the w direction by setting $u = u_i$ $(i = 0, 1, \ldots, n)$. If we regard $x_{u_{i,j}}$ $(i = 0, 1, \ldots, n; j = 0, 1, \ldots, m)$, provided by the result of the first step and boundary conditions (4.67), as the function values, and $x_{uw_{i,j}}$ as the derivatives, we may construct $(n + 1)$ partial derivative curves $x_u(u_i, w)$ $(i = 0, 1, \ldots, n)$, whose mixed partial derivative relation equations are

$$\lambda_j x_{uw_{i,j-1}} + 2x_{uw_{i,j}} + \mu_j x_{uw_{i,j+1}} = C_{i,j} \tag{4.73}$$

in which λ_j, μ_j are the same as defined in (4.71)

$$C_{i,j} = 3 \left(\lambda_j \frac{x_{u_{i,j}} - x_{u_{i,j-1}}}{k_j} + \mu_j \frac{x_{u_{i,j+1}} - x_{u_{i,j}}}{k_{j+1}} \right)$$

All of the mixed partial derivatives at net points are now obtained.

Note that the roles of u and w in steps 3 and 4 may be interchanged; in other words, firstly the mixed partial derivatives at internal knot points of two w boundaries of the composite surface may be calculated; then the remaining x_{uw} parts may be calculated. The results are the same.

We see now that $x_{u_{i,j}}, x_{w_{i,j}}$ and $x_{uw_{i,j}}$ at the net points $x_{i,j}$ can be calculated by (4.70), (4.71), (4.72) and (4.73). These results are needed just to determine the corner information matrix (4.65). Then, according to (4.64), we obtain piecewise and continuous patches $x_{i,j}(u, w)$. The bi-cubic function can be expressed as

$$x(u, w) = x_{i,j}(u, w) \qquad (i = 1, 2, \ldots, n; j = 1, 2, \ldots, m) \tag{4.74}$$

The bi-cubic spline function $x(u, w)$ holds for the following three conditions:

- $x(u, w)$ passes through given data points $x_{i,j}$ $(i = 0, 1, \ldots, n; j = 0, 1, \ldots, m)$,
- $x(u, w)$ possesses up to C^2 continuity of the partial derivatives x_{uu} and x_{ww}, and up to C^4 continuity of the mixed partial derivative x_{uuww},
- $x(u, w)$ is a piecewise bi-cubic polynomials.

$y(u, w)$, $z(u, w)$ are also constructed by using similar formulae given in (4.64)–(4.72). The entire bi-cubic spline surface $\mathbf{r}(u, w)$ is therefore determined.

Bi-cubic spline surfaces form the theoretical basis of the Numerical Master Geometry System developed by Sabin at the British Aircraft Corporation (Weybridge) and the Cambridge Computer-Aided Design Centre's Polysurf system.

4.5.3 Parametrization of bi-cubic spline surfaces

Parametrization of the cubic spline curve described in subsection 4.3.1 usually employs accumulated chord length as the parameter. We will now examine how to parametrize a bi-cubic spline surface, in other words, how to determine the parametric plane (uw plane; see Fig. 4.16).

Fig. 4.16 shows that there are $(m + 1)$ spline curves in the u direction, and $(n + 1)$ in the w direction. Unfortunately, the patch equation (4.61) requires parameters u and w to vary over the same range along opposite patch boundaries, so that we can choose only a set of points in the u direction and a set of points in the w direction to determine the accumulated chord lengths in the u direction and the w direction, respectively. Usually the data points of the two sets should be as even as possible, producing a non-uniform form.

If the data points are fairly uniform, we can assign integer values $u = 0, 1, \ldots, n$; $w = 0, 1, \ldots, m$ as the parameter values. This is the simplest way for parametrization; it is called the uniform form.

If the disposition of points is even in the u direction, but is uneven in the w direction, we can choose a uniform parameter in the u direction, and a non-uniform parameter in the w direction.

If the disposition of points is very uneven, we have to adjust the data points, unless this will cause unwanted flat regions on long spans, oscillations and even loops on short spans.

4.6 EXAMPLE

Fig. 4.17 shows a composite surface of an aircraft fuselage, which includes 15 cross-sections along the axis of the aircraft fuselage. These cross-sections have been discussed in subsection 4.3.2.

Known data points may be expressed in a cylindrical coordinate system as

$$(\theta_i, x_j, \rho_{ij}) \qquad (i = 0, 1, \ldots, 10; \ j = 0, 1, \ldots, 14)$$

in which θ and x are parameters. We will construct a bi-cubic spline surface

$$\rho = \rho(\theta, x) \qquad (0° \leqslant \theta \leqslant 75°; \ x_0 \leqslant x \leqslant x_{14}) \tag{4.75}$$

Then the surface parameter equations may be described by

$$x = x$$

$$y = \rho(\theta, x) \cos \theta$$

$$z = \rho(\theta, x) \sin \theta \tag{4.76}$$

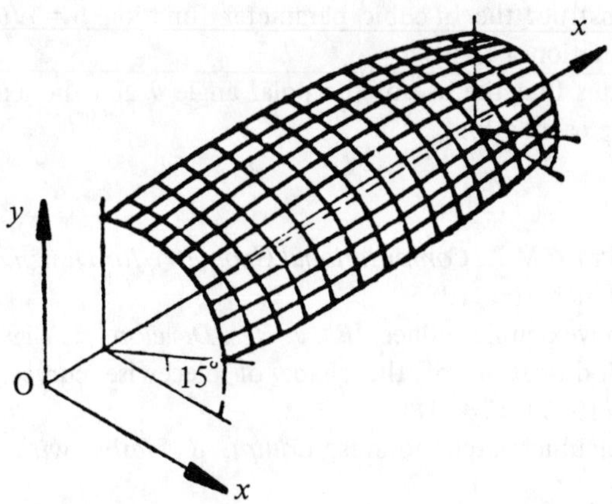

Fig. 4.17 A composite surface of an aircraft fuselage

so that the key is to construct equation $\rho(\theta, x)$.

The interpolation conditions are provided by

$$\rho(\theta_i, x_j) = \rho_{ij} \qquad (i = 0, 1, \ldots, 10;\ j = 0, 1, \ldots, 14) \tag{4.77}$$

They are similar to (4.66).

The boundary conditions may be obtained according to the shape of the fuselage.

Setting $x = x_j$, the $\rho(\theta, x_j)$ is a function of the single variable θ; we obtain from sub-section 4.3.2

$$\frac{\partial \rho(\theta_0, x_j)}{\partial \theta} = 0, \qquad \frac{\partial \rho(\theta_{10}, x_j)}{\partial \theta} = 0 \qquad (j = 0, 1, \ldots, 14) \tag{4.78}$$

These conditions are similar to (4.67).

Setting $\theta = \theta_i$, the $\rho(\theta_i, x)$ is a function of the single variable x; we can obtain from the drawing

$$\frac{\partial \rho(\theta_i, x_0)}{\partial x}, \qquad \frac{\partial \rho(\theta_i, x_{14})}{\partial x} \qquad (i = 0, 1, \ldots, 10) \tag{4.79}$$

These conditions are similar to (4.68).

Letting the mixed partial derivatives at the four corners of the composite surface be zero

$$\frac{\partial \rho(\theta_i, x_j)}{\partial \theta \partial x} = 0 \qquad (i = 0, 10;\ j = 0, 14) \tag{4.80}$$

The above assumptions can be adopted, since these mixed partial derivatives are the rate of change of $\partial \rho / \partial \theta$ with respect to x; $\partial \rho / \partial \theta$ are all zero (see equation (4.78)), and their rate of change is, of course, also zero.

The interpolation conditions (4.77), and boundary conditions (4.78)–(4.80) are now known, so we may construct the bi-cubic parameter function $\rho = \rho(\theta, x)$, and finally obtain the parameter functions (4.76).

The example illustrates that the use of the polar angle θ and the axis coordinate x as parameters simplifies the calculation.

REFERENCES

[1] Faux, I.D. and Pratt, M.J., *Computational Geometry for Design and Manufacture*, Ellis Horwood, Chichester, 1985.

[2] Dimsdale, B., Convex cubic splines, *IBM J. Res. Develop.*, **22** (1978), 168–178.

[3] Coons, S.A., Modification of the shape of piecewise curves, *Computer-aided Design*, **9**, no. 3 (1977), 178–180.

[4] Dimsdale, B., Bicubic patch bounds, *Compt. & Maths. with Appl.*, **3** (1977), 95–104.

[5] Adams, J.A., The intrinsic method for curve definition, *Computer-aided Design*, **7**, No. 4 (1975), 243–249.

[6] Cox, M.G., An algorithm for spline interpolation, *J. Inst. Math. Applic.*, **15** (1975), 95–108.

[7] Manning, J.R., Continuity conditions for spline curves, *Comput. J.*, **17** (1974), 181–186.

[8] Schoenberg, I.J., Cardinal spline interpolation, *SIAM*, Philadelphia (1973).

[9] Forrest, A.R., Mathematical principles for curve and surface representation, in *Proc. Curved Surfaces in Eng.* (Churchill College, Cambridge), IPC Science and Technology Press, 1972.

[10] Forrest, A.R., On Coons' and other methods for the representation of curved surfaces, *Computer Graphics and Image Processing*, **1** (1972), 341–359.

[11] Nutbourne, A.W., McLellan, P.M. and Kensit, R.M.L., Curvature profiles for plane curves, *Computer-aided Design*, **4**, No. 4 (1972), 176–184.

[12] Forrest, A.R., Computational geometry, *Proc. Roy. Soc. London*, **A321** (1971), 187–195.

[13] Gordon, W.J., Spline-blended surface interpolation through curve networks, *J. Math. and Mech.*, **18**, No. 10 (1969), 931–952.

[14] Forrest, A.R., Curves and surfaces for computer-aided design, PhD thesis, University of Cambridge, 1968.

[15] Ahuja, D.V., An algorithm for generating spline-like curves, *IBM Syst. J.*, **3 & 4** (1968), 206–217.

[16] Ahuja, D.V. & Coons, S.A., Geometry for construction and display, *IBM Syst. J.*, **3 & 4** (1968), 188–205.

[17] Coons, S.A., Surfaces for computer aided design of space forms, *Report MAC-TR-41*, project MAC, MIT (1967).

[18] Ahlberg, J.H., Nilson, E.N. and Walsh, J.L., *The Theory of Splines and their Applications*, Academic Press, London, 1967.

[19] Ferguson, J.C., Multivariable curve interpolation, *J. ACM*, **11**, No. 2 (1964), 221–228.

[20] Ferguson, J.C., Multivariable curve interpolation, *Report No. D2-22504*, The Boeing Co., Seattle, Washington (1963).

[21] Schoenberg, I.J. and Whitney, A., On polya frequency functions III: the positivity of translation determinants with an application to the interpolation problem by spline curves, *Trans. Amer. Math. Soc.,* **74** (1953), 246–259.

5

Bezier Curves and Surfaces

5.1 INTRODUCTION

Bezier's technique is one of the most famous in computer-aided geometric design. P. Bezier (French automobile company of Renault) set out in the early 1960s to find curves and surface which only approximate or approach the given points, rather than passing through them. This 'approach' scheme is more convenient to the designer and the design process than the interpolate scheme mentioned in Chapter 4. The result of Bezier's work was the UNISURF system, used by Renault since 1972 to design the sculptured surfaces of many of their automobile bodies.

The underlying mathematical theory of Bezier's technique is based on the concept of Bernstein polynomials. The relationship between Bezier's work and Bernstein polynomials was established by R. Forrest, de Casteljau, W.J. Gordon, and R.F. Riesenfeld developed the Bezier technique.

Bezier curves and surfaces are now established as the mathematical basis of many CAD/CAM systems; they have also become a major tool for the development of new methods for curve and surface descriptions.

A standard form of a polynomial curve of degree n can be expressed as

$$\mathbf{r}(u) = \sum_{i=0}^{n} \mathbf{b}_i u^i \tag{5.1}$$

where $\mathbf{b}_i$ is the coefficient vector, u is the local parameter of the segment under consideration, and $u \in [0, 1]$. The vector $\mathbf{b}_i$ does not possess any intuitive insight into the shape of the curve beyond the point $u = 0$. The form is not suitable for the discussion of smoothness properties of piecewise curves.

To avoid the two drawbacks, J.C. Ferguson used a representation in terms of piecewise Hermite polynomials. The cubic parametric curve is given by

$$\mathbf{r}(u) = \mathbf{r}(0)\, F_0(u) + \mathbf{r}(1)\quad F_1(u) + \mathbf{r}'(0)\quad G_0(u) + \mathbf{r}'(1)\quad G_1(u)$$

$$= \begin{bmatrix} 1 & u & u^2 & u^3 \end{bmatrix} \begin{bmatrix} 1 & 0 & 0 & 0 \\ 0 & 0 & 1 & 0 \\ -3 & 3 & -2 & -1 \\ 2 & -2 & 1 & 1 \end{bmatrix} \begin{bmatrix} \mathbf{r}(0) \\ \mathbf{r}(1) \\ \mathbf{r}'(0) \\ \mathbf{r}'(1) \end{bmatrix} \tag{5.2}$$

where $F_0(u)$, $F_1(u)$, $G_0(u)$ and $G_1(u)$ are cubic blending functions discussed in Chapter 4. $\mathbf{r}(0)$ and $\mathbf{r}(1)$ are the position vectors of end points of the curve segment; $\mathbf{r}'(0)$ and $\mathbf{r}'(1)$ are the tangent vectors of end points of the curve segment. The method is not suitable for interactive design, because derivative vector magnitudes are often unmanageable. For example, if we try to change the shape of a spline-interpolated curve by moving one or more of the interpolating points, we may produce unexpected perturbations and inflections, both locally and remotely.

Bezier's technique can control curve and surface shape in a predictable way by changing only a few simple control points. It partially satisfies the need of interactive design.

Chapter 5 presents the definition and properties of the Bezier curves; it introduces the de Casteljau algorithm, and the subdivision technique, degree elevation, and the inverse algorithm; it gives the condition of composite Bezier curves; and, finally, it discusses Bezier surface patches and composite Bezier surfaces. This will enable us to select the best application for their use.

5.2 BEZIER CURVES

5.2.1 Bezier cubic curves

The Ferguson cubic parameter curve is defined by two position vectors $\mathbf{r}(0)$, $\mathbf{r}(1)$ and two tangent vectors $\mathbf{r}'(0)$, $\mathbf{r}'(1)$ at the curve segment ends. Bezier chose a family of functions called Bernstein polynomials as blending functions. A Bezier curve can be defined by a set of control points called Bezier points or vertices. This alternative approach defines a curve that only approximates to these given control points. For example, the Bezier cubic curve is determined by two end point vectors $\mathbf{V}_0$, $\mathbf{V}_3$ and two control point vectors $\mathbf{V}_2$, $\mathbf{V}_3$, which do not lie on the curve (see Fig. 5.1).

A Bezier curve of degree n is determined by a set of control points $\mathbf{V}_i$ $(i = 0, 1, \ldots, n)$; they form a characteristic polygon called the Bezier polygon, which reflects the shape of the Bezier curve.

Using the linear combination between Bernstein polynomials and the vertices of the characteristic polygon, we obtain the Bezier curve of degree n as

$$\mathbf{r}(u) = \sum_{i=0}^{n} B_{n,i}(u)\, \mathbf{V}_i \qquad (0 \leqslant u \leqslant 1) \tag{5.3}$$

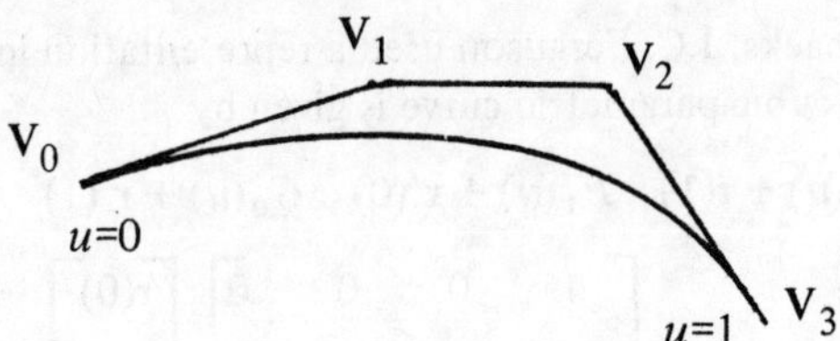

Fig. 5.1 Bezier cubic curve

where $B_{n,i}(u)$ is the Bernstein function

$$B_{n,i}(u) = C(n,\, i)\, u^i (1-u)^{n-i} \tag{5.4}$$

$C(n,\, i)$ is the familiar binomial coefficient

$$C(n,\, i) = \frac{n!}{i!\,(n-i)!} \tag{5.5}$$

Note that when $i = 0$ and $u = 0$, $u^i = 1$; $0! = 1$. It is evident that $B_{n,i}(u)$ is an nth-degree polynomial.

Now let us discuss equations (5.3) and (5.4) for a Bezier curve of degree 3 defined by four vertices, so that we become familiar with the polynomial forms.

From (5.4), we obtain 3rd-degree Bernstein functions (see Fig. 5.2) as follows:

$$B_{3,0}(u) = C(3,\, 0)\, u^0 (1-u)^3 = (1-u)^3$$

$$B_{3,1}(u) = C(3,\, 1)\, u^1 (1-u)^2 = 3u(1-u)^2$$

$$B_{3,2}(u) = C(3,2\,)\, u^2 (1-u) = 3u^2 (1-u)$$

$$B_{3,3}(u) = C(3,\, 3)\, u^3 (1-u)^0 = u^3 \tag{5.6}$$

Substituting (5.6) into (5.3), we obtain the Bezier cubic curve as

$$\mathbf{r}(u) = (1-u)^3\,\mathbf{V}_0 + 3u(1-u)^2\,\mathbf{V}_1 + 3u^2(1-u)\mathbf{V}_2 + u^3\mathbf{V}_3 \tag{5.7}$$

It can be rewritten in matrix form:

$$\mathbf{r}(u) = \begin{bmatrix} 1 & u & u^2 & u^3 \end{bmatrix} \begin{bmatrix} 1 & 0 & 0 & 0 \\ -3 & 3 & 0 & 0 \\ 3 & -6 & 3 & 0 \\ -1 & 3 & -3 & 1 \end{bmatrix} \begin{bmatrix} \mathbf{V}_0 \\ \mathbf{V}_1 \\ \mathbf{V}_2 \\ \mathbf{V}_3 \end{bmatrix} \tag{5.8}$$

$$= \begin{bmatrix} 1 & u & u^2 & u^3 \end{bmatrix} M_{\mathrm{be}} \begin{bmatrix} \mathbf{V}_0 & \mathbf{V}_1 & \mathbf{V}_2 & \mathbf{V}_3 \end{bmatrix}^{\mathrm{T}}$$

$$= U M_{\mathrm{be}} \begin{bmatrix} \mathbf{V}_0 & \mathbf{V}_1 & \mathbf{V}_2 & \mathbf{V}_3 \end{bmatrix}^{\mathrm{T}}$$

Here, $U M_{\mathrm{be}}$ is the blending function matrix and $\begin{bmatrix} \mathbf{V}_0 & \mathbf{V}_1 & \mathbf{V}_2 & \mathbf{V}_3 \end{bmatrix}^{\mathrm{T}}$ is the vertex information matrix.

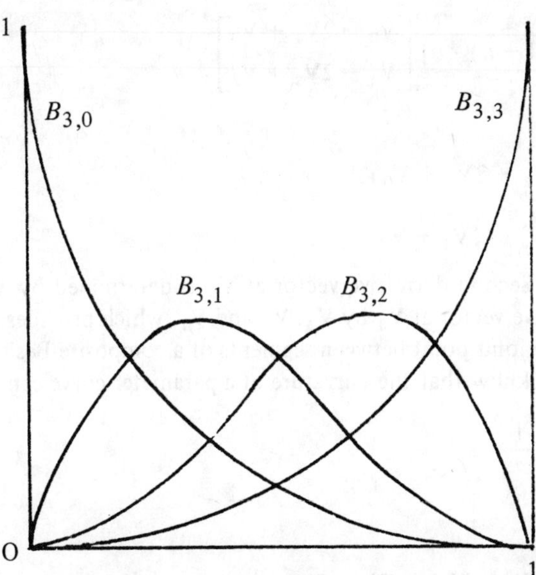

Fig. 5.2 3rd-degree Bernstein functions

The Bernstein functions, which were chosen as the blending functions, are the key to the behaviour of Bezier curves. We will discuss the properties of Bezier curves of degree 3 according to equation (5.7) or (5.8).

Equation (5.8) yields the following results, when $u = 0$ and $u = 1$:

$$r(0) = V_0$$

$$r(1) = V_3 \tag{5.9}$$

This shows that the curve starts on V_0 and ends on V_3 (see Fig. 5.1).

On differentiating (5.8), and rearranging terms, we obtain

$$r'(u) = 3[(1-u)^2 \quad 2u(1-u) \quad u^2] \begin{bmatrix} V_1 - V_0 \\ V_2 - V_1 \\ V_3 - V_2 \end{bmatrix} \tag{5.10}$$

When $u = 0$, and $u = 1$, we obtain from (5.10)

$$r'(0) = 3(V_1 - V_0)$$

$$r'(1) = 3(V_3 - V_2) \tag{5.11}$$

This shows that the tangent vector at V_0 is given by $V_1 - V_0$, and the tangent vector at V_3 by $V_3 - V_2$. This gives us direct control of the tangent to the curve at each end. On differentiating (5.10), and rearranging items, we obtain

$$\mathbf{r}''(u) = 6\left[(1-u) \quad u\right] \begin{bmatrix} \mathbf{V}_2 - 2\mathbf{V}_1 + \mathbf{V}_0 \\ \mathbf{V}_1 - 2\mathbf{V}_2 + \mathbf{V}_3 \end{bmatrix} \tag{5.12}$$

thus

$$\mathbf{r}''(0) = 6(\mathbf{V}_2 - 2\mathbf{V}_1 + \mathbf{V}_0)$$

$$\mathbf{r}''(1) = 6(\mathbf{V}_1 - 2\mathbf{V}_2 + \mathbf{V}_3) \tag{5.13}$$

This shows that the second derivative vector at $\mathbf{V}_0$ is determined by $\mathbf{V}_0$, $\mathbf{V}_1$ and $\mathbf{V}_2$, and the second derivative vector at $\mathbf{V}_3$ by $\mathbf{V}_3$, $\mathbf{V}_2$ and $\mathbf{V}_1$, which provides us with control of the continuity of the joint point between segments of a composite Besier curve.

From Chapter 1 we know that the curvature of a parameter curve can be expressed as

$$\kappa = \frac{|\mathbf{r}' \times \mathbf{r}''|}{|\mathbf{r}'|^3} \tag{5.14}$$

thus

$$\kappa(0) = \frac{2}{3} \frac{|(\mathbf{V}_1 - \mathbf{V}_0) \times (\mathbf{V}_2 - \mathbf{V}_1)|}{|\mathbf{V}_1 - \mathbf{V}_0|^3}$$

$$\kappa(1) = \frac{2}{3} \frac{|(\mathbf{V}_2 - \mathbf{V}_1) \times (\mathbf{V}_3 - \mathbf{V}_2)|}{|\mathbf{V}_3 - \mathbf{V}_2|^3} \tag{5.15}$$

and the binormal vector, which is the normal of the osculating plane of the curve, is

$$\mathbf{B} = \mathbf{r}' \times \mathbf{r}'' \tag{5.16}$$

Thus the curvature and osculating plane at each end are also determined by its three neighbouring vertices.

We will now discuss the key role of blending functions. Fig. 5.2 shows 3rd-degree blending functions $B_{3,i}(u)$, $i = 0, 1, 2,$. The vertex $\mathbf{V}_0$, whose contribution to the Bezier curve shape is propagated by $B_{3,0}(u)$, is most influential when $u = 0$. The other vertices do not contribute to $\mathbf{r}(u)$ at $u = 0$, since their associated blending functions are each zero. A symmetrical situation occurs for $\mathbf{V}_3$ at $u = 1$. The vertices $\mathbf{V}_1$ and $\mathbf{V}_2$ are most influential at $u = \frac{1}{3}$ and $\frac{2}{3}$, respectively.

Each vertex $\mathbf{V}_i$ is weighted by the associated blending function. The maximal weight applied to $\mathbf{V}_0$ is when $u = 0$, to $\mathbf{V}_1$ when $u = \frac{1}{3}$, to $\mathbf{V}_2$ when $u = \frac{2}{3}$ and to $\mathbf{V}_3$ when $u = 1$.

We thus observe that the disposition of a set of vertices determines the shape of the Bezier curve. For example, to design a Bezier cubic curve, we choose two end points of the curve as $\mathbf{V}_0$ and $\mathbf{V}_3$, $\mathbf{V}_1$ and $\mathbf{V}_2$ determine the direction of the tangent vectors at the two end points, and the internal shape of the curve. Fig. 5.3(a) shows that the disposition of vertices generates a smooth uninflected curve, while in Fig. 5.3(b) an inflected curve is generated. Note that in these three cases, the curves are tangent to the lines joining $\mathbf{V}_1 - \mathbf{V}_0$ and $\mathbf{V}_3 - \mathbf{V}_2$.

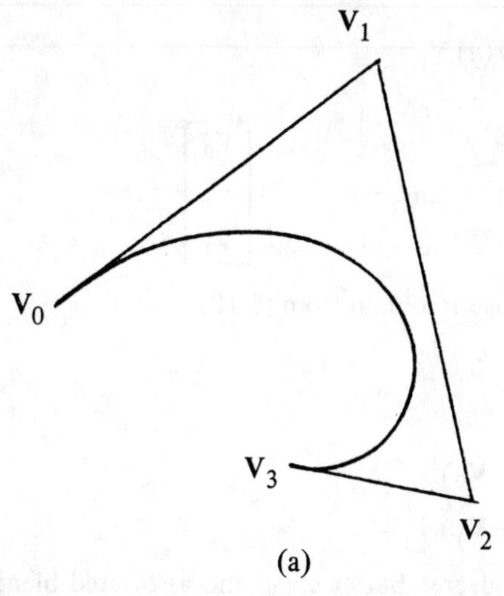

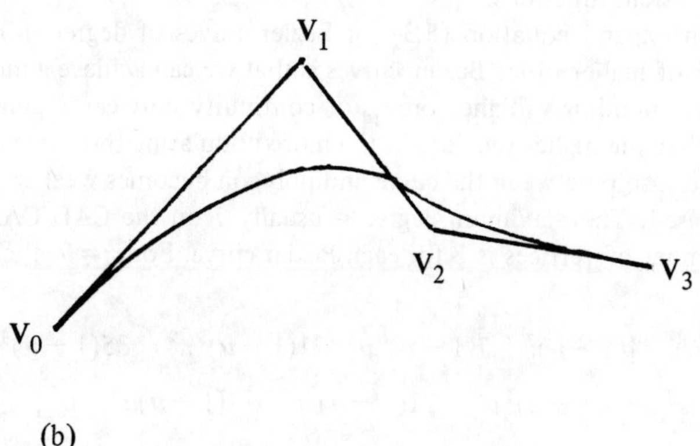

Fig. 5.3 Bezier cubic curve

5.2.2 Bezier curves of degree n

We are now familiar with the Bezier cubic curve; this is a very useful step in understanding an nth-degree Bezier curve.

Equations (5.3) and (5.4) yield a 1st-degree Bezier curve, when $n = 1$.

$$\mathbf{r}(u) = \sum_{i=0}^{1} \mathbf{B}_{1,i}(u)\, \mathbf{V}_i$$

$$= [(1-u) \quad u] \begin{bmatrix} \mathbf{V}_0 \\ \mathbf{V}_1 \end{bmatrix} = \mathbf{V}_0 + (\mathbf{V}_1 - \mathbf{V}_0)\,u \tag{5.17}$$

This shows that the 1st-degree Bezier curve is a straight line joining $\mathbf{V}_0$ and $\mathbf{V}_1$.

Similarly, the 2nd-degree Bezier curve can be obtained from (5.3) and (5.4), when $n = 2$.

$$r(u) = \sum_{i=0}^{2} B_{2,i}(u)\, \mathbf{V}_i$$

$$= [(1-u)^2 \quad 2u(1-u) \quad u^2] \begin{bmatrix} \mathbf{V}_0 \\ \mathbf{V}_1 \\ \mathbf{V}_2 \end{bmatrix} \tag{5.18}$$

The following results are easy to obtain from (5.18):

$$\mathbf{r}(0) = \mathbf{V}_0$$
$$\mathbf{r}(1) = \mathbf{V}_1$$
$$\mathbf{r}'(0) = 2(\mathbf{V}_1 - \mathbf{V}_0)$$
$$\mathbf{r}'(1) = 2(\mathbf{V}_2 - \mathbf{V}_1) \tag{5.19}$$

Fig. 5.4 shows the 2nd-degree Bezier curve and associated blending functions, that is, 2nd-degree Bernstein functions.

Readers can expand equation (5.3) for Bezier curves of degree n, $n = 4, 5, 6, 7 \ldots$. The advantage of higher order Bezier curves is that we can achieve a more complex curve shape and correspondingly higher orders of continuity between segments of compound curves. Note that the higher the degree, the more undulating the curve is likely to be, and the shape relationship between the curve and polygon becomes weaker as the order of the curve is increased. The maximum degree is usually 7 on the CAD/CAM systems, so the maximum number of vertices is 8 for each Bezier curve. For $n = 7$, that is, 8 vertices, the Bezier curve

$$\mathbf{r}(u) = [(1-u)^7 \quad 7(1-u)^6 u \quad 21(1-u)^5 u^2 \quad 35(1-u)^4 u^3$$
$$35(1-u)^3 u^4 \quad 21(1-u)^2 u^5 \quad 7(1-u)u^6 \quad u^7]$$
$$[\mathbf{V}_0 \quad \mathbf{V}_1 \ldots \mathbf{V}_7]^{\mathrm{T}} \tag{5.20}$$

The properties of the Bezier cubic curve mentioned in subsection 5.2.1 can be extended to the nth-degree case. As we have seen for the Bezier cubic curve, the Bernstein functions are the key to the behaviour of curves. We will start with the Bernstein functions, and then analyse the important properties of the Bezier curve.

The Bernstein functions chosen as the blending functions for the Bezier curves possess the following properties.

Positivity

$$0 \leqslant B_{n,i}(u) \leqslant 1 \quad u \in [0,1] \tag{5.21}$$

when $i = 0$ and $i = n$, equation (5.21) yields

$$B_{n,0}(0) = B_{n,n}(1) = 1$$
$$B_{n,0}(1) = B_{n,n}(0) = 0$$

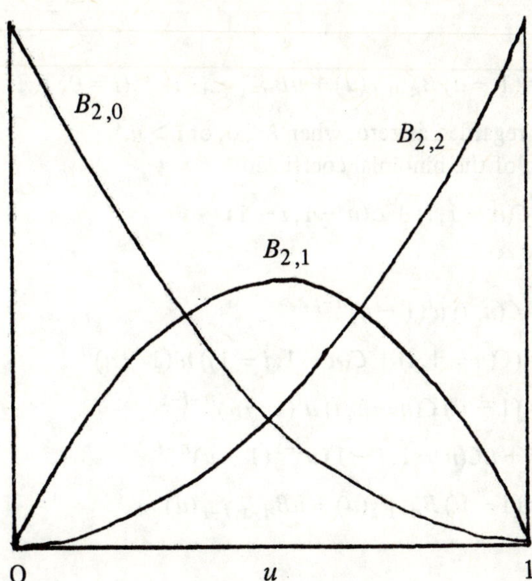

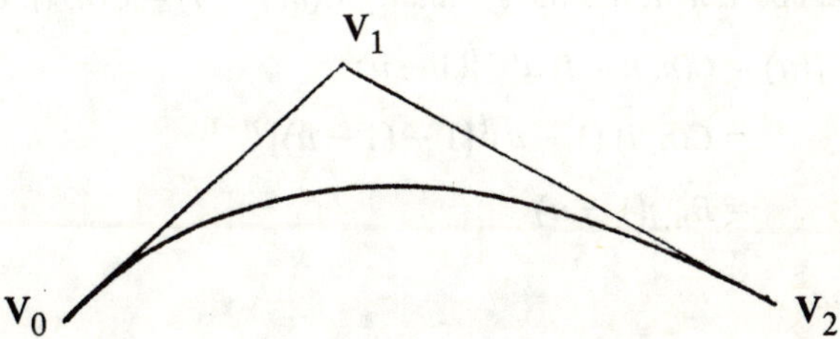

Fig. 5.4 2nd-degree Bernstein functions (a) and 2nd-degree Bezier curve (b)

when $i = 1, 2, \ldots, (n-1)$

$$B_{n,i}(0) = B_{n,i}(1) = 0$$

Partition of unity

$$\sum_{i=0}^{n} B_{n,i}(u) \equiv 1 \quad u \in [0, 1] \tag{5.22}$$

Since expansion of the binomial $[u + (1-u)]^n$ yields $B_{n,i}(u)$ $(i = 0, 1, \ldots, n)$, the value of the binomial, of course, equals 1.

$$\sum_{i=0}^{n} B_{n,i}(u) = \sum_{i=0}^{n} C(n, i)\, u^i (1-u)^{n-i} = [u + (1-u)]^n = 1$$

Recursion

$$B_{n,i}(u) = (1-u)B_{n-1,i}(u) + uB_{n-1,i-1}(u) \quad (i = 0, 1, \ldots, n) \tag{5.23}$$

Note that $B_{n,i}(u)$ are regarded as zero, when $i < 0$, or $i > n$.

Since the recursion of the binomial coefficient

$$C(n, i) = C(n-1, i) + C(n-1, i-1)$$

we obtain

$$\begin{aligned}
B_{n,i}(u) &= C(n, i)\, u^i (1-u)^{n-i} \\
&= (C(n-1, i) + C(n-1, i-1))\, u^i (1-u)^{n-i} \\
&= (1-u)\, C(n-1, i)\, u^i (1-u)^{n-i-1} \\
&\quad + uC(n-1, i-1)\, u^{i-1}(1-u)^{n-i} \\
&= (1-u)\, B_{n-1,i}(u) + uB_{n-1,i-1}(u)
\end{aligned}$$

Symmetry

$$B_{n,n-i}(u) = B_{n,i}(1-u) \tag{5.24}$$

Since the binomial coefficient has the symmetry $C(n, n-i) = C(n, i)$, then

$$\begin{aligned}
B_{n,n-i}(u) &= C(n, n-i)\, u^{n-i}(1-u)^i \\
&= C(n, i)\, (1-u)^i [1 - (1-u)]^{n-i} \\
&= B_{n,i}(1-u)
\end{aligned}$$

Derivative function

$$B'_{n,i}(u) = n\left\{ B_{n-1,i-1}(u) - B_{n-1,i}(u) \right\} \quad (i = 0, 1, \ldots, n) \tag{5.25}$$

Since

$$B'_{n,i}(u) = C(n, i)\, iu^{i-1}(1-u)^{n-i} - C(n, i)u^i(n-i)(1-u)^{n-i-1}$$

and

$$C(n, i)i = \frac{n!\, i}{i!(n-i)!} = \frac{n(n-1)!}{(i-1)!(n-i)!} = nC(n-1, i-1)$$

$$C(n, i)(n-i) = \frac{n!(n-i)}{i!(n-i)!} = \frac{n(n-1)!}{i!(n-i-1)!} = nC(n-1, i)$$

then

$$\begin{aligned}
B'_{n,i}(u) &= nC(n-1, i-1)u^{i-1}(1-u)^{n-i} - nC(n-1, i)u^i(1-u)^{n-i-1} \\
&= n\left\{ B_{n-1,i-1}(u) - B_{n-1,i}(u) \right\}
\end{aligned}$$

These properties of Bernstein functions ensure the following geometric properties of Bezier curves.

The geometric properties of end points
According to the positivity of Bernstein functions, we obtain directly

$$\mathbf{r}(0) = \mathbf{V}_0$$
$$\mathbf{r}(1) = \mathbf{V}_n \tag{5.26}$$

Using the formula of the derivative functions (5.25), we obtain

$$\mathbf{r}'(u) = \sum_{i=0}^{n} B'_{n,i}(u)\,\mathbf{V}_i = n \sum_{i=0}^{n} \mathbf{V}_i \left\{ B_{n-1,i-1}(u) - B_{n-1,i}(u) \right\}$$

$$= n \sum_{i=1}^{n} (\mathbf{V}_i - \mathbf{V}_{i-1})\, B_{n-1,i-1}(u) \tag{5.27}$$

thus

$$\mathbf{r}'(0) = n(\mathbf{V}_1 - \mathbf{V}_0)$$
$$\mathbf{r}'(1) = n(\mathbf{V}_n - \mathbf{V}_{n-1}) \tag{5.28}$$

Similarly

$$\mathbf{r}''(0) = n(n-1)\,[(\mathbf{V}_2 - \mathbf{V}_1) - (\mathbf{V}_1 - \mathbf{V}_0)]$$
$$\mathbf{r}''(1) = n(n-1)\,[(\mathbf{V}_n - \mathbf{V}_{n-1}) - (\mathbf{V}_{n-1} - \mathbf{V}_{n-2})] \tag{5.29}$$

The binormal vector at end points is, respectively,

$$\mathbf{B}(0) = \mathbf{r}'(0) \times \mathbf{r}''(0) = n^2(n-1)\,(\mathbf{V}_1 - \mathbf{V}_0) \times (\mathbf{V}_2 - \mathbf{V}_1)$$

$$\mathbf{B}(1) = \mathbf{r}'(1) \times \mathbf{r}''(1) = n^2(n-1)\,(\mathbf{V}_{n-1} - \mathbf{V}_{n-2}) \times (\mathbf{V}_n - \mathbf{V}_{n-1}) \tag{5.30}$$

The kth derivative vector at end points is, respectively,

$$\mathbf{r}^{(k)}(0) = \frac{n!}{(n-k)!} \sum_{i=0}^{k} (-1)^{k-i} C(k, i)\, \mathbf{V}_i$$

$$\mathbf{r}^{(k)}(1) = \frac{n!}{(n-k)!} \sum_{i=0}^{k} (-1)^{i} C(k, i)\, \mathbf{V}_{n-i} \tag{5.31}$$

These reveal that the Bezier curve starts on the first vertex $\mathbf{V}_0$, and ends on the last vertex $\mathbf{V}_n$ (see equation (5.26)); that the tangent vector at the start point is determined by the first edge of the characteristic polygon, that is, $\mathbf{V}_1 - \mathbf{V}_0$, and the tangent vector at the last point by the last edge, that is, $\mathbf{V}_n - \mathbf{V}_{n-1}$; that the length of the tangent vector at the two end points is n times the length of the first or last edge of the characteristic polygon, respectively (see equation (5.28)); that the osculating plane of the curve at start point is the plane defined by the first two edges of the characteristic polygon; that the osculating plane at the last point is defined by the last two edges (see equation (5.30)); that the kth derivative vector at each end is determined only by its $(k + 1)$ neighbouring vertices (see equation (5.31)).

The property of multiple vertices

By multiple vertices we mean that some of the neighbouring vertices are coincident. Multiple vertices will 'pull' the Bezier curve in closer and closer to the space position of multiple vertices. To do this, we have to correspondingly increase the degree of the Bezier curve. This provides a useful and interesting tool to change the shape of the Bezier curve without changing the shape of the characteristic polygon.

If the first and last vertices of the characteristic polygon are coincident, we will obtain a closed Bezier curve.

Symmetry property

Setting $\mathbf{V}_i^* = \mathbf{V}_{n-i}(i = 0, 1, \ldots, n)$ without changing the shape of the characteristic polygon, using $\{\mathbf{V}_i^*\}$ $(i = 0, 1, \ldots, n)$, we construct a new Bezier curve $\mathbf{r}^*(u)$:

$$\mathbf{r}^*(u) = \sum_{i=0}^{n} B_{n,i}(u)\,\mathbf{V}_i^* = \sum_{i=0}^{n} B_{n,i}(u)\,\mathbf{V}_{n-i}$$

It can be rewritten, if we set $i = n - j$, as

$$\mathbf{r}^*(u) = \sum_{j=0}^{n} B_{n,n-j}(u)\,\mathbf{V}_j$$

Using (5.24), the result is

$$\mathbf{r}^*(u) = \sum_{j=0}^{n} B_{n,j}(1-u)\,\mathbf{V}_j = \mathbf{r}(1-u) \tag{5.32}$$

This shows that the new Bezier curve $\mathbf{r}^*(u)$ defined by $\{\mathbf{V}_i^*\}$ and the original Bezier curve $\mathbf{r}(u)$ defined by $\{\mathbf{V}_i\}$ are the same in shape, and differ only in choosing which end point is the start point of the curve (see Fig. 5.5).

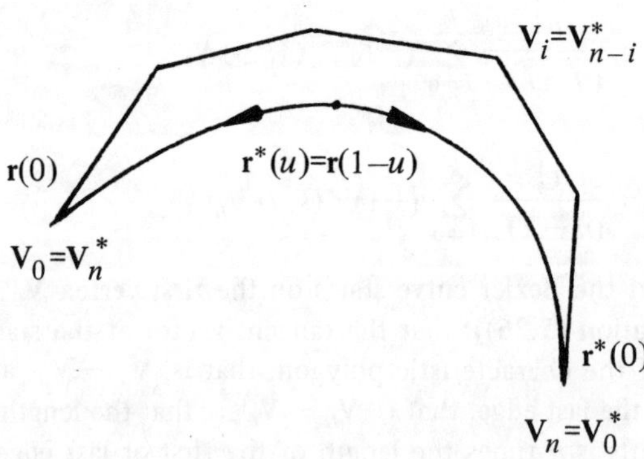

Fig. 5.5

Convex hull property

The positivity (5.21) guarantees that the Bezier curve lies completely within the convex hull of the vertices $\mathbf{V}_i$. The Bezier curve $\mathbf{r}(u)$ defined by (5.3) is just a weighted average of the vertices, so that blending functions $B_{n,i}(u)$ are also called weight functions. Each of the blending functions ranges in value from 0 to 1 (see equation (5.21)) and their sum is 1 for $u \in [0, 1]$ (see equation (5.22)). It can be shown that the weighted average of $(n + 1)$ vertices falls within the convex hull of the $(n + 1)$ vertices. The convex hull bounds the Bezier curve (see Fig. 5.6). Intuitively, the convex hull in a plane is the area defined by a rubber band stretched around all the vertices, and, in 3-D space, by a balloon tightly stretched around all the vertices. The convex hull can be seen intuitively by setting $n = 1$ and $n = 2$, and then generalizing. For $n = 1$, the convex hull is a straight line joining $\mathbf{V}_0$ and $\mathbf{V}_1$; for $n = 2$ it is a triangle $\Delta \mathbf{V}_0 \mathbf{V}_1 \mathbf{V}_2$.

The convex hull is a useful tool in designing a curve, clipping a curve against a window or view volume, calculating intersections and in hidden curve removal.

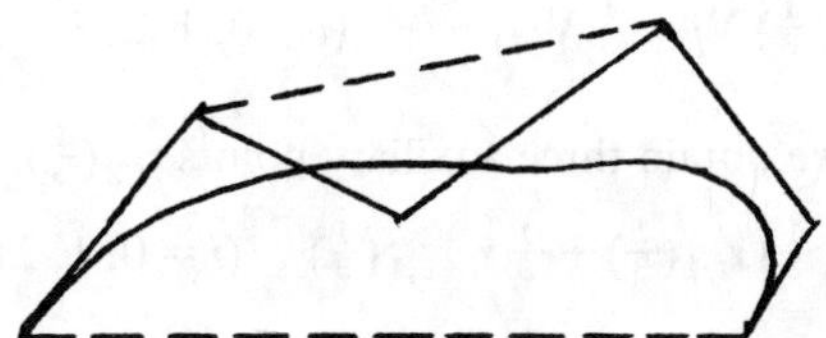

Fig. 5.6 Convex hull

Geometry invariant property
The shape of the Bezier curve defined by (5.3) is determined only by its vertices, and is not related to the coordinate system.

The partition of unity (5.22) ensures that the relationship between the Bezier curve and the vertices of the characteristic polygon is invariant under coordinate system transformation.

This property is called the geometry invariant property.

Linear interpolation property
The recursion (5.23) can be used to construct the $B_{n,i}(u)$ by the repeated linear interpolation property.

Variation diminishing property
No plane has more intersections with the Bezier curve than with its characteristic polygon. This property means that the Bezier curve never oscillates wildly away from its defining vertices.

These properties of the Bezier curve make it an effective interactive design tool.

5.3 BEZIER CURVE ALGORITHMS

5.3.1 The de Casteljau algorithm
The recursion of Bernstein functions leads directly to the de Casteljau algorithm for the calculation of $\mathbf{r}(u)$ at a given value u.

$$\mathbf{r}_{i,l}(u) = (1-u)\,\mathbf{r}_{i,l-1}(u) + u\,\mathbf{r}_{i+1,l-1}(u) \tag{5.33}$$

$$(0 \leqslant u \leqslant 1) \quad (i = 0, 1, \ldots, n-1; \quad l = 1, 2, \ldots, n)$$

where $\mathbf{r}_{i,0} = \mathbf{V}_i$ ($i = 0, 1, \ldots, n$). The subscript l denotes the order of the recursion; the subscript i denotes the order of auxiliary points.

An interesting plotting procedure (see Fig. 5.7) illustrates the recursion algorithm. We given an example ($n = 4, u = \frac{1}{3}$) for illustration.

We start with $\mathbf{V}_i$ ($i = 0, 1, \ldots, 4$) for the evaluation of $\mathbf{r}(\frac{1}{3})$.

1st step: using (5.33), we obtain four auxiliary points $\mathbf{r}_{i,1}(\frac{1}{3})$:

$$\mathbf{r}_{i,1}(\tfrac{1}{3}) = (1 - \tfrac{1}{3})\,\mathbf{r}_{i,0} + \tfrac{1}{3}\,\mathbf{r}_{i+1,0}$$

$$= (1 - \tfrac{1}{3})\,\mathbf{V}_i + \tfrac{1}{3}\,\mathbf{V}_{i+1} \qquad (i = 0, 1, 2, 3)$$

2nd step: using (5.33), we obtain three auxiliary points $\mathbf{r}_{i,2}(\frac{1}{3})$:

$$\mathbf{r}_{i,2}(\tfrac{1}{3}) = (1 - \tfrac{1}{3})\,\mathbf{r}_{i,1}(\tfrac{1}{3}) + \tfrac{1}{3}\,\mathbf{r}_{i+1,1}(\tfrac{1}{3}) \quad (i = 0, 1, 2)$$

3rd step: repeating (5.33), two auxiliary points $\mathbf{r}_{i,3}(\frac{1}{3})$ can be obtained:

$$\mathbf{r}_{i,3}(\tfrac{1}{3}) = (1 - \tfrac{1}{3})\,\mathbf{r}_{i,2}(\tfrac{1}{3}) + \tfrac{1}{3}\,\mathbf{r}_{i+1,2}(\tfrac{1}{3}) \quad (i = 0, 1)$$

Last step: we obtain the point $\mathbf{r}_{i,0}(\frac{1}{3})$ which lies on the Bezier curve:

$$\mathbf{r}_{i,4}(\tfrac{1}{3}) = (1 - \tfrac{1}{3})\,\mathbf{r}_{i,3}(\tfrac{1}{3}) + \tfrac{1}{3}\,\mathbf{r}_{i+1,3}(\tfrac{1}{3}) \quad (i = 0)$$

Here, $\mathbf{r}_{i,4}$ is the point on the Bezier curve, and $n\mathbf{r}_{0,3}\,\mathbf{r}_{1,3}$ is the tangent vector at the point.

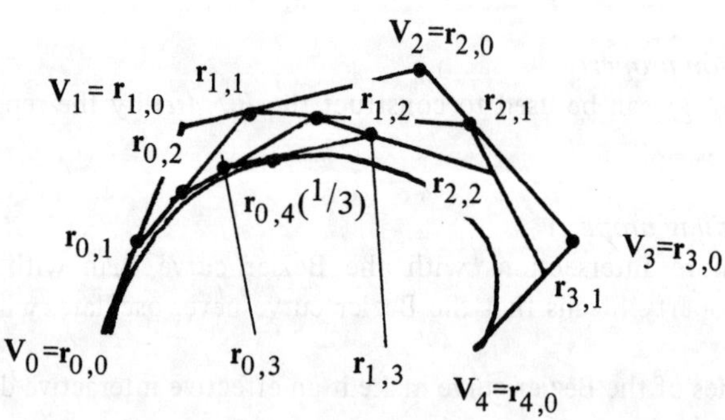

Fig. 5.7 de Casteljau algorithm for $n = 4, u = \frac{1}{3}$

This algorithm is both a very stable method and an important theoretical tool for the following application.

Let us prove that the final result $\mathbf{r}_{0,n}(u)$ of the de Casteljau algorithm is just the point $\mathbf{r}(u)$ of the Bezier curve by the inductive method.

$$\mathbf{r}_{0,n}(u) = \sum_{i=0}^{n} B_{n,i}(u)\, \mathbf{V}_i \tag{5.34}$$

When $n = 1$, the above equation is valid, because the 1st-degree Bezier curve and its characteristic polygon are coincident.

Assuming for a polygon $\mathbf{V}_0\mathbf{V}_1\dots\mathbf{V}_{n-1}$, repeating the calculation (5.33), the final result is

$$\mathbf{r}_{0,n-1}(u) = \sum_{i=0}^{n-1} B_{n-1,i}(u)\, \mathbf{V}_i = \sum_{i=0}^{n} B_{n-1,i}(u)\, \mathbf{V}_i$$

since $B_{n-1,n}(u) = 0$.

For another polygon $\mathbf{V}_1\mathbf{V}_2\dots\mathbf{V}_n$, we similarly obtain

$$\mathbf{r}_{1,n-1}(u) = \sum_{i=0}^{n-1} B_{n-1,i}(u)\, \mathbf{V}_{i+1} = \sum_{i=1}^{n} B_{n-1,i-1}(u)\, \mathbf{V}_i = \sum_{i=0}^{n} B_{n-1,i-1}(u)\, \mathbf{V}_i$$

since $B_{n-1,-1}(u) = 0$.

According to equation (5.33)

$$\mathbf{r}_{0,n}(u) = (1-u)\, \mathbf{r}_{0,n-1}(u) + u\, \mathbf{r}_{1,n-1}(u)$$

$$= (1-u) \sum_{i=0}^{n} B_{n-1,i}(u)\, \mathbf{V}_i + u \sum_{i=0}^{n} B_{n-1,i-1}(u)\, \mathbf{V}_i$$

$$= \sum_{i=0}^{n} \left\{ (1-u)\, B_{n-1,i}(u) + u B_{n-1,i-1}(u) \right\} \mathbf{V}_i$$

Then, using the recursion of Bernstein functions, we obtain

$$\mathbf{r}_{0,n}(u) = \sum_{i=0}^{n} B_{n,i}(u)\, \mathbf{V}_i$$

Thus equation (5.34) is proved.

Now let us prove that $n\, \mathbf{r}_{0,n-1}\mathbf{r}_{1,n-1}$ is the tangent vector at the corresponding point. Differentiating (5.34)

$$\mathbf{r}'_{0,n}(u) = \sum_{i=0}^{n} B'_{n,i}(u)\, \mathbf{V}_i \tag{5.35}$$

Substituting (5.25) into (5.35)

$$\mathbf{r}'_{0,n}(u) = n \sum_{i=0}^{n} \left\{ B_{n-1,i-1}(u) - B_{n-1,i}(u) \right\} \mathbf{V}_i$$

$$= n \left\{ \mathbf{r}_{1,n-1}(u) - \mathbf{r}_{0,n-1}(u) \right\}$$

$$= n\, \mathbf{r}_{0,n-1}\, \mathbf{r}_{1,n-1} \tag{5.36}$$

Thus the above conclusion is valid.

We now see that the recursion of the binomial coefficients ensures the recursion of the Bernstein functions (see equation (5.23)); further, the recursion of the Bernstein functions guarantees the recursion of the de Casteljau algorithm (see equation (5.33)).

The de Casteljau algorithm is the theoretical basis for subdivision.

5.3.2 Subdivision algorithm

The result of repeating the de Casteljau algorithm is the curve point $\mathbf{r}(u)$. In this process, we obtain two sets of auxiliary vertices: one is $\mathbf{r}_{0,0}, \mathbf{r}_{0,1}, \mathbf{r}_{0,2}, \mathbf{r}_{0,3}$ and $\mathbf{r}_{0,4}$; and the other is $\mathbf{r}_{0,4}, \mathbf{r}_{1,3}, \mathbf{r}_{2,2}, \mathbf{r}_{3,1}$ and $\mathbf{r}_{4,0}$, which define two new Bezier curves (see Fig. 5.7 and Fig. 5.8). In other words, the point $\mathbf{r}(u)$ subdivides a Bezier curve into two Bezier curves without changing their degree.

The subdivision point may be chosen according to requirements, usually $u = \frac{1}{2}$. The process may be repeated: if the set of subdivision points is dense in $(0 \leqslant u \leqslant 1)$, the final sequence of polygons converges to the original Bezier curve. The convergence is extremely fast, so that we often regard the final sequence of polygons as the Bezier curve in the CAD system.

The subdivision algorithm may be extended to the Bezier surface case. The B-spline curve and surface mentioned in the next chapter also have a similar subdivision algorithm.

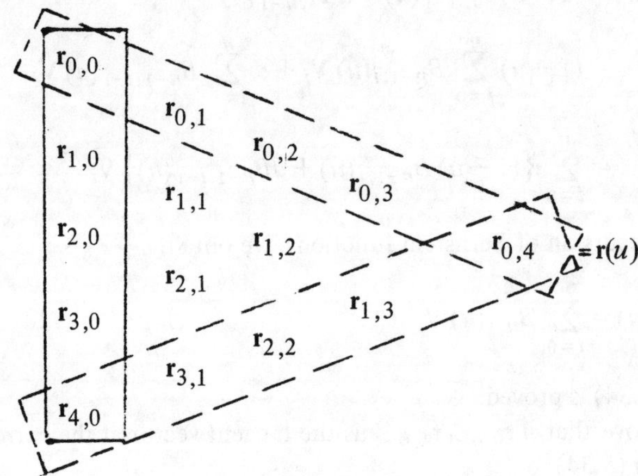

Fig. 5.8 Subdivision algorithm scheme

5.3.3 Degree elevation

A Bezier curve of degree n can be expressed as a Bezier curve of degree $n + 1$.

$$\mathbf{r}(u) = \sum_{i=0}^{n} B_{n,i}(u)\,\mathbf{V}_i = \sum_{i=0}^{n+1} B_{n+1,i}(u)\,\mathbf{V}_i^* \tag{5.37}$$

$\mathbf{V}_i^*$ can be calculated according to the following formula:

$$\mathbf{V}_i^* = \lambda_i \mathbf{V}_{i-1} + (1 - \lambda_i)\,\mathbf{V}_i \quad (i = 0, 1, \ldots, n + 1) \tag{5.38}$$

in which $\lambda_i = i/(n + 1)$.

Two sets of vertices, $\mathbf{V}_i$ $(i = 0, 1, \ldots, n)$ and $\mathbf{V}_i^*$ $(i = 0, 1, \ldots, n+1)$, define the Bezier curve with the same shape, but different degree (see Fig. 5.9). The process of degree elevation may be repeated.

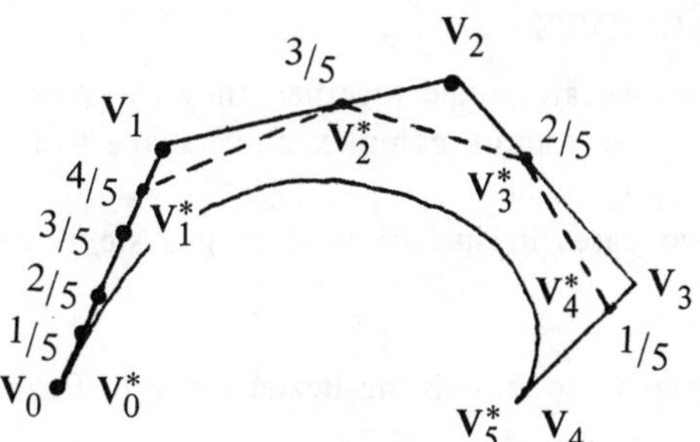

Fig. 5.9   Degree elevation from $n = 3$ to $n = 4$

5.3.4. The inverse algorithm

The Bezier approach defines a curve that only approximates to the given points. In engineering applications, we sometimes require a Bezier curve which also passes exactly through the given points. In this case, the inverse algorithm can satisfy this requirement.

Assuming the data points $\{\mathbf{r}_i\}$ $(r = 0, 1, \ldots, n)$ are provided by the designer, we construct a Bezier curve of degree n, passing through the given points $\mathbf{r}_i$.

We may decompose the procedure into two steps: firstly, using the given points $\mathbf{r}_i$, calculate the vertices $\mathbf{V}_i$; secondly, using $\mathbf{V}_i$, construct a Bezier curve which will, of course, pass through the original data points.

According to (5.3) and (5.19), we obtain the following equations:

$$\mathbf{r}_0 = \mathbf{V}_0$$

$$\mathbf{r}_j = \sum_{i=0}^{n} B_{n,i}(u_j)\, \mathbf{V}_i \qquad (j = 1, 2, \ldots, n-1) \tag{5.39}$$

$$\mathbf{r}_n = \mathbf{V}_n$$

Resolving the set of equations above by an iteration technique, we may obtain the required $\{\mathbf{V}_i\}$ $(i = 0, 1, \ldots, n)$. The natural way is to choose the $\mathbf{r}_i$ as a starting approximation for the vertices, because the $\mathbf{r}_i$ are very close to the vertices.

In equation (5.39), how shall we determine the corresponding parameter value u_j for r_j?

When the disposition of the given points is even, $u_j = j/n$. When the disposition is uneven, the chord length can be chosen as the parameter, that is, setting

$$u_j = \begin{cases} 0 & j = 0 \\[2mm] \displaystyle\sum_{k=1}^{j} l_k \Big/ \sum_{k=1}^{n} l_k & j = 1, 2, \ldots, n-1 \\[2mm] 1 & j = n \end{cases} \tag{5.40}$$

where $l_k = |\mathbf{r}_k - \mathbf{r}_{k-1}|$.

We now see that the inverse algorithm makes it possible for the Bezier technique to be used to interpolate a given set of points.

5.4 COMPOSITE BEZIER CURVES

When two or more Bezier curves are joined together, they form a continuous composite Bezier curve, which can express a more complex curve shape to fit the design requirements.

We often encounter two cases in surface modelling systems based on the Bezier technique.

- Adding a new Bezier curve to an existing Bezier curve to form a composite Bezier curve.
- Blending a new Bezier curve between two existing Bezier curves to form a composite Bezier curve consisting of three segments.

We start with the first case, and state the problem by using a Bezier cubic curve as an example.

Two curves joined at a common end point have at least C^0 continuity at their junction. They form the simplest kind of composite curve. C^1 continuity requires a common tangent line at their junction, but the lengths of tangent vectors at their junction do not have to be equal. We can imagine that we join two curves and then rotate them about their junction until they are tangent to each other while preserving the internal shape of each. Thus C^1 continuity implies sharing a common tangent line at their joint. C^2 continuity, i.e. curvature continuity, requires not only that the curvature vectors at the junction have the same direction, but that the curvature centres coincide.

Denote $\mathbf{r}^{(1)}(u_1)$ as the existing Bezier curve, and $\mathbf{r}^{(2)}(u_2)$ as the new Bezier curve. To ensure C^0, C^1 and C^2, the following conditions must exist:

$$\mathbf{r}^{(2)}(0) = \mathbf{r}^{(1)}(1) \tag{5.41}$$

$$\mathbf{r}^{(2)'}(0) = k_1\,\mathbf{r}^{(1)'}(1) \tag{5.42}$$

$$\mathbf{r}^{(2)''}(0) = k_2\,\mathbf{r}^{(1)''}(1) \tag{5.43}$$

Substituting (5.9) into (5.41), we obtain

$$\mathbf{V}_0^{(2)} = \mathbf{V}_3^{(1)} \tag{5.44}$$

Substituting (5.11) into (5.42) yields

$$3(\mathbf{V}_1^{(2)} - \mathbf{V}_0^{(2)}) = 3k_1(\mathbf{V}_3^{(1)} - \mathbf{V}_2^{(1)}) \tag{5.45}$$

thus

$$\mathbf{V}_1^{(2)} = k_1(\mathbf{V}_3^{(1)} - \mathbf{V}_2^{(1)}) + \mathbf{V}_0^{(2)} \tag{5.46}$$

Equations (5.44) and (5.46) show that the three vertices $\mathbf{V}_2^{(1)}$, $\mathbf{V}_3^{(1)} = \mathbf{V}_0^{(2)}$ and $\mathbf{V}_1^{(2)}$ must be collinear (see Fig. 5.10).

Substituting (5.13) into (5.43), we obtain

$$6(\mathbf{V}_2^{(2)} - 2\mathbf{V}_1^{(2)} + \mathbf{V}_0^{(2)}) = 6k_2(\mathbf{V}_1^{(1)} - 2\mathbf{V}_2^{(1)} + \mathbf{V}_3^{(1)}) \qquad (5.47)$$

thus

$$\mathbf{V}_2^{(2)} = k_2(\mathbf{V}_1^{(1)} - 2\mathbf{V}_2^{(1)} + \mathbf{V}_3^{(1)}) + 2\mathbf{V}_1^{(2)} - \mathbf{V}_0^{(2)}$$

then substituting (5.44) and (5.46) into the above equation, we obtain

$$\mathbf{V}_2^{(2)} = k_2\mathbf{V}_1^{(1)} - 2(k_1 + k_2)\,\mathbf{V}_2^{(1)} + (1 + 2k_1 + k_2)\,\mathbf{V}_3^{(1)} \qquad (5.48)$$

Equations (5.44), (5.46) and (5.48) show that $\mathbf{V}_0^{(2)}$ has been fixed by the condition for positional continuity, $\mathbf{V}_1^{(2)}$ has also been fixed by the condition for gradient continuity, $\mathbf{V}_2^{(2)}$ has been determined by the condition for curvature continuity. Only the fourth vertex $\mathbf{V}_3^{(2)}$ and k_1, k_2 can be freely chosen for shape determination (see Fig. 5.10).

If $\mathbf{V}_3^{(1)}$ is subtracted from both sides of (5.48), the right-hand side may be expressed as a combination of $(\mathbf{V}_3^{(1)} - \mathbf{V}_2^{(1)})$ and $(\mathbf{V}_2^{(1)} - \mathbf{V}_1^{(1)})$.

$$\mathbf{V}_2^{(2)} - \mathbf{V}_3^{(1)} = (2k_1 + k_2)\,(\mathbf{V}_3^{(1)} - \mathbf{V}_2^{(1)}) - k_2(\mathbf{V}_2^{(1)} - \mathbf{V}_1^{(1)}) \qquad (5.49)$$

This shows that $\mathbf{V}_1^{(1)}$, $\mathbf{V}_2^{(1)}$, $\mathbf{V}_3^{(1)} = \mathbf{V}_0^{(2)}$, $\mathbf{V}_1^{(2)}$, and $\mathbf{V}_2^{(2)}$ must be coplanar (see Fig. 5.10). This also means that the osculating plane of the two curves at the common point must coincide or their binormals must be collinear.

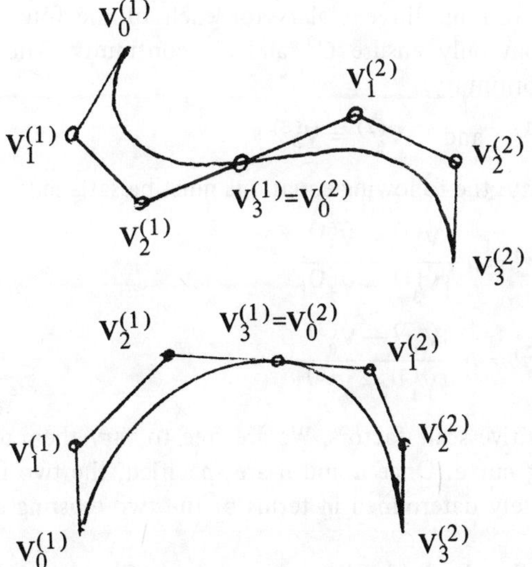

Fig. 5.10 Conditions for C^0, C^1, C^2 continuity

Using (5.44), (5.46) and (5.48), we may construct a composite Bezier curve with positional, gradient and curvature continuity. We start at one end point of curve $\mathbf{r}^{(1)}(u_1)$, adding one new curve $\mathbf{r}^{(2)}(u_2)$ at a time.

We now discuss blending a new Bezier curve $\mathbf{r}^{(2)}(u_2)$ between two existing Bezier curves $\mathbf{r}^{(1)}(u_1)$ and $\mathbf{r}^{(3)}(u_3)$ to form a composite Bezier curve (see Fig. 5.11).

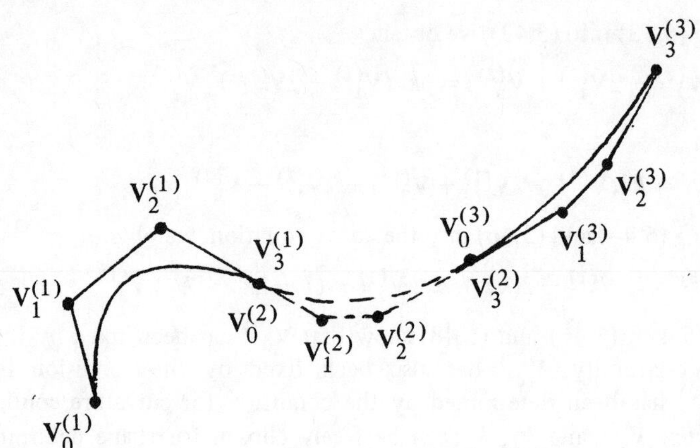

Fig. 5.11 Blending a new Bezier curve between two existing Bezier curves

We can only blend a plane Bezier cubic curve with positional, gradient and curvature continuity between two existing plane Bezier curves. In the plane, a position vector is determined by two scalars, the direction of a tangent by one, and a radius of curvature by the other. We have eight scalars, which suffice to determine the four 2-D vertices defining the new blending plane curve.

Each position vector or curvature vector requires three scalars, and a tangent direction requires two scalars for their specification. Thus we have 16 conditions to satisfy, but only 12 degrees of freedom, three scalars for each of the four vertices defining the blending curve. We can only ensure C^0 and C^1 continuity. The following equations guarantee positional continuity:

$$V_0^{(2)} = V_3^{(1)} \quad \text{and} \quad V_3^{(2)} = V_0^{(3)}$$

To ensure C^1 continuity, the following equations must be satisfied:

$$V_1^{(2)} - V_0^{(2)} = a \, \frac{V_3^{(1)} - V_2^{(1)}}{|V_3^{(1)} - V_2^{(1)}|} \tag{5.50}$$

$$V_3^{(2)} - V_2^{(2)} = b \, \frac{V_1^{(3)} - V_0^{(3)}}{|V_1^{(3)} - V_0^{(3)}|} \tag{5.51}$$

where a and b are positive scale factors. We are free to vary them to change the internal shape of the blending curve. Once a and b are specified, the two internal vertices $V_1^{(2)}$ and $V_2^{(2)}$ are immediately determined in terms of the two existing curves by (5.50) and (5.51).

It is apparent that the above blending curves ensure C^1 continuity, but do not ensure C^2 continuity. However, the usefulness of C^2 continuity is sometimes limited. Most mechanical parts do not require it, since fillets or rounded edges usually blend directly into plane faces.

In design for vehicle contours, C^2 continuity is usually required. More freedom is available if the high-order Bezier curves are used. The reader may do the necessary analysis for C^2 continuity referring to the procedure discussed above.

5.5 BEZIER SURFACES

The underlying principle in defining a Bezier surface is that we let a point trace out a Bezier curve, then let this curve sweep out a Bezier surface. Such a procedure will be described in more detail in the following subsection.

5.5.1 Bezier bi-cubic surfaces

We set 16 control vertices $\mathbf{V}_{i,j}$ ($i = 0, 1, 2, 3; j = 0, 1, 2, 3$), and put them in order to form a 4 × 4 matrix

$$\mathbf{V} = \begin{bmatrix} \mathbf{V}_{00} & \mathbf{V}_{01} & \mathbf{V}_{02} & \mathbf{V}_{03} \\ \mathbf{V}_{10} & \mathbf{V}_{11} & \mathbf{V}_{12} & \mathbf{V}_{13} \\ \mathbf{V}_{20} & \mathbf{V}_{21} & \mathbf{V}_{22} & \mathbf{V}_{23} \\ \mathbf{V}_{30} & \mathbf{V}_{31} & \mathbf{V}_{32} & \mathbf{V}_{33} \end{bmatrix}$$

This is called a vertex information matrix, which defines a characteristic polyhedron in a geometric space (see Fig. 5.12).

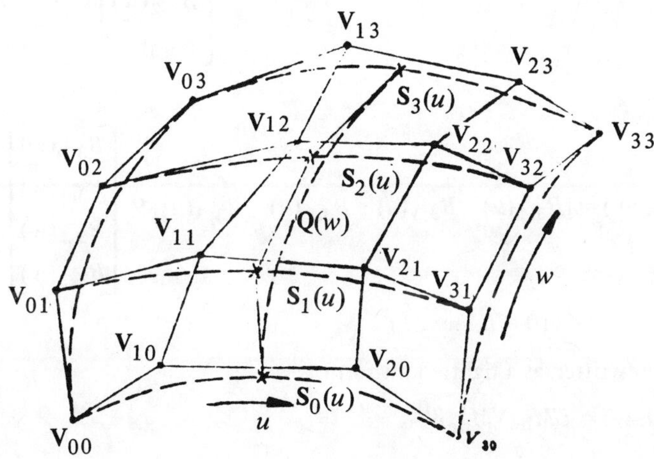

Fig. 5.12 Bezier bi-cubic surface and its characteristic polyhedron

Now using four vertices, which are matrix elements in the same column, to define a Bezier cubic curve, we obtain its matrix representation as follows:

$$S_0(u) = \sum_{i=0}^{3} B_{3,i}(u)\, \mathbf{V}_{i0}$$

$$S_1(u) = \sum_{i=0}^{3} B_{3,i}(u)\, \mathbf{V}_{i1}$$

$$S_2(u) = \sum_{i=0}^{3} B_{3,i}(u) \, V_{i2}$$

$$S_3(u) = \sum_{i=0}^{3} B_{3,i}(u) \, V_{i3} \qquad (0 \leqslant u \leqslant 1)$$

Choosing any value of the parameter u between zero and one, i.e. $u = u^*$, we can regard $S_0(u^*)$, $S_1(u^*)$, $S_2(u^*)$ and $S_3(u^*)$ as four vertices of the characteristic polygon and then construct a Bezier cubic curve with parameter w:

$$Q(w) = \sum_{j=0}^{3} B_{3,j}(w) \, S_j(u^*) \qquad (0 \leqslant w \leqslant 1)$$

Let the Bezier cubic curve $Q(w)$ sweep out a Bezier bi-cubic surface, i.e. let parameter u^* vary between zero and one. Such a procedure can be mathematically described by substituting $S_0(u)$, $S_1(u)$, $S_2(u)$ and $S_3(u)$ into the above equation. The result is

$$\mathbf{r}(u, w) = [\mathbf{S}_0(u) \quad \mathbf{S}_1(u) \quad \mathbf{S}_2(u) \quad \mathbf{S}_3(u)] \begin{bmatrix} B_{3,0}(w) \\ B_{3,1}(w) \\ B_{3,2}(w) \\ B_{3,3}(w) \end{bmatrix}$$

that is

$$\mathbf{r}(u,w) = [B_{3,0}(u) \quad B_{3,1}(u) \quad B_{3,2}(u) \quad B_{3,3}(u)] \, \mathbf{V} \begin{bmatrix} B_{3,0}(w) \\ B_{3,1}(w) \\ B_{3,2}(w) \\ B_{3,3}(w) \end{bmatrix} \qquad (5.52)$$

$$(0 \leqslant u, \ w \leqslant 1)$$

(5.52) may be rewritten as a tightly knit form:

$$\mathbf{r}(u, w) = U M_{be} \mathbf{V} M_{be}^{T} W^{T} \qquad (5.53)$$

Its three component equations are

$$x(u, w) = U M_{be} \mathbf{V}_x M_{be}^{T} W^{T}$$

$$y(u, w) = U M_{be} \mathbf{V}_y M_{be}^{T} W^{T}$$

$$z(u, w) = U M_{be} \mathbf{V}_z M_{be}^{T} W^{T} \qquad (5.54)$$

(5.52) can also be expressed as

$$\mathbf{r}(u, w) = \sum_{i=0}^{3} \sum_{j=0}^{3} B_{3,i}(u) \, B_{3,j}(w) \mathbf{V}_{ij} \qquad (5.55)$$

These products $B_{3,i}(u) \, B_{3,j}(w)$ are the basic functions for the Bezier bi-cubic surface. Note that despite our derivation from parameter u to w or w to u, the result is the same.

The following results are easily obtained from (5.52):

$$\mathbf{r}(0, 0) = \mathbf{V}_{00} \qquad \mathbf{r}(0, 1) = \mathbf{V}_{03}$$

$$\mathbf{r}(1, 0) = \mathbf{V}_{30} \qquad \mathbf{r}(1, 1) = \mathbf{V}_{33}$$

This illustrates that the Bezier bi-cubic surface passes through four vertices, that is, its four corner points coincide with $\mathbf{V}_{00}$, $\mathbf{V}_{03}$, $\mathbf{V}_{30}$ and $\mathbf{V}_{33}$ (see Fig. 5.12).

The four boundaries of the Bezier bi-cubic surface are respectively

$$\mathbf{r}(u, 0) = \sum_{i=0}^{3} B_{3, i}(u)\, \mathbf{V}_{i0}$$

$$\mathbf{r}(u, 1) = \sum_{i=0}^{3} B_{3, i}(u)\, \mathbf{V}_{i3}$$

$$\mathbf{r}(0, w) = \sum_{j=0}^{3} B_{3, j}(w)\, \mathbf{V}_{0j}$$

$$\mathbf{r}(1, w) = \sum_{j=0}^{3} B_{3, j}(w)\, \mathbf{V}_{3j}$$

The boundaries of the Bezier bi-cubic surface are Bezier cubic curves whose vertices of the characteristic polygon are the corresponding boundary vertices of the characteristic polyhedron.

5.5.2 The relationship between Bezier form and Ferguson form

A bi-cubic parametric surface patch may be expressed in the Ferguson form, mentioned in Chapter 4, or Bezier form. For the same patch,

$$UM_{\mathrm{c}}\mathbf{B}\, M_{\mathrm{c}}^{\mathrm{T}} W^{\mathrm{T}} = UM_{\mathrm{be}}\mathbf{V}\, M_{\mathrm{be}}^{\mathrm{T}} W^{\mathrm{T}} \tag{5.56}$$

where $\mathbf{B}$ is the corner information matrix.

Eliminating U and W^{T} in the above equation, we obtain

$$M_{\mathrm{c}}\mathbf{B}M_{\mathrm{c}}^{\mathrm{T}} = M_{\mathrm{be}}\mathbf{V}\, M_{\mathrm{be}}^{\mathrm{T}}$$

$\mathbf{B}$ can be expressed in terms of $\mathbf{V}$:

$$\mathbf{B} = (M_{\mathrm{c}}^{-1} M_{\mathrm{be}})\, \mathbf{V}(M_{\mathrm{c}}^{-1} M_{\mathrm{be}})^{\mathrm{T}}$$

Denoting the new coefficient matrix

$$k = M_{\mathrm{c}}^{-1} M_{\mathrm{be}} = \begin{bmatrix} 1 & 0 & 0 & 0 \\ 0 & 0 & 0 & 1 \\ -3 & 3 & 0 & 0 \\ 0 & 0 & -3 & 3 \end{bmatrix}$$

we obtain

$$\mathbf{B} = k\mathbf{V}k^{\mathrm{T}} \tag{5.57}$$

that is

$$
\begin{bmatrix}
\mathbf{r}(0,0) & \mathbf{r}(0,1) & \mathbf{r}_w(0,0) & \mathbf{r}_w(0,1) \\
\mathbf{r}(1,0) & \mathbf{r}(1,1) & \mathbf{r}_w(1,0) & \mathbf{r}_w(1,1) \\
\mathbf{r}_u(0,0) & \mathbf{r}_u(0,1) & \mathbf{r}_{uw}(0,0) & \mathbf{r}_{uw}(0,1) \\
\mathbf{r}_u(1,0) & \mathbf{r}_u(1,1) & \mathbf{r}_{uw}(1,0) & \mathbf{r}_{uw}(1,1)
\end{bmatrix}
$$

$$
=
\begin{bmatrix}
\mathbf{V}_{00} & \mathbf{V}_{03} & 3(\mathbf{V}_{01}-\mathbf{V}_{00}) \\
\mathbf{V}_{30} & \mathbf{V}_{33} & 3(\mathbf{V}_{31}-\mathbf{V}_{30}) \\
3(\mathbf{V}_{10}-\mathbf{V}_{00}) & 3(\mathbf{V}_{13}-\mathbf{V}_{03}) & 9(\mathbf{V}_{00}-\mathbf{V}_{01}-\mathbf{V}_{10}+\mathbf{V}_{11}) \\
3(\mathbf{V}_{30}-\mathbf{V}_{20}) & 3(\mathbf{V}_{33}-\mathbf{V}_{23}) & 9(\mathbf{V}_{20}-\mathbf{V}_{30}-\mathbf{V}_{21}+\mathbf{V}_{31})
\end{bmatrix}
$$

$$
\left.
\begin{matrix}
3(\mathbf{V}_{03}-\mathbf{V}_{02}) \\
3(\mathbf{V}_{33}-\mathbf{V}_{32}) \\
9(\mathbf{V}_{13}-\mathbf{V}_{03}-\mathbf{V}_{12}+\mathbf{V}_{02}) \\
9(\mathbf{V}_{33}-\mathbf{V}_{23}-\mathbf{V}_{32}+\mathbf{V}_{22})
\end{matrix}
\right]
\tag{5.58}
$$

We examine one of four corner points of the surface patch. The following four equations can be obtained by equating the corresponding elements of both sides in (5.58).

$$
\mathbf{r}(0,0) = \mathbf{V}_{00}
$$

$$
\mathbf{r}_u(0,0) = 3(\mathbf{V}_{10}-\mathbf{V}_{00})
$$

$$
\mathbf{r}_w(0,0) = 3(\mathbf{V}_{01}-\mathbf{V}_{00})
$$

$$
\mathbf{r}_{uw}(0,0) = 9\left[(\mathbf{V}_{00}-\mathbf{V}_{01})+(\mathbf{V}_{11}-\mathbf{V}_{10})\right]
\tag{5.59}
$$

(5.59) illustrates the relationship between corner information and vertex information (see Fig. 5.13). The position of the corner point is determined by the corresponding vertex. The tangent vector at the corner point is the tangent vector at the end point of the corresponding boundary curve. The twist vector $\mathbf{r}_{uw}(0,0)$ at the patch corner is determined by the corresponding four vertices $\mathbf{V}_{00}$, $\mathbf{V}_{01}$, $\mathbf{V}_{10}$ and $\mathbf{V}_{11}$. Adjusting $\mathbf{V}_{11}$ means altering the twist vector at the patch corner without changing the boundary curves. Fig. 5.13 shows the geometric mean of the twist vector at the patch corner.

The above relationship at patch corner $\mathbf{r}(0,0)$ is valid for other patch corners.

The Bezier approach has the great virtue that only the position vectors $\mathbf{V}_{ij}$ of the 16 vertices of the polyhedron need be specified. These have a fairly obvious geometrical implication, and the surface design system is therefore suitable for use by a designer with no advanced mathematical training. The Ferguson–Coons approach has to supply both gradients and twist vectors in constructing a surface patch. It is very difficult to supply twist vectors, so that Ferguson suggested setting $\mathbf{r}_{uw} = 0$ to patch corners. Coons came to the same result, but the pseudo-flats at the corners were considered a drawback.

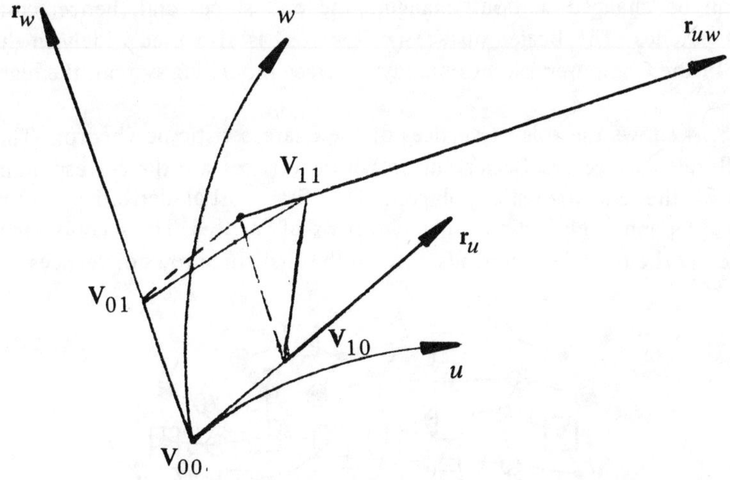

Fig. 5.13 Twist vector

5.5.3 Bezier surfaces

We may describe the Bezier surface of $(n + 1) \times (m + 1)$ order by the position vectors $\mathbf{V}_{ij}$ $(i = 0, 1, \ldots, n;\ j = 0, 1, \ldots, m)$ of the vertices of the characteristic polyhedron; they form the following vertex information matrix.

$$\mathbf{V} = \begin{bmatrix} \mathbf{V}_{00} & \mathbf{V}_{01} & \cdots\cdots & \mathbf{V}_{0m} \\ \mathbf{V}_{10} & \mathbf{V}_{11} & \cdots\cdots & \mathbf{V}_{1m} \\ \cdots & \cdots & \cdots\cdots & \cdots \\ \mathbf{V}_{n0} & \mathbf{V}_{n1} & \cdots\cdots & \mathbf{V}_{nm} \end{bmatrix}$$

They define the Bezier surface as

$$\mathbf{r}(u, w) = [B_{n,0}(u)\quad B_{n,1}(u)\quad \ldots\quad B_{n,n}(u)]\, \mathbf{V} \begin{bmatrix} B_{m,0}(w) \\ B_{m,1}(w) \\ \vdots \\ B_{m,m}(w) \end{bmatrix} \tag{5.60}$$

$$(0 \leqslant u,\ w \leqslant 1)$$

or

$$\mathbf{r}(u, w) = \sum_{i=0}^{n} \sum_{j=0}^{m} B_{n,i}(u)\, B_{m,j}(w)\, \mathbf{V}_{ij} \quad (0 \leqslant u,\ w \leqslant 1) \tag{5.61}$$

If $n = m = 3$, equation (5.60) or (5.61) presents the Bezier bi-cubic surface.

In Bezier's UNISURF system, designers choose $n = m = 4$ in most cases. The advantage of a five-vertex boundary curve over a four-vertex curve is that a change in the third or middle vertex of the curve does not affect the slope at either end. Thus, patch shape can be changed without changing the end slopes and, hence, continuity with adjacent patches. The Bezier surface ($n = m = 6$) is also used widely in the UNISURF system. In the Computervision Company's surface modelling system, the highest degree is $n = m = 7$.

Fig. 5.14 shows the role of vertices of the characteristic polyhedron. The boundaries of the Bezier surface are Bezier curves whose vertices are the corresponding boundary vertices of the characteristic polygon. The first partial derivative vector across the boundary depends only on the first two rows of vertices. The second partial derivative vector across the boundary depends only on the first three rows of vertices.

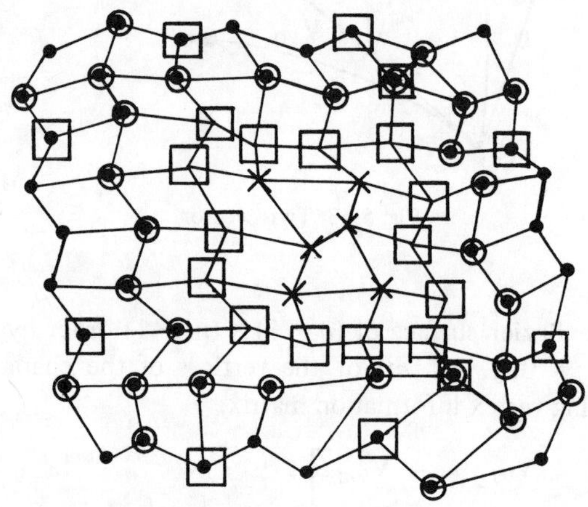

Fig. 5.14 The role of vertices of the characteristic polyhedron
● vertices defining the boundary curves
◉ vertices defining the cross-boundary slopes
▣ vertices defining the cross-boundary curvatures
✕ vertices affecting the inter-shape without changing the boundary curves, cross-boundary slopes and curvatures

Many properties and algorithms of Bezier curves are easily extended to the case of Bezier surfaces. The Bezier surface lies in the convex hull of its characteristic polyhedron. The relationship between the surface and its polyhedron is invariant. Subdivision of the surface (by the de Casteljau algorithm) is performed on rows and then on columns, or in the reverse order. The degree elevations and inverse algorithm for Bezier curves are valid for Bezier surfaces.

5.6 COMPOSITE BEZIER SURFACES

By analogy to curves it is also possible to build up complex surfaces from a number of Bezier patches. The conditions for continuity of adjacent surface patches can be derived from those for curves. Let us now consider how C^0 and C^1 continuity may be achieved for a composite Bezier surface (see Fig. 5.15).

The positional continuity across the boundary is

$$\mathbf{r}^{(1)}(1, w) = \mathbf{r}^{(2)}(0, w) \qquad (0 \leqslant w \leqslant 1) \tag{5.62}$$

that is

$$\mathbf{V}^{(1)}_{3j} = \mathbf{V}^{(2)}_{0j} \qquad (j = 0, 1, 2, 3) \tag{5.63}$$

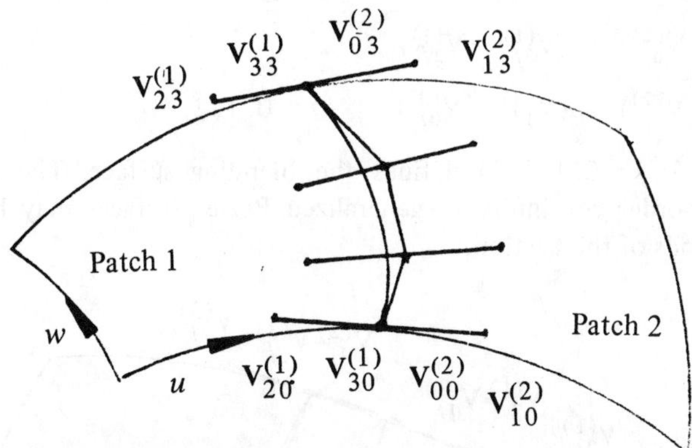

Fig. 5.15 C^1 continuity for a composite Bezier surface

The gradient continuity across the boundary is

$$\mathbf{r}^{(2)}_u(0, w) \times \mathbf{r}^{(2)}_w(0, w) = \lambda(w)\, \mathbf{r}^{(1)}_u(1, w) \times \mathbf{r}^{(1)}_w(1, w) \tag{5.64}$$

(5.64) means that the tangent plane of patch 1 on $u = 1$ must coincide with that of patch 2 on $u = 0$; in other words, the direction of the surface normal must be continuous across the boundary. $\lambda(w)$ is a positive-valueed scalar function, which provides a 'freedom' for the difference in the magnitude of the surface normal vector.

Since

$$\mathbf{r}^{(2)}_w(0, w) = \mathbf{r}^{(1)}_w(1, w)$$

then (5.64) yields

$$\mathbf{r}^{(2)}_u(0, w) = \lambda(w)\, \mathbf{r}^{(1)}_u(1, w) \tag{5.65}$$

This implies that all parameter curves with u in the composite surface will have continuity of gradient direction. Setting $\lambda(w) = \lambda$, a positive constant, and using the partial derivative equation of a Bezier surface, we obtain from (5.65)

$$[0 \quad 1 \quad 0 \quad 0]M_{be}V^{(2)}M^{T}_{be}W^{T} = \lambda[0 \quad 1 \quad 2 \quad 3]M_{be}V^{(1)}M^{T}_{be}W^{T} \tag{5.66}$$

(5.66) must hold for all relevant w, and therefore we equate coefficients and post-multiply by $(M^{T}_{BE})^{-1}$ to obtain the four equations

$$(V^{(2)}_{1j} - \mathbf{V}^{(2)}_{0j}) = \lambda(V^{(1)}_{3j} - \mathbf{V}^{(1)}_{2j}) \qquad (j = 0, 1, 2, 3) \tag{5.67}$$

(5.67) shows that the four pairs of polyhedron edges, which meet at the boundary, must be collinear (see Fig. 5.15). (5.67) gives the conditions for C^1 continuity in the u

direction. In general, two Bezier patches have C^r continuity if all rows (or columns, respectively) of the two Bezier polydedra are Bezier polygons of C^r continuous curves.

We will now discuss blending a new Bezier $\mathbf{r}^{(2)}(u_2, w_2)$ between existing Bezier surfaces $\mathbf{r}^{(1)}(u_1, w_1)$ and $\mathbf{r}^{(3)}(u_3, w_3)$ to form a composite Bezier surface (see Fig. 5.16). The conditions of C^1 for blending a new Bezier surface are

$$(\mathbf{V}^{(2)}_{1j} - \mathbf{V}^{(2)}_{0j}) = \lambda(\mathbf{V}^{(1)}_{3j} - \mathbf{V}^{(1)}_{2j})$$

$$(\mathbf{V}^{(2)}_{3j} - \mathbf{V}^{(2)}_{2j}) = \mu(\mathbf{V}^{(3)}_{1j} - \mathbf{V}^{(3)}_{0j}) \qquad (j = 0, 1, 2, 3) \qquad (5.68)$$

$\mathbf{V}^{(2)}_{ij}$ $(i = 0, 1, 2, 3; j = 0, 1, 2, 3)$ defines the blending surface. The conditions of second- and higher-order continuity of generalized Bezier surfaces may be derived by extending the methods of this section.

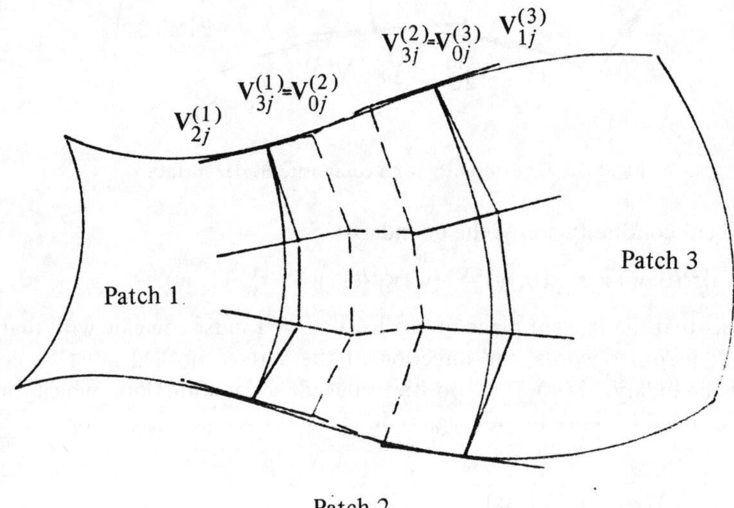

Fig. 5.16   Blending Bezier surfaces

5.7 THREE FORMS OF BEZIER CURVES (APPENDIX)

In this chapter, we employ the Bernstein–Bezier form

$$\mathbf{r}(u) = \sum_{i=0}^{n} B_{n,i}(u)\, \mathbf{V}_i$$

where $n = 3$ (see Fig. 5.17(a))

$$\mathbf{r}(u) = (1 - u)^3 \mathbf{V}_0 + 3u(1 - u)^2 \mathbf{V}_1 + 3u^2(1 - u)\mathbf{V}_2 + u^3 \mathbf{V}_3 \qquad (5.69)$$

The above equation may be rewritten as

$$\mathbf{r}(u) = \mathbf{a}_0 + (3u - 3u^2 + u^3)\,\mathbf{a}_1 + (3u^2 - 2u^3)\,\mathbf{a}_2 + u^3 \mathbf{a}_3 \qquad (5.70)$$

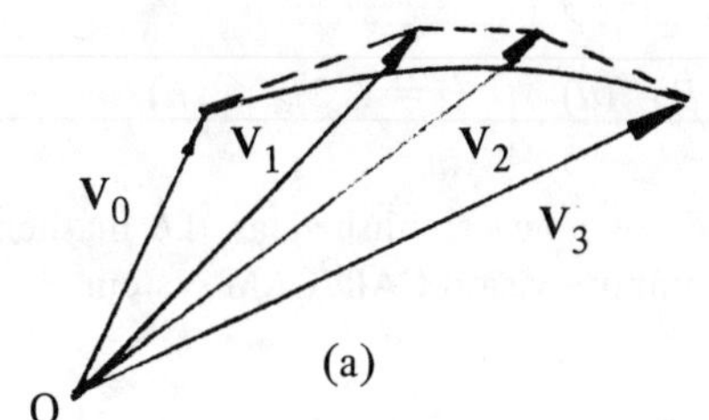
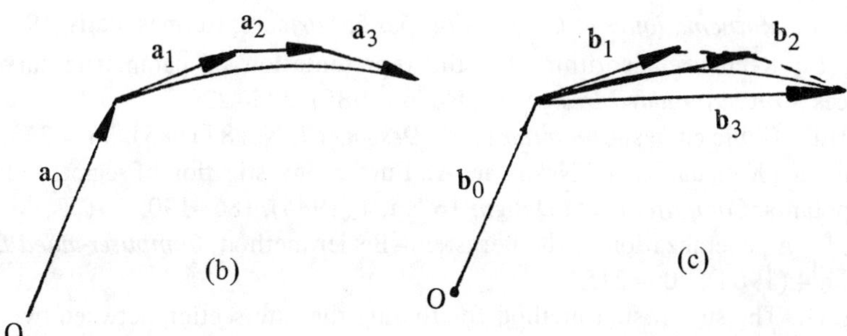

Fig. 5.17　Three forms of Bezier curve

where a_i $(i = 1, 2, 3)$ is the edge vector of the characteristic polygon. The relationship between V_i and a_i is (see Fig. 5.17(b))

$$a_i = V_i - V_{i-1} \quad (i = 1, 2, 3)$$

In general, the Bezier form may be expressed as

$$r(u) = \sum_{i=0}^{n} f_{n,i}(u)\, a_i \tag{5.71}$$

in which $f_{u,i}(u)$ is called a Bezier function; its equations are

$$f_{n,0}(u) = 1$$

$$f_{n,i}(u) = \frac{(-u)^i}{(i-1)!} \frac{d^{i-1}}{du^{i-1}} \frac{(1-u)^n - 1}{u} \quad (i = 1, 2, \ldots, n) \tag{5.72}$$

Equation (5.69) can also be rewritten as (see Fig. 5.17(c))

$$r(u) = V_0 + 3u(1-u)^2 (V_1 - V_0) + 3u^2(1-u)(V_2 - V_0) + u^3(V_3 - V_0)$$

$$= b_0 + 3u(1-u)^2 b_1 + 3u^2(1-u) b_2 + u^3 b_3 \tag{5.73}$$

The three forms (5.69), (5.70) and (5.73) are equivalent. The Bernstein–Bezier form is generally adopted by most workers in computer-aided geometric design.

The relationship between Bernstein functions $B_{n,i}(u)$ and their Bezier functions $f_{n,i}(u)$ may be proved to be

$$f_{n,i}(u) = 1 - \sum_{j=0}^{i-1} B_{n,j}(u) \qquad (i = 1, 2, \ldots, n) \tag{5.74}$$

Bezier curves and surfaces are now established as the mathematical basis of many CAD/CAM systems, e.g. the Computervision CAD/CAM system.

REFERENCES

[1] Bezier, P., *Mathematical Basis of Unisurf CAD System*, Butterworth, Borough Green, Sevenoaks, Kent, 1986.

[2] Bezier, P., *Mathematiques et C.A.O.; Courbes et Surfaces*, Hermes, Paris, 1986.

[3] Piegl, L., Recursive algorithms for the representation of parametric curves and surfaces, *Computer-aided Design, 17*, No. 5 (1985), 225–229.

[4] Bez, H.E., Cubic curves, *Computer-aided Design, 17*, No. 8 (1985), 367–368.

[5] Harada, K., Kaneda, K. and Nakamae, A., Further investigation of segmented Bezier interpolants, *Computer-aided Design, 16* No. 4 (1984), 186–190.

[6] Piegl, L., A generalization of the Bernstein–Bezier method, *Computer-aided Design, 16*, No. 4 (1984), 209–215.

[7] Wang, G., The subdivision method for finding the intersection between two Bezier curves or surfaces, *Zhejiang University Journal*: Special Issue on Computational Geometry, China (1984).

[8] Boehm, W. & Farin, G., Subdivision algorithm (letter to the editor), *Computer-aided Design, 15*, No. 5 (1983), 260–261.

[9] Hering, L., Closed Bezier and B-spline curves with given tangent polygons, *Computer-aided Design, 15*, No. 1 (1983), 3–6.

[10] Goldman, R.N., Using degenerate Bezier triangles and tetrahedra to subdivide Bezier curves, *Computer-aided Design, 14*, No. 6 (1982), 307–311.

[11] Chang, G.Z., Matrix formulations of Bezier technique, *Computer-aided Design, 14*, No. 6 (1982), 345–350.

[12] Chang, G.Z. and Wu, J. H., Mathematical foundations of Bezier's technique, *Computer-aided Design, 13*, No. 3 (1981), 133–136.

[13] Timmer, H.G., Alternative representation for parametric cubic curves and surfaces, *Computer-aided Design, 12*, No. 1 (1980), 25–28.

[14] Bezier, P., Essai de definition numerique des courbes et des surfaces experimentales, *Thesis*, Unversité de Paris VI, 1977.

[15] Bezier, P., Mathematical and practical possibilities of UNISURF, in *Computer-aided Geometric Design*, Academic Press, New York, 1974.

[16] Bezier, P., UNISURF system: principles, program, language, *Proc. PROLAMAT Conf., Budapest*, North Holland, Amsterdam, 1974.

[17] Bezier, P., *Numerical Control: Mathematics and Applications*, John Wiley & Sons, London, 1972.

[18] Bezier, P., Example of an existing system in the motor industry: the UNISURF system, *Proc. Roy. Soc. London, A321* (1971), 207–218.

[19] Bezier, P., How Renault uses numerical control for car body design and tooling, *SAE Paper 680010* (1968).

6

B-spline Curves and Surfaces

6.1 INTRODUCTION

In the previous chapter, the Bezier curve was discussed. It was shown that from a given set of vertices of the characteristic polygon (V_i) $(i = 0\ 1, \ldots, n)$ and Bernstein functions $J_{n,i}(u)$ $(i = 0, 1, \ldots, n)$, the Bezier curve can be obtained. The visuality and simplicity of the Bezier curve simplifies computer interactive geometric design. Sometimes, however, the Bezier curve and its characteristic polygon are far apart, and once the position of one vertex is altered, the whole curve has to be recalculated.

During the years 1972–1974, Riesenfeld, Gordon and Forrest popularized the Bezier curve. By replacing Bernstein functions with B-spline functions in the Bezier curve formula, a B-spline curve can be obtained.

The B-spline was proposed by I.J. Schoenberg as early as 1946. Thanks to the extensive research done by many mathematicians, the B-spline curves and surfaces have their own well-based theory. B-spline curves and surfaces possess excellent geometric properties. They retain the visuality and overcome the shortcoming of the Bezier method. The B-spline curve and its characteristic polygon keep close to each other; local alterations can be made without recalculating the whole curve.

During the last few years, many departments have been studying and applying B-spline curves and surfaces with good results, and B-spline curves and surfaces are proving to be a very promising geometrical tool in Computer-Aided Geometric Design (CAGD).

6.2 B-SPLINES (1)

In this section, B-splines are introduced in a simple form, because of their importance in CAGD. Then a span of a cubic B-spline curve is constructed by using B-splines as blending functions, and the continuity conditions between each span are discussed. Finally, B-splines are derived from the continuity conditions.

6.2.1 Cubic B-splines

B-splines can be derived by many methods, such as de Boor and Cox's recursion formula, divided difference of the truncated power function, continuity conditions, etc. The representations of B-splines are very different according to the ways in which they are derived, but the nature is exactly the same. The matrix forms of cubic B-spline functions are now being introduced, but their derivation will not appear until the end of this section. B-splines are expressed in the algebraic form

$$N_{4,0}(u) = \frac{1}{3!}\,(1 - 3u + 3u^2 - u^3)$$

$$N_{4,1}(u) = \frac{1}{3!}\,(4 - 6u^2 + 3u^3)$$

$$N_{4,2}(u) = \frac{1}{3!}\,(1 + 3u + 3u^2 - 3u^3)$$

$$N_{4,3}(u) = \frac{1}{3!}\,(u^3) \qquad\qquad (0 \leqslant u \leqslant 1)$$

They may be expressed in the matrix form

$$[N_{4,0}(u) \quad N_{4,1}(u) \quad N_{4,2}(u) \quad N_{4,3}(u)]$$

$$= [1 \quad u \quad u^2 \quad u^3]\,\frac{1}{3!}\begin{bmatrix} 1 & 4 & 1 & 0 \\ -3 & 0 & 3 & 0 \\ 3 & -6 & 3 & 0 \\ -1 & 3 & -3 & 1 \end{bmatrix} \qquad\qquad (6.1)$$

or

$$= [1 \quad u \quad u^2 \quad u^3]M_{\mathrm{b}}$$

or

$$= UM_{\mathrm{b}} \qquad\qquad (0 \leqslant u \leqslant 1)$$

where a subscript 4 means that the B-splines are functions of order 4 (degree 3). If we have a set of vectors $\mathbf{V}_i$, $\mathbf{V}_{i+1}$, $\mathbf{V}_{i+2}$ and $\mathbf{V}_{i+3}$, we use the linear combination between blending functions $N_{4,j}(u)$ and vertices $\mathbf{V}_{i+j}(j = 0, 1, 2, 3)$ to construct a cubic B-spline curve span.

6.2.2 The cubic B-spline curve span

The cubic B-spline curve span $\mathbf{r}_i(u)$ is defined as

$$r_i(u) = [N_{4,0}(u) \quad N_{4,1}(u) \quad N_{4,2}(u) \quad N_{4,3}(u)] \begin{bmatrix} V_i \\ V_{i+1} \\ V_{i+2} \\ V_{i+3} \end{bmatrix} \qquad (6.2)$$

Its geometric properties are as follows:

At $u = 0$ and $u = 1$, (6.2) gives

$$r_i(0) = [1 \quad 0 \quad 0 \quad 0] M_B \begin{bmatrix} V_i \\ V_{i+1} \\ V_{i+2} \\ V_{i+3} \end{bmatrix}$$

$$= [\tfrac{1}{6} \quad \tfrac{4}{6} \quad \tfrac{1}{6} \quad 0] \begin{bmatrix} V_i \\ V_{i+1} \\ V_{i+2} \\ V_{i+3} \end{bmatrix}$$

$$= \tfrac{2}{3} V_{i+1} + \tfrac{1}{3} \left(\frac{V_i + V_{i+2}}{2} \right) \qquad (6.3)$$

Similarly

$$r_i(1) = \tfrac{2}{3} V_{i+2} + \tfrac{1}{3} \left(\frac{V_{i+1} + V_{i+3}}{2} \right)$$

and hence by setting $t = \tfrac{1}{3}$, then

$$r_i(t) = (1 - t) V_{i+1} + t \left(\frac{V_i + V_{i+2}}{2} \right)$$

The linear relationship above shows that the starting point is one-third of the way along the straight line joining V_{i+1} to the mid-point of the line joining V_i and V_{i+2}.

On differentiating (6.2)

$$r_i'(u) = [0 \quad 1 \quad 2u \quad 3u^2] M_b \begin{bmatrix} V_i \\ V_{i+1} \\ V_{i+2} \\ V_{i+3} \end{bmatrix}$$

then at $u = 0$ and $u = 1$, we obtain

$$\mathbf{r}_i'(0) = \tfrac{1}{2}\,(\mathbf{V}_{i+2} - \mathbf{V}_i)$$

$$\mathbf{r}_i'(1) = \tfrac{1}{2}\,(\mathbf{V}_{i+3} - \mathbf{V}_{i+1}) \tag{6.4}$$

On differentiating $\mathbf{r}_i'(u)$

$$\mathbf{r}_i''(u) = \begin{bmatrix} 0 & 0 & 2 & 6u \end{bmatrix} M_{\mathrm{b}} \begin{bmatrix} \mathbf{V}_i \\ \mathbf{V}_{i+1} \\ \mathbf{V}_{i+2} \\ \mathbf{V}_{i+3} \end{bmatrix}$$

then at $u = 0$ and $u = 1$, we obtain

$$\mathbf{r}_i''(0) = (\mathbf{V}_{i+2} - \mathbf{V}_{i+1}) - (\mathbf{V}_{i+1} - \mathbf{V}_i)$$

$$\mathbf{r}_i''(1) = (\mathbf{V}_{i+3} - \mathbf{V}_{i+2}) - (\mathbf{V}_{i+2} - \mathbf{V}_{i+1}) \tag{6.5}$$

The tangent vector at the starting point of the curve span is parallel to the line joining $\mathbf{V}_i$ and $\mathbf{V}_{i+2}$. The curvature vector at the starting point is along the line joining $\mathbf{V}_{i+1}$ and $\mathbf{V}_m$. The tangent plane starting point of the curve span is the plane, which is defined by $\mathbf{V}_i, \mathbf{V}_{i+1}$ and $\mathbf{V}_{i+2}$; the same relationship exists at another end point $\mathbf{r}_i(1)$.

The position, tangent and curvature vectors of end points of a curve span are as shown in Fig. 6.1.

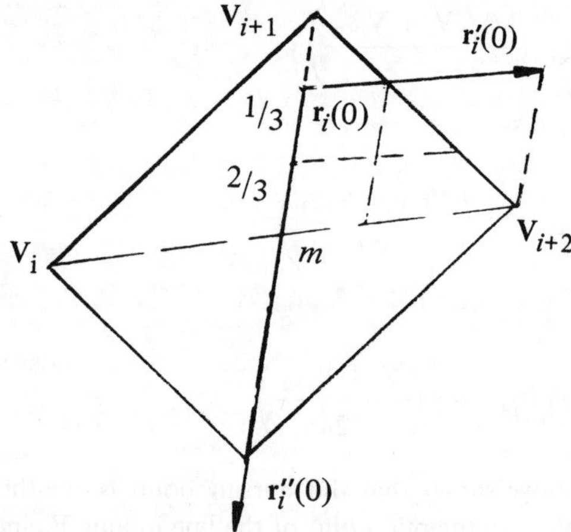

Fig. 6.1 The cubic B-spline curve span

6.2.3 Continuity conditions between spans

By adding one vertex to a characteristic polygon, we may obtain correspondingly one new span of the cubic B-spline curve.

The cubic B-spline curve and its characteristic polygon are as shown in Fig. 6.2. Each span of the cubic B-spline curve is determined by at most four consecutive vertices of its defining characteristic polygon.

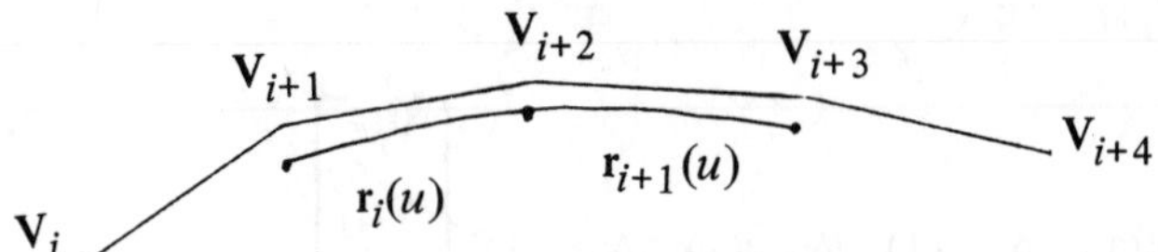

Fig. 6.2 A cubic B-spline curve and its characteristic polygon

In order to ensure up to second-order continuity at a joint point, we require:

$$\mathbf{r}_i(1) = \mathbf{r}_{i+1}(0)$$

$$\mathbf{r}_i'(1) = \mathbf{r}_{i+1}'(0)$$

$$\mathbf{r}_i''(1) = \mathbf{r}_{i+1}''(0) \tag{6.6}$$

According to formulae (6.3), (6.4) and (6.5), we can see that the representations of the end point of the ith span are related only to vertices $\mathbf{V}_{i+1}$, $\mathbf{V}_{i+2}$ and $\mathbf{V}_{i+3}$. The representations of the start point of the $(i+1)$th span are also related to vertices $\mathbf{V}_{i+1}$, $\mathbf{V}_{i+2}$ and $\mathbf{V}_{i+3}$; moreover, the position, tangent and curvature vectors at jointed points are equal. This illustrates that a cubic B-spline curve defined by (6.2) ensures automatically up to second-order continuity everywhere on the curve. By contrast, if a polygon has more than three sides, the cubic Bezier technique will require a composite curve, with the associated problem of matching curvature at joint points between spans, if second-order continuity is required.

6.2.4 From continuity conditions to B-splines

Readers now may ask how B-splines originate? They may be derived and proved from continuity requirements. This is an easy approach to B-splines, because it has a clear geometric meaning.

Assuming blending functions $N_{4,j}(u)$ $(j = 0, 1, 2, 3)$ are unknown cubic polynomials, we may express them in the form

$$N_{4,j}(u) = a_j + b_j u + c_j u^2 + d_j u^3 \qquad (j = 0, 1, 2, 3) \tag{6.7}$$

There are 16 coefficients which are unknown in (6.7). If a set of vertices $\mathbf{V}_i$ $(i = 0, 1, \ldots, n+1)$ is provided, we may use the linear combination between $N_{4,j}(u)$ and $\mathbf{V}_{i+j}(j = 0, 1, 2, 3)$ to construct a cubic B-spline curve

$$\mathbf{r}_i(u) = [N_{4,0}(u) \quad N_{4,1}(u) \quad N_{4,2}(u) \quad N_{4,3}(u)] \begin{bmatrix} \mathbf{V}_i \\ \mathbf{V}_{i+1} \\ \mathbf{V}_{i+2} \\ \mathbf{V}_{i+3} \end{bmatrix} \tag{6.8}$$

The cubic B-spline curve contains $(n-1)$ curve spans.

We now derive the 16 unknown coefficients from the continuity conditions between spans. Firstly in order to ensure position continuity, we should have

$$\mathbf{r}_i(1) - \mathbf{r}_{i+1}(0) = 0$$

i.e.

$$[N_{4,0}(1) \quad N_{4,1}(1) \quad N_{4,2}(1) \quad N_{4,3}(1)] \begin{bmatrix} \mathbf{V}_i \\ \mathbf{V}_{i+1} \\ \mathbf{V}_{i+2} \\ \mathbf{V}_{i+3} \end{bmatrix}$$

$$- [N_{4,0}(0) \quad N_{4,1}(0) \quad N_{4,2}(0) \quad N_{4,3}(0)] \begin{bmatrix} \mathbf{V}_{i+1} \\ \mathbf{V}_{i+2} \\ \mathbf{V}_{i+3} \\ \mathbf{V}_{i+4} \end{bmatrix} = 0$$

we obtain from the above equation

$$N_{4,0}(1) = 0$$
$$N_{4,1}(1) = N_{4,0}(0)$$
$$N_{4,2}(1) = N_{4,1}(0) \tag{6.9}$$
$$N_{4,3}(1) = N_{4,2}(0)$$
$$N_{4,3}(0) = 0$$

Similarly in order to ensure first-order continuity, we should have

$$\mathbf{r}_i'(1) - \mathbf{r}_{i+1}'(0) = 0$$

we obtain from the above equation

$$N_{4,0}'(1) = 0$$
$$N_{4,1}'(1) = N_{4,0}'(0)$$
$$N_{4,2}'(1) = N_{4,1}'(0) \tag{6.10}$$
$$N_{4,3}'(1) = N_{4,2}'(0)$$
$$N_{4,3}'(0) = 0$$

Similarly in order to ensure second-order continuity

$$\mathbf{r}_i''(1) - \mathbf{r}_{i+1}''(0) = 0$$

we obtain

$$N_{4,0}''(1) = 0$$
$$N_{4,1}''(1) = N_{4,0}''(0)$$
$$N_{4,2}''(1) = N_{4,1}''(0) \tag{6.11}$$
$$N_{4,3}''(1) = N_{4,2}''(0)$$
$$N_{4,3}''(0) = 0$$

Finally, considering the case in which four consecutive vertices coincide, the ith span is reduced to one point, i.e.

$$\mathbf{r}_i(u) = \mathbf{V}_i$$

thus we obtain an additional equation

$$N_{4,0}(u) + N_{4,1}(u) + N_{4,2}(u) + N_{4,3}(u) \equiv 1 \tag{6.12}$$

Sixteen equations are provided from (6.9)–(6.12), which form a linear system.

The 16 coefficients are determined uniquely by resolving this linear system; then the four blending functions are just cubic B-splines which were introduced in formula (6.1). This shows that cubic B-splines ensure up to second-order continuity of a cubic B-spline curve (6.8); inversion, cubic B-splines may be derived according to curve continuity requirements.

6.3 B-SPLINE CURVES

In this section we discuss some of the important geometric properties and basic algorithms of cubic B-spline curves from the engineering point of view.

6.3.1 Geometric properties of a B-spline curve

A cubic B-spline curve is a polynomial curve

$$\mathbf{r}_i(u) = \sum_{j=0}^{3} N_{4,j}(u)\, \mathbf{V}_{i+j} \qquad (i = 0, 1, \ldots, n-2;\ 0 \leqslant u \leqslant 1) \tag{6.13}$$

The cubic B-splines $N_{4,j}(u)$ are polynomials of degree 3 (or order 4). Vertices $\mathbf{V}_i$ $(i = 0, 1, \ldots, n+1)$ are also called control points or de Boor points; they form the characteristic polygon of a B-spline curve.

Features

Approximate property is the first important feature. Four useful facts are:

- the curve passes through the points from formula (6.3)

$$\mathbf{r}_i(0) = \tfrac{2}{3}\, \mathbf{V}_{i+1} + \tfrac{1}{3}\left(\frac{\mathbf{V}_i + \mathbf{V}_{i+2}}{2}\right)$$

  for $i = 0, 1, \ldots, n-2$. These points are one-third the way along the straight line joining $\mathbf{V}_{i+1}$ to the mid-point of the line joining $\mathbf{V}_i$ and $\mathbf{V}_{i+2}$, as shown in Fig. 6.1;
- the curve passes close to the mid-point of each side of the characteristic polygon, as shown in Fig. 6.2;
- the tangent direction of the curve at $\mathbf{r}_i(0)$ is determined by formula (6.4);
- the direction of the curvature vector of the curve at $\mathbf{r}_i(0)$ is determined by formula (6.5). This means that the direction of the curvature vector of the curve at the joining point and the direction of bending of the polygon are the same.

From these four characteristics, it is quite easy to sketch a cubic B-spline curve for any given polygon.

Theoretical analysis and engineering experience show that the cubic B-spline curve may be regarded as an approximation to the polygon, but the approximation of the cubic B-spline curve is better than that of the Bezier curve.

Local adjustment property is the second interesting feature. We see that the cubic B-spline curve span $r_i(u)$ is only determined by the four consecutive vertices V_i, V_{i+1}, V_{i+2} and V_{i+3}; in other words, a change in one vertex only alters four spans of the curve — for example, a change in vertex V_{i+3} only alters spans $r_{i+1}(u)$, $r_{i+2}(u)$, $r_{i+3}(u)$ and $r_{i+4}(u)$. This means the B-spline curve has the advantage that local adjustments can be made without disturbing the rest of the curve. We may make such local modifications to the curve by moving some vertices without having to recompute it completely. Such a feature is desirable in any design system.

Note that the Bezier curve does not possess the local adjustment property. So the B-spline curve is more powerful than the Bezier curve for design.

Flexibility is the third useful feature. When three successive vertices V_i, V_{i+1} and V_{i+2} are collinear, the starting point of a curve span lies on the straight line joining V_i and V_{i+2}, the tangent vector at the starting point coincides with the line joining V_i and V_{i+2}, and, moreover, the curvature vector equals zero at the starting point. Using the last property, the turning point may be designed if necessary.

When four successive vertices V_i, V_{i+1}, V_{i+2} and V_{i+3} are collinear, the corresponding B-spline curve span is reduced to a straight line segment.

When three successive vertices V_i, V_{i+1} and V_{i+2} coincide, there will be a sharp point in the B-spline curve.

As most products with complex shape consist of curve spans, straight lines, turning points and sharp points, a B-spline curve provides enough flexibility for this design need.

Convex hull property is also an interesting geometrical property of B-spline curves. Each curve span is determined by at most four consecutive vertices. As we know, the values of the four corresponding B-splines are positive and sum to unity. Thus for any u, $r_i(u)$ is a weighted average of these four vertices, and the entire span must lie inside what is called their convex hull. Similar to the case of the Bezier curve, the convex hull of vertices in a plane is the area defined by a rubber band stretched around all the vertices, or in 3-D, by a bollen tightly stretched around all the vertices. The convex hull is useful in clipping a curve against a window or view volume.

6.3.2 Algorithms of B-spline curves

A B-spline curve can be defined by two sets of points: by vertices V_i of the characteristic polygon or by junction points r_i which lie on the curve. If vertices V_i are provided, junction points r_i and any points on the curve can be determined by using formula (6.8); this procedure is called approximation, or the positive algorithm. If junction points r_i are points given, vertices V_i can be calculated by solving the linear system (6.14); this procedure is called interpolation; it is also called the inverse algorithm.

The positive algorithm

This calculation procedure is simply provided by formula (6.8), so there is no need for detailed discussion. Note that a practical implementation of the procedure is the divided difference method, when intervals of parameter u are constant, e.g. in numerical control draughting and machining. The divided difference method provides high calculating speed for the user.

The inverse algorithm

The complete cubic interpolating B-spline curve may be constructed by using $(n + 1)$ junction points $\mathbf{r}_i$ $(i = 0, 1, \ldots, n)$ and two other items of information. This method is usually used in engineering practice. Assuming $(n + 1)$ consecutive junction points $\mathbf{r}_i$ are known, in order to determine values of vertex vectors of the control polygon $\mathbf{V}_i$ $(i = -1, 1, 0, \ldots, n + 1)$, $(n + 3)$ equations are required.

According to the properties of the B-spline curve discussed in section 6.2.2, that is, a junction point of the B-spline curve is determined by three consecutive vertices, we have $(n + 1)$ equations as follows:

$$\tfrac{1}{6}(\mathbf{V}_{i-1} + 4\mathbf{V}_i + \mathbf{V}_{i+1}) = \mathbf{r}_i \quad (i = 0, 1, \ldots, n) \tag{6.14}$$

The two additional relations chosen will depend upon physical or other considerations in any specific application. The possibilities include:

1. Free ends: no curvature of the curve at $\mathbf{r}_0$ and $\mathbf{r}_n$; we suggest setting

    $$\mathbf{V}_{-1} = \mathbf{V}_0, \quad \mathbf{V}_{n+1} = \mathbf{V}_n \tag{6.15}$$

    Equations (6.14) and (6.15) form a linear system which includes $(n + 3)$ equations. We note that the matrix of coefficients of this sytem is tridiagonal (having non-zero elements only on the leading diagonal and immediately to either side of it). A solution to such a system may be computed accurately and efficiently using a standard algorithm which may be found in most books on linear algebra.

2. Built-in ends: specified tangent vectors at the ends of the curve, $\mathbf{r}_0$ and $\mathbf{r}_n$. Additional conditions may be

    $$\tfrac{1}{2}(\mathbf{V}_1 - \mathbf{V}_{-1}) = \mathbf{r}_0'$$

    $$\tfrac{1}{2}(\mathbf{V}_{n+1} - \mathbf{V}_{n-1}) = \mathbf{r}_n' \tag{6.16}$$

    Using the first equation of both (6.14) and (6.16), after deleting $\mathbf{V}_1$, the following equation may be obtained:

    $$\tfrac{2}{6}\mathbf{V}_{-1} + \tfrac{4}{6}\mathbf{V}_0 = \mathbf{r}_0 - \tfrac{1}{3}\mathbf{r}_0' \tag{6.17}$$

    Using the last equation of both (6.14) and (6.16), after deleting $\mathbf{V}_{n-1}$, the following equation may be obtained:

    $$\tfrac{4}{6}\mathbf{V}_n + \tfrac{2}{6}\mathbf{V}_{n+1} = \mathbf{r}_n + \tfrac{1}{3}\mathbf{r}_n' \tag{6.18}$$

(6.14), (6.17) and (6.18) form a tridiagonal linear system; it may be computed using a standard algorithm.

3.   Closed ends: in order to smooth the curve at start and end points, we should choose

$$\mathbf{V}_{n+1} = \mathbf{V}_0, \quad \mathbf{V}_n = \mathbf{V}_{-1} \tag{6.19}$$

Equations (6.14) and (6.19) form a linear system, but not a tridiagonal linear system. It may be solved by evaluating inverse matrices which may be found in most books on linear algebra.

The numerical solution of three linear systems may also be achieved by the Newton–Raphson method. A reasonable starting approximation to vertices is a prerequisite for the success of this method. The best way is by choosing the values of junction points as starting approximation to vertices, because the $\mathbf{r}_i$ are very close to the $\mathbf{V}_i$. This method usually gives the required solutions to any desired accuracy with great efficiency.

We have seen that a cubic B-spline curve can be defined by two sets of points. From eqaution (6.14), $\mathbf{r}_i$ is determined only by vertices $\mathbf{V}_{i-1}$, $\mathbf{V}_i$ and $\mathbf{V}_{i+1}$; in other words, altering one $\mathbf{V}_i$ affects only three junction points $\mathbf{r}_{i-1}$, $\mathbf{r}_i$ and $\mathbf{r}_{i+1}$, i.e. only a limited local part of the curve is affected. Altering one $\mathbf{r}_i$ (and subsequent resolving of the linear system) will influence the whole curve. We should note that there is an approximate representation of $\mathbf{V}_i$ with $\mathbf{r}_i$ according to the principle of the combination for solution of a system of linear equations.

$$\mathbf{V}_i = \sqrt{3} \quad \mathbf{r}_i + \sum_{j=1}^{4} (\mathbf{r}_{i+j} + \mathbf{r}_{i-j}) \lambda^j \qquad (i = 4, \ldots, n-4) \tag{6.20}$$

where

$$\lambda \simeq 0.268000$$

$$\lambda^2 \simeq 0.071800$$

$$\lambda^3 \simeq 0.019200$$

$$\lambda^4 \simeq 0.000515$$

We see from (6.20) that $\mathbf{V}_i$ is mainly determined by $\mathbf{r}_{i-1}$, $\mathbf{r}_i$ and $\mathbf{r}_{i+1}$; the influence of $\mathbf{r}_{i+j}$ and $\mathbf{r}_{i-j}$ $(j = 2, 3, \ldots)$ on $\mathbf{V}_i$ is reduced according to λ^j. Equation (6.20) provides an efficient method for calculating directly the starting approximation values to vertices without an inversion procedure.

6.3.3 The fitting and design procedure

The fitting procedure contains the following steps:

(i)   the designer specifies a set of points $\mathbf{r}_i$ which lie exactly on the desired curve;

(ii)   the computer uses an inversion procedure to determine the vertices of the control polygon which corresponds to the interpolated curve;

(iii)   the computer uses these vertices to calculate any points of the curve for numerical controlled draughting and machining.

Note that in some cases, the inversion procedure will cause the curve to oscillate. This effect can be reduced by specifying more points $\mathbf{r}_i$ for the same products.

The design procedure consists of the following steps:

(i)   the designer specifies a set of points $\mathbf{r}_i$ which lie approximately on the desired curve;

(ii)   the computer uses an approximate method to determine the vertices, according to the formula (6.20);

(iii)   the designer now works with the polygon, moving individual vertices, to adjust the initial curve into what he considers to be a more satisfactory shape;

(iv)   the computer uses these vertices to calculate any points on the curve for draughting or machining.

6.4 B-SPLINES (2)

The B-splines which were introduced in section 6.2 are widely used as blending functions (or so-called weight functions) to construct the B-spline curve. This section outlines some of the underlying ideas, and is intended as a basic and theoretical introduction to non-uniform B-splines. One of the reasons is that non-uniform B-splines are the generalization of uniform B-splines; in other words, the uniform B-spline is the simplest form. Another reason is that non-uniform B-splines are also widely used in more complex cases.

We will endeavour to avoid tedious and trivial derivation, so that the geometric ideas can be emphasized.

Non-uniform B-splines were first presented by I.J. Schoenberg in 1964, and have been investigated in more detail. This provides a strong theoretical basis for constructing B-spline curves and surfaces.

As we know, the junction points lie on the desired curve, and the vertices are control points of the characteristic polygon. The concept of the knot is now introduced for defining B-spline functions. The knots x_i are points which lie on the parametric axis. If the intervals between knots x_i are equal, they are called uniform knots; if the intervals are not equal, they are called non-uniform knots.

The present standard method for a non-uniform B-spline depends upon the following recurrence relation, due independently to Cox (1972) and de Boor (1972):

$$N_{m,i}(x) = \frac{x - x_i}{x_{i+m-1} - x_i} \cdot N_{m-1,i}(x) + \frac{x_{i+m} - x}{x_{i+m} - x_{i+1}} \cdot N_{m-1,i+1}(x) \quad (6.21)$$

where

$$N_{1,i}(x) = \begin{cases} 1 & x \in [x_i, \ x_{i+1}] \\ 0 & x \in [x_i, \ x_{i+1}] \end{cases}$$

and m is the order of the B-spline, and is a positive integer.

The subscript i of a B-spline $N_{m,i}(x)$ is that of the left end knot x_i of its support. This asymmetrical notation simplifies some formulae.

Note that the B-spline function $N_{m,i}(x)$ is a piecewise polynomial of degree $(m-1)$ and only non-zero on its support $[x_i, x_{i+m}]$.

The geometric concepts 'movement', 'enhancement' and 'combination' can be applied to the important recursion formula (6.21).

'Movement' means that the support of $N_{i,m-1}(x)$ is $[x_i, x_{i+m-1}]$, but that of $N_{i+1,m-1}(x)$ is just $[x_{i+1}, x_{i+m}]$.

'Enhancement' means that the B-spline of order $(m-1)$ is multiplied by the linear function whose parameter is x.

'Combination' means that after 'movement' and 'enhancement', the B-spline of order m can be obtained by 'combination'.

We now discuss the B-spline from degree zero to three in more detail by using the geometric idea of the recurrence formula.

The B-spline of degree 0 (order 1)

$$N_{1,i}(x) = \begin{cases} 1 & x \in [x_i, \quad x_{i+1}] \\ 0 & x \in [x_i, \quad x_{i+1}] \end{cases} \tag{6.22}$$

The B-spline of degree 0 is as shown in Fig. 6.3. In this diagram, the B-spline $N_{1,i}(x)$ is only non-zero on the support $[x_i, x_{i+1}]$, and its function value equals constant 1. This means that it is a polynomial of degree 0. It is called 'the floor function'.

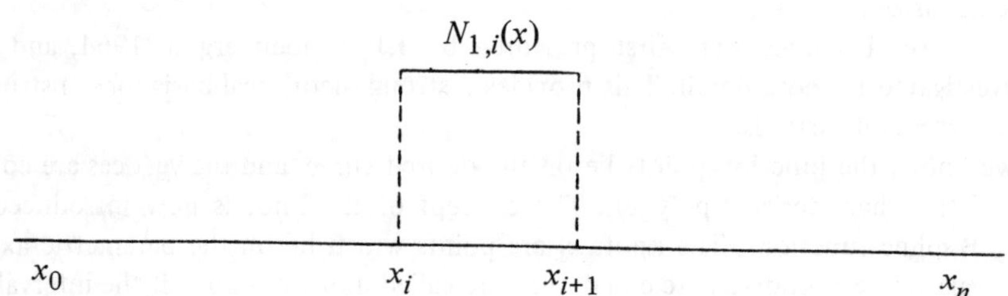

Fig. 6.3 The B-spline of degree 0 (order 1)

The B-spline of degree 1 (order 2)
'Movement' of $N_{1,i}(x)$ (see (6.22)) may produce

$$N_{1,i+1}(x) = \begin{cases} 1 & x \in [x_{i+1}, \quad x_{i+2}] \\ 0 & x \in [x_{i+1}, \quad x_{i+2}] \end{cases}$$

along the parametric axis x.

We substitute $N_{1,i}(x)$ and $N_{1,i+1}(x)$ into the recurrence formula (6.21) and obtain

$$N_{2,i}(x) = \begin{cases} \dfrac{x - x_i}{x_{i+1} - x_i} & x \in [x_i,\ x_{i+1}] \\[2ex] \dfrac{x_{i+2} - x}{x_{i+2} - x_{i+1}} & x \in [x_{i+1},\ x_{i+2}] \\[2ex] 0 & x \notin [x_i,\ x_{i+2}] \end{cases} \qquad (6.23)$$

$N_{1,i}(x)$, $N_{1,i+1}(x)$ and $N_{2,i}(x)$ are as shown in Fig. 6.4. $N_{2,i}(x)$ is only non-zero on the support $[x_i,\ x_{i+2}]$, and is a polynomial of degree 1. It is also called 'the top function'.

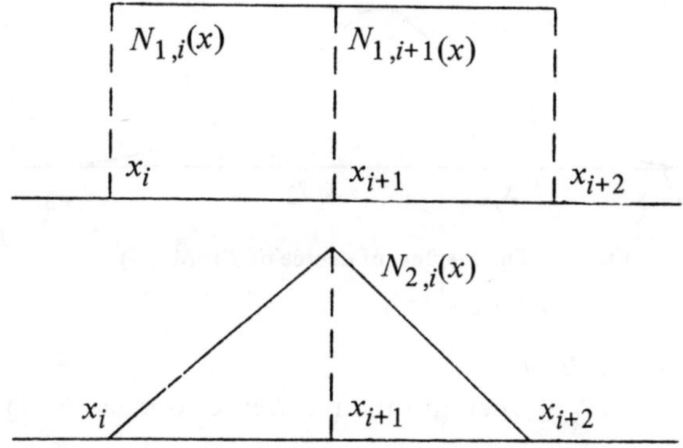

Fig. 6.4 The B-spline of degree 1 (order 2)

The B-spline of degree 2 (order 3)

Changing subscript i of formula (6.23) into subscript $i + 1$ produces the representation of $N_{2,i+1}(x)$. We then substitute $N_{2,i}(x)$ and $N_{2,i+1}(x)$ into recurrence formula (6.21) and obtain

$$N_{3,i}(x) = \begin{cases} \dfrac{(x - x_i)^2}{(x_{i+2} - x_i)(x_{i+1} - x_i)} & x \in [x_i,\ x_{i+1}] \\[3ex] \dfrac{(x - x_i)^2}{(x_{i+2} - x_i)(x_{i+1} - x_i)} \\[3ex] \quad + \dfrac{(x_{i+3} - x_i)(x - x_{i+1})^2}{(x_{i+3} - x_{i+1})(x_{i+2} - x_{i+1})(x_i - x_{i+1})} & x \in [x_{i+1},\ x_{i+2}] \\[3ex] \dfrac{(x_{i+3} - x)^2}{(x_{i+3} - x_{i+2})(x_{i+3} - x_{i+1})} & x \in [x_{i+2},\ x_{i+3}] \\[3ex] 0 & x \notin [x_i,\ x_{i+3}] \end{cases} \qquad (6.24)$$

$N_{2,i}(x)$, $N_{2,i+1}(x)$ and $N_{3,i}(x)$ are as shown in Fig. 6.5. Note that $N_{3,i}(x)$ is only non-zero on the support $[x_i, x_{i+3}]$, and is a polynomial of degree 2. It is also called 'the ancient clock function'.

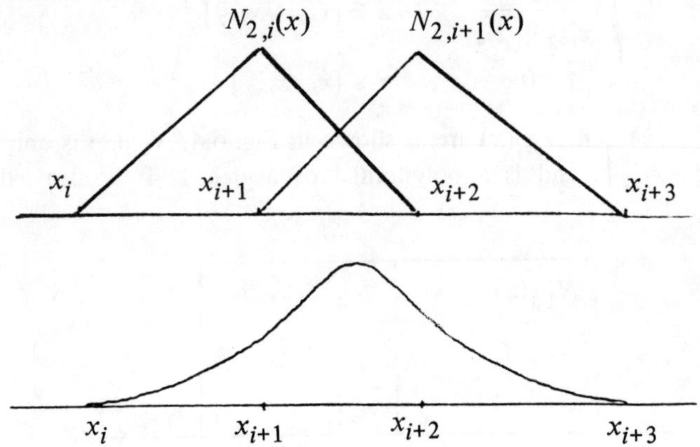

Fig. 6.5 The B-spline of degree of 2 (order 3)

The B-spline of degree 3 (order 4)
We substitute $N_{3,i}(x)$ and $N_{3,i+1}(x)$ into the recurrence formula (6.21) and obtain after some simplification

$$
N_{4,i}(x) = \begin{cases}
\dfrac{(x-x_i)^3}{(x_{i+3}-x_i)(x_{i+2}-x_i)(x_{i+1}-x_i)} & x \in [x_i,\ x_{i+1}] \\[3ex]
\begin{aligned}
&\dfrac{(x-x_i)^3}{(x_{i+3}-x_i)(x_{i+2}-x_i)(x_{i+1}-x_i)} \\
&+ \dfrac{(x-x_{i+1})^3(x_{i+4}-x_i)}{(x_{i+1}-x_i)(x_{i+1}-x_{i+2})(x_{i+1}-x_{i+3})(x_{i+1}-x_{i+4})}
\end{aligned} & x \in [x_{i+1}, x_{i+2}] \\[5ex]
\begin{aligned}
&\dfrac{(x_{i+3}-x)^3(x_{i+4}-x_i)}{(x_{i+3}-x_i)(x_{i+3}-x_{i+1})(x_{i+3}-x_{i+2})(x_{i+3}-x_{i+4})} \\
&+ \dfrac{(x_{i+4}-x)^3}{(x_{i+4}-x_{i+1})(x_{i+4}-x_{i+2})(x_{i+4}-x_{i+3})}
\end{aligned} & x \in [x_{i+2},\ x_{i+3}] \\[5ex]
\dfrac{(x_{i+4}-x)^3}{(x_{i+4}-x_{i+1})(x_{i+4}-x_{i+2})(x_{i+4}-x_{i+3})} & x \in [x_{i+3},\ x_{i+4}] \\[3ex]
0 & x \in [x_i,\ x_{i+4}]
\end{cases}
$$

$$(6.25)$$

$N_{3,i}(x)$, $N_{3,i+1}(x)$ and $N_{4,i}(x)$ are shown in Fig. 6.6. Note that $N_{4,i}(x)$ is only non-zero on the support $[x_i, x_{i+4}]$, and is a polynomial of degree 3. It is also called 'the straw hat function', and is used widely in engineering design.

It is possible to calculate the B-spline for any degree by recurrence of formula (6.21). Fortunately, the B-spline of degree 3 provides enough flexibility for the requirements of engineering design; there is no need to discuss B-splines of higher degree than three.

We now provide two examples of non-uniform B-splines.

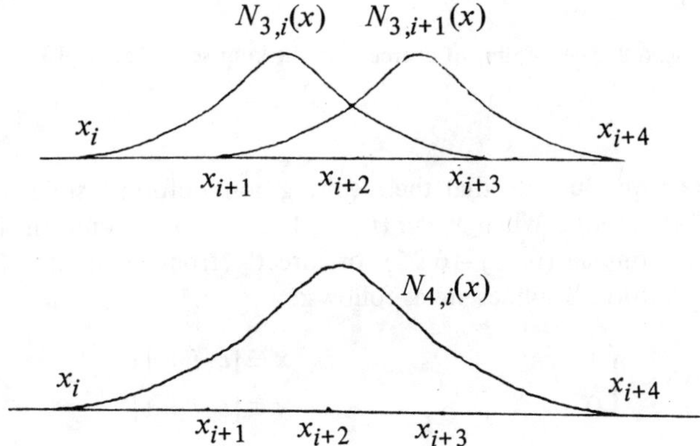

Fig. 6.6 The B-spline of degree 3 (order 4)

Example 1
The B-spline of degree 2 is as shown in Fig. 6.7, which may be constructed on the knot set 0, 1, 3, 6.

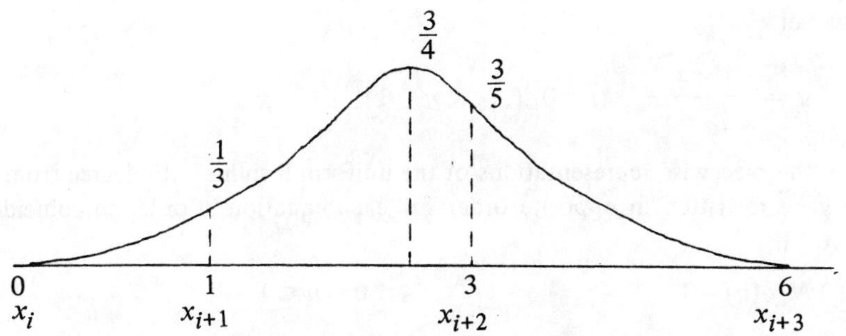

Fig. 6.7 The B-spline of degree 2 on the knot set 0, 1, 3, 6

Example 2
The B-spline of degree 3, which may be constructed on the knot set 0, 1, 3, 6, 10, is shown in Fig. 6.8.

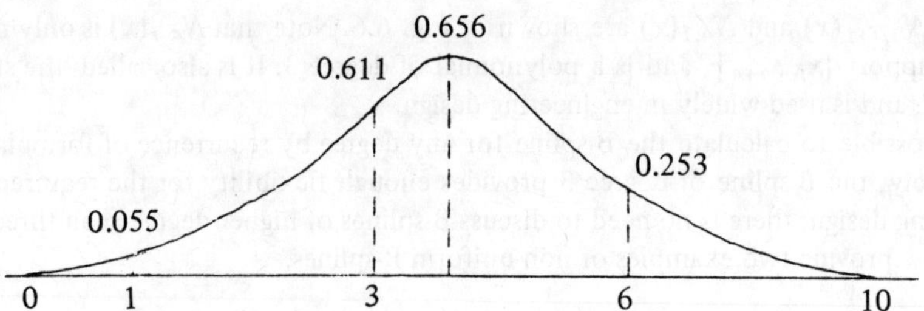

Fig. 6.8 The B-spline of degree 3 on the knot set 0, 1, 3, 6, 10

The examples above illustrate that the resulting non-uniform B-spline closely depends on the values of the knots. When $x_i = i$ $(i = 0, 1, 2, \ldots, n)$, a uniform B-spline can be constructed from formulae (6.23)–(6.25), or directly from recurrence formula (6.21). The formulae for uniform B-splines are as follows:

$$N_{1,i}(x) = \begin{cases} 1 & x \in [i,\ i+1] \\ 0 & x \notin [i,\ i+1] \end{cases}$$

$$N_{2,i}(x) = \begin{cases} x-i & x \in [i,\ i+1] \\ (i+2)-x & x \in [i+1, i+2] \\ 0 & x \notin [i,\ i+2] \end{cases}$$

The representations of the uniform B-spline $N_{3,i}(x)$, $N_{4,i}(x)$ may be written by readers themselves.

Replacing the parameter x by u, since u will be used as a curve parameter in what follows, we set

$$u = \frac{x - x_i}{x_{i+1} - x_i} \qquad (i = 0, 1, \ldots, n-1)$$

and obtain the piecewise representations of the uniform B-spline with degree from 0 to 3 which may be rewritten in opposite order for each equation in order to coincide with equation (6.1).

$$N_{1,i}(u) = 1 \qquad\qquad 0 \leqslant u \leqslant 1 \qquad\qquad (6.26)$$

$$N_{2,i}(u) = \begin{cases} 1-u \\ u \end{cases} \qquad 0 \leqslant u \leqslant 1 \qquad\qquad (6.27)$$

$$N_{3,i}(u) = \begin{cases} \frac{1}{2}(1 - 2u + u^2) \\ \frac{1}{2}(1 + 2u - 2u^2) \\ \frac{1}{2}(u^2) \end{cases} \qquad 0 \leqslant u \leqslant 1 \qquad\qquad (6.28)$$

$$N_{4,i}(u) = \begin{cases} \frac{1}{6}(1 - 3u + 3u^2 - u^3) \\ \frac{1}{6}(4 - 6u^2 + 3u^3) \\ \frac{1}{6}(1 + 3u + 3u^2 - 3u^3) \\ \frac{1}{6}(u^3) \end{cases} \quad 0 \leqslant u \leqslant 1 \tag{6.29}$$

These representations above may be expressed in terms of matrices as follows:

$$N_{2,i}(u) = \begin{bmatrix} 1 & u \end{bmatrix} \frac{1}{(2-1)!} \begin{bmatrix} 1 & 0 \\ -1 & 1 \end{bmatrix} \quad 0 \leqslant u \leqslant 1 \tag{6.30}$$

$$N_{3,i}(u) = \begin{bmatrix} 1 & u & u^2 \end{bmatrix} \frac{1}{(3-1)!} \begin{bmatrix} 1 & 1 & 0 \\ -2 & 2 & 0 \\ 1 & -2 & 1 \end{bmatrix} \quad 0 \leqslant u \leqslant 1 \tag{6.31}$$

$$N_{4,i}(u) = \begin{bmatrix} 1 & u & u^2 & u^3 \end{bmatrix} \frac{1}{(4-1)!} \begin{bmatrix} 1 & 4 & 1 & 0 \\ -3 & 0 & 3 & 0 \\ 3 & -6 & 3 & 0 \\ -1 & 3 & -3 & 1 \end{bmatrix} \quad 0 \leqslant u \leqslant 1$$

$$\tag{6.32}$$

Formula (6.32) is exactly the same as (6.1).

We infer that the uniform B-spline of order m may be written in the form

$$N_{m,i}(u) = \begin{bmatrix} 1 & u \dots u^{m-2} & u^{m-1} \end{bmatrix} \frac{1}{(m-1)!} A^{[m]} \tag{6.33}$$

where A is a matrix of order m.

We have proved the recursion formula of the elements of this coefficient matrix as follows:

$$a_{i,j}^m = a_{i,j}^{m-1} - a_{i,j-1}^{m-1} + (j-1)\, a_{i-1,j}^{m-1} + (m-j+1)\, a_{i-1,j-1}^{m-1} \tag{6.34}$$

where $a_{i,j}^m$ is the element in the ith row and jth column of the coefficient matrix, and

$$a_{0,j}^{m-1} = a_{i,0}^{m-1} = a_{m,j}^{m-1} = a_{i,m}^{m-1} = 0$$

The recursion formula is both interesting and useful, but space limitations permit no detailed discussions of the proof.

The B-splines $N_{m,i}(x)$ are piecewise polynomials of degree $(m-1)$ that are defined over the knots $\dots < x_0 < x_1 < x_2 < \dots$ and have the following properties.

- local support: $N_{m,i}(x) = 0$ if $x \in [x_i,\ x_{i+m}]$
- positivity: $N_{m,i}(x) \geqslant 0$

- partition of unity: $\sum_i N_{m,i}(x) \equiv 1$

- continuity: $N_{m,l}(x)$ is continuously differentiable $(m-2)$ times.

If knots $x_i = \ldots = x_{i+p-1}$ coincide, the B-spline may become only C^{m-1-p} continuous at knot x_i. In order to ensure that a B-spline has a non-vanishing support, one has to demand that $p \leqslant m$, so that the recursion formula remains valid.

6.5 NON-UNIFORM B-SPLINE CURVES

From the foregoing, we see that the uniform B-spline curves can be constructed by using the linear combination between vertices and uniform B-splines. In this section we will introduce non-uniform B-spline curves with degree from one to three.

6.5.1 Non-uniform B-spline curves with degree 1

A B-spline is said to be a spline of minimal support, its support being the number of spans over which a spline in non-zero. For example, $N_{2,i-1}(x)$ and $N_{2,i}(x)$ are non-zero on their supports $[x_{i-1}, x_{i+1}]$ and $[x_i, x_{i+2}]$ as shown in Fig 6.9.

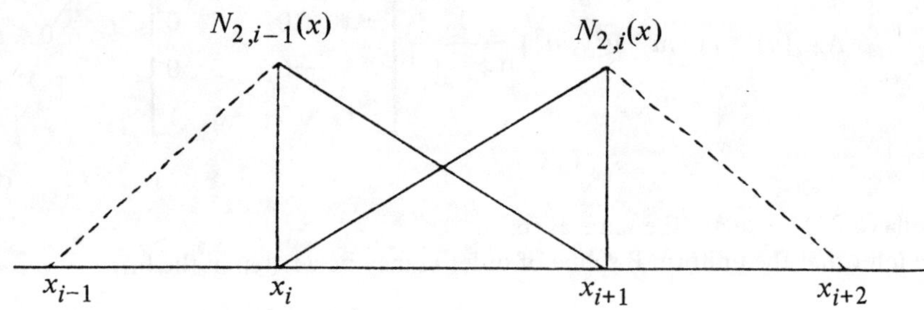

Fig. 6.9

By providing a set of vertices $\mathbf{V}_i$ $(i = 0, 1, \ldots, n)$, we may use the linear combination between non-uniform B-splines with degree one and vertices to construct a non-uniform B-spline curve with degree one on the interval $[x_i, x_{i+1}]$:

$$\mathbf{r}_i(x) = \mathbf{V}_i(x_{i+1} - x)/(x_{i+1} - x_i) + \mathbf{V}_{i+1}(x - x_i)/(x_{i+1} - x_i) \tag{6.35}$$

$$(i = 0, 1, \ldots, n-1; \; x_i \leqslant x \leqslant x_{i+1})$$

Note that the subscript should be replaced correspondingly for the representation of B-spline $N_{2,i-1}(x)$ from formula (6.23).

By setting

$$u = \frac{x - x_i}{x_{i+1} - x_i}$$

we may write

$$\mathbf{r}_i(u) = \mathbf{V}_i \cdot (1 - u) + \mathbf{V}_{i+1} \cdot u \tag{6.36}$$

$$(i = 0, 1, \ldots, n-1; \; 0 \leqslant u \leqslant 1)$$

which has a matrix form

$$\mathbf{r}_i(u) = \begin{bmatrix} 1 & u \end{bmatrix} M_2 \begin{bmatrix} \mathbf{V}_i \\ \mathbf{V}_{i+1} \end{bmatrix} \tag{6.37}$$

where

$$M_2 = \begin{bmatrix} 1 & 0 \\ -1 & 1 \end{bmatrix}$$

It is obvious that the non-uniform B-spline curve is coincident with the polygon of vertices.

6.5.2 Non-uniform B-spline curves with degree 2

We know that $N_{3,i}(x)$ is non-zero on its support $[x_i, x_{i+3}]$, similarly, support $[x_{i-1}, x_{i+2}]$ for $N_{3,i-1}(x)$, $[x_{i-2}, x_{i+1}]$ for $N_{3,i-2}(x)$; so three are simultaneously non-zero on the interval $[x_i, x_{i+1}]$, as shown in Fig. 6.10.

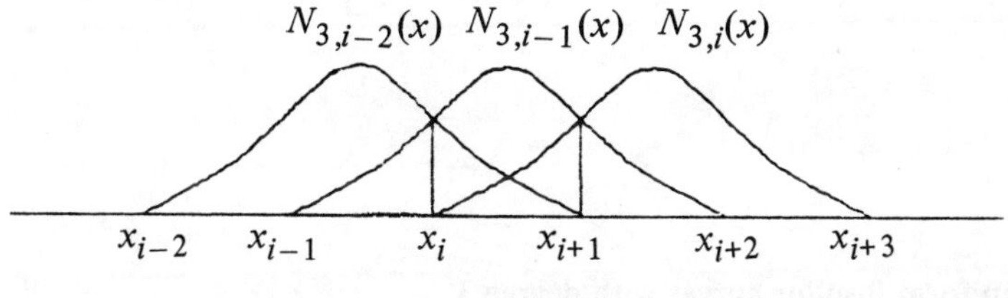

Fig. 6.10

A non-uniform B-spline curve with degree 2 can be constructed by using the linear combination between B-spline $N_{3,i-2}(x)$, $N_{3,i-1}(x)$, $N_{3,i}(x)$ and vertices $\mathbf{V}_i$, $\mathbf{V}_{i+1}$ and $\mathbf{V}_{i+2}$ on interval $[x_i, x_{i+1}]$. After subscript transformations and parametric transformations, we obtain

$$\mathbf{r}_i(u) = \begin{bmatrix} 1 & u & u^2 \end{bmatrix} M_3 \begin{bmatrix} \mathbf{V}_i \\ \mathbf{V}_{i+1} \\ \mathbf{V}_{i+2} \end{bmatrix} \qquad (i = 0, 1, \ldots, n-2; \ 0 \leqslant u \leqslant 1) \tag{6.38}$$

where

$$
M_3 = \begin{bmatrix} m_{11} = \dfrac{x_{i+1} - x_i}{x_{i+1} - x_{i-1}} \\[2ex] m_{21} = -2m_{11} \\[2ex] m_{31} = m_{11} \end{bmatrix}
$$

$$
m_{12} = \frac{x_i - x_{i-1}}{x_{i+1} - x_{i-1}}
$$

$$
m_{22} = 2m_{11}
$$

$$
m_{32} = \frac{(x_{i+1} - x_i)}{(x_i - x_{i-1})} \cdot \left(\frac{(x_{i+1} - x_{i-1})}{(x_{i+1} - x_i)} - \frac{(x_{i+2} - x_{i-1})}{(x_{i+2} - x_i)} \right)
$$

$$
m_{13} = 0
$$

$$
m_{23} = 0
$$

$$
m_{33} = \frac{x_{i+1} - x_i}{x_{i+2} - x_i} \tag{6.39}
$$

6.5.3 Non-uniform B-spline curves with degree 3

Using the linear combination between B-spline $N_{4,i-3}(x)$, $N_{4,i-2}(x)$, $N_{4,i-1}(x)$ and $N_{4,i}(x)$, which are as shown in Fig. 6.11, and vertices $\mathbf{V}_i$, $\mathbf{V}_{i+1}$, $\mathbf{V}_{i+2}$ and $\mathbf{V}_{i+3}$ on interval $[x_i, x_{i+1}]$, we obtain the non-uniform B-spline curve with degree 3 after subscript transformations and parametric transformations.

$$
\mathbf{r}_i(u) = \begin{bmatrix} 1 & u & u^2 & u^3 \end{bmatrix} M_4 \begin{bmatrix} \mathbf{V}_i \\ \mathbf{V}_{i+1} \\ \mathbf{V}_{i+2} \\ \mathbf{V}_{i+3} \end{bmatrix} \tag{6.40}
$$

$$
(i = 0, 1, \ldots, n-3; \ 0 \leqslant u \leqslant 1)
$$

where M_4 is a 4×4 matrix with elements which are as follows:

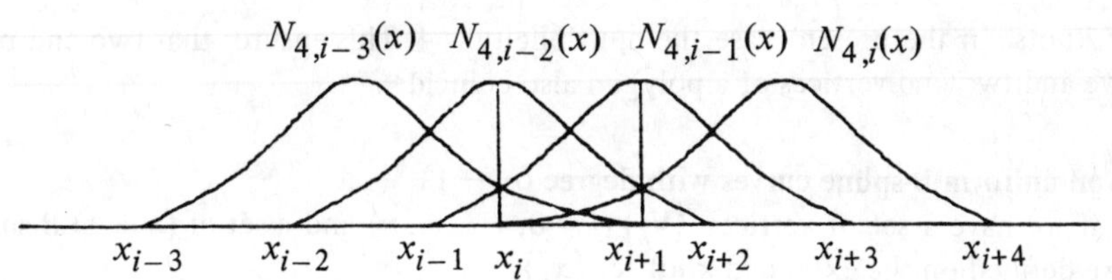

Fig. 6.11

$$m_{11} = \frac{(x_i - x_{i+1})^2}{(x_{i+1} - x_{i-2})(x_{i+1} - x_{i-1})} \qquad m_{21} = -3m_{11}$$

$$m_{12} = 1 - (m_{11} + m_{13}) \qquad m_{22} = -(m_{21} + m_{23})$$

$$m_{13} = \frac{(x_{i-1} - x_i)^2}{(x_{i-1} - x_{i+2})(x_{i-1} - x_{i+1})} \qquad m_{23} = \frac{3(x_{i+1} - x_i)(x_i - x_{i-1})}{(x_{i-1} - x_{i+2})(x_{i-1} - x_{i+1})}$$

$$m_{14} = 0 \qquad m_{24} = 0$$

$$m_{31} = 3m_{11} \qquad m_{41} = -m_{11}$$

$$m_{32} = -(m_{31} + m_{33}) \qquad m_{42} = -(m_{41} + m_{43} + m_{44})$$

$$m_{33} = \frac{3(x_{i+1} - x_i)^2}{(x_{i-1} - x_{i+2})(x_{i-1} - x_{i+1})} \qquad m_{43} = -(x_{i+1} - x_i)^2 \left[\frac{1}{(x_{i-1} - x_{i+1})(x_{i-1} - x_{i+2})} \right.$$

$$m_{34} = 0 \qquad \qquad + \frac{1}{(x_i - x_{i+2})(x_i - x_{i+3})}$$

$$m_{44} = \frac{(x_{i+1} - x_i)^2}{(x_i - x_{i+3})(x_i - x_{i+2})} \qquad \left. + \frac{1}{(x_{i+2} - x_{i-1})(x_{i+2} - x_i)} \right] \qquad (6.41)$$

These elements of the coefficient matrix depend upon the values of knots x_i. If the interval between each two neighbouring knots is equal, the non-uniform B-spline curve is reduced to the uniform B-spline curve.

We confine our attention to the cubic case, as it has been widely used in computer-aided geometric design. If $x_i = i$, $i = 0, 1, \ldots, n$, i.e. the case of the integer knot set, it defines uniform cubic B-spline curves. If a set of knots has unequal spacing, it defines non-uniform cubic B-spline curves. Gordon and Riesenfeld experimented along these lines, relating distances between knots to the lengths of the corresponding sides of the control polygon. The authors have also experimented along these lines, relating distances between knots to the lengths of the corresponding chord of the curve, i.e. the lengths of straight line between junction points. Both approaches have been implemented in engineering design.

The most convenient way to extend the original knots is to choose multiple knots. Then the extra spans introduced all have length zero, and the two end knots become multiple knots. In the present case the multiplicity is 4. This ensures that two end points of a curve and two end vertices of a polygon also coincide.

6.5.4 Non-uniform B-spline curves with degree $(m-1)$

Finally, if we have a set of vertices $\{V_i\}$ $(i = 0, 1, \ldots, n)$ and a set of $(n+1)$ B-splines, which are defined on the extended knot set $\{x_i\}$:

$$\underbrace{x_0, \ldots, x_0,}_{m} \quad x_1, \ldots, x_{n-m}, \quad x_{n-(m-1)}, \quad \underbrace{x_{n-(m-2)}, \ldots, x_{n-(m-2)}}_{m}$$

we may use them to construct a non-uniform B-spline curve with degree $(m-1)$ by defining

$$\mathbf{r}_{m,i}(x) = \sum_{i}^{i+m-1} N_{m,i}(x)\,\mathbf{V}_i \quad (i = 0, 1, \ldots, n-(m-1)) \tag{6.42}$$

where

$$n \geqslant m-1$$

$\mathbf{r}(x)$ is a piecewise polynomial with degree $(m-1)$, and possesses continuity up to C^{m-2}.

The theoretical analyses and experimental investigations illustrate that the non-uniform B-spline curves closely resemble the corresponding uniform curves except in cases of considerable disparity between the lengths of the polygon sides.

6.6 B-SPLINE CURVES WITH MULTIPLE VERTICES

The properties of multiple vertices are very useful. In this section, using formulae (6.33) and (6.34), we will discuss the general case of B-spline curves with multiple vertices.

As we know, a span of B-splines of order m (degree $m-1$) is a linear combination of B-splines of order m and m vertices of the characteristic polygon, where matrix representation is

$$\mathbf{r}_{m,i}(u) = [N_{m,i}(u) \quad \ldots \quad N_{m,i+m-1}(u)]\,\mathbf{V} \tag{6.43}$$

where $\mathbf{V}$ is a column vector, which consists of m vertices $\mathbf{V}_i, \mathbf{V}_{i+1}, \ldots, \mathbf{V}_{i+m-1}$ in space.

Let us now discuss the case of m, $(m-1)$, $(m-2)$ and $(m-3)$ multiple vertices, in order.

m Multiple vertices

We substitute (6.33) into (6.43) and obtain

$$\mathbf{r}_{m,i}(u) = [1 \quad \ldots \quad u^{m-1}]\frac{1}{(m-1)!}A^{[m]}\,[\mathbf{V}_i \quad \ldots \quad \mathbf{V}_{i+m-1}]^{\mathrm{T}} \tag{6.44}$$

When

$$\mathbf{V}_i = \ldots = \mathbf{V}_{i+m-1}$$

we obtain

$$\mathbf{r}_{m,i}(u) = \mathbf{V}_i \frac{1}{(m-1)!} \sum_{i=1}^{m} u^{i-1} \sum_{j=1}^{m} a_{i,j} \qquad (6.45)$$

Because

$$\sum_{j=1}^{m} a_{i,j} = 0 \quad (i = 2, \ldots, m)$$

and

$$\sum_{j=1}^{m} a_{1,j} = (m-1)!$$

the result is

$$\mathbf{r}_{m,i}(u) = \mathbf{V}_i \qquad (6.46)$$

Equation (6.46) shows that the span of a B-spline curve is reduced to the vertex $\mathbf{V}_i$ with multiplicity m, where multiplicity m means $\mathbf{V}_i = \mathbf{V}_{i+1} = \ldots = \mathbf{V}_{i+m-1}$.

$(m-1)$ Multiple vertices
We now have m vertices, which are $\mathbf{V}_i$, and $\mathbf{V}_{i+1}$ with multiplicity $(m-1)$, where $\mathbf{V}_{i+1} = \mathbf{V}_{i+2} = \ldots = \mathbf{V}_{i+m-1}$, constructing a span of a B-spline curve of order m.
   From (6.44), we obtain

$$\mathbf{r}_{m,i}(u) = \mathbf{V}_{i+1} + \frac{\mathbf{V}_i - \mathbf{V}_{i+1}}{(m-1)!} (1-u)^{m-1} \qquad (6.47)$$

at $u = 0$, and $u = 1$, we have

$$\mathbf{r}_{m,i}(0) = \mathbf{V}_{i+1} + \frac{\mathbf{V}_i - \mathbf{V}_{i+1}}{(m-1)!}$$

and

$$\mathbf{r}_{m,i}(1) = \mathbf{V}_{i+1} \qquad (6.48)$$

Equation (6.47) illustrates that a span of a B-spline curve may be reduced to a linear section, which is a useful feature from the design point of view, and that the length of the straight line is

$$\frac{1}{(m-1)!} (\mathbf{V}_i - \mathbf{V}_{i+1})$$

where $(\mathbf{V}_i - \mathbf{V}_{i+1})$ is the length of the corresponding edge of the polygon.
   Similarly, we construct the span of the B-spline curve of order m, using m vertices, which are $\mathbf{V}_{i+1}$ with $(m-1)$ multiple vertices and $\mathbf{V}_{i+2}$, and obtain another straight line. $\mathbf{V}_{i+1}$ with multiplicity $(m-1)$ is a sharp point with discontinuity of direction, which is also a useful feature for design, as shown in Fig. 6.12.

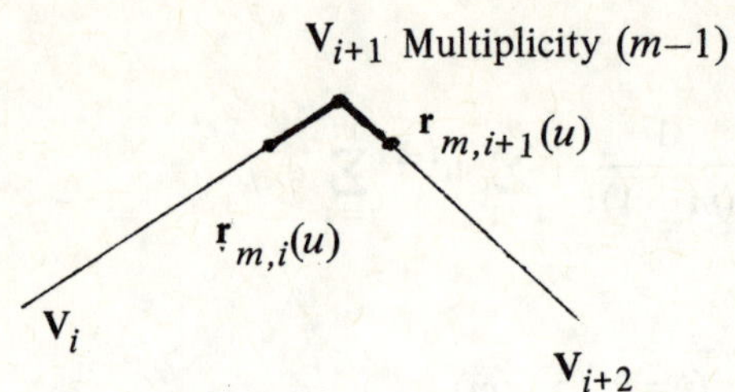

Fig. 6.12

(m − 2) Multiple vertices

We have m vertices, which are $\mathbf{V}_i$, $\mathbf{V}_{i+1}$ with multiplicity $(m-2)$, and $\mathbf{V}_{i+2}$, constructing a span of a B-spline curve of order m. Equation (6.44) gives, after some simplification,

$$\mathbf{r}_{m,i}(u) = \mathbf{V}_{i+1} + \frac{\mathbf{V}_i - \mathbf{V}_{i+1}}{(m-1)!}(1-u)^{m-1} + \frac{\mathbf{V}_{i+2} - \mathbf{V}_{i+1}}{(m-1)!}u^{m-1} \tag{6.49}$$

On differentiating (6.49), we obtain

$$\mathbf{r}'_{m,i}(u) = \frac{\mathbf{V}_{i+1} - \mathbf{V}_i}{(m-2)!}(1-u)^{m-2} + \frac{\mathbf{V}_{i+2} - \mathbf{V}_{i+1}}{(m-2)!}u^{m-2} \tag{6.50}$$

At $u =$, and $u = 1$, from (6.49) and (6.50), we obtain

$$\mathbf{r}_{m,i}(0) = \mathbf{V}_{i+1} + \frac{\mathbf{V}_i - \mathbf{V}_{i+1}}{(m-1)!}$$

$$\mathbf{r}_{m,i}(1) = \mathbf{V}_{i+1} + \frac{\mathbf{V}_{i+2} - \mathbf{V}_{i+1}}{(m-1)!} \tag{6.51}$$

$$\mathbf{r}'_{m,i}(0) = \frac{\mathbf{V}_{i+1} - \mathbf{V}_i}{(m-2)!}$$

and

$$\mathbf{r}'_{m,i}(1) = \frac{\mathbf{V}_{i+2} - \mathbf{V}_{i+2}}{(m-2)!}$$

Equations (6.51) illustrate that the span of the B-spline curve of order m is tangent to the edges of the polygon at the start point and the end point of the span of the curve, as shown in Fig. 6.13.

If we choose $\mathbf{V}_{i+1}$ with multiplicity $(m-2)$, $\mathbf{V}_{i+2}$ and $\mathbf{V}_{i+3}$, and construct another span $\mathbf{r}_{m,i+1}(u)$, the spans are tangent to each other at the junction point. This is a turning point which may be controlled, according to the need of a designer.

(m − 3) Multiple vertices

We have m vertices, which are $\mathbf{V}_i$, $\mathbf{V}_{i+1}$ with multiplicity $(m-3)$, $\mathbf{V}_{i+2}$ and $\mathbf{V}_{i+3}$, constructing a span of a B-spline curve of order m. From (6.44), at $u = 0$, we obtain

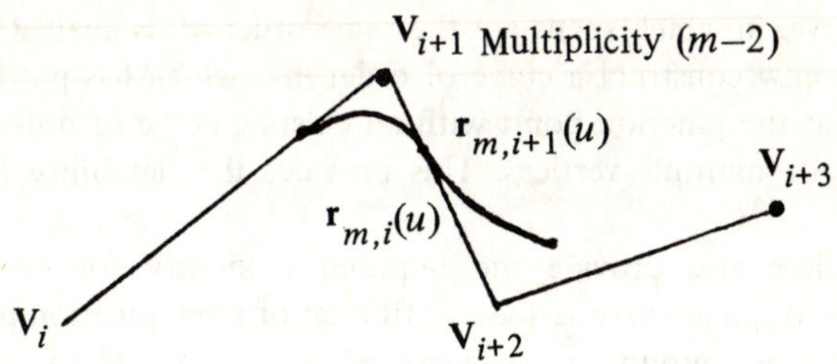

Fig. 6.13

$$\mathbf{r}_{m,i}(0) = V_{i+1} + \frac{2}{(m-1)!} \left[\tfrac{1}{2}(V_i + V_{i+2}) - V_{i+1} \right]$$

the start point of the span of the curve is $2/(m-1)!$ of the way along the straight line joining V_{i+1} to the mid-point of the line joining V_i and V_{i+2}.

By differentiating formula (6.44), at $u = 0$, we obtain

$$\mathbf{r}'_{m,i}(0) = \frac{1}{(m-2)!}(V_{i+2} - V_i)$$

$$\mathbf{r}''_{m,i}(0) = \frac{1}{(m-3)!}\left[(V_{i+2} - V_{i+1}) - (V_{i+1} - V_i)\right]$$

and

$$\mathbf{r}'_{m,i}(0) \times \mathbf{r}''_{m,i}(0) = \frac{2}{(m-2)!\,(m-3)!}(V_{i+1} - V_i) \times (V_{i+2} - V_i)$$

We see that the tangent vector at the start point of the span of the curve is parallel to the line joining V_i and V_{i+2}. The tangent plane at the start point of the span of the curve is the plane, which is defined by V_i, V_{i+1} and V_{i+2} as shown in Fig. 6.14.

We can also consider $(m-4),\ldots$ multiple vertices, but their geometric properties are not simple or obvious. Fortunately, multiplicity m, $(m-1)$, $(m-2)$ and $(m-3)$ provides enough tools for computer-aided geometric design.

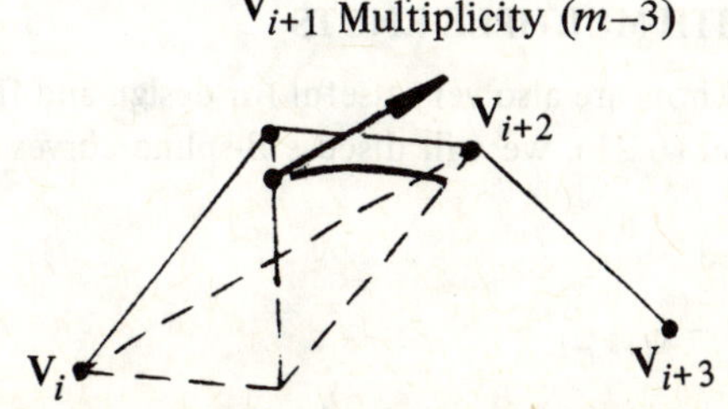

Fig. 6.14

The composite curve, in which spans are the same order m, is dealt within works on the B-spline. We can now construct a curve of order m_2, which has position, slope and curvature continuity at the junction point with an existing curve of order m_1, using the geometric properties of multiple vertices. This provides the flexibility for designing a composite curve.

The multiple vertices also provide the required flexibility for curve fitting. As mentioned earlier, the B-spline curve is used to fit a set of given junction points $\mathbf{r}_i$, which provide one linear equation group for the involved vertices $\mathbf{V}_i$. The vertices $\mathbf{V}_i$ can be computed by solving the linear system.

In the case of multiple vertices, the procedure for solving the linear system will cause the curve to oscillate or inflect. The difficulty is overcome by using the properties of multiple vertices.

The method is that we add equations of multiple vertices into the linear system. For example, at $m = 4$, according to the property of curves with multiplicity $(m - 1)$, we have

$$\mathbf{V}_{i-1} = \mathbf{V}_i = \mathbf{V}_{i+1} = \mathbf{r}_i$$

Let

$$\mathbf{V}_i = \mathbf{r}_i$$

at the ith row of the linear system, and add

$$\mathbf{V}_{i-1} - \mathbf{V}_i = 0$$

$$\mathbf{V}_i - \mathbf{V}_{i+1} = 0$$

at the $(i - 1)$th row and the $(i + 1)$th row respectively, subsequently resolve the linear system with the addition of the above two equations.

The inversion procedure determines the polygon with multiple vertices which corresponds to the fitted curve with the discontinuity of direction, avoiding unwanted oscillations or inflections.

In an analogous way to the discontinuity of tangents, the discontinuity of curvatures can be solved, but using the property of $(m - 2)$ multiple vertices.

It is therefore possible, by using multiple vertices, to represent a highly complex curve by means of a single equation such as (6.43).

6.7 B-SPLINE CURVES WITH MULTIPLE KNOTS

The properties of multiple knots are also very useful for design and fitting; in this section, using the recurrence relation (6.21), we will discuss B-spline curves defined by B-splines with multiple knots.

Multiple knots are defined

$$x_i = x_{i+1} = \ldots = x_{i+k_i-1}$$

where k_i is called the multiplicity of knots. In the case of a non-multiple knot, $k_i = 1$. Note that the multiplicity k_i must be less than or equal to the order m of the B-spline.

Using the de Boor–Cox recurrence relation (6.21) and assuming $0/0 = 0$, a B-spline with multiple knots can be represented as follows:

If $k_i = m$, we obtain

$$N_{m,i}(x) = \left(\frac{x_{i+m} - x}{x_{i+m} - x_{i+m-1}} \right)^{m-1} \qquad x \in [x_{i+m-1},\ x_{i+m}] \qquad (6.52)$$

The following results can easily be derived from (6.52):

$$N_{m,i}(x_i) = N_{m,i}(x_{i+1}) = \ldots = N_{m,i}(x_{i+m-2}) = 0$$

only

$$N_{m,i}(x_{i+m-1}) = 1$$

$N_{2,i}(x), N_{3,i}(x)$ and $N_{4,i}(x)$ are as shown in Fig. 6.15.

If $k_i < m$, the following results can be obtained:

$$N_{m,i}(x_i) = N_{m,i}(x_{i+1}) = \ldots = N_{m,i}(x_{i+k_i-1}) = 0$$

$N_{3,i}(x)$ and $N_{4,i}(x)$ at $k_i = 2$ are as shown in Fig. 6.16. $N_{4,i}(x)$ at $k_i = 3$ is as shown in Fig. 6.17.

Two important properties of B-splines with multiple knots may be explained from Figs. 6.15–6.17. One is that the width of support of a B-spline may be reduced when the multiplicity of knots k_i is increased. In order to ensure that a B-spline has a non-vanishing

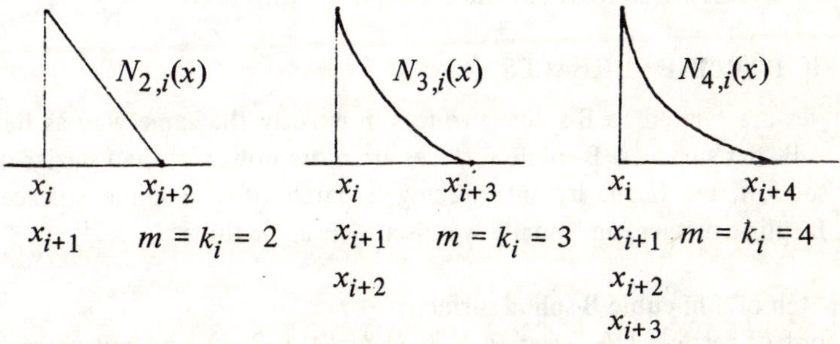

Fig. 6.15

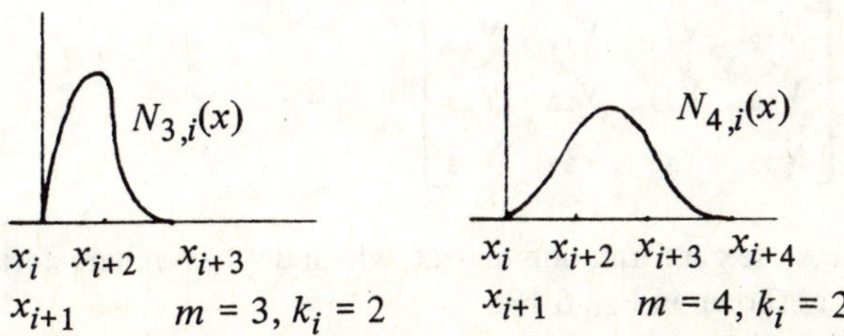

Fig. 6.16

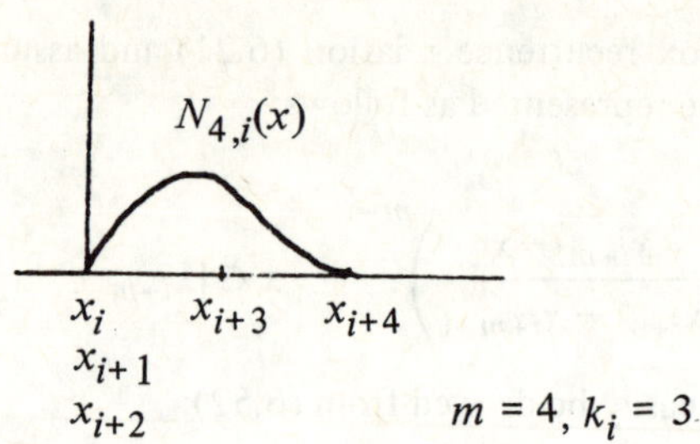

Fig. 6.17

support, one has to demand that $k_i \leqslant m$ (such that the recursion formula remains valid). Another is that the B-spline may become only C^{m-k_i-1} continuous at multiple knots.

It is easy to understand that the B-spline curve, which is defined by the B-spline with multiple knots, becomes C^{m-k_i-1} continuous at junction points between the spans of a curve. We may use this property to design a complex curve.

In the case of a B-spline curve of order 4 (degree 3), if $k_i = 2$, the continuity of the curve is $C^{m-k_i-1} = C^{4-2-1} = C^1$, i.e. first-order continuity, such as the junction point between a span of a straight line and a span of a curve. If $k_i = 3$, the continuity is C^0, i.e. zero-order continuity; this means that there is a sharp point between spans. If $k_i = 4$, the continuity is C^{-1}; this means that the curve is separated. These facilities are needed to design products with a highly complex curve.

In sections 6.6 and 6.7, we outline two widely used practical curve design and fitting methods; their effects are similar, but the concepts are different.

6.8 BI-CUBIC B-SPLINE SURFACES

B-spline curves are related to B-spline surfaces in exactly the same way as Bezier curves are related to Bezier surfaces. B-spline surfaces are more powerful than Bezier surfaces.

In this section, we begin by introducing a patch of a B-spline surface, then we construct a B-spline surface, and finally we discuss its algorithms.

6.8.1 The patch of a bi-cubic B-spline surface

We set 16 control vertices $(\mathbf{V}_{i,j})$ $(i = 0, 1, 2, 3; j = 0, 1, 2, 3)$, and put them in order to form a 4×4 matrix

$$
\mathbf{V} = \begin{bmatrix}
\mathbf{V}_{00} & \mathbf{V}_{01} & \mathbf{V}_{02} & \mathbf{V}_{03} \\
\mathbf{V}_{10} & \mathbf{V}_{11} & \mathbf{V}_{12} & \mathbf{V}_{13} \\
\mathbf{V}_{20} & \mathbf{V}_{21} & \mathbf{V}_{22} & \mathbf{V}_{23} \\
\mathbf{V}_{30} & \mathbf{V}_{31} & \mathbf{V}_{32} & \mathbf{V}_{33}
\end{bmatrix}
$$

This is called the vertex information matrix, which defines a characteristic polyhedron in geometric space, as shown in Fig. 6.18.

Now, using four vertices, which are matrix elements in the same column, to define a span of a cubic B-spline curve, we obtain its matrix representation as follows:

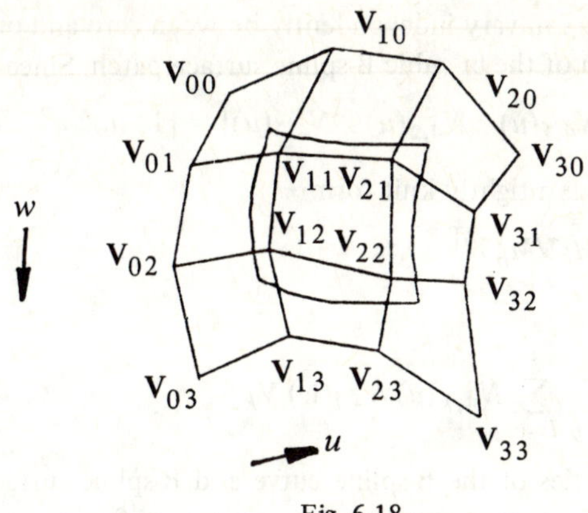

Fig. 6.18

$$S_j(u) = [N_{4,0}(u) \quad N_{4,1}(u) \quad N_{4,2}(u) \quad N_{4,3}(u)] \begin{bmatrix} V_{0,j} \\ V_{1,j} \\ V_{2,j} \\ V_{3,j} \end{bmatrix}$$

$$(j = 0, 1, 2, 3, \quad 0 \leqslant u \leqslant 1)$$

This means that four B-spline curve spans have been defined which are parallel topologically; their representations may be rewritten as

$$[S_0(u) \quad S_1(u) \quad S_2(u) \quad S_3(u)]$$

$$= [N_{4,0}(u) \quad N_{4,1}(u) \quad N_{4,2}(u) \quad N_{4,3}(u)] \, V$$

Choosing any value of the parameter u between zero and one, we can regard $S_0(u)$, $S_1(u)$, $S_2(u)$ and $S_3(u)$ as four vertices of the characteristic polygon and then construct a span of a cubic B-spline curve with parameter w:

$$r(u, w) = [S_0(u) \quad S_1(u) \quad S_2(u) \quad S_3(u)] \begin{bmatrix} N_{4,0}(w) \\ N_{4,1}(w) \\ N_{4,2}(w) \\ N_{4,3}(w) \end{bmatrix}$$

We substitute $S_j(u)$ $(j = 0, 1, 2, 3)$ into the above representation and obtain

$$r(u, w) = [N_{4,0}(u) \quad N_{4,1}(u) \quad N_{4,2}(u) \quad N_{4,3}(u)] \, V \begin{bmatrix} N_{4,0}(w) \\ N_{4,1}(w) \\ N_{4,2}(w) \\ N_{4,3}(w) \end{bmatrix} \qquad (6.53)$$

$$(0 \leqslant u, \ w \leqslant 1)$$

The parameters u and w can vary independently between zero and one in formula (6.53), which is a representation of the bi-cubic B-spline surface patch. Since

$$[N_{4,0}(u) \quad N_{4,1}(u) \quad N_{4,2}(u) \quad N_{4,3}(u)] = [1 \quad u \quad u^2 \quad u^3]\, M_b$$

(6.53) may be rewritten as a tightly knit form

$$\mathbf{r}(u, w) = U M_b \mathbf{V} M_b^{\mathrm{T}} W^{\mathrm{T}} \tag{6.54}$$

or

$$\mathbf{r}(u, w) = \sum_{k=0}^{3} \sum_{l=0}^{3} N_{4,k}(u)\, N_{4,l}(w)\, \mathbf{V}_{k,l} \tag{6.55}$$

According to the properties of the B-spline curve and B-spline surface patch, we can see that the patch does not in general pass through vertices; its four corner points are close to vertices $\mathbf{V}_{11}$, $\mathbf{V}_{12}$, $\mathbf{V}_{21}$, $\mathbf{V}_{22}$, as shown in Fig. 6.18. By changing the order of constructing the surface patch, i.e. first row direction then column direction, the same result is obtained. So it may be said that a B-spline surface patch is defined only by 16 vertices of the characteristic polyhedron.

6.8.2 Bi-cubic B-spline surfaces

We set $(n + 1) \times (m + 1)$ control vertices $\mathbf{V}_{i,j}$ $(i = 0, 1, \ldots, n; \; j = 0, 1, \ldots, m)$, and put them in order to form an $(n + 1) \times (m + 1)$ matrix, which is a characteristic polyhedron in geometric space. The bi-cubic B-spline surface may be represented by

$$\mathbf{r}_{i,j}(u, w) = U M_b \mathbf{V}_{i,j} M_b^{\mathrm{T}} W^{\mathrm{T}} \tag{6.56}$$

$$(0 \leqslant u, \; w \leqslant 1; \; i = 0, 1, \ldots, n - 3; \; j = 0, 1, \ldots, m - 3)$$

It includes $(n - 2) \times (m - 2)$ patches. Since B-splines possess second-order continuity, this ensures that there is automatic second-order continuity between patches mentioned above.

A bi-cubic Bezier surface patch is based on a characteristic polyhedron defined by just 16 vertices. A single patch of this type can only represent a surface element having a simple topography. By contrast, there is no limit on the number of vertices defining the characteristic polyhedron by a bi-cubic B-spline surface; therefore, by choosing a sufficiently complex polyhedron, a highly convoluted surface can be represented by means of a single equation such as (6.56).

Like the B-spline curves, the B-spline surfaces also possess a local adjustment property. This means that changing a single vertex only alters that part of the B-spline surface related to the vertex; the rest remains unaltered.

These advantages make the B-spline surface as the mathematical basis of surface modelling in many CAD/CAM systems.

6.8.3 Algorithms of bi-cubic and B-spline surfaces

The positive algorithm
The calculation procedure is clear from formula (6.55); there is no need for more detailed

discussion. We will discuss only the algorithm of the normal vector of points on the surface; this must be known in order to define an offset of the surface.

On differentiating formula (6.55) with respect to u, we obtain

$$\frac{\partial}{\partial u}\mathbf{r}(u, w) = \sum_{k=0}^{2} \sum_{l=0}^{3} N_{3,k}(u)\, N_{4,l}(w)\, \mathbf{V}_{i,j}^{k} \tag{6.57}$$

where

$$\mathbf{V}_{i,j}^{k} = \mathbf{V}_{i+k+1,\, j+l} - \mathbf{V}_{i+k,\, j+l} \quad (k = 0, 1, 2; \quad l = 0, 1, 2, 3)$$

Similarly

$$\frac{\partial}{\partial w}\mathbf{r}(u, w) = \sum_{k=0}^{3} \sum_{l=0}^{2} N_{4,k}(u)\, N_{3,l}(w)\, \mathbf{V}_{i,j}^{l} \tag{6.58}$$

where

$$\mathbf{V}_{i,j}^{l} = \mathbf{V}_{i+k,\, j+l+1} - \mathbf{V}_{i+k,\, j+l} \quad (k = 0, 1, 2, 3; \quad l = 0, 1, 2)$$

The normal vector of surface points may be obtained by the vector product of the two differentiating vectors mentioned above.

The inverse algorithm

Drawings of products provide much section information in most cases; the section information includes coordinate values of points.

The inverse algorithm means that vertices $\mathbf{V}_{i,j}$ of a characteristic polyhedron may be calculated by solving a system depending on the given section information.

Firstly, using the inverse algorithm of a B-spline curve with parameter u (see subsection 6.3.2), from section information of set $(m + 1)$, we may obtain the vertices of the characteristic polygon; this procedure is repeated $(m + 1)$ times, resulting in

$$\mathbf{Q}_{i,j} \begin{pmatrix} i = -1, 0, 1, \ldots, n,\ n + 1 \\ j = 0, 1, \ldots, m \end{pmatrix}$$

Then $\mathbf{Q}_{i,j}$ may be regarded as a point of sets $(n + 3)$, using the inverse algorithm of the B-spline curve with parameter w; this procedure is repeated $(n + 3)$ times and the results are

$$\mathbf{V}_{i,j} \begin{pmatrix} i = -1, 0, 1, \ldots, n,\ n + 1 \\ j = -1, 0, 1, \ldots, m,\ m + 1 \end{pmatrix}$$

These $\mathbf{V}_{i,j}$ are merely the vertices of the characteristic polyhedron of the bi-cubic B-spline surface.

We can see that the inverse algorithm of the B-spline surface consists of the inverse algorithm of the B-spline curve repeated $(m + 1) \times (n + 3)$ times [or $(n + 1) \times (m + 3)$ times]. This requires the repeated application of subroutines. A complex question is how to deal with boundary conditions correctly. The authors have presented a method which may be used to deal with the boundary conditions correctly and which has been used in engineering design.

The section information $r_{i,j}$ $(i = 0, 1, \ldots, n; \; j = 0, 1, \ldots, m)$ and the boundary conditions are as shown in Fig 6.19.

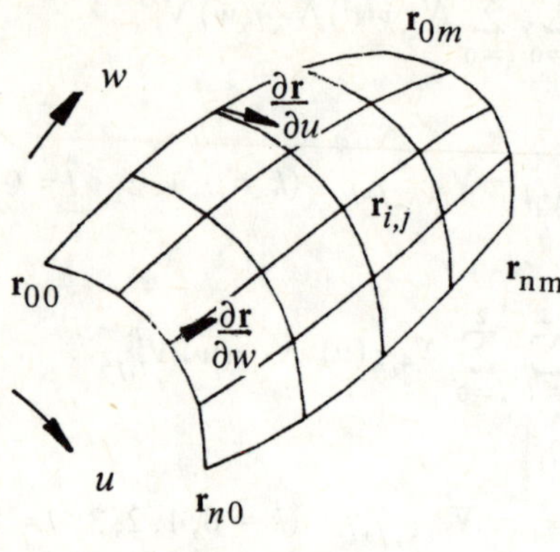

Fig. 6.19

It is clear that the end conditions, which are needed for the inverse algorithm of curves with parameter u, are

$$\frac{\partial r}{\partial u} \quad (i = 0, n; \; j = 0, 1, \ldots, m)$$

Since $r_{i,j}$ and $\partial r/\partial u$ are known, we may obtain $Q_{i,j}$.

According to the boundary conditions

$$\frac{\partial r}{\partial w} \quad (i = 0, 1, \ldots, n; \; j = 0, m)$$

and

$$\frac{\partial r}{\partial u \partial w} \quad (i = 0, n; \; j = 0, m)$$

we will translate them into end conditions $Q'_{i,j} (i = -1, 0, \ldots, n, n + 1; j = 0, m)$, which are needed for the inverse algorithm of curves with parameter w.

Fig. 6.20 clearly illustrates the relationships between $r_{i,j}$, $Q_{i,j}$ and $V_{i,j}$.

The translation method is based on the following fact for the inverse algorithm of the B-spline curve with parameter w; the $Q_{i,j}$ are regarded as curve points and $V_{i,j}$ regarded as vertices of the curves. From the property of the cubic B-spline curve, we can see that

$$Q'_{i,0} = \tfrac{1}{2} (V_{i,1} - V_{i,-1})$$

This means that if $(V_{i,1} - V_{i,-1}) (i = -1, 0, \ldots, n, n + 1)$ are known, $Q'_{i,0}$ are also known.

Using the B-spline surface equation (6.56), we obtain

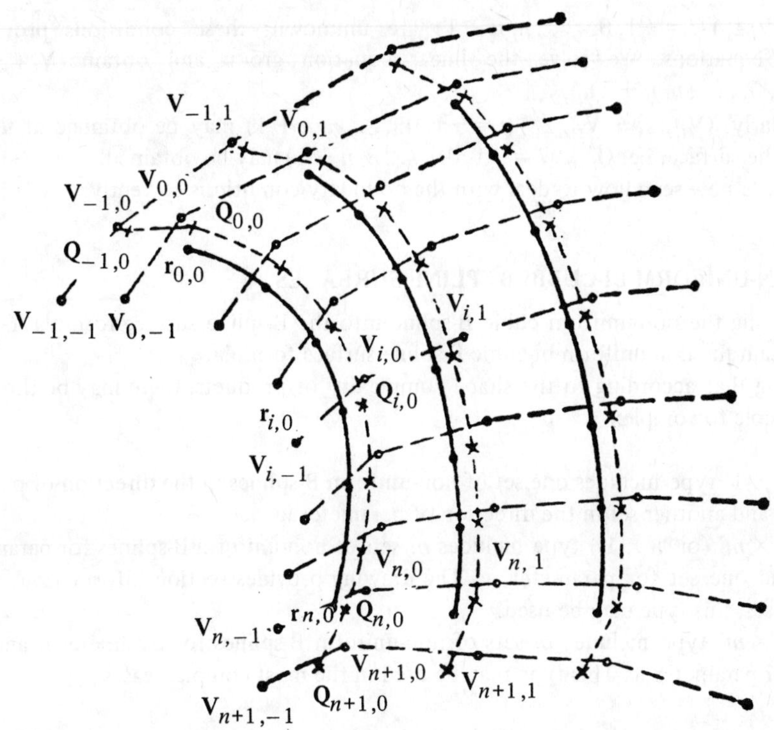

Fig. 6.20

● - - - - $r_{i,j}$ given points on surfaces $(i = 0, \ldots, n; j = 0, \ldots, m)$ ✳ - - - Vertices $Q_{i,j}$ of B-spline curves with parameter u $(i = -1, 0, \ldots, n + 1; j = 0, \ldots, m)$ ○ - - - Vertices $V_{i,j}$ of B-spline surfaces $(i = -1, 0, \ldots, n + 1; j = -1, 0, \ldots, m + 1)$

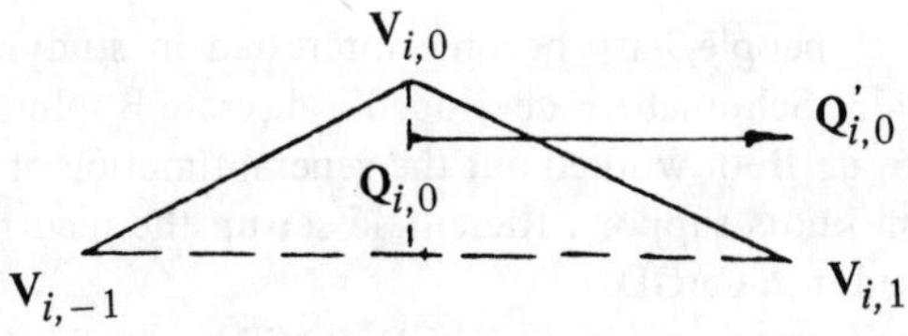

Fig. 6.21

$$\frac{\partial \mathbf{r}}{\partial w}_{i,0} = \tfrac{1}{12}\left(V_{i-1,1} - V_{i-1,-1}\right) + \tfrac{1}{3}\left(V_{i,1} - V_{i,-1}\right) + \tfrac{1}{12}\left(V_{i+1,1} - V_{i+1,-1}\right)$$

$$(i = 0, 1, \ldots, n)$$

$$\frac{\partial \mathbf{r}}{\partial u \partial w_{i,0}} = -\tfrac{1}{4}\left(V_{i-1,1} - V_{i-1,-1}\right) + \tfrac{1}{4}\left(V_{i+1,1} - V_{i+1,-1}\right) \quad (i = 0, n)$$

$(\mathbf{V}_{i,1} - \mathbf{V}_{i,-1})$ $(i = -1, 0, \ldots, n, n + 1)$ are unknown; these conditions provide just $(n + 3)$ equations. We solve the linear equation group and obtain $(\mathbf{V}_{i,1} - \mathbf{V}_{i,-1})$ $(i = -1, 0, \ldots, n, n + 1)$.

Similarly, $(\mathbf{V}_{i,n+1} - \mathbf{V}_{i,n-1})$ $(i = -1, 0, \ldots, n, n + 1)$ may be obtained at the other side of the surface, i.e. $\mathbf{Q}'_{i,m}$ $(i = -1, 0, \ldots, n, n + 1)$ may be obtained.

We have now seen how to deal with the boundary conditions correctly.

6.9 NON-UNIFORM BI-CUBIC B-SPLINE SURFACES

Substituting the non-uniform cubic B-spline into the B-spline surface formula (6.53), we may obtain the non-uniform bi-cubic B-spline surface formula.

Noting that according to the shape complexity of products, there may be three cases, from simple to complex.

'1 × 1' type includes one set of non-uniform B-splines in the direction of parameter u, and another set in the direction of parameter w.

'1 × m' (or 'n × 1') type includes m sets of non-uniform B-splines for parameter u, and one set for parameter w. The drawing provides section information. In most cases, this type may be used.

'n × m' type includes m sets of non-uniform B-splines for parameter u and n sets for parameter w. This type may be used in the most complex cases.

These concepts, such as multiple vertices and multiple knots, are suitable for the B-spline surface. This method of dealing with boundary conditions for the bi-cubic B-spline surface may also be used for non-uniform B-spline surfaces.

These methods and concepts are applied in software for surface modelling.

6.10 FURTHER ASPECTS OF B-SPLINES

An increasing number of people have become interested in studying and applying the discrete B-spline. In 1973, Schumaberg developed a discrete B-spline defined on uniform knots support. In 1976, de Boor worked out the general function of the discrete B-spline defined on non-uniform knots support. Riesenfeld set up the recurrence formula of the discrete B-spline and used it in CAGD.

Although the B-spline is very popular in CAGD, it still has its limitations:

- Too much work is involved in calculating the intersection between curves, or surfaces, and the process is slow.
- The finished designs cannot be treated conveniently in a systematic way because of the heterogeneity of the models in different stages of designing, displaying and plotting.

The discrete B-spline offers quite satisfactory solutions to these two problems. Moreover, the discrete B-spline makes piecewise treatments and local adjustments much easier. Since the discrete form of B-spline expresses and treats the continuous B-spline with the method of the discrete form, it is especially suitable for interactive design by computer.

While the discrete form of B-spline mainly concerns itself with the application of B-spline theory in engineering by discrete treatment, the multivariate B-spline is to develop the theory further.

Based on its solid theoretical foundation, the B-spline is developing further both in its theory and in its application. It is a very promising geometrical tool for designing. It is not only popular in CAGD, but also widely applicable in other areas such as data processing and finite element analysis.

REFERENCES

[1] Böehm, W. and Prautzsch, H., The insertion algorithm, *Computer-aided Design,* **17**, No. 2 (1985), 58–59.

[2] Hölzle, G. E., Knot placement for piecewise polynomial approximation of curves, *Computer-aided Design,* **15**, No. 5 (1983), 295–296.

[3] Barsky, B. A. and Greenberg, D. P., Interactive surface representation system using a B-spline formulation with interpolation capability, *Computer-aided Design,* **14**, No. 4 (1982), 187–194.

[4] Frain, G., Visually C^2 cubic splines, *Computer-aided Design,* **14**, No. 3 (1982), 137–140.

[5] Wang, C. Y., Shape classification of the parametric cubic curve and parametric B-spline cubic curve, *Computer-aided Design,* **13**, No. 4 (1981), 199–206.

[6] Böehm, W., Generating the Bezier points of B-spline curves and surfaces, *Computer-aided Design,* **13**, No. 6 (1981), 365–366.

[7] Loh, R., Convex B-spline surfaces, *Computer-aided Design,* **13**, No. 3 (1981), 145–150.

[8] Barsky, B. A. and Greenberg, D. P., Determining a set of B-spline control vertices to generate an interpolating surface, *Computer Graphics and Image Processing,* **14**, No. 3 (1980), 203–226.

[9] Cohen, E., Lyche, T. and Riesenfeld, R. F., Discrete B-splines and subdivision techniques in computer-aided geometric design and computer graphics, *Computer Graphics and Image Processing,* **14**, Oct. (1980), 87–111.

[10] Lane, J. M. and Riesenfeld, R. F., A theoretical development for the computer generation of piecewise polynomial surfaces, *IEEE Transactions on Pattern Analysis and Machine Intelligence, PAMI 2* (1980), 35–46.

[11] Böehm, W., Inserting new knots into B-spline curves, *Computer-aided Design,* **12**, No. 4, July (1980), 199–201.

[12] Rogers, D. F., B-spline curves and surfaces for ship hull design, *Proc. ACM Siggraph,* 1980.

[13] de Boor, C., A practical guide to splines, *Applied Mathematical Sciences,* **27**, Springer-Verlag, Bedford, U.K., 1978.

7

Rational Curves and Surfaces

7.1 BALL CURVES

Rational curves and surfaces are currently the most general curves and surfaces used. They offer more degrees of freedom for shaping curves and surfaces, so they have a wide range of applications in the new generation of systems of surface modelling.

In this chapter we will begin with Ball curves, then introduce rational Ball curves, and discuss the rational extension of other curves, and finally provide the concepts, formulae and applications of rational surfaces.

Ball [1] has provided one of the cubic parametric curves (PC stands for a parametric curve later) which is described by the eqaution of the form

$$r(u) = [1 \quad u \quad u^2 \quad u^3] \, M_{bl} \begin{bmatrix} V_1 \\ V_2 \\ V_3 \\ V_4 \end{bmatrix} \quad (0 \leqslant u \leqslant 1) \tag{7.1}$$

where M_{bl} is a 4×4 matrix of coefficients of blending functions, V_i ($i = 1, 2, 3, 4$) are vertices of a characteristic polygon of a Ball curve.

Four conditions to define the segment of a Ball curve are as follows:

$$r(0) = V_1$$

$$r(1) = V_4$$

$$r'(0) = 2(V_2 - V_1)$$

and

$$\mathbf{r}'(1) = 2(\mathbf{V}_4 - \mathbf{V}_3)$$

Thus the Ball curve will pass through the vertices $\mathbf{V}_1$ and $\mathbf{V}_4$, and have a tangent at $\mathbf{V}_1$ in the direction from $\mathbf{V}_1$ to $\mathbf{V}_2$ and have a tangent at $\mathbf{V}_4$ in the direction from $\mathbf{V}_3$ to $\mathbf{V}_4$ (see Fig. 7.1).

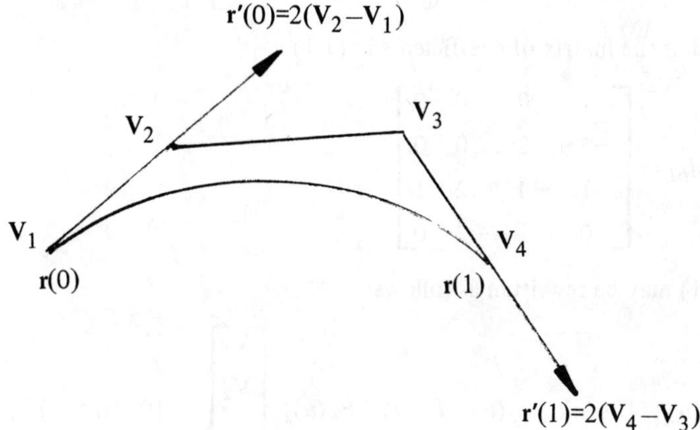

Fig. 7.1

The matrix form of four conditions defining a Ball curve is

$$\begin{bmatrix} \mathbf{r}(0) \\ \mathbf{r}(1) \\ \mathbf{r}'(0) \\ \mathbf{r}'(1) \end{bmatrix} = \begin{bmatrix} 1 & 0 & 0 & 0 \\ 0 & 0 & 0 & 1 \\ -2 & 2 & 0 & 0 \\ 0 & 0 & -2 & 2 \end{bmatrix} \begin{bmatrix} \mathbf{V}_1 \\ \mathbf{V}_2 \\ \mathbf{V}_3 \\ \mathbf{V}_4 \end{bmatrix}$$

The general equation of a cubic PC is presented in Chapter 4, section 2 as follows:

$$\mathbf{r}(u) = \begin{bmatrix} 1 & u & u^2 & u^3 \end{bmatrix} M_c \begin{bmatrix} \mathbf{r}(0) \\ \mathbf{r}(1) \\ \mathbf{r}'(0) \\ \mathbf{r}'(1) \end{bmatrix} \tag{7.2}$$

where

$$M_c = \begin{bmatrix} 1 & 0 & 0 & 0 \\ 0 & 0 & 1 & 0 \\ -3 & 3 & -2 & -1 \\ 2 & -2 & 1 & 1 \end{bmatrix}$$

Substituting the above four conditions defining the Ball curve into (7.2) we obtain the following result after multiplication of the matrices:

$$\mathbf{r}(u) = \begin{bmatrix} 1 & u & u^2 & u^3 \end{bmatrix} \begin{bmatrix} 1 & 0 & 0 & 0 \\ -2 & 2 & 0 & 0 \\ 1 & -4 & 2 & 1 \\ 0 & 2 & -2 & 0 \end{bmatrix} \begin{bmatrix} \mathbf{V}_1 \\ \mathbf{V}_2 \\ \mathbf{V}_3 \\ \mathbf{V}_4 \end{bmatrix}$$

We now see that the matrix of coefficients in (7.1) is

$$M_{bl} = \begin{bmatrix} 1 & 0 & 0 & 0 \\ -2 & 2 & 0 & 0 \\ 1 & -4 & 2 & 1 \\ 0 & 2 & -2 & 0 \end{bmatrix}$$

Equation (7.1) may be rewritten as follows:

$$\mathbf{r}(u) = \begin{bmatrix} F_1(u) & F_2(u) & F_3(u) & F_4(u) \end{bmatrix} \begin{bmatrix} \mathbf{V}_1 \\ \mathbf{V}_2 \\ \mathbf{V}_3 \\ \mathbf{V}_4 \end{bmatrix} \qquad (0 \leqslant u \leqslant 1) \qquad (7.3)$$

where

$$F_1(u) = (1-u)^2$$
$$F_2(u) = 2u(1-u)^2$$
$$F_3(u) = 2u^2(1-u)$$
$$F_4(u) = u^2 \qquad\qquad (7.4)$$

It is evident that the blending functions of the Ball curve possess the following properties:

- $$F_i(u) \geqslant 0 \qquad\qquad (i = 1, 2, 3, 4) \quad (0 \leqslant u \leqslant 1)$$

- $$\sum_{i=1}^{4} F_i(u) \equiv 1$$

The geometric concepts and formulae of Ball curves discussed above are very helpful to readers to understand the rational extension of Ball curves.

7.2 RATIONAL BALL CURVES

The rational ball cubic PC is a rational extension of the Ball cubic PC, as each vertex $\mathbf{V}_i$ of a characteristic polygon is assigned a weight H_i ($i = 1, 2, 3, 4$).

The general rational curve is defined by rational polynomials, that is, by the algebraic ratio of two polynomial functions. It may be described by an equation of the form

$$\mathbf{r}(u) = \mathbf{R}(u)/H(u) \tag{7.5}$$

where $\mathbf{r}(u)$ is an algebraic ratio; its numerator $\mathbf{R}(u)$ is a vector-valued polynomial function, but its denominator $H(u)$ is a scalar polynomial function. Equation (7.5) is important, and it will be discussed in more detail in this chapter.

A complete formal derivation of equation (7.5) requires the use of homogeneous coordinates. As is well known, the equation of a curve may be expressed in three-dimensional space, that is, the Cartesian coordinate system

$$\mathbf{r}(u) = [x(u) \quad y(u) \quad z(u)]$$

where $x(u)$, $y(u)$ and $z(u)$ are elements of the vector function $\mathbf{r}(u)$. The equation of a curve may also be described in four-dimensional space, that is, a homogeneous coordinate system

$$\mathbf{r}(u) = [x(u) \quad y(u) \quad z(u) \quad 1] \tag{7.6}$$

From (7.6) it can be seen that the first three coordinates are equal to Cartesian coordinates, respectively, if the fourth coordinate is one.

According to the rule of homogeneous coordinates, the representation of a vector is no longer unique; in each case, only the ratios of elements are important.

The product of (7.6) and $H(u)$ is

$$\mathbf{R}(u) = [x(u)\,H(u) \quad y(u)\,H(u) \quad z(u)\,H(u) \quad H(u)] \tag{7.7}$$

which is directly equivalent to equation (7.6). Remember, the polynomial function $H(u)$ is the fourth coordinate of $\mathbf{R}(u)$. Because we are concerned with the dimensional properties of curves and surfaces, we need to relate the $\mathbf{R}(u)$ to $\mathbf{r}(u)$. The values of the Cartesian coordinates may be recovered from equation (7.7) by division by its fourth coordinate $H(u)$; thus the relation is just the equation (7.5).

We now derive representations of $\mathbf{R}(u)$ and $H(u)$ for a rational Ball cubic PC. The four conditions necessary to define the segment of a rational Ball cubic PC are as follows:

$$\mathbf{R}(0) = H_1\mathbf{V}_1$$

$$\mathbf{R}(1) = H_4\mathbf{V}_4$$

$$\mathbf{R}'(0) = 2(H_2\mathbf{V}_2 - H_1\mathbf{V}_1)$$

$$\mathbf{R}'(1) = 2(H_4\mathbf{V}_4 - H_3\mathbf{V}_3)$$

in which $\mathbf{V}_i = (x_i, y_i, z_i, 1)$ $(i = 1, 2, 3, 4)$.

Note that each vertex $\mathbf{V}_i$ of the characteristic polygon is assigned a weight H_i $(i = 1, 2, 3, 4)$.

Substituting the above four conditions into the general equation of a cubic PC, we obtain

$$\mathbf{R}(u) = \begin{bmatrix} 1 & u & u^2 & u^3 \end{bmatrix} M_c \begin{bmatrix} H_1\mathbf{V}_1 \\ H_4\mathbf{V}_4 \\ 2(H_2\mathbf{V}_2 - H_1\mathbf{V}_1) \\ 2(H_4\mathbf{V}_4 - H_3\mathbf{V}_3) \end{bmatrix}$$

$$= \begin{bmatrix} 1 & u & u^2 & u^3 \end{bmatrix} M_c \begin{bmatrix} 1 & 0 & 0 & 0 \\ 0 & 0 & 0 & 1 \\ -2 & 2 & 0 & 0 \\ 0 & 0 & -2 & 2 \end{bmatrix} \begin{bmatrix} H_1\mathbf{V}_1 \\ H_2\mathbf{V}_2 \\ H_3\mathbf{V}_3 \\ H_4\mathbf{V}_4 \end{bmatrix}$$

$$= \begin{bmatrix} 1 & u & u^2 & u^3 \end{bmatrix} M_{bl} \begin{bmatrix} H_1\mathbf{V}_1 \\ H_2\mathbf{V}_2 \\ H_3\mathbf{V}_3 \\ H_4\mathbf{V}_4 \end{bmatrix} \tag{7.8}$$

The representation (7.8) is similar to (7.1), except that each vertex $\mathbf{V}_i$ in a column is assigned a weight H_i.

By using the representation of blending functions (7.4), equation (7.8) may be rewritten as

$$\mathbf{R}(u) = \sum_{i=1}^{4} F_i(u)\, H_i\, \mathbf{V}_i \tag{7.9}$$

Because $\mathbf{V}_i = (x_i, y_i, z_i, 1)$ in homogeneous coordinates, equation (7.9) may be rewritten as

$$R(u) = \begin{bmatrix} \displaystyle\sum_{i=1}^{4} F_i(u)\, H_i x_i & \displaystyle\sum_{i=1}^{4} F_i(u)\, H_i y_i \\[2em] \displaystyle\sum_{i=1}^{4} F_i(u)\, H_i z_i & \displaystyle\sum_{i=1}^{4} F_i(u)\, H_i \end{bmatrix} \tag{7.10}$$

According to (7.10), we see that the fourth coordinate is

$$H(u) = \sum_{i=1}^{4} F_i(u)\, H_i$$

$$= \begin{bmatrix} 1 & u & u^2 & u^3 \end{bmatrix} M_{bl} \begin{bmatrix} H_1 \\ H_2 \\ H_3 \\ H_4 \end{bmatrix} \tag{7.11}$$

The equation of the fourth coordinate is also similar to (7.1), except that each vertex V_i in the column is exchanged with weight H_i.

From the representations of a rational cubic PC which are (7.5), (7.8) and (7.11), we know that the Ball cubic PC may be rationalized, as each vertex is assigned a weight H_i. Each segment of a rational cubic PC possesses four weights, which can be adjusted by the user; in other words, the segement of a rational cubic PC can be altered by changing the individual weights.

If $H_i = H$ ($i = 1, 2, 3, 4$), then substituting them into (7.8) and (7.11),

$$\mathbf{R}(u) = [1 \quad u \quad u^2 \quad u^3] M_{bl} \begin{bmatrix} HV_1 \\ HV_2 \\ HV_3 \\ HV_4 \end{bmatrix}$$

$$H(u) = [1 \quad u \quad u^2 \quad u^3] M_{bl} \begin{bmatrix} H \\ H \\ H \\ H \end{bmatrix} = H$$

then substituting them into (7.5), we obtain

$$\mathbf{r}(u) = [1 \quad u \quad u^2 \quad u^3] M_{bl} \begin{bmatrix} V_1 \\ V_2 \\ V_3 \\ V_4 \end{bmatrix}$$

Thus if the weights H_i are all equal, the Ball cubic PC is recovered. At $u = 0$ and $u = 1$ respectively, by using (7.5) the following results can be obtained:

$$\mathbf{r}(0) = \mathbf{V}_1$$

$$\mathbf{r}(1) = \mathbf{V}_4$$

On differentiating formula (7.5) with respect to u, that is

$$\frac{d}{du}(\mathbf{r}(u)) = \frac{d}{du}(\mathbf{R}(u))/H(u) + \frac{d}{du}\left(\frac{1}{H(u)}\right)\mathbf{R}(u)$$

we obtain after some simplification

$$\mathbf{r}'(u) = [\mathbf{R}'(u) - \mathbf{r}(u)H'(u)]/H(u) \tag{7.12}$$

At $u = 0$ and $u = 1$ respectively, by using (7.12) the results are as follows:

$$\mathbf{r}'(0) = 2\frac{H_2}{H_1}(\mathbf{V}_2 - \mathbf{V}_1)$$

$$\mathbf{r}'(1) = 2\,\frac{H_3}{H_4}\,(\mathbf{V}_4 - \mathbf{V}_3)$$

Thus the characteristic polygon for a rational Ball cubic PC defined by $\mathbf{V}_i$ ($i = 1, 2, 3, 4$) has the same geometric significance as one for a Ball cubic PC, and the rational Ball cubic PC passes through the vertices $\mathbf{V}_1$ and $\mathbf{V}_4$, has a tangent at $\mathbf{V}_1$ in the direction from $\mathbf{V}_1$ to $\mathbf{V}_2$, and at $\mathbf{V}_4$ has a tangent in the direction from $\mathbf{V}_3$ to $\mathbf{V}_4$ except that we now have freedom to adjust the weights H_i ($i = 1, 2, 3, 4$) according to the shape requirements of the user (see Fig. 7.2).

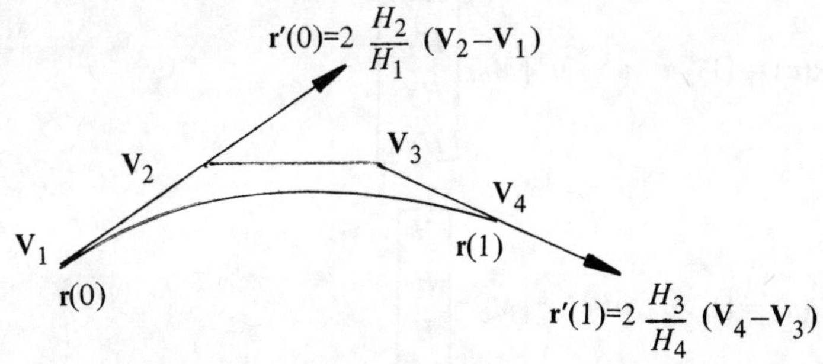

Fig. 7.2

Comparing Figs. (7.1) and (7.2), it is clear that the tangent vector of the end points of a rational Ball cubic PC includes the weight ratio H_2/H_1 or H_3/H_4 respectively, and that increasing the ratio H_2/H_1 or H_3/H_4 gives greater fullness to the curve segment.

All standard algorithms (de Boor etc.) discussed in Chapter 6 are applied simultaneously to the numerator and to the denominator of the representation (7.5).

7.3 RATIONAL EXTENSION OF OTHER CURVES

7.3.1 Rational Bezier curves

We will now derive the representations of $\mathbf{R}(u)$ and $H(u)$ for a rational Bezier cubic PC. The four conditions to define a segment of a rational Bezier cubic PC are as follows:

$$\mathbf{R}(0) = H_1\mathbf{V}_1$$

$$\mathbf{R}(1) = H_4\mathbf{V}_4$$

$$\mathbf{R}'(0) = 3(H_2\mathbf{V}_2 - H_1\mathbf{V}_1)$$

$$\mathbf{R}'(1) = 3(H_4\mathbf{V}_4 - H_3\mathbf{V}_3)$$

Note that each vertex $\mathbf{V}_i(x_i, y_i, z_i, 1)$ of the characteristic polygon is assigned a weight H_i ($i = 1, 2, 3, 4$).

Substituting the four conditions above into the general equation of a cubic PC we obtain

$$\mathbf{R}(u) = \begin{bmatrix} 1 & u & u^2 & u^3 \end{bmatrix} M_c \begin{bmatrix} H_1\mathbf{V}_1 \\ H_4\mathbf{V}_4 \\ 3(H_2\mathbf{V}_2 - H_1\mathbf{V}_1) \\ 3(H_4\mathbf{V}_4 - H_3\mathbf{V}_3) \end{bmatrix}$$

$$= \begin{bmatrix} 1 & u & u^2 & u^3 \end{bmatrix} M_c \begin{bmatrix} 1 & 0 & 0 & 0 \\ 0 & 0 & 0 & 1 \\ -3 & 3 & 0 & 0 \\ 0 & 0 & -3 & 3 \end{bmatrix} \begin{bmatrix} H_1\mathbf{V}_1 \\ H_2\mathbf{V}_2 \\ H_3\mathbf{V}_3 \\ H_4\mathbf{V}_4 \end{bmatrix}$$

$$= \begin{bmatrix} 1 & u & u^2 & u^3 \end{bmatrix} M_{be} \begin{bmatrix} H_1\mathbf{V}_1 \\ H_2\mathbf{V}_2 \\ H_3\mathbf{V}_3 \\ H_4\mathbf{V}_4 \end{bmatrix} \tag{7.13}$$

where

$$M_{be} = \begin{bmatrix} 1 & 0 & 0 & 0 \\ -3 & 3 & 0 & 0 \\ 3 & -6 & 3 & 0 \\ -1 & 3 & -3 & 1 \end{bmatrix}$$

which is a coefficient matrix of cubic Bernstein functions.

The fourth coordinate of equation (7.13) is

$$H(u) = \begin{bmatrix} 1 & u & u^2 & u^3 \end{bmatrix} M_{be} \begin{bmatrix} H_1 \\ H_2 \\ H_3 \\ H_4 \end{bmatrix} \tag{7.14}$$

Equation (7.5) represents a rational Bezier cubic PC, as its denominator $H(u)$ is expressed by equation (7.14) and its numerator $\mathbf{R}(u)$ is expressed by equation (7.13).

At $u = 0$ and $u = 1$, we obtain from (7.5), (7.13) and (7.14)

$$\mathbf{r}(0) = \mathbf{V}_1$$

$$\mathbf{r}(1) = \mathbf{V}_4$$

and from (7.12), we obtain

$$\mathbf{r}'(0) = 3\,\frac{H_2}{H_1}(\mathbf{V}_2 - \mathbf{V}_1)$$

$$\mathbf{r}'(1) = 3\,\frac{H_3}{H_4}\,(\mathbf{V}_4 - \mathbf{V}_3)$$

Comparing Fig. 7.4 with Fig. 7.3, we now see that the characteristic polygon of a rational Bezier curve defined by $\mathbf{V}_i$ has the same geometric significance as one for a Bezier curve, and the rational Bezier cubic PC passes through the vertices $\mathbf{V}_1$ and $\mathbf{V}_4$, has a tangent at $\mathbf{V}_1$ in the direction from $\mathbf{V}_1$ to $\mathbf{V}_2$, which includes a weight ratio H_2/H_1, and at $\mathbf{V}_4$ has a tangent in the direction from $\mathbf{V}_3$ to $\mathbf{V}_4$, which includes a weight ratio of H_3/H_4. Users have freedom to adjust the weights H_i ($i = 1, 2, 3, 4$). Increasing the weights H_2 (or the ratio H_2/H_1) and H_3 (or the ratio H_3/H_4) will give greater fullness to the curve segment.

If the weights H_i ($i = 1, 2, 3, 4$) are all equal, the rational Bezier cubic PC is reduced to the Bezier cubic PC again.

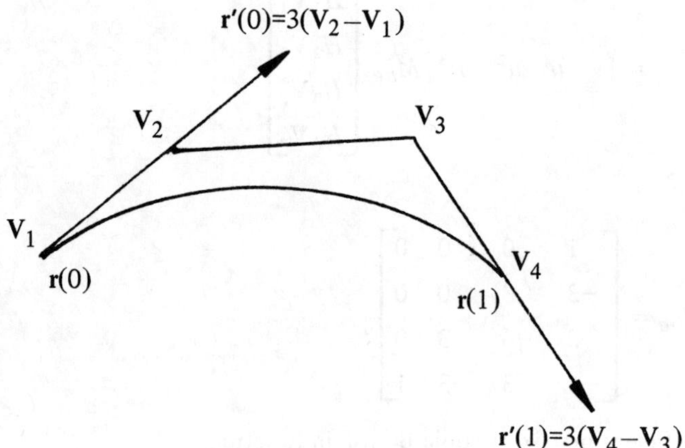

Fig. 7.3 Bezier cubic PC

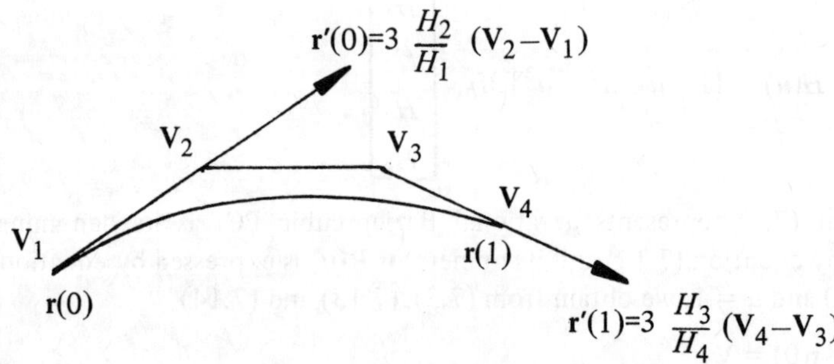

Fig. 7.4 Rational Bezier cubic PC

7.3.2 Rational B-spline curves

The rational extension from the B-spline curve to the rational B-spline curve is similar to the rational extension discussed in section 7.3.1. The four conditions to define the segment of a rational B-spline curve are as follows:

$$\mathbf{R}(0) = \tfrac{1}{6}\,(H_1\mathbf{V}_1 + 4H_2\mathbf{V}_2 + H_3\mathbf{V}_3)$$

$$\mathbf{R}(1) = \tfrac{1}{6}\,(H_2\mathbf{V}_2 + 4H_3\mathbf{V}_3 + H_4\mathbf{V}_4)$$

$$\mathbf{R}'(0) = \tfrac{1}{2}\,(H_3\mathbf{V}_3 - H_1\mathbf{V}_1)$$

$$\mathbf{R}'(1) = \tfrac{1}{2}\,(H_4\mathbf{V}_4 - H_2\mathbf{V}_2)$$

Here, each vertex $\mathbf{V}_i(x_i,\,y_i,\,z_i,\,1)$ of the characteristic polygon is assigned a weight $H_i\ (i = 1, 2, 3, 4)$.

Substituting the four conditions above into the general equation of a cubic PC, we obtain

$$\mathbf{R}(u) = \begin{bmatrix} 1 & u & u^2 & u^3 \end{bmatrix} M_c \begin{bmatrix} \tfrac{1}{6} & \tfrac{4}{6} & \tfrac{1}{6} & 0 \\ 0 & \tfrac{1}{6} & \tfrac{4}{6} & \tfrac{1}{6} \\ -\tfrac{1}{2} & 0 & \tfrac{1}{2} & 0 \\ 0 & -\tfrac{1}{2} & 0 & \tfrac{1}{2} \end{bmatrix} \begin{bmatrix} H_1\mathbf{V}_1 \\ H_2\mathbf{V}_2 \\ H_3\mathbf{V}_3 \\ H_4\mathbf{V}_4 \end{bmatrix}$$

$$= \begin{bmatrix} 1 & u & u^2 & u^3 \end{bmatrix} M_b \begin{bmatrix} H_1\mathbf{V}_1 \\ H_2\mathbf{V}_2 \\ H_3\mathbf{V}_3 \\ H_4\mathbf{V}_4 \end{bmatrix} \tag{7.15}$$

where

$$M_b = \tfrac{1}{6} \begin{bmatrix} 1 & 4 & 1 & 0 \\ -3 & 0 & 3 & 0 \\ 3 & -6 & 3 & 0 \\ -1 & 3 & -3 & 1 \end{bmatrix}$$

which is a coefficient matrix of the cubic B-spline functions.

The fourth coordinate of equation (7.15) is

$$H(u) = \begin{bmatrix} 1 & u & u^2 & u^3 \end{bmatrix} M_b \begin{bmatrix} H_1 \\ H_2 \\ H_3 \\ H_4 \end{bmatrix} \tag{7.16}$$

Equation (7.5) represents a rational B-spline cubic PC, as its denominator $H(u)$ is expressed by (7.16), and its numerator $\mathbf{R}(u)$ is expressed by (7.15).

Users now have the freedom to adjust the shape of the curve segment, by changing the value of weights H_i without moving any of the vertices themselves. If the weights $H_i\ (i = 1, 2, 3, 4)$ are all equal, the rational B-spline PC is reduced to the B-spline PC again.

Finally, a brief introduction to non-uniform rational B-spline curves is offered here. If M_b in equations (7.15) and (7.16) is the coefficient matrix of the non-uniform B-spline cubic functions mentioned earlier in Chapter 6, section 5, then equation (7.15) stands for a non-uniform rational B-spline curve, which is the mathematical basis of the new generation of surface modellers.

To summarize parametric curves — including Ball curves, Bezier curves and B-spline curves — may be extended to form rational parametric curves by assigning them weights. Rational parametric curves possess some distinguishing features as follows:

1. Assigning weights. Rational parametric curves are the most general curve scheme, in that they include piecewise polynomial curves as well as piecewise conic sections and mixed curve forms by changing weights; the method of changing weights will be discussed in later sections.

2. Rational parametric curves are most succinctly represented in terms of homogeneous coordinates, that is, in four-dimensional homogeneous space as

$$\mathbf{R}(u) = [H(u)\,x(u) \quad H(u)\,y(u) \quad H(u)\,z(u) \quad H(u)]$$

or

$$\mathbf{R}(u) = H(u)\,[x(u) \quad y(u) \quad z(u)\, 1]$$

or

$$\mathbf{R}(u) = H(u) \cdot \mathbf{r}(u)$$

3. Rational parametric curves in three-dimensional space are, again, obtained by dividing each of the first three coordinates of a curve given by the above equation by the fourth homogeneous coordinate, i.e. equation (7.5). Although the rational parametric curve equation includes denominator and numerator, which are all functions of parametric u, the denominator is just the fourth homogeneous coordinate; thus the calculation of the rational curve is not complex.

7.4 DEGENERATE RATIONAL CURVES

Note that in a complex and powerful interactive surface-modelling system, it is likely that we will create degenerate conditions that may arise by design. The modelling system must

recognize these conditions and deal with them. We will take only a brief look at some of the more obvious cases of degenerate rational curves. We will focus on the coefficients of a single rational PC.

The rational cubic PC may be described in three-dimensional space as

$$\mathbf{r}(u) = \frac{\mathbf{A} + \mathbf{B}u + \mathbf{C}u^2 + \mathbf{D}u^3}{a + bu + cu^2 + du^3} \tag{7.17}$$

which is directly equivalent to equation (7.5). According to (7.17), we see the following results.

1.   The rational cubic PC becomes a normal cubic PC, if

$$b = c = d = 0$$

2.   The rational cubic PC degenerates to a rational quadric PC, if

$$\mathbf{D} = 0 \quad \text{and} \quad d = 0$$

3.   If

$$\frac{\mathbf{A}}{a} = \frac{\mathbf{B}}{b} = \frac{\mathbf{C}}{c} = \mathbf{N},$$

that is, $\mathbf{A}$, $\mathbf{B}$ and $\mathbf{C}$ are collinear, then equation (7.17) may be rewritten as

$$\mathbf{r}(u) = \frac{(a + bu + cu^2)\,\mathbf{N} + u^3\mathbf{D}}{a + bu + cu^2 + du^3}$$

$$= \mathbf{N} + \frac{u^3}{a + bu + cu^2 + du^3}\,(\mathbf{D} - d\mathbf{N}) \tag{7.18}$$

thus the $\mathbf{r}(u)$ is reduced to a space straight line, which starts from the point represented by the vector $\mathbf{N}$ and is parallel to the vector $(\mathbf{D} - d\mathbf{N})$.

4.   If

$$\frac{\mathbf{A}}{a} = \frac{\mathbf{B}}{b} = \frac{\mathbf{C}}{c} = \frac{\mathbf{D}}{d} = \mathbf{N}$$

then

$$\mathbf{r}(u) = \frac{(a + bu + cu^2 + du^3)\,\mathbf{N}}{a + bu + cu^2 + du^3} = \mathbf{N} \tag{7.19}$$

This curve degenerates to the point represented by the vector $\mathbf{N}$.

The brief analyses offered above show that the rational cubic PC can represent a normal cubic PC, a quadric PC, a straight line and a point, and that degenerate conditions exist when one or more of the coefficients are zero or linearly related to another coefficient.

By using equations (7.8) and (7.11), we obtain the following.

1.   The rational Ball cubic PC becomes a normal Ball cubic PC, if

$$H_1 = H_2 = H_3 = H_4$$

2.   This curve degenerates to a rational quadric PC, if

$$H_2 = H_3 \quad \text{and} \quad V_2 = V_3$$

This may be proved as follows. By substituting H_2 for H_3 into (7.11)

$$H(u) = \begin{bmatrix} 1 & u & u^2 & u^3 \end{bmatrix} M_{bl} \begin{bmatrix} H_1 \\ H_2 \\ H_2 \\ H_4 \end{bmatrix}$$

Then rewriting the equation above after some matrix manipulation, we obtain

$$H(u) = \begin{bmatrix} 1 & u & u^2 \end{bmatrix} \begin{bmatrix} 1 & 0 & 0 \\ -2 & 2 & 0 \\ 1 & -2 & 1 \end{bmatrix} \begin{bmatrix} H_1 \\ H_2 \\ H_4 \end{bmatrix} \tag{7.20}$$

By substituting H_2 and V_2 for H_3 and V_3 into (7.8), respectively

$$R(u) = \begin{bmatrix} 1 & u & u^2 & u^3 \end{bmatrix} M_{bl} \begin{bmatrix} H_1 V_1 \\ H_2 V_2 \\ H_2 V_2 \\ H_4 V_4 \end{bmatrix}$$

Then rewriting the equation above after matrix manipulation

$$R(u) = \begin{bmatrix} 1 & u & u^2 & u^3 \end{bmatrix} M_{bl} \begin{bmatrix} H_1 & 0 & 0 & 0 \\ 0 & H_2 & 0 & 0 \\ 0 & 0 & H_2 & 0 \\ 0 & 0 & 0 & H_4 \end{bmatrix} \begin{bmatrix} V_1 \\ V_2 \\ V_2 \\ V_4 \end{bmatrix}$$

$$= \begin{bmatrix} 1 & u & u^2 \end{bmatrix} \begin{bmatrix} 1 & 0 & 0 \\ -2 & 2 & 0 \\ 1 & -2 & 1 \end{bmatrix} \begin{bmatrix} H_1 & 0 & 0 \\ 0 & H_2 & 0 \\ 0 & 0 & H_4 \end{bmatrix} \begin{bmatrix} V_1 \\ V_2 \\ V_4 \end{bmatrix}$$

$$= \begin{bmatrix} 1 & u & u^2 \end{bmatrix} \begin{bmatrix} 1 & 0 & 0 \\ -2 & 2 & 0 \\ 1 & -2 & 1 \end{bmatrix} \begin{bmatrix} H_1 V_1 \\ H_2 V_2 \\ H_4 V_4 \end{bmatrix} \tag{7.21}$$

Equations (7.5), (7.20) and (7.21) represent a rational quadric PC. At $u = 0$ and $u = 1$, the results from equations (7.5), (7.20) and (7.21) are

$$\mathbf{r}(0) = V_1$$

$$\mathbf{r}(1) = V_4$$

$$\mathbf{r}'(0) = 2 \frac{H_2}{H_1} (V_2 - V_1)$$

$$\mathbf{r}'(1) = 2\,\frac{H_2}{H_4}\,(\mathbf{V}_4 - \mathbf{V}_2)$$

Increasing the weight H_2 will give greater fullness to the rational curve segment (see Fig. 7.5).

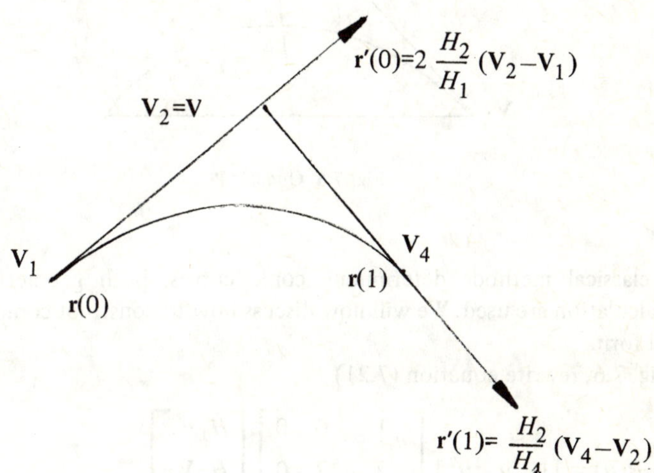

Fig. 7.5 Rational quadric PC

3.   If $H_2 = H_3 = 0$ and $H_1 = H_4$ then

$$\mathbf{r}(u) = \mathbf{V}_1 + \frac{u^2}{1 - 2u + 2u^2}\,(\mathbf{V}_4 - \mathbf{V}_1)$$

This curve becomes a straight line joining $\mathbf{V}_1$ and $\mathbf{V}_4$.

4.   This curve degenerates to a point, if $H_1 = H_2 = H_3 = H_4$ and

$$\mathbf{V}_1 = \mathbf{V}_2 = \mathbf{V}_3 = \mathbf{V}_4$$

In the four cases discussed above, the rational quadric PC is a very useful and interesting form. Conic curves have been widely applied in aircraft design for many years. In order to describe the segment of the conic curve shown in Fig. 7.6, designers provide three vertices $\mathbf{V}_1$, $\mathbf{V}_2$ and $\mathbf{V}_T$. The segment of the conic curve passes through vertices $\mathbf{V}_1$ and $\mathbf{V}_2$, but $\mathbf{V}_T$ is the intersection of two tangents at end points. Designers also provide a parameter ρ:

$$\rho = sm/\mathbf{V}_T m$$

where m is the mid-point of the line joining $\mathbf{V}_1$ and $\mathbf{V}_2$, s is called the shoulder point of the segment, and $\mathbf{V}_T$ is called the hardpoint.

ρ determines the type of conic curve; in other words, for a parabola $\rho = \frac{1}{2}$, whereas $\rho < \frac{1}{2}$ gives an ellipse and $\rho > \frac{1}{2}$ a hyperbola.

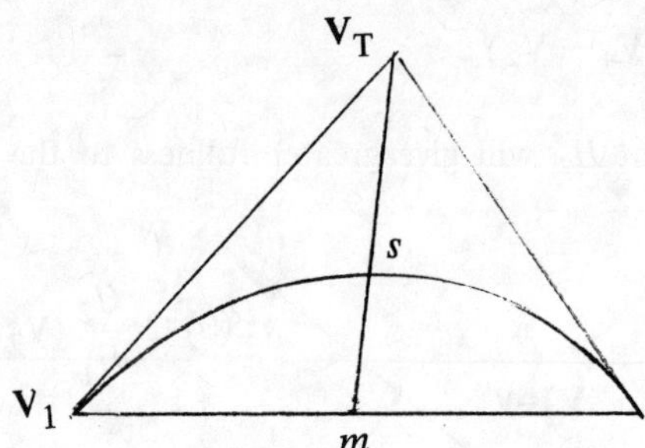

Fig. 7.6 Quadric PC

In the classical methods determining conic curves, both geometric drawing and algebraic calculation are used. We will now discuss how to construct conic curves by using the rational form.

From Fig. 7.6, rewrite equation (7.21)

$$\mathbf{R}(u) = \begin{bmatrix} 1 & u & u^2 \end{bmatrix} \begin{bmatrix} 1 & 0 & 0 \\ -2 & 2 & 0 \\ 1 & -2 & 1 \end{bmatrix} \begin{bmatrix} H_1 \mathbf{V}_1 \\ H_T \mathbf{V}_T \\ H_2 \mathbf{V}_2 \end{bmatrix} \tag{7.22}$$

Equation (7.22) defines a rational quadric PC and possesses three weights H_1, H_T and H_2. The three weights mean that the curve segment possesses three degress of freedom.

There are so many that it is not easy to choose them.

If we assume that

$$H_1 = 1 - \rho$$

$$H_T = \rho$$

and

$$H_2 = 1 - \rho$$

then the number of surplus degrees of freedom is only one, and the equation of the rational quadric curve is as follows:

$$\mathbf{r}(u) = \begin{bmatrix} 1 & u & u^2 \end{bmatrix} \begin{bmatrix} 1 & 0 & 0 \\ -2 & 2 & 0 \\ 1 & -2 & 1 \end{bmatrix} \begin{bmatrix} (1-\rho)\mathbf{V}_1 \\ \rho\mathbf{V}_T \\ (1-\rho)\mathbf{V}_2 \end{bmatrix} \bigg/ H(u) \tag{7.23}$$

where $H(u)$ is the fourth coordinate of the numerator.

It is evident that increasing the value of weight ρ $(0 < \rho < 1)$ will give greater fullness to the curve segment (see Fig. 7.6).

It is easy to prove that the parabola has $\rho = \frac{1}{2}$, whereas $\rho < \frac{1}{2}$ gives an ellipse and $\rho > \frac{1}{2}$ a hyperbola, so that equation (7.23) is also called a conic PC.

The rational Ball quadric PC (or Bezier quadric PC) may represent any conic segment, whereas the Ball (or Bezier) quadric PC represents only a parabola.

7.5 SPECIAL RATIONAL CURVES

7.5.1 The generalized conic segment

Note that a rational cubic PC possesses four weights, which means that each segment possesses four degrees of freedom — so many that it is not easy to control them.

If we assume that

$$H_1 = (1 - f)$$

$$H_2 = f$$

$$H_3 = f$$

$$H_4 = (1 - f) \quad (0 < f < 1)$$

then substituting them into equation (7.8), the rational Ball cubic PC retains one weight f only. This curve equation is as follows:

$$\mathbf{r}(u) = [1 \quad u \quad u^2 \quad u^3] M_{bl} \begin{bmatrix} (1-f)\mathbf{V}_1 \\ f\mathbf{V}_2 \\ f\mathbf{V}_3 \\ (1-f)\mathbf{V}_4 \end{bmatrix} \Big/ H(u) \qquad (7.24)$$

in which $H(u)$ is the fourth coordinate of the numerator.

Increasing the value of weight f will give greater fullness to the curve segment, because the magnitudes of the tangent vector at end points are determined by the weight f.

$$\mathbf{r}'(0) = 2 \frac{f}{1-f} (\mathbf{V}_2 - \mathbf{V}_1)$$

$$\mathbf{r}'(1) = 2 \frac{f}{1-f} (\mathbf{V}_4 - \mathbf{V}_3)$$

The curve segment can therefore by shaped by changing the weight f.

Usually in engineering design the user provides values for the end point vectors $\mathbf{V}_1$ and $\mathbf{V}_4$, and the corresponding tangent vectors $\mathbf{T}_1$ and $\mathbf{T}_4$ at end points to define a curve segment.

Setting $\mathbf{V}_2$ and $\mathbf{V}_3$ according to the conditions required by the user

$$\mathbf{V}_2 = \mathbf{V}_1 + \lambda \mathbf{T}_1 / |\mathbf{T}_1|$$

$$\mathbf{V}_3 = \mathbf{V}_4 - \mu \mathbf{T}_4 / |\mathbf{T}_4| \qquad (7.25)$$

then vertices $\mathbf{V}_2$ and $\mathbf{V}_3$ are points lying on the circle of intersection of the cones obtained by rotating the vectors $\mathbf{T}_1$ and $\mathbf{T}_4$ about the line joining the end points $\mathbf{V}_1$ and $\mathbf{V}_4$ (see Fig. 7.7).

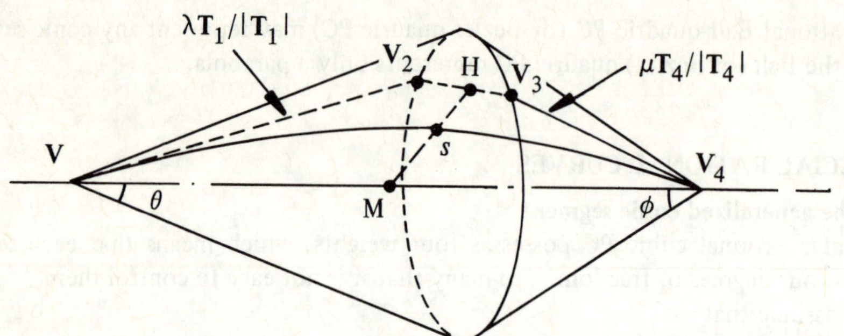

Fig. 7.7 Generalized conic segment

Let the semi-angles of the cones with vertices $\mathbf{V}_1$ and $\mathbf{V}_4$ be θ and ϕ respectively. Then

$$\lambda \cos \theta + \mu \cos \phi = d$$

$$\lambda \sin \theta - \mu \sin \phi = 0$$

where

$$d = |\mathbf{V}_4 - \mathbf{V}_1|$$

Hence

$$\lambda = \frac{d \sin \phi}{\sin (\theta + \phi)}, \qquad \mu = \frac{d \sin \theta}{\sin (\theta + \phi)} \tag{7.26}$$

The curve segment defined by (7.24), (7.25) and (7.26) is the special rational Ball cubic PC bounded by two right circular cones (see Fig. 7.7).

At $u = \frac{1}{2}$ from (7.24) the result is

$$\mathbf{r}\left(\tfrac{1}{2}\right) = (1 - f)\left(\frac{\mathbf{V}_1 + \mathbf{V}_4}{2}\right) + f\left(\frac{\mathbf{V}_2 + \mathbf{V}_3}{2}\right)$$

so the curve segment crosses the line joining the mid-point $M[(\mathbf{V}_1 + \mathbf{V}_4)/2]$ and the mid-point $H[(\mathbf{V}_2 + \mathbf{V}_3)/2]$ at a point which divides MH in the ratio $f:(1-f)$ (see Fig. 7.7). We see that this is a straightforward generalization of the $\rho : (1 - \rho)$ used to specify the fullness of the plane conic curve mentioned in section 7.4.

Thus the special rational cubic PC is called a *generalized conic segment*.

7.5.2 The linear parameter segment

The other special rational cubic PC is the *linear parameter segment* in which a fixed axis direction $\mathbf{n}$ is given. Then the position vector $\mathbf{r}$ of a point on the curve is required to have a component $\mathbf{r} . \mathbf{n}$ which increases linearly with the curve parameter u. Thus

$$\mathbf{r} . \mathbf{n} = k_1(1 - u) + k_2 u \tag{7.27}$$

where k_2 and k_1 are constants $(k_1 \neq k_2)$. Then

$$\mathbf{R} \cdot \mathbf{n} = H(u) \left[k_1 (1-u) + k_2 u \right]$$

where $\mathbf{R} \cdot \mathbf{n}$ is a scalar product of the homogeneous vectors.

By writing down the cubic expressions for $\mathbf{R}(u)$ and $H(u)$, expanding the both sides, setting $H_2 = H_3$ and equating coefficients, the following conditions are obtained for the linear parameter segment:

$$2H_2 (\mathbf{V}_2 - \mathbf{V}_1) \cdot \mathbf{n} = H_1 (\mathbf{V}_4 - \mathbf{V}_1) \cdot \mathbf{n}$$

and

$$2H_3 (\mathbf{V}_3 - \mathbf{V}_4) \cdot \mathbf{n} = H_4 (\mathbf{V}_1 - \mathbf{V}_4) \cdot \mathbf{n}$$

To simplify the use of this segment by setting $H_1 = H_4 = f$ and $H_2 = H_3 = (1-f)$, a simple inear parameter segment is defined in which the user provides values for the end point vectors $\mathbf{V}_1$ and $\mathbf{V}_4$ and corresponding tangent vectors $\mathbf{T}_1$ and $\mathbf{T}_4$ and the f-ratio as described below.

$$\mathbf{V}_2 = \mathbf{V}_1 + \alpha_1 \mathbf{T}_1$$

$$\mathbf{V}_3 = \mathbf{V}_4 - \alpha_4 \mathbf{T}_4 \tag{7.28}$$

where

$$\alpha_1 = \frac{f}{2(1-f)} \frac{(\mathbf{V}_4 - \mathbf{V}_1) \cdot \mathbf{n}}{\mathbf{T}_1 \cdot \mathbf{n}}$$

$$\alpha_4 = \frac{f}{2(1-f)} \frac{(\mathbf{V}_4 - \mathbf{V}_1) \cdot \mathbf{n}}{\mathbf{T}_4 \cdot \mathbf{n}} \tag{7.29}$$

We see that increasing the f-ratio moves $\mathbf{V}_2$ and $\mathbf{V}_3$ farther along the tangents, and thus gives greater fullness to the segment. Note that the linear parameter segment is very important in fitting a curve along the longitudinal direction of the fuselage of an aircraft. A cross-section is just a PC with parameter w, and parameter u is a constant.

7.6 RATIONAL SPLINES

7.6.1 Rational splines

By giving a set of points $\{\mathbf{P}_i\}$ $(i = 0, 1, \ldots, n)$ and tangent vectors at end points $\mathbf{T}_0$ and $\mathbf{T}_n$, and constructing a cubic parametric spline, the tangent vector at any points $\mathbf{T}_i$ $(i = 1, \ldots, n-1)$ can be obtained (see Chapter 4, section 2). We now discuss the rational extension of a cubic parametric spline.

The procedure of rational extension contains the following steps:

1. Calculating the coefficients λ_i, μ_i according to formula (7.26), because points $\mathbf{P}_{i-1}$ and $\mathbf{P}_i$ and tangent vectors $\mathbf{T}_{i-1}$ and $\mathbf{T}_i$ are provided by the fitting of a cubic parametric spline

$$\lambda_i = \frac{d_i \sin \phi_i}{\sin (\theta_{i-1} + \phi_i)}$$

$$\mu_i = \frac{d_i \sin \theta_{i-1}}{\sin (\theta_{i-1} + \phi_i)} \qquad (7.30)$$

where $d_i = |\mathbf{P}_i - \mathbf{P}_{i-1}|$.

θ_{i-1} and ϕ_i are the angles between the chord and tangents (see Fig. 7.8).

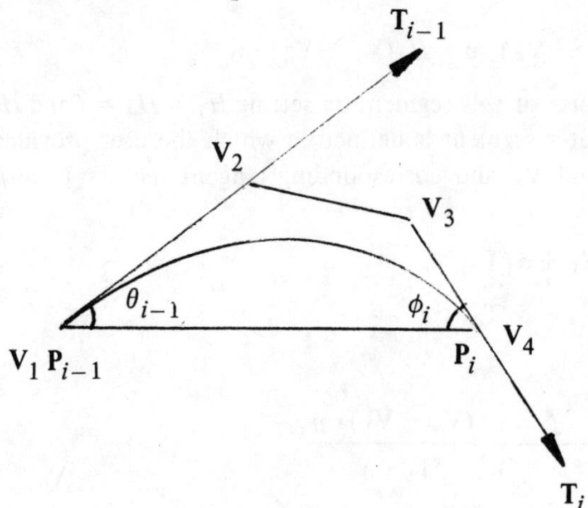

Fig. 7.8 Segment of rational spline

2. Calculating the vertices of the generalized conic segment, according to formula (7.25)

$$\mathbf{V}_2 = \mathbf{V}_1 + \lambda_i\, \mathbf{T}_{i-1} / |\mathbf{T}_{i-1}|$$

$$\mathbf{V}_3 = \mathbf{V}_4 - \mu_i\, \mathbf{T}_i / |\mathbf{T}_i|$$

where

$$\mathbf{V}_1 = \mathbf{P}_{i-1} \quad \text{and} \quad \mathbf{V}_4 = \mathbf{P}_i$$

3. Calculating any points of the segment for numerically controlled draughting according to the formula (7.24).

   Steps 1–3 are repeated for each segment ($i = 1, \ldots, n$).

4. The designer now works with the rational spline, changing individual values of f_i to adjust the initial curve into what he considers to be a more satisfactory shape. If $f = 0.5$, the rational spline curve is reduced to the ordinary spline curve.

These steps form a procedure in which the cubic parametric spline is extended to the rational cubic parametric spline that possesses the flexibilities for controlling the shape; consequently some of the latest surface modelling systems employ the rational spline.

7.6.2 The rational fitting of circular arcs and straight lines

A plane curve consists of N segments of circular arcs and straight lines, which are tangent to each other (see Fig. 7.9). A set of points $\{P_i\}$ $(i = 0, 1, \ldots, n)$ including the starting point P_0, tangent points $\{P_i\}$ $(i = 1, \ldots, n - 1)$ and end point P_n should be provided by the designer. They may be fitted by using the rational functions.

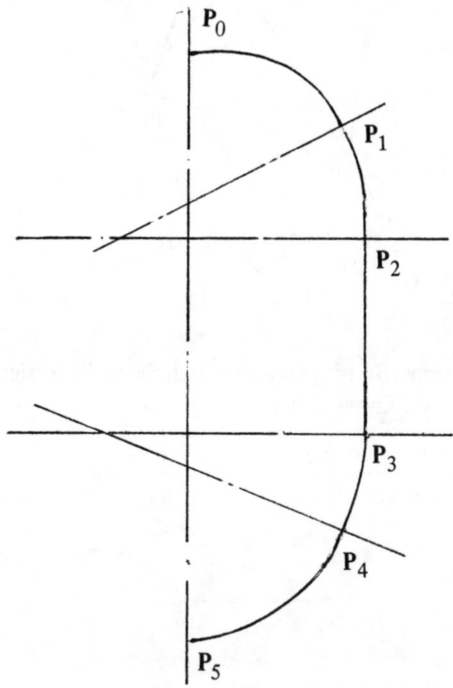

Fig. 7.9 A section

We have mentioned in section 7.4 that when $H_2 = H_3$, and $V_2 = V_3$, the rational cubic curve is reduced to the rational quadric curve.

Since three vertices define a plane, a quadric curve is always a plane curve. Moreover, a circular arc is rational; for symmetry reasons the distances of A from P_{i-1} and P_i should be equal; see Fig. 7.10.

The argument above shows that the circular arcs may be represented by using the rational functions.

Take the circular arc $P_{i-1}P_i$ as an example, as shown in Fig. 7.10.

If we suppose that the unit tangent vector T_{i-1} at point P_{i-1} of the circular arc $P_{i-1}P_i$ is known, and setting

$$Q_i = P_i - P_{i-1}$$

the angle β_i between the tangent vector T_{i-1} and the chord vector Q_i may be calculated by using the scalar product of T_{i-1} and Q_i, that is

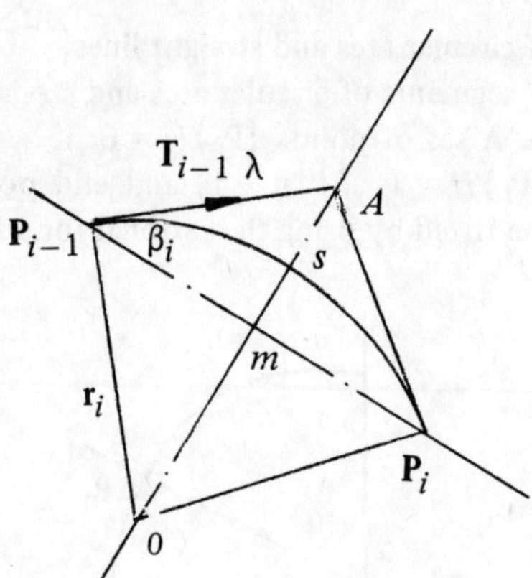

Fig. 7.10 A circular arc

$$\cos \beta_i = \frac{\mathbf{T}_{i-1} \cdot \mathbf{Q}_i}{|\mathbf{Q}_i|}$$

Then according to the geometric properties of a circle and the significance of parameter f mentioned in section 7.4 we know that

$$f_i = \frac{sm}{Am} = \frac{r_i\,(1 - \cos \beta_i)}{\lambda_i \sin \beta_i}$$

because

$$\frac{r_i}{\lambda_i} = \frac{\cos \beta_i}{\sin \beta_i}$$

thus

$$f_i = \frac{(1 - \cos \beta_i) \cdot \cos \beta_i}{(\sin \beta_i)^2} = \frac{(1 - \cos \beta_i) \cdot \cos \beta_i}{1 - (\cos \beta_i)^2} = \frac{\cos \beta_i}{1 + \cos \beta_i} \qquad (7.31)$$

According to the symmetry property, we obtain

$$\lambda_i = \mu_i = \frac{|\mathbf{Q}_i|}{2 \cos \beta_i} \qquad (7.32)$$

Finally, the generalized conic segment defined by equations (7.24), (7.25) (7.31) and (7.32) represents the circular arc exactly.

According to the vector relationship shown in Fig. 7.10 and equation (7.32) we obtain

$$\mathbf{Q}_i = \lambda_i \cdot \mathbf{T}_{i-1} + \mu_i \cdot \mathbf{T}_i$$

thus

$$\mathbf{T}_i = \frac{\mathbf{Q}_i}{\lambda_i} - \mathbf{T}_{i-1} \qquad (7.33)$$

$\mathbf{T}_i$ $(i = 1, \ldots, n)$ may be calculated by using (7.33) in order.

These equations for circular arcs are also efficient for a straight line.

It has been proved that the formulae for a generalized conic segment may represent exactly cubic splines, general conics (ellipse, hyperbola, parabola), circular arcs and straight lines. The aircraft configuration drawing and manual lofting consist only of these curves. There is a wide range of applications, since one form can represent both conic and cubic curves.

7.7 RATIONAL SURFACES

As we know, the PC form is defined by straight polynomials, but a generalization of the straight polynomial produces the rational PC form.

The rational PC form as the following advantages:

- It contains a greater supply of shapes than straight polynomials.
- Conic sections can be represented exactly in rational form.
- Simple matrix representations exist in homogeneous coordinates.

The rational form in modelling provides greater flexibility of shapes. Some of the surface modelling of the latest generation based on the rational form has already been applied in practice. Great care has been taken in providing the associated geometric database and the intelligent user interfaces for driving the rational form systems.

In this section we will give a brief survey of rational surfaces; two aspects will be emphasized: how to choose weights and how to apply rational surfaces.

7.7.1 Rational surface patch with sixteen weights

The rational bi-cubic surface patch is a rational extension of a bi-cubic parametric surface patch, as each vertex $\mathbf{V}_{i,j}$ of the characteristic polyhedron is assigned a weight $H_{i,j}$ $(i = 1, 2, 3, 4; j = 1, 2, 3, 4)$ (see Fig. 7.11). The general rational surface patch is defined by rational polynomials, that is, by the algebraic ratio of two polynomial functions. It may be described as an equation of the homogeneous coordinate form.

$$\mathbf{R}(u, w) = \begin{bmatrix} 1 & u & u^2 & u^3 \end{bmatrix} M_{bl} \begin{bmatrix} H_{11}\mathbf{V}_{11} & H_{12}\mathbf{V}_{12} & H_{13}\mathbf{V}_{13} & H_{14}\mathbf{V}_{14} \\ H_{21}\mathbf{V}_{21} & H_{22}\mathbf{V}_{22} & H_{23}\mathbf{V}_{23} & H_{24}\mathbf{V}_{24} \\ H_{31}\mathbf{V}_{31} & H_{32}\mathbf{V}_{32} & H_{33}\mathbf{V}_{33} & H_{34}\mathbf{V}_{34} \\ H_{41}\mathbf{V}_{41} & H_{42}\mathbf{V}_{42} & H_{43}\mathbf{V}_{43} & H_{44}\mathbf{V}_{44} \end{bmatrix}$$

$$M_{bl}^{\mathrm{T}} \begin{bmatrix} 1 \\ w \\ w^2 \\ w^3 \end{bmatrix} \tag{7.34}$$

Its fourth coordinate is

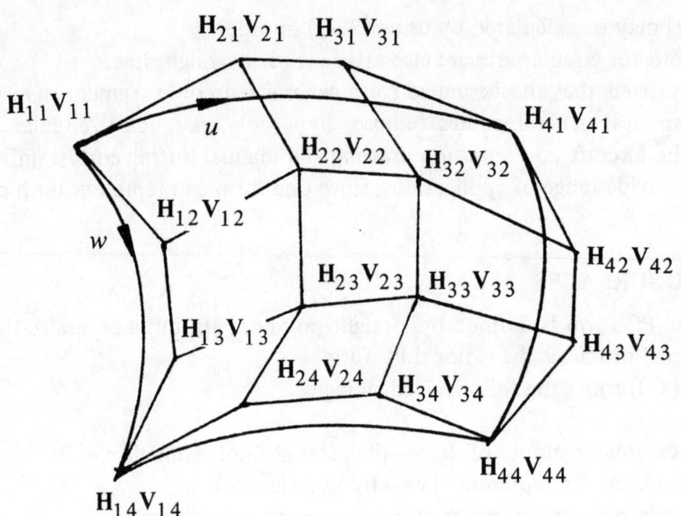

Fig. 7.11

$$H(u, w) = \begin{bmatrix} 1 & u & u^2 & u^3 \end{bmatrix} M_{bl} \begin{bmatrix} H_{11} & H_{12} & H_{13} & H_{14} \\ H_{21} & H_{22} & H_{23} & H_{24} \\ H_{31} & H_{32} & H_{33} & H_{34} \\ H_{41} & H_{42} & H_{43} & H_{44} \end{bmatrix} M_{bl}^{\mathrm{T}} \begin{bmatrix} 1 \\ w \\ w^2 \\ w^3 \end{bmatrix}$$

(7.35)

Then the equation of a rational surface patch may be expressed as

$$\mathbf{r}(u, w) = \frac{\mathbf{R}(u, w)}{H(u, w)}$$

(7.36)

in which numerator $\mathbf{R}(u, w)$ stands for (7.34), and denominator $H(u, w)$ stands for (7.35). The first three coordinates of $\mathbf{r}(u, w)$ are Cartesian coordinates of the rational surface patch.

Replacing M_{bl}, M_{bl}^{T} in equations (7.34), (7.35) by M_{be}, $M_{\mathrm{be}}^{\mathrm{T}}$ and M_b, M_b^{T}, we can obtain the rational Bezier surface patch and the rational B-spline surface patch, respectively.

We can see that 16 weights $H_{i,j}$ ($i = 1, 2, 3, 2$; $j = 1, 2, 3, 4$) are involved in the patch definition, so the rational bi-cubic surface patch is more flexible.

It is evident that great flexibility results from the use of the rational polynomial patch. One problem which arises is that the very generality of these functions presents difficulties in the design of a practical system for specifying surfaces. It is required that any such system can be operated by a non-mathematician, and also it is necessary that it should be obvious how all the available degrees of freedom can be incorporated into the system so that each has a clear geometrical significance.

7.7.2 Rational surface patch with eight weights

We examine now the rational surface patch in the way described in section 6.8.

Ball curves are related to Ball surface patches in exactly the same way as B-spline curves are related to B-spline surface patches.

Firstly using four vertices, which are matrix elements in the same column, to define a span of a Ball cubic PC, we obtain its matrix representation as follows:

$$\mathbf{S}_j(u) = [\,1 \quad u \quad u^2 \quad u^3\,]\, M_{\mathrm{b1}} \begin{bmatrix} \mathbf{V}_{1j} \\ \mathbf{V}_{2j} \\ \mathbf{V}_{3j} \\ \mathbf{V}_{4j} \end{bmatrix} \qquad (0 \leqslant u \leqslant 1;\; j = 1, 2, 3, 4)$$

Selecting any value of parameter u between 0 and 1, we can regard $\mathbf{S}_j(u)\,(j = 1, 2, 3, 4)$ as four vertices of the characteristic polygon and then construct a span of a Ball curve with parameter w.

$$\mathbf{r}(u, w) = [\,\mathbf{S}_1(u) \quad \mathbf{S}_2(u) \quad \mathbf{S}_3(u) \quad \mathbf{S}_4(u)\,]\, M_{bl}^{\mathrm{T}} \begin{bmatrix} 1 \\ w \\ w^2 \\ w^3 \end{bmatrix}$$

or

$$= [\,1 \quad u \quad u^2 \quad u^3\,]\, M_{bl}\, \mathbf{V} M_{bl}^{\mathrm{T}} \begin{bmatrix} 1 \\ w \\ w^2 \\ w^3 \end{bmatrix} \tag{7.37}$$

where

$$\mathbf{V} = \{\mathbf{V}_{i,j}\} \quad (i = 1, 2, 3, 4;\; j = 1, 2, 3, 4)$$

is a matrix of vertices of a characteristic polyhedron. The parameters u and w can vary independently between zero and one in formula (7.37), which is a representation of the Ball bi-cubic surface patch.

The rational extension of a Ball surface is closely related to the corresponding rational extension of a Ball curve. We may therefore construct a rational Ball bi-cubic parametric surface patch — first by constructing four rational Ball cubic PC segments with parameter u. Their matrix representation may be described in the form

$$\mathbf{r}_j(u) = [\,1 \quad u \quad u^2 \quad u^3\,]\, M_{bl} \begin{bmatrix} (1 - g_j)\,\mathbf{V}_{1j} \\ g_j \qquad \mathbf{V}_{2j} \\ g_j \qquad \mathbf{V}_{3j} \\ (1 - g_j)\,\mathbf{V}_{4j} \end{bmatrix} \Big/ H(u) \tag{7.38}$$

$$(0 \leqslant u \leqslant 1;\; j = 1, 2, 3, 4)$$

Selecting any value of parameter u between zero and one, we also regard $\mathbf{r}_j(u)$ $(j = 1, 2, 3, 4)$ as four vertices of the characteristic polygon and then construct a span of a rational Ball curve with parameter w:

$$\mathbf{r}(u, w) = \begin{bmatrix} 1 & w & w^2 & w^3 \end{bmatrix} M_{bl} \begin{bmatrix} (1 - f(u))\,\mathbf{r}_1(u) \\ f(u)\,\mathbf{r}_2(u) \\ f(u)\,\mathbf{r}_3(u) \\ (1 - f(u))\,\mathbf{r}_4(u) \end{bmatrix} \Big/ H(u, w) \tag{7.39}$$

where the denominator of the above equation is

$$H(u, w) = \begin{bmatrix} 1 & w & w^2 & w^3 \end{bmatrix} M_{bl} \begin{bmatrix} 1 - f(u) \\ f(u) \\ f(u) \\ 1 - f(u) \end{bmatrix} \tag{7.40}$$

and $f(u)$ in equations (7.39) and (7.40) may be defined as

$$f(u) = \begin{bmatrix} 1 & u & u^2 & u^3 \end{bmatrix} M_{bl} \begin{bmatrix} f_1 \\ f_2 \\ f_3 \\ f_4 \end{bmatrix} \tag{7.41}$$

Note that the g_j $(j = 1, 2, 3, 4)$ f_i $(i = 1, 2, 3, 4)$ are weights with directions u and w respectively as shape-modifying parameters, as shown in Fig. 7.12.

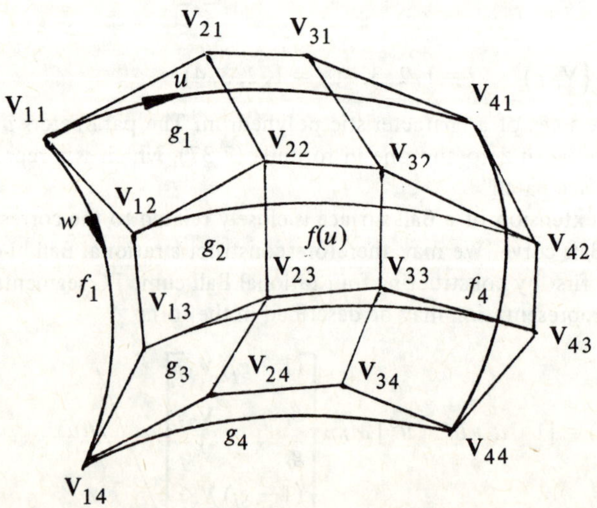

Fig. 7.12

The rational surface patch defined by (7.38)–(7.41) has the properties that the patch corners coincide with the polyhedron vertices V_{11}, V_{14}, V_{41} and V_{44}, while the tangent vectors r_u and r_w at the patch corners are in the directions of the corresponding polyhedron edges, and that each of its boundary curves is a rational curve whose weights are g_1, g_4, f_1 and f_4, respectively.

Replacing M_{bl} in equations (7.38)–(7.41) by M_{be} and M_b, we can correspondingly obtain the rational Bezier and B-spline surface patches respectively.

Eight weights – g_j $(j = 1, 2, 3, 4)$ and f_i $(i = 1, 2, 3, 4)$ – have obvious geometrical significance (see Fig. 7.12), the g_j as shape-modifying parameters in the u direction, and f_i in the w direction. Eight weights are also too many for convenient adjustment of a surface patch.

7.7.3 Rational surface patch with four weights

When $g_j = \frac{1}{2}$ $(j = 1, 2, 3, 4)$, equations (7.38) are reduced to a Ball cubic PC. In this case, equations (7.39)–(7.41) represent only the rational surface patch with four weights f_i $(i = 1, 2, 3, 4)$.

It is evident that boundaries $r(u, 0)$ and $r(u, 1)$ are fixed but boundaries $r(0, w)$ and $r(1, w)$ may be adjusted, and that the surface patch may be adjusted only in the w direction (see Fig. 7.13).

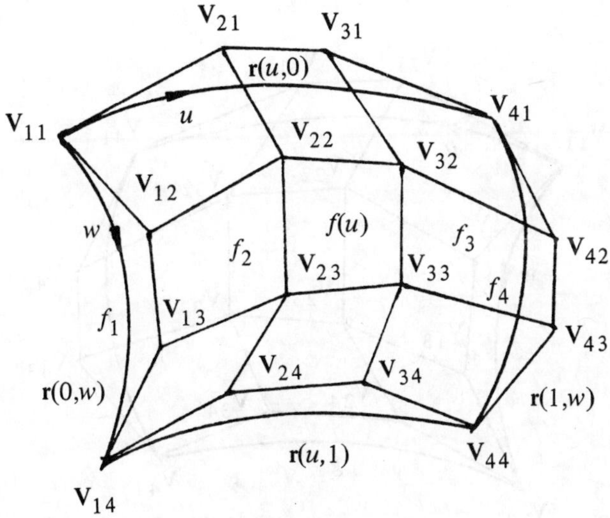

Fig. 7.13

7.7.4 Rational surface patch with two weights

When $g_j = g$ $(j = 1, 2, 3, 4)$ and $f_i = f$ $(i = 1, 2, 3, 4)$, g and f are positive-valued constants, we obtain from (7.41) and (7.40)

$$f(u) = f \tag{7.42}$$

and

$$H(u, w) = H(w)$$

then we obtain from (7.38) and (7.39)

$$r_j(u) = \begin{bmatrix} 1 & u & u^2 & u^3 \end{bmatrix} M_{bl} \begin{bmatrix} (1-g)\,\mathbf{V}_{1j} \\ g\mathbf{V}_{2j} \\ g\mathbf{V}_{3j} \\ (1-g)\,\mathbf{V}_{4j} \end{bmatrix} \Big/ H(u) \tag{7.43}$$

and

$$r(u, w) = \begin{bmatrix} 1 & w & w^2 & w^3 \end{bmatrix} M_{bl} \begin{bmatrix} (1-f)\,\mathbf{r}_1(u) \\ f\,\mathbf{r}_2(u) \\ f\,\mathbf{r}_3(u) \\ (1-f)\,\mathbf{r}_4(u) \end{bmatrix} \Big/ H(w) \tag{7.44}$$

The shape-modifying parameters g and f control the shape of the surface patch in the u direction and w direction; they have a fairly obvious geometrical significance (see Fig. 7.14). It is very easy for the user to control them.

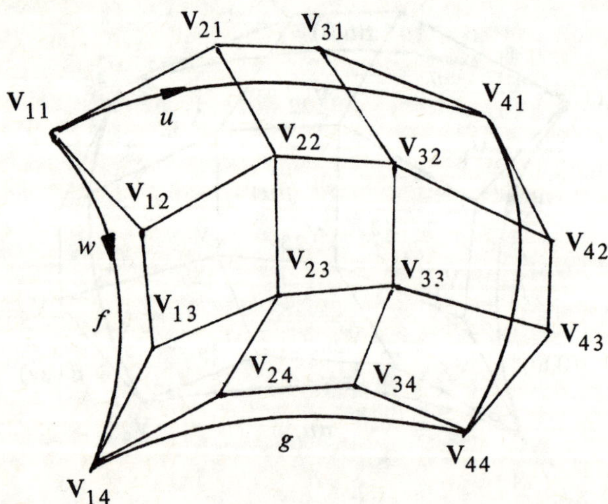

Fig. 7.14

7.7.5 Applications

In aircraft configuration drawings, a number of plane curves are defined at specific controlling sections, and a smooth surface is constructed through by joining them with longitudinal stream lines (see Fig. 7.15).

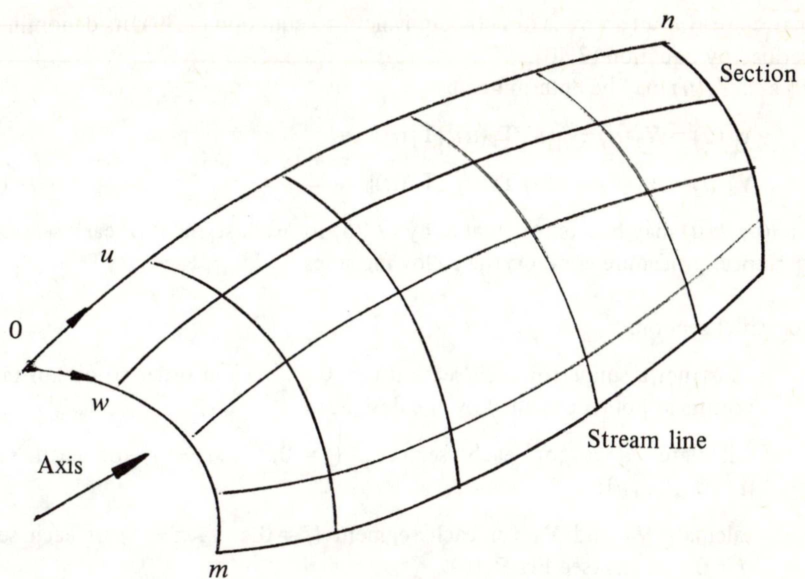

Fig. 7.15 Surfaces of an aircraft

The total surface would be divided into a range of surface patches by a number of net-lines. Curves on each controlling section act as the cross-net-lines which are arranged from 0 to N. Some specific points from each controlling section are taken, and corresponding points located on each controlling section are connected to form a range of longitudinal net-lines. The sequential numbers of these net-lines are arranged from 0 to m. Then the surface is consequently divided into $m \times n$ surface patches, or m stripes (see Fig. 7.15).

Ball (formerly of British Aircraft Corporation) described in his CONSURF system composite rational surfaces that are built up from the two types of rational cubic PC discussed in section 7.5. Smooth composite generalized conic sections are blended together by linear parameter segments. Each stripe of the surface is computed from the segmented rational end point lines $\mathbf{V}_i(u)$ and $\mathbf{V}_{i+1}(u)$, the hard point line $\mathbf{T}_i(u)$ and the should line $\mathbf{S}_i(u)$.

Ball's 'lofting' principle is similar to a draughtsman's working method.

Li JianXin (Chengdu Aircraft Corporation, China) described in the C-SURF system composite rational surfaces that can be denoted in the form

$$r(u,\, w) = \mathbf{R}(u,\, w)/H(u,\, w) \tag{7.45}$$

in which

$$\mathbf{R}(u,\, w) = \begin{bmatrix} 1 & w & w^2 & w^3 \end{bmatrix} M_{bl} \begin{bmatrix} (1 - f(u))\,\mathbf{V}_1(u) \\ f(u) \qquad \mathbf{V}_2(u) \\ f(u) \qquad \mathbf{V}_3(u) \\ (1 - f(u))\,\mathbf{V}_4(u) \end{bmatrix} \tag{7.46}$$

The equation of $\mathbf{r}(u, w)$ above is directly equivalent to equation (7.39); its denominator is still described by equation (7.40).

$\mathbf{V}_2(u)$ and $\mathbf{V}_3(u)$ may be determined by

$$\mathbf{V}_2(u) = \mathbf{V}_1(u) + \lambda(u)\, \mathbf{T}_1(u)/|\mathbf{T}_1(u)|$$

$$\mathbf{V}_3(u) = \mathbf{V}_4(u) - \mu(u)\, \mathbf{T}_4(u)/|\mathbf{T}_4(u)| \qquad (7.47)$$

in which $\lambda(u)$, $\mu(u)$ may be first calculated by (7.26) for each segment of each section.

The practical procedure contains the following steps:

1.　Construct sections:

- construct a spline for each section ($i = 0, \ldots, n$) in order to obtain tangent vectors at points provided by the designer;

- Calculate λ, μ for each segment ($j = 0, \ldots, m - 1$) of each section ($i = 0, \ldots, n$);

- calculate $\mathbf{V}_2$ and $\mathbf{V}_3$ for each segment ($j = 0, \ldots, m - 1$) of each section ($i = 0, \ldots, n$) (see Fig. 7.16).

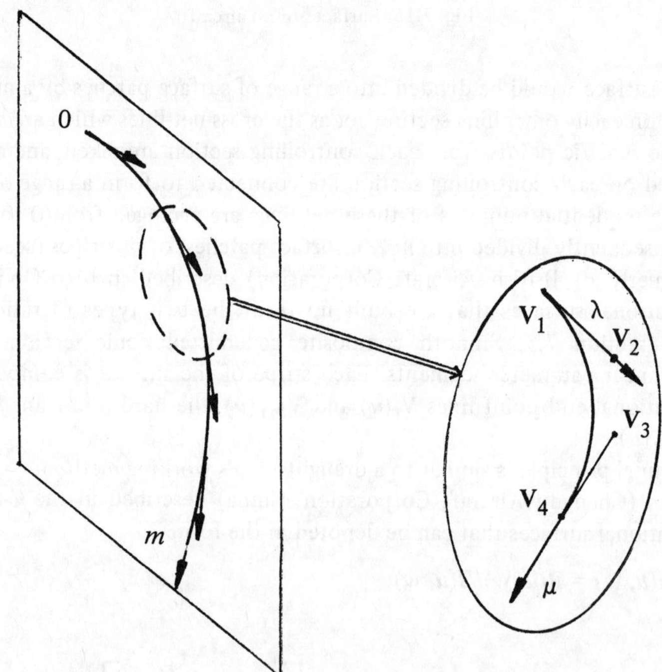

Fig. 7.16　A section

2.　Construct longitudinal stream lines:

- construct $\mathbf{V}_1(u)$ and $\mathbf{V}_4(u)$ mentioned in section 7.5.2;

- construct $\mathbf{V}_2(u)$ and $\mathbf{V}_3(u)$;

- Construct $\mathbf{F}(u) = [\,f(u)\ \ \lambda(u)\ \ \mu(u)\,]$ $f(u)$, $\lambda(u)$ and $\mu(u)$ may be assumed to be the three components of an imaginary vector $\mathbf{F}(u)$.

  Then each stripe of the surface has five longitudinal curves, which are $\mathbf{V}_1(u)$, $\mathbf{V}_4(u)$, $\mathbf{V}_2(u)$, $\mathbf{V}_3(u)$ and $\mathbf{F}(u)$. They are all cubic splines or linear parameter segments (see Fig. 7.17).

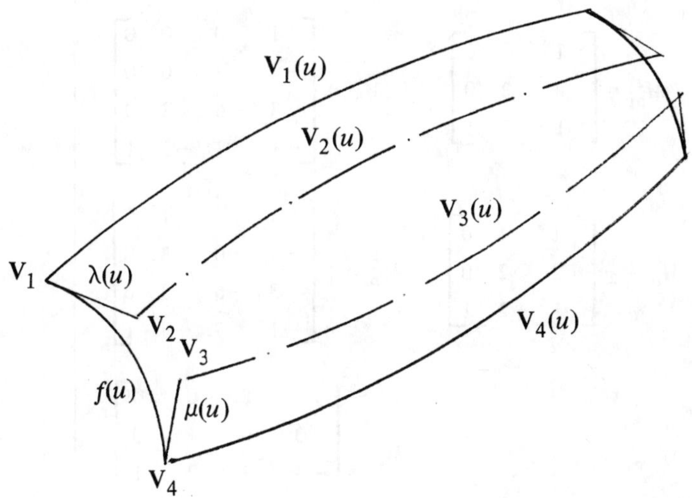

Fig. 7.17 A stripe of a rational surface

3.   Construct rational surfaces:

   each surface patch may be defined by equations (7.45)–(7.47).

4.   The designer now shapes the rational surface, to adjust the initial surface into what he considers to be a more satisfactory shape.

Finally, the computer uses the rational surfaces to calculate any information on the surface for draughting or machining.

We now see that rational surfaces may be constructed by choosing different blending functions and different numbers of weights, as needed in practical engineering. This is why there are many different rational surface systems on the market. The non-uniform rational B-spline surface is perhaps the latest method for surface modelling. The NURBS system by Computervision is of this type. Moreover, the rational surface in modelling provides greater flexibility of shapes for all geometric entities from ruled surfaces through sculptured surfaces to solid modelling, but this is beyond the scope of this text.

7.8 FAMILY OF RATIONAL CURVES IN CAGD (APPENDIX)

See pages 206–208.

Coefficient matrix of blending functions

$$M_{bl}^2 = \begin{bmatrix} 1 & 0 & 0 \\ -2 & 2 & 0 \\ 1 & -2 & 1 \end{bmatrix} \qquad M_{bl}^3 = \begin{bmatrix} 1 & 0 & 0 & 0 \\ -2 & 2 & 0 & 0 \\ 1 & -4 & 2 & 1 \\ 0 & 2 & -2 & 0 \end{bmatrix}$$

$$M_{be}^2 = \begin{bmatrix} 1 & 0 & 0 \\ -2 & 2 & 0 \\ 1 & -2 & 1 \end{bmatrix} \qquad M_{be}^3 = \begin{bmatrix} 1 & 0 & 0 & 0 \\ -3 & 3 & 0 & 0 \\ 3 & -6 & 3 & 0 \\ -1 & 3 & -3 & 1 \end{bmatrix}$$

$$M_b^2 = \tfrac{1}{2}\begin{bmatrix} 1 & 1 & 0 \\ -2 & 2 & 0 \\ 1 & -2 & 1 \end{bmatrix} \qquad M_b^3 = \tfrac{1}{6}\begin{bmatrix} 1 & 4 & 1 & 0 \\ -3 & 0 & 3 & 0 \\ 3 & -6 & 3 & 0 \\ -1 & 3 & -3 & 1 \end{bmatrix}$$

$$M_c = \begin{bmatrix} 1 & 0 & 0 & 0 \\ 0 & 0 & 1 & 0 \\ -3 & 3 & -2 & -1 \\ 2 & -2 & 1 & 1 \end{bmatrix}$$

Generalized conic segment
$$\begin{cases} \mathbf{V}_2 = \mathbf{V}_1 + \lambda\mathbf{T}_1/|\mathbf{T}_1| \\ \mathbf{V}_3 = \mathbf{V}_4 - \mu\mathbf{T}_4/|\mathbf{T}_4| \end{cases}$$

$$\mathbf{r}(u) = [1 \quad u \quad u^2 \quad u^3]M_{bl}^3\begin{bmatrix} (1-f)\mathbf{V}_1 \\ f\mathbf{V}_2 \\ f\mathbf{V}_3 \\ (1-f)\mathbf{V}_4 \end{bmatrix} \Bigg/ [1 \quad u \quad u^2 \quad u^3]M_{bl}^3\begin{bmatrix} 1-f \\ f \\ f \\ 1-f \end{bmatrix}$$

$$H_1 = H_4 = 1 - f$$

Linear parameter segment
$$\begin{cases} \mathbf{V}_1 = \mathbf{V}_1 + \alpha_1\mathbf{T}_1/|\mathbf{T}_1| \\ \mathbf{V}_3 = \mathbf{V}_4 - \alpha_4\mathbf{T}_4/|\mathbf{T}_4| \end{cases}$$

$$\mathbf{r}(u) = [1 \quad u \quad u^2 \quad u^3]M_{bl}^3\begin{bmatrix} f\mathbf{V}_1 \\ (1-f)\mathbf{V}_2 \\ (1-f)\mathbf{V}_3 \\ f\mathbf{V}_4 \end{bmatrix} \Bigg/ [1 \quad u \quad u^2 \quad u^3]M_{bl}^3\begin{bmatrix} f \\ 1-f \\ 1-f \\ f \end{bmatrix}$$

$$H_2 = H_3 = 1 - f$$

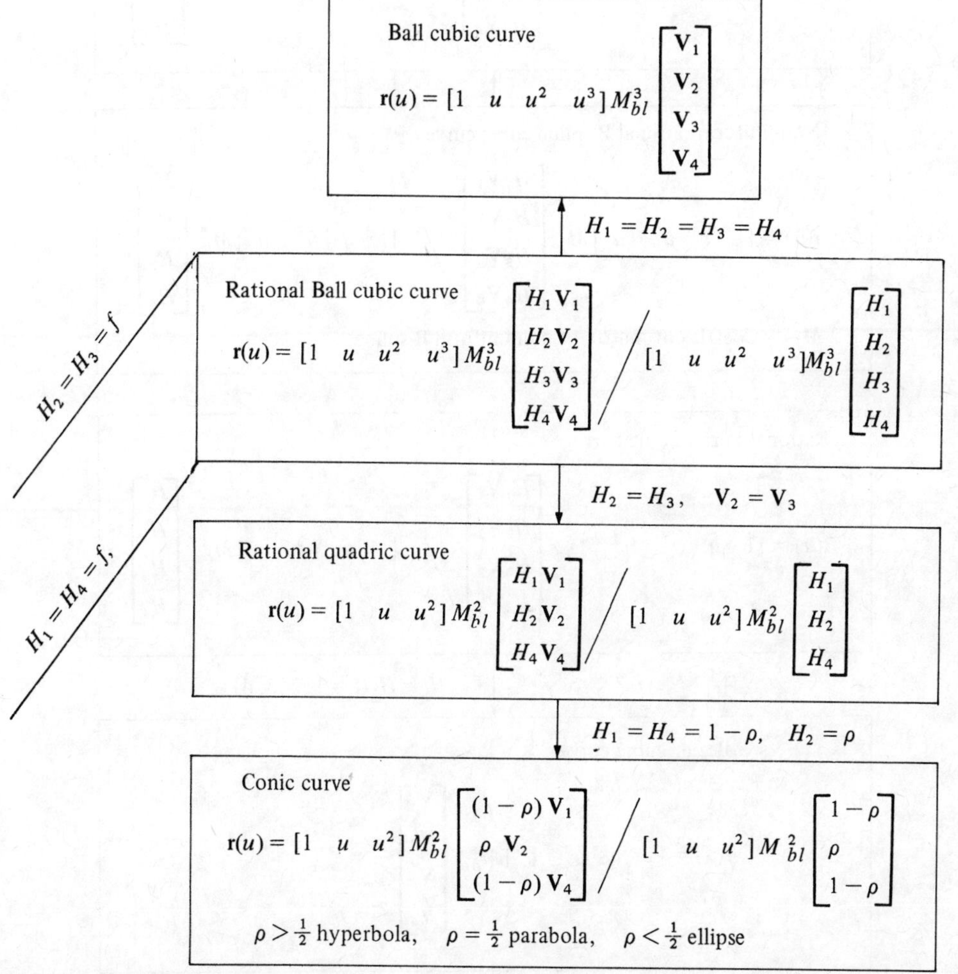
Ball cubic curve

$$\mathbf{r}(u) = \begin{bmatrix} 1 & u & u^2 & u^3 \end{bmatrix} M_{bl}^3 \begin{bmatrix} \mathbf{V}_1 \\ \mathbf{V}_2 \\ \mathbf{V}_3 \\ \mathbf{V}_4 \end{bmatrix}$$

$H_1 = H_2 = H_3 = H_4$

Rational Ball cubic curve

$$\mathbf{r}(u) = \begin{bmatrix} 1 & u & u^2 & u^3 \end{bmatrix} M_{bl}^3 \begin{bmatrix} H_1\mathbf{V}_1 \\ H_2\mathbf{V}_2 \\ H_3\mathbf{V}_3 \\ H_4\mathbf{V}_4 \end{bmatrix} \Big/ \begin{bmatrix} 1 & u & u^2 & u^3 \end{bmatrix} M_{bl}^3 \begin{bmatrix} H_1 \\ H_2 \\ H_3 \\ H_4 \end{bmatrix}$$

$H_2 = H_3 = f$

$H_2 = H_3, \quad \mathbf{V}_2 = \mathbf{V}_3$

Rational quadric curve

$$\mathbf{r}(u) = \begin{bmatrix} 1 & u & u^2 \end{bmatrix} M_{bl}^2 \begin{bmatrix} H_1\mathbf{V}_1 \\ H_2\mathbf{V}_2 \\ H_4\mathbf{V}_4 \end{bmatrix} \Big/ \begin{bmatrix} 1 & u & u^2 \end{bmatrix} M_{bl}^2 \begin{bmatrix} H_1 \\ H_2 \\ H_4 \end{bmatrix}$$

$H_1 = H_4 = f,$

$H_1 = H_4 = 1 - \rho, \quad H_2 = \rho$

Conic curve

$$\mathbf{r}(u) = \begin{bmatrix} 1 & u & u^2 \end{bmatrix} M_{bl}^2 \begin{bmatrix} (1-\rho)\mathbf{V}_1 \\ \rho\,\mathbf{V}_2 \\ (1-\rho)\mathbf{V}_4 \end{bmatrix} \Big/ \begin{bmatrix} 1 & u & u^2 \end{bmatrix} M_{bl}^2 \begin{bmatrix} 1-\rho \\ \rho \\ 1-\rho \end{bmatrix}$$

$\rho > \tfrac{1}{2}$ hyperbola, $\quad \rho = \tfrac{1}{2}$ parabola, $\quad \rho < \tfrac{1}{2}$ ellipse

B-spline cubic curve

$$\mathbf{r}(u) = \begin{bmatrix} 1 & u & u^2 & u^3 \end{bmatrix} M_b^3 \begin{bmatrix} \mathbf{V}_1 \\ \mathbf{V}_2 \\ \mathbf{V}_3 \\ \mathbf{V}_4 \end{bmatrix}$$

$H_i = H \ (i = 1, 2, 3, 4)$

Rational B-spline cubic curve

$$\mathbf{r}(u) = \begin{bmatrix} 1 & u & u^2 & u^3 \end{bmatrix} M_b^3 \begin{bmatrix} H_1\mathbf{V}_1 \\ H_2\mathbf{V}_2 \\ H_3\mathbf{V}_3 \\ H_4\mathbf{V}_4 \end{bmatrix} \Bigg/ \begin{bmatrix} 1 & u & u^2 & u^3 \end{bmatrix} M_b^3 \begin{bmatrix} H_1 \\ H_2 \\ H_3 \\ H_4 \end{bmatrix}$$

Non-uniform rational B-spline cubic curve

$$\mathbf{r}(u) = \begin{bmatrix} 1 & u & u^2 & u^3 \end{bmatrix} M_b^* \begin{bmatrix} H_1\mathbf{V}_1 \\ H_2\mathbf{V}_2 \\ H_3\mathbf{V}_3 \\ H_4\mathbf{V}_4 \end{bmatrix} \Bigg/ \begin{bmatrix} 1 & u & u^2 & u^3 \end{bmatrix} M_b^* \begin{bmatrix} H_1 \\ H_2 \\ H_3 \\ H_4 \end{bmatrix}$$

M_B^* – Coefficient matrix of non-uniform B-spline

Rational Bezier cubic curve

$$\mathbf{r}(u) = \begin{bmatrix} 1 & u & u^2 & u^3 \end{bmatrix} M_{be}^3 \begin{bmatrix} H_1\mathbf{V}_1 \\ H_2\mathbf{V}_2 \\ H_3\mathbf{V}_3 \\ H_4\mathbf{V}_4 \end{bmatrix} \Bigg/ \begin{bmatrix} 1 & u & u^2 & u^3 \end{bmatrix} M_{be}^3 \begin{bmatrix} H_1 \\ H_2 \\ H_3 \\ H_4 \end{bmatrix}$$

$H_i = H \ (i = 1, 2, 3, 4)$

Bezier cubic curve

$$\mathbf{r}(u) = \begin{bmatrix} 1 & u & u^2 & u^3 \end{bmatrix} M_{be}^3 \begin{bmatrix} \mathbf{V}_1 \\ \mathbf{V}_2 \\ \mathbf{V}_3 \\ \mathbf{V}_4 \end{bmatrix}$$

REFERENCES

[1] Ball, A.D., CONSURF Part 1: Introduction of the conic lofting tile, *Computer-aided Design,* **6**, No. 4 (1974), 243–249.

[2] Ball, A.A., CONSURF Part 2: Description of the algorithms, *Computer-aided Design,* **7**, No. 4 (1975), 237–242.

[3] Ball, A.A., CONSURF Part 3: How the program is used, *Computer-aided Design,* **9**, No. 1 (1977), 9–12.

[4] Ball, A.A., A simple specification of the parametric cubic segment, *Computer-aided Design,* **10**, No. 3 (1978), 181–182.

[5] Faux, I.D. and Pratt, M.J., *Computational Geometry for Design and Manufacture,* Ellis Horwood, Chichester, 1985.

[6] Mortensen, M.E., *Geometric Modelling,* John Wiley and Sons, New York, 1985.

[7] Versprille, K.J., Computer-aided design applications of the rational B-spline approximation form, *Diss.*, Syracuse University, 1975.

[8] Böehm, W., Frain, G. and Kahmann, J., *A Survey of Curve and Surface Methods in CAGD,* Elsevier, B. V. North-Holland, Amsterdam, 1984.

[9] Tiller, W., Rational B-splines for curves and surface representation. IEEE Computer Graphics and Applications, **3**, No. 6 (1983), 61–69.

8

Fairing of Curves and Surfaces

8.1 CONCEPTS OF FAIRING

8.1.1 Design and fairing

Modern vehicles such as aircraft, ship hulls or cars possess an aesthetic contour shape. The development of the contour shape definition generally proceeds through first the design and then the fairing of the contour shape. During the design stage, an initial contour shape is generated, usually to a relatively small scale, in accordance with given form requirements. The objective of this stage is primarily to meet the desired shape characteristics and to try to reconcile potentially conflicting requirements. The fairing stage has a different principal objective, which is to refine the shape quality in terms of some criteria of surface fairness or smoothness while conserving the significant shape characteristics. In other industries, a similar two-stage process is observed (see Fig. 8.1).

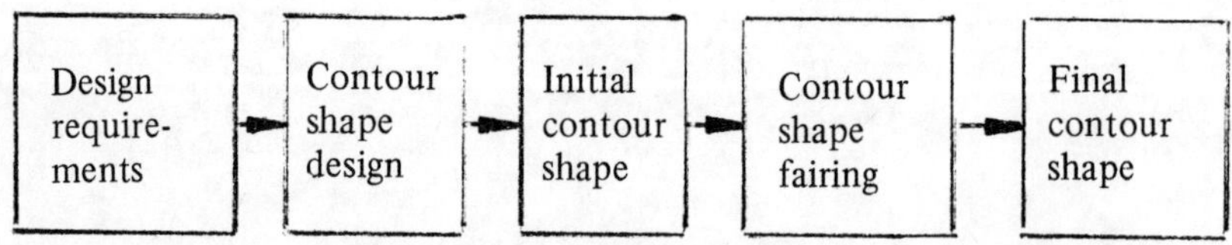

Fig. 8.1 Design and fairing

8.1.2 Mathematical fairing

Before the days of computers, vehicles such as ship hulls or aircraft fuselages were usually designed in terms of parallel plane cross-sections at a number of longitudinal stations.

Once these curves were specified, longitudinal curves were constructed to blend them together into a three-dimensional shape. Traditionally, these curves were drawn, usually to relatively small scale at the design stage, or full size at the fairing stage, with the assistance of *mechanical splines*. The techniques of manual fairing of these curves were based on the experience developed by skilful draughtsmen over many centuries in the ship industry. This technique was used by much of the aircraft industry during the fifties and early sixties.

Manual fairing techniques are inadequate for modern manufacturing industry for two reasons. Firstly, manual fairing was perhaps more of an art than a science; there were no quantitative criteria of the 'fairing' of these curves, since aesthetic judgement may be involved and fairness often lies in the craftsman's eye. Secondly, manual fairing has been a lengthy and meticulous process involving a great deal of trial and error.

With the advent of powerful computers it became possible to automate the fairing process by modern mathematical methods for the development and representation of vehicle contour shapes. In fact, some mathematical fairing procedures combine human experience and intuition with mathematical tools provided by interactive surface modelling systems. To date, the great majority of existing surface fairing systems are based on curve fairing.

8.1.3 Fairing criteria

In order to apply more rigorous mathematical emthods to surface fairing, fairing criteria have to be defined. Curve fairing is the basis of surface fairing; curve fairing criteria may be summed up as follows:

- Curves should be smooth and usually possess C^2 continuity. In a few cases, C^1 continuity may be allowed.
- Curves have no unwanted inflection points.
- Curvature change of the curves should be gradual.

Criterion 1 means that the curve does not include a cusp, as shown in Fig. 8.2(a). Criterion 2 avoids local concave shapes. If there are unwanted inflection points, the local concave case may occur, as shown in Fig. 8.2(b). Criterion 3 provides a limitation to local flatness. If there are more than two limit value points of the curve curvature, a local flat area will arise, as shown in Fig. 8.2(c).

These criteria will be formulated to automate the fairing process in the following sections.

The geometric concepts of curve fairing criteria are also suitable for surface fairing.

8.2 THE LOCAL SPRING-BACK METHOD

Mathematical fairing using the local spring-back method usually simulates the behaviour of the draughtsman's mechanical elastic spline supported at certain points by weights (called ducks). The mathematical spline function, that is a piecewise continuous polynomial, is used in an interpolating sense, so that poor data points must be adjusted automatically according to the fairing criteria.

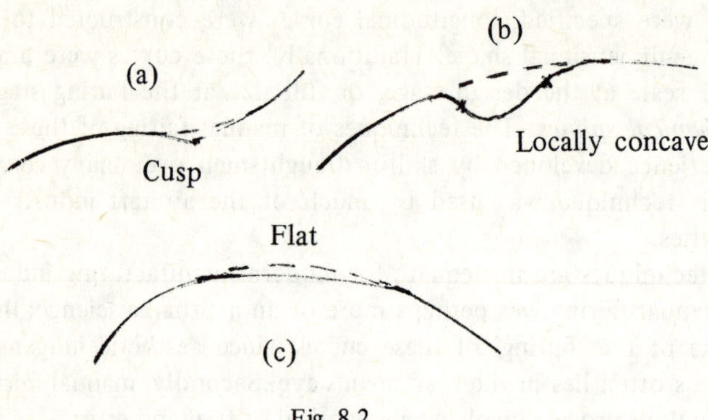

Fig. 8.2

8.2.1 Generating a spline

It should be apparent that splines have the great advantage that second-order continuity is attained, that is, curvature is continuous. Using the data points given by the user, we construct a cubic spline. Although it possesses C^2 continuity, it often does not satisfy the fairing criteria. The poor data points within the cubic spline will be adjusted, until the cubic spline satisfies the fairing criteria.

8.2.2 Indicators of the fairing

The fairing process is divided into two stages: rough fairing and finish fairing. Their indicators are as follows.

Indicators of rough fairing

Firstly, the curve is segmented according to the inflection points required by the designer. Each segment should be convex or concave (see Fig. 8.3).

We denote the sign of the second-order derivative in convex segments as $P = -1$, and the sign in concave segments as $P = 1$.

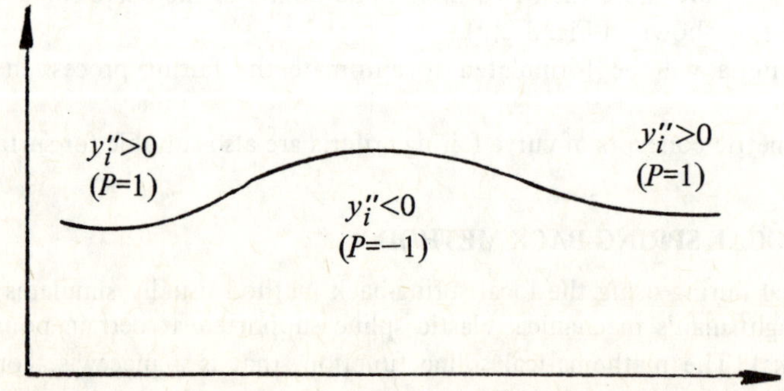

Fig. 8.3

If we find

$$P \cdot y_i'' < 0 \quad (i = 1, 2, \ldots, n)$$

then the point within this segment is a poor data point. It is observed that when the curvature is very small, viz. y_i'' is very small, convergence of the iterative process in terms of the above indicator will be much slower.

In order to avoid this case, it usually is suggested that if

$$|y_i''| \leqslant 10^{-4}$$

the iterative process should be stopped. The indicators of rough fairing therefore may be redefined as:

$$P \cdot y_i'' > 0$$

$$|y_i''| \leqslant 10^{-4} \quad (i = 1, 2, \ldots, n) \tag{8.1}$$

Indicator of finish fairing

It can be seen that the indicator of finish fairing is that the case

$$(y_{i+1}'' - y_i'')(y_i'' - y_{i-1}'') < 0 \tag{8.2}$$

will be allowed to arise only once at most in a single convex segment (or a single concave segment), unless the curve is not smooth.

8.2.3 Adjusting the poor data points

Many of the poor data points may be found according to the above fairing indicators. We always hope that the worst data point can be adjusted initially. In a physical spline, the internal energy is decreased by decreasing the shear forces applied to it. Mathematically this can be seen as decreasing the difference in third derivatives on both sides of a data point. The difference between the shear forces at a data point joining two spans of a spline is

$$N_i = y_{i,\text{right}}''' - y_{i,\text{left}}'''$$

Then the worst data point should satisfy

$$N = \max_j |y_{j,\text{right}}''' - y_{j,\text{left}}'''| \quad (j = 1, \ldots, k) \tag{8.3}$$

where k is the number of poor data points.

The adjusting process is divided into two stages: rough adjusting and finish adjusting.

Rough adjusting

Let the program generate a new spline without the worst data point $(x_{\text{poor}}, y_{\text{poor}})$ then interplate with the new spline at x_{poor}, and obtain the y_{poor}^*. Note that the data point $(x_{\text{poor}}, y_{\text{poor}})$ lies on the original spline curve, but the data point $(x_{\text{poor}}, y_{\text{poor}}^*)$ lies on the new spline curve. The value $(y_{\text{poor}}^* - y_{\text{poor}})$ is called the amount of the spring-back adjustment.

Adding a coefficient α to control the value of the adjustment gives

$$\Delta y_{\text{poor}} = \alpha(y_{\text{poor}}^* - y_{\text{poor}}) \tag{8.4}$$

For fairing an aircraft contour, $\alpha = 0.3$ can be used.

Replace the poor data point $(x_{\text{poor}}, y_{\text{poor}})$ by the point $(x_{\text{poor}}, y_{\text{poor}} + \Delta y_{\text{poor}})$. Let the program generate a new spline.

Repeat the search for poor data points according to the indicators of rough fairing and adjust the worst data point, until the indicators of the rough fairing are satisfied.

Finish adjusting

Search for poor data points according to the indicator of the finish fairing, then determine the worst data point using the same procedure as outlined in rough fairing.

The original spline passing through the worst data point (x_i, y_i) possesses the equation mentioned in Chapter 4.

$$\mu_i y_{i-1}'' + 2y_i'' + \lambda_i y_{i+1}'' = d_i \tag{8.5}$$

in which

$$d_i = 3\left\{\left(\frac{y_{i+1} - y_i}{h_{i+1}} - \frac{y_i - y_{i-1}}{h_i}\right)\Bigg/\frac{h_i + h_{i+1}}{2}\right\}$$

and $h_i = x_i - x_{i-1}$; $h_{i+1} = x_{i+1} - x_i$.

After adjusting the worst data point, which is moved to (x_i, y_i^*), we have the equation

$$\mu_i y_{i-1}''^* + 2y_i''^* + \lambda_i y_{i+1}''^* = d_i^*$$

since

$$y_{i-1}''^* \simeq y_{i-1}'' \quad \text{and} \quad y_{i+1}''^* \simeq y_{i+1}''$$

we obtain

$$\mu_i y_{i-1}'' + 2y_i''^* + \lambda_i y_{i+1}'' = d_i^* \tag{8.6}$$

where

$$d_i^* = 3\left\{\left(\frac{y_{i+1} - y_i^*}{h_{i+1}} - \frac{y_i^* - y_{i-1}}{h_i}\right)\Bigg/\frac{h_i + h_{i+1}}{2}\right\}$$

Subtracting equation (8.6) from equation (8.5) leaves, after some simplification,

$$y_i^* = y_i + \tfrac{1}{3}(y_i'' - y_i''^*)h_i h_{i+1}$$

in which

$$y_i''^* = (h_{i+1} y_{i-1}'' + h_i y_{i+1}'')/(h_{i+1} + h_i) \tag{8.7}$$

This means that a limit point of the second-order derivative at (x_i, y_i^*) has been removed.

Adding a coefficient ω to control the value of the adjustment gives

$$y_i^* = y_i + \tfrac{1}{3}\omega(y_i'' - y_i''^*)h_i h_{i+1} \tag{8.8}$$

For fairing an aircraft contour, setting $\omega = 0.3$ is suitable.

Replacing the poor data point (x_i, y_i) by the point (x_i, y_i^*), let the program generate a new spline.

Repeating the search for poor data points according to the indicator of the finish fairing and adjust the worst data point, until the indicator of the finish fairing is satisfied.

8.2.4 Application

The above study is adequate for a plane curve. A space curve may be projected onto two coordinate planes, and then may be carried out in each coordinate plane.

When a spline is being faired interactively by adjusting the positions of data points, a sufficient method is that the fairing software generates a curve showing the curvature of the original spline. This is a κ-curve which shows a variation of curvature along the spline to be faired. Any oscillations or inflexions are easily detected with the help of this curve.

To sum up, there are two things that a system ought to be able to help the designer with:

- measuring the smoothness of the spline;
- adjusting the positions of data points so that the spline gets smoother.

8.3 THE CIRCLE RATE METHOD

In some of the new approaches to the problem of increasing the smoothness of curves by adjusting the position of data points, the circle rate method is often used in practical applications. This is probably due to its simple mathematics and ease of computation.

8.3.1 Calculating circle rates

A set of data points $\mathbf{P}_i\,(x_i, y_i)\,(i = 0, 1, \ldots, n)$ and tangents m_0 and m_n at end points are provided by the user.

As we know, a circle can be determined by three successive data points $\mathbf{P}_{i-1}$, $\mathbf{P}_i$ and $\mathbf{P}_{i+1}$. The circle rate k_i at $\mathbf{P}_i$ may be calculated by the following formula:

$$k_i = \frac{\Delta x_i \Delta y_{i+1} - \Delta y_i \Delta x_{i+1}}{L_1 L_2 L_3} \qquad (i = 1, 2, \ldots, n-1) \tag{8.9}$$

in which

$$L_1 = \sqrt{\Delta x_i^2 + \Delta y_i^2}$$

$$L_2 = \sqrt{\Delta x_{i+1}^2 + \Delta y_{i+1}^2}$$

$$L_3 = \sqrt{(\Delta x_i + \Delta x_{i+1})^2 + (\Delta y_i + \Delta y_{i+1})^2}$$

$$\Delta x_i = x_i - x_{i-1}$$

$$\Delta y_i = y_i - y_{i-1} \qquad (i = 1, \ldots, n)$$

The circle rate k_0 at end point $\mathbf{P}_0$ can be determined by two data points $\mathbf{P}_0$, $\mathbf{P}_1$ and tangent m_0 at end point $\mathbf{P}_0$. It can be represented by

$$k_0 = \frac{2(\Delta y_1 - m_0 \, \Delta x_1)}{\sqrt{1 + m_0^2}(\Delta x_1^2 + \Delta y_1^2)} \qquad (8.10)$$

There is the same relation for the circle rate k_n at end point $\mathbf{P}_n$.

$$k_n = \frac{2(m_n \Delta x_n - \Delta y_n)}{\sqrt{1 + m_n^2} \, (\Delta x_n^2 + \Delta y_n^2)} \qquad (8.11)$$

Using formulae (8.9)–(8.11), we obtain a set of circle rates $\{k_i\}$ corresponding to a set of data points $\mathbf{P}_i \, (x_i, y_i)$.

We also know from the three formulae above that the sign of the circle rate is based on the sign of the numerator in the corresponding formula.

8.3.2 Indicators of the fairing

The fairing process is also divided into two stages: rough fairing and finish fairing. Their indicators are as follows.

Indicator of rough fairing

We denote the sign of the circle rate of $\mathbf{P}_i \, (x_i, y_i)$ as minus when the circular arc defined by three points $\mathbf{P}_{i-1}$, $\mathbf{P}_i$ and $\mathbf{P}_{i+1}$ is clockwise, and positive when anti-clockwise. We will now discuss the sign of the circle rates $\{\text{sign}\,(k_i)\}$.

It is evident that if the following conditions exist simultaneously

$$k_{i-1} \cdot k_i < 0$$

$$k_i \cdot k_{i+1} < 0 \qquad (8.12)$$

then the $\mathbf{P}_i$ must be a poor data point, which leads to a local convex or concave portion of the curve. The rough fairing will move the positions of poor data points to eliminate the local convex or concave portions.

Indicator of finish fairing

We now consider the sign of the first differences of the circle rates $\{\text{sign}\,(\Delta k_i)\}$.

If the following conditions exist simultaneously:

$$\Delta k_{i-1} \cdot \Delta k_i < 0$$

and

$$\Delta k_i \cdot \Delta k_{i+1} < 0 \qquad (8.13)$$

then the $\mathbf{P}_i$ must be a poor data point and the change of curvature is not even.

Finish fairing will adjust the position of poor data points to give a better and smoother curve.

8.3.3 Adjusting the position of data points

The second difference of the circle rate at point $\mathbf{P}_i$ can be defined as

$$D_i = \lambda_i k_{i-1} - k_i + \mu_i k_{i+1} \qquad (8.14)$$

where

$$\lambda_i = l_{i+1}/(l_i + l_{i+1})$$

$$\mu_i = l_i/(l_i + l_{i+1})$$

$$l_i = |\mathbf{P}_i - \mathbf{P}_{i-1}|$$

Then (8.4) may be rewritten as

$$D_i = \frac{l_i\, l_{i+1}}{l_i + l_{i+1}} \left(\frac{k_{i+1} - k_i}{l_{i+1}} - \frac{k_i - k_{i-1}}{l_i} \right) \tag{8.15}$$

The second difference D_i of the circle rate possesses the same geometric significance as the difference in third derivatives on both sides of a data point. In a curve, energy is decreased by decreasing the absolute value $|D_i|$. The worst data point may be found according to $|D_i|_{\max}$. Making the second difference D_i of the circle rate zero gives a better and smoother curve, whose circle rate is more even.

Using the indicator of the fairing we may look for poor data points, in which the worst data point can be found from the condition of $|D_i|_{\max}$.

Let the worst data point $\mathbf{P}_i\,(x_i,\, y_i)$ be replaced by the point $\mathbf{P}_i^*(x_i,\, y_i^*)$,

$$y_i^* = y_i + \rho_i$$

ρ_i is called the adjusting value.

From the geometric relation we have

$$\rho_i = -\frac{l_i\, l_{i+1}}{g_i}\, D_i \tag{8.16}$$

in which D_i is the second difference of the circle rate at the point $\mathbf{P}_i\,(x_i,\, y_i)$, and the coefficient g_i can be calculated (see Fig. 8.4).

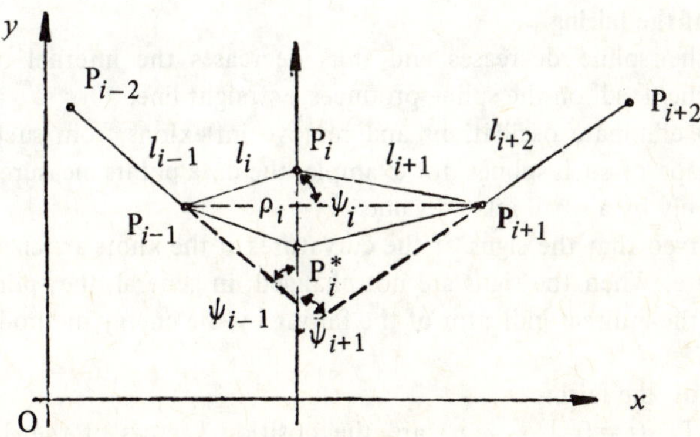

Fig. 8.4

$$g_i = 2 \left(\sin \psi_i + \frac{l_{i+1}}{l_{i-1} + l_i} \lambda_i \sin \psi_{i-1} + \frac{l_i}{l_{i+1} + l_{i+2}} \mu_i \sin \psi_{i+1} \right) \qquad (8.17)$$

If the distribution of data points is even for a plane linear elastic beam, then $g_i \simeq 3$. Adding a coefficient α to control the value of the adjustment gives

$$\rho_i = - \frac{l_i \, l_{i+1}}{g_i} D_i \cdot \alpha \qquad (8.18)$$

In practical applications, $\alpha = 0.2$ for the rough fairing, and $\alpha = 0.7$ for the finish fairing.

The circle rate method is a typical geometric adjusting method without calculating spline interpolation; it is suitable for any plane curve including closed curves. The design of plane curves plays a prominent role in some design procedures.

8.4 ENERGY METHOD

As discussed in Chapter 4, the physical spline, which is a traditional curve-fitting tool, is composed of a thin strip of wood or plastic fixed at several points (called knots) by lead weights (called ducks). By manipulating the ducks, the draughtsman created smooth curves. These wooden splines have now been replaced by the mathematical spline. The mathematical spline is an approximate model for a thin wooden spline which is not bent too sharply. Under these simplifying assumptions, the mathematical spline behaves like a thin elastic beam with the point supports of classical mechanics.

A thin elastic beam with point supports conforms to a shape which minimizes its internal bending energy subject to the constraints of point supports at the knots.

Moving ducks in the physical spline, equivalent to adjusting the data points in the mathematical spline, decreasing the 'load' on the beam, that is, minimizing the internal bending energy, gives a better and smoother curve after each iteration. This is the basis of the energy method for curve fairing.

8.4.1 Indicator of the fairing

The 'load' on the spline decreases and thus decreases the internal bending energy. Removing all of the 'load' on the spline produces a straight line.

We require to eliminate oscillations and remove inflexions from such splines, while preserving the shape of such splines; for example, the data points measured from a model can be adjusted only by a small related value.

It is also observed that the signs of the curvatures at the knots are changed during the iterative procedure. When the signs are not changed, in general, the splines are smooth. This is chosen as the indirect indicator of the fairing by the energy method.

8.4.2 Equations of the fairing

Assuming that P_i $(i = 0, 1, \ldots, n)$ are the position vectors of the data points, and P_i' $(i = 0, 1, \ldots, n)$ are tangent vectors at corresponding data points, we may express each span of the spline as follows:

$$r(u) = P_{i-1} F_0(u) + P_i F_1(u) + h_i [P'_{i-1} G_0(u) + P'_i G_1(u)] \qquad (8.19)$$

$$(0 \leqslant u \leqslant 1) \quad (i = 1, \ldots, n)$$

in which

$$P_{i-1}, P_i$$

are position vectors of the data points.

P'_{i-1}, P'_i are tangent vectors with respect to the accumulated chord length b of the spline.

$F_0(u), F_1(u), G_0(u)$ and $G_1(u)$ are the cubic blending functions mentioned in Chapter 4.

$$h_i = b_i - b_{i-1}, \quad b = b_{i-1} + uh_i \quad (0 \leqslant u \leqslant 1)$$

$\{b_i\} (i = 0, 1, \ldots, n)$ are the accumulated chord lengths at knots of the spline.

The ith span of the spline can be expressed as

$$r_i(u) = r_i(b_{i-1} + uh_i)$$

The function of the tangent vector with respect to the parameter u of the spline is

$$r'_i(u) = r'_i(b) h_i$$

We use B_i, C_i to denote tangent vectors with respect to the parameter u at points P_{i-1}, P_i respectively (see Fig. 8.5), that is

$$B_i = R'_i(0) = P'_{i-1} \cdot h_i$$

$$C_i = R'_i(1) = P'_i \cdot h_i$$

or

$$P'_{i-1} = B_i/h_i, \quad P'_i = C_i/h_i$$

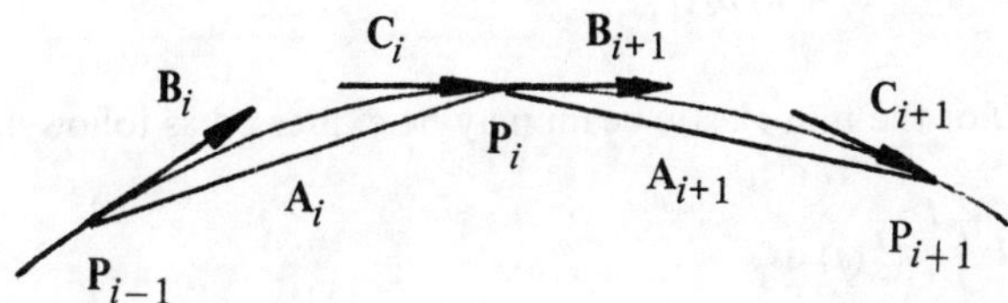

Fig. 8.5

Substituting them into equation (8.19), we obtain

$$r_i(u) = P_{i-1} F_0(u) + P_i F_1(u) + B_i G_0(u) + C_i G_1(u) \qquad (8.20)$$

Since

$$C_i = P'_i \cdot h_i = P'_i \cdot h_{i+1} \cdot h_i/h_{i+1}$$

and

$$\mathbf{B}_{i+1} = \mathbf{P}_i' \cdot h_{i+1}$$

denoting

$$k_i = h_i / h_{i+1}$$

we obtain

$$\mathbf{C}_i = k_i \cdot \mathbf{B}_{i+1} \qquad (8.21)$$

Note that when $i = n$, setting $k_i = 1$, then $\mathbf{C}_n = \mathbf{B}_{n+1}$. And since

$$F_0(u) = 1 - F_1(u) \qquad (8.22)$$

denoting

$$\mathbf{A}_i = \mathbf{P}_i - \mathbf{P}_{i-1} \qquad (8.23)$$

substituting results in (8.21), (8.22) and (8.23) above into equation (8.20), we finally obtain

$$\mathbf{r}_i(u) = \mathbf{P}_{i-1} + \mathbf{A}_i F_1(u) + \mathbf{B}_i G_0(u) + k_i \mathbf{B}_{i+1} G_1(u) \qquad (8.24)$$

Equation (8.24) may be rewritten as follows:

$$\mathbf{r}_i(u) = \mathbf{Q}_{i,0} + \mathbf{Q}_{i,1} u + \mathbf{Q}_{i,2} u^2 + \mathbf{Q}_{i,3} u^3 \qquad (8.25)$$
$$(0 \leqslant u \leqslant 1) \quad (i = 1, \ldots, n)$$

in which

$$\mathbf{Q}_{i,0} = \mathbf{P}_{i-1}$$

$$\mathbf{Q}_{i,1} = \mathbf{B}_i$$

$$\mathbf{Q}_{i,2} = 3\mathbf{A}_i - 2\mathbf{B}_i - k_i \mathbf{B}_{i+1}$$

$$\mathbf{Q}_{i,3} = -2\mathbf{A}_i + \mathbf{B}_i + k_i \mathbf{B}_{i+1} \qquad (8.26)$$

The bending energy U of the thin elastic beam may be expressed as follows:

$$U = \tfrac{1}{2} EJ \int_0^l \kappa^2(s) \, \mathrm{d}s \qquad (8.27)$$

where

l is the spline length

s is the accumulated arc length

$\kappa(s)$ is the curvature at a point with the arc length s

EJ is the bending constant.

The accumulated arc length s may be conveniently replaced by the accumulated chord length, that is $\mathrm{d}s \simeq \mathrm{d}b$. Then

$$\kappa^2(s) = \left(\frac{d^2\mathbf{r}}{ds^2}\right)^2 \simeq \left(\frac{d^2\mathbf{r}}{db^2}\right)^2$$

Since $du/db = 1/h_i$, the curvature vector may be rewritten as

$$\kappa(s) \simeq \mathbf{r}_i''(b) = \mathbf{r}_i''(u)\left(\frac{du}{db}\right)^2 = \frac{1}{h_i^2}\,\mathbf{r}_i''(u)$$

The bending energy of the ith span is

$$U_i = \frac{EJ}{2h_i^3}\int_0^1 \mathbf{r}_i''^2(u)\,du \tag{8.28}$$

Differentiating (8.25) we obtain

$$\mathbf{r}_i''(u) = 2\mathbf{Q}_{i,2} + 6\mathbf{Q}_{i,3}u$$

then

$$\mathbf{r}_i''^2(u) = 4(\mathbf{Q}_{i,2}^2 + 6u\mathbf{Q}_{i,2}\cdot\mathbf{Q}_{i,3} + 9u^2\mathbf{Q}_{i,3}^2)$$

Substituting the equation above into (8.28), we obtain

$$U_i = \frac{2EJ}{h_i^3}(\mathbf{Q}_{i,2}^2 + \mathbf{Q}_{i,2}\cdot\mathbf{Q}_{i,3} + 3\mathbf{Q}_{i,3}^2) \tag{8.29}$$

The bending energy U of the thin elastic beam is the sum of the bending energies of each span.

$$U = \sum_{i=1}^{n} U_i \tag{8.30}$$

The position vector $\mathbf{P}_i$ and tangent vector $\mathbf{B}_i$ are regarded as adjusting values. Minimizing the bending energy gives the following two equations:

$$\frac{\partial U}{\partial \mathbf{B}_i} = 0, \qquad \frac{\partial U}{\partial \mathbf{P}_i} = 0 \tag{8.31}$$

Note than when adjusting $\mathbf{P}_i$, $\mathbf{B}_i$, we may presume h_i unchanged then k_i is also unchanged.

From equations (8.29) and (8.26), we see that U_{i-1} and U_i include the tangent vector $\mathbf{B}_i$; the other items in (8.30) are not related to $\mathbf{B}_i$. Thus

$$\frac{\partial U}{\partial \mathbf{B}_i} = \frac{\partial U_{i-1}}{\partial \mathbf{B}_i} + \frac{\partial U_i}{\partial \mathbf{B}_i} = 0 \tag{8.32}$$

From (8.29) and (8.32), we obtain

$$\frac{k_{i-1}}{h_{i-1}^3}(\mathbf{Q}_{i-1,2} + 3\mathbf{Q}_{i-1,3}) - \frac{1}{h_i^3}\mathbf{Q}_{i,2} = 0$$

and hence

$$\mathbf{Q}_{i-1,2} + 3\mathbf{Q}_{i-1,3} - k_{i-1}^2 \mathbf{Q}_{i,2} = 0$$

Substituting coefficient vectors $\mathbf{Q}_{i-1,2}$, $\mathbf{Q}_{i-1,3}$, and $\mathbf{Q}_{i,2}$ into the above equation, we obtain

$$\mathbf{B}_{i-1} + 2k_{i-1}(1+k_{i-1})\mathbf{B}_i + k_{i-1}^2 k_i \mathbf{B}_{i+1} = 3(\mathbf{A}_{i-1} + k_{i-1}^2 \mathbf{A}_i)$$

$$(i = 2, 3, \ldots, n)$$

Replacing the subscript i by the subscript $i+1$, the result is

$$\mathbf{B}_i + 2k_i(1+k_i)\mathbf{B}_{i+1} + k_i^2 k_{i+1} \mathbf{B}_{i+2} = 3(\mathbf{A}_i + k_i^2 \mathbf{A}_{i+1}) \tag{8.33}$$

$$(i = 1, 2, \ldots, n-1)$$

Equation (8.33) is the knot relation equation of the cubic parametric spline mentioned in Chapter 4.

This means that a thin beam with point supports conforms to a shape which minimizes its bending energy; in doing so it satisfies the simple differential equation

$$\mathbf{r}''''(u) = 0$$

in each of the spans between adjacent knots; it passes through the point supports, and it has continuous tangent and curvature at each knot. In other words, the spline satisfies the minimizing 'bending' energy of the curve.

From (8.29) and (8.26), we see that U_i and U_{i+1} in equation (8.30) are related only to $\mathbf{P}_i$. Thus

$$\frac{\partial U}{\partial \mathbf{P}_i} = \frac{\partial U_i}{\partial \mathbf{P}_i} + \frac{\partial U_{i+1}}{\partial \mathbf{P}_i} = 0$$

From (8.29) and (8.26), we obtain

$$\frac{1}{h_i^3}\mathbf{Q}_{i,3} - \frac{1}{h_{i+1}^3}\mathbf{Q}_{i+1,3} = 0$$

and hence

$$\mathbf{Q}_{i,3} - k_i^3 \mathbf{Q}_{i+1,3} = 0$$

Substituting the corresponding coefficient vectors into the above equation, the result is

$$-2\mathbf{P}_{i-1} + 2(1+k_i^3)\mathbf{P}_i - 2k_i^3\mathbf{P}_{i+1} = \mathbf{B}_i + (1-k_i^2)k_i\mathbf{B}_{i+1} - k_i^3 k_{i+1}\mathbf{B}_{i+2}$$

$$(i = 1, 2, \ldots, n-1) \tag{8.34}$$

The fairing equations consist of (8.33) and (8.34). Assuming $\mathbf{P}_0$, $\mathbf{P}_n$, $\mathbf{B}_1$ and $\mathbf{B}_{n+1}$ are unchanged, calculating (8.33) and (8.34), we obtain the solution $\{\mathbf{B}_i\}$ $(i = 2, 3, \ldots, n)$ and $\{\mathbf{P}_i\}$ $(i = 1, 2, \ldots, n-1)$, respectively.

Because $\mathbf{B}_1$ and $\mathbf{B}_{n+1}$ are unchanged, the 1st and $(n-1)$th equations in (8.33) may be rewritten as follows:

$$2k_1(1 + k_1)\mathbf{B}_2 + k_1^2 k_2 \mathbf{B}_3 = 3(\mathbf{A}_1 + k_1^2 \mathbf{A}_2) - \mathbf{B}_1$$

$$\mathbf{B}_{n-1} + 2k_{n-1}(1 + k_{n-1})\mathbf{B}_n = 3(\mathbf{A}_{n-1} + k_{n-1}^2 \mathbf{A}_n) - k_{n-1}^2 k_n \mathbf{B}_{n+1}$$

the coefficient matrix of equation (8.33) is given by

$$\begin{bmatrix} 2k_1(1+k_1) & k_1^2 k_2 & & & & \\ 1 & 2k_2(1+k_2) & k_2^2 k_3 & & & 0 \\ & & \ddots & \ddots & \ddots & \\ & & 1 & 2k_{n-2}(1+k_{n-2}) & k_{n-2}^2 k_{n-1} \\ 0 & & & 1 & 2k_{n-1}(1+k_{n-1}) \end{bmatrix}$$

Because $\mathbf{P}_0$ and $\mathbf{P}_n$ are unchanged, the 1st and $(n-1)$th equations in (8.34) may be rewritten as follows:

$$2(1 + k_1^3)\mathbf{P}_1 - 2k_1^3 \mathbf{P}_2 = \mathbf{B}_1 + (1 - k_1^2)k_1 \mathbf{B}_2 - k_1^3 k_2 \mathbf{B}_3 + 2\mathbf{P}_0$$

$$-2\mathbf{P}_{n-2} + 2(1 + k_{n-1}^3)\mathbf{P}_{n-1} = \mathbf{B}_{n-1} + (1 - k_{n-1}^2)k_{n-1}\mathbf{B}_n - k_{n-1}^3 k_n \mathbf{B}_{n-1}$$

$$+ 2k_{n-1}^3 \mathbf{P}_n$$

The coefficient matrix of equation (8.34) is given by

$$\begin{bmatrix} 2(1+k_1^3) & -2k_1^3 & & & & \\ -2 & 2(1+k_2^3) & -2k_2^3 & & & 0 \\ & & \ddots & \ddots & \ddots & \\ & & -2 & 2(1+k_{n-2}^3) & -2k_{n-2}^3 \\ 0 & & & -2 & 2(1+k_{n-1}^3) \end{bmatrix}$$

The two linear systems are tridiagonal and they may be calculated using a standard algorithm.

A fairing calculation can be divided into three steps: constructing a spline curve, checking the spline curve, and adjusting the spline curve.

Constructing a spline curve
According to the initial conditions (or adjusting results), including the position vectors

of the data points and the end tangent vectors, calculating the tridiagonal linear system
(8.33) gives a set of tangent vectors $\mathbf{B}_i$ $(i = 1, 2, \ldots, n + 1)$.

Checking the signs of the curvatures
The curvature signs of project curves of the spline, for example in the xOy and yOz
coordinate plane, should be checked simultaneously.

Adjusting the spline curve
Calculating the tridiagonal linear system (8.34) gives a set of new position vectors
$\{\mathbf{P}_i\}$ $(i = 0, 1, \ldots, n)$.

Three coordinates x, y and z may be adjusted simultaneously. In fact, we only need to
adjust the coordinate y for a plane curve, and coordinates y and z for a space curve. It is
not necessary to calculate the component x of the vectors.

The curve may be segmented at some points and then faired separately if these
controlled data points cannot be changed in the design procedure.

Each fairing circulation gives a better and smoother curve. Fig. 8.6 shows the fairing
effect. C_1 is the initial curve, C_2 is the faired curve, $C_3 - C_5$ show further steps in fairing.

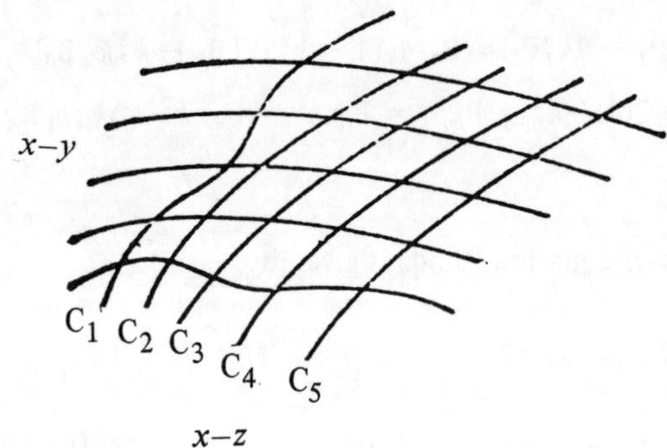

Fig. 8.6

8.4.3 Fairing with weights
Adding a small spring to each knot of the spline curve will give an additional elastic
restriction (see Fig. 8.7).

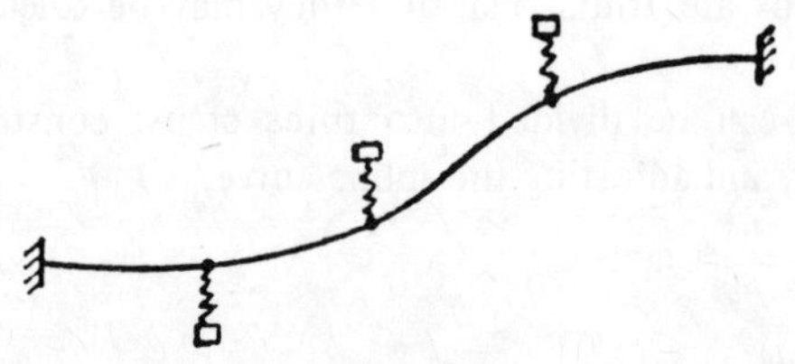

Fig. 8.7

The system consisting of a thin beam and constrained by springs as shown in Fig. 8.7 possesses two kinds of energy: beam bending energy and spring potential energy, so the total energy of the system is given by

$$U = \tfrac{1}{2} \sum_{i=0}^{n} C_i (\mathbf{P}_i - \mathbf{Q}_i)^2 + \tfrac{1}{2} EJ \int_0^l \kappa^2(s)\, ds \qquad (8.35)$$

where

$\mathbf{Q}_i$ — initial position vectors

$\mathbf{P}_i$ — position vectors after adjustment

C_i — elastic coefficients of the springs

EJ — bending constant of the beam

$\kappa(s)$ — curvature at a point with arc length s.

Minimizing the energy of the system, that is using (8.31), we obtain

$$\mathbf{B}_i + 2k_i(1 + k_i)\mathbf{B}_{i+1} + k_i^2 k_{i+1} \mathbf{B}_{i+2} = 3[(\mathbf{P}_i - \mathbf{P}_{i-1}) + k_i^2(\mathbf{P}_{i+1} - \mathbf{P}_i)] \qquad (8.36)$$

and

$$\mathbf{P}_i - \mathbf{Q}_i + 6\lambda_i \big\{ [2(\mathbf{P}_i - \mathbf{P}_{i-1}) - \mathbf{B}_i - k_i \mathbf{B}_{i+1}]/h_i^3$$
$$- [2(\mathbf{P}_{i+1} - \mathbf{P}_i) - \mathbf{B}_{i+1} - k_{i+1} \mathbf{B}_{i+2}]/h_{i+1}^3 \big\} = 0$$

where $\lambda_i = EJ/C_i$.

The above equation may be rewritten after some simplification as follows:

$$-2\mathbf{P}_{i-1} + 2(1 + k_i^3 + h_i^3/(12\lambda_i))\mathbf{P}_i - 2k_i^3 \mathbf{P}_{i+1}$$
$$= (\mathbf{B}_i + k_i \mathbf{B}_{i+1}) - (\mathbf{B}_{i+1} + k_{i+1} \mathbf{B}_{i+2})k_i^3 + k_i^3 \mathbf{Q}_i/(6\lambda_i) \qquad (8.37)$$
$$(i = 1, 2, \ldots, n-1)$$

Comparing (8.36), (8.37) with (8.33), (8.34) respectively, we find that (8.36) and (8.33) are the same, and that (8.37) and (8.34) are also the same, if $C_i \to 0$, $\lambda_i \to \infty$ in (8.37).

Using (8.36) and (8.37), we may fair the spline curve, and control the position vectors by the weight coefficient λ_i.

8.5 SURFACE MESH FAIRING

A surface mesh consists of two sets of curves: a fairing surface mesh is a two-dimensional extension of curve fairing. As the smoothness of the mesh increases, the smoothness of the surface defined by the mesh increases.

We discuss mesh fairing by the energy method. The surface defined by the mesh may be regarded as two sets of thin elastic beams. Let

$\mathbf{Q}_{ij}$ $-$ initial position vectors of the data points

$\mathbf{P}_{ij}$ $-$ the position vectors after adjusting

$\mathbf{r}_{ij}^{uu}$ $-$ the second-order tangent vectors with respect to u at mesh point $\mathbf{P}_{ij}$

$\mathbf{r}_{ij}^{ww}$ $-$ the second-order tangent vectors with respect to w at mesh point $\mathbf{P}_{ij}$

h_i^j $= |\mathbf{P}_{ij} - \mathbf{P}_{i-1,j}|$

h_j^i $= |\mathbf{P}_{ij} - \mathbf{P}_{i,j-1}|$

To simplify the formulae let

$$\Delta_u^2 f_{ij} = (f_{i+1,j} - f_{ij})/h_{i+1}^j - (f_{ij} - f_{i-1,j})/h_i^j$$

$$\Delta_w^2 f_{ij} = (f_{i,j+1} - f_{ij})/h_{j+1}^i - (f_{ij} - f_{i,j-1})/h_j^i$$

(f_{ij} may be regarded as $\mathbf{Q}_{ij}$, $\mathbf{r}_{ij}^{uu}$ or $\mathbf{r}_{ij}^{ww}$)

Adding a small spring to each mesh point, we now express the energy of the system, which consists of two sets of elastic beams and some springs, as follows:

$$U = \tfrac{1}{2} \sum_{ij} C_{ij}(\mathbf{P}_{ij} - \mathbf{Q}_{ij})^2 + \tfrac{1}{2} EJ \left(\sum_i \int_{C_i} \kappa^2 \, ds + \sum_j \int_{D_j} \kappa^2 \, ds \right) \tag{8.38}$$

where C_i and D_j respectively represent two sets of curves.

As for the nergy method for the fairing curve, we obtain three equations

$$\mathbf{P}_{ij} = \mathbf{Q}_{ij} - \lambda_{ij} (\Delta_u^2 \mathbf{r}_{ij}^{uu} + \Delta_w^2 \mathbf{r}_{ij}^{ww}) \tag{8.39}$$

$$h_i^j \mathbf{r}_{i-1,j}^{uu} + 2\mathbf{r}_{ij}^{uu}(h_i^j + h_{i+1}^j) + h_{i+1}^j \mathbf{r}_{i+1,j}^{uu} + 6\Delta_u^2(\lambda_{ij}\Delta_u^2 \mathbf{r}_{ij}^{uu}) = 6\Delta_u^2 \mathbf{Q}_{ij} \tag{8.40}$$

$$h_j^i \mathbf{r}_{i,j-1}^{ww} + 2\mathbf{r}_{ij}^{ww}(h_j^i + h_{j+1}^i) + h_{j+1}^i \mathbf{r}_{i,j+1}^{ww} + 6\Delta_w^2(\lambda_{ij}\Delta_w^2 \mathbf{r}_{ij}^{ww}) = 6\Delta_w^2 \mathbf{Q}_{ij}$$

$$\tag{8.41}$$

$\mathbf{r}_{ij}^{uu}$ and $\mathbf{r}_{ij}^{ww}$ may be calculated by using (8.40) and (8.41).

Then substituting $\mathbf{r}_{ij}^{uu}$ and $\mathbf{r}_{ij}^{ww}$ into (8.39), we obtain the new data mesh points $\mathbf{P}_{ij}$. Repeating the iteration procedure gives a better and smoother surface mesh. In design and fairing, the maximum value of the allowed adjustment should be specified by the designer. It is evident that a fair surface is a result of smooth mesh curves.

8.6 SURFACE FAIRING

8.6.1 Energy method

A mathematical surface behaves like a thin rectangular elastic plate of small defleciton. A thin elastic plate with mesh point supports conforms to a shape which minimizes its internal strain energy subject to the constraints of the point supports. The strain energy of flexure and torsion in an elastic plate may be represented by

$$U = C \cdot \int_0^a \int_0^b \left[\left(\frac{\partial^2 f}{\partial x^2} + \frac{\partial^2 f}{\partial y^2} \right)^2 - 2(1 - \nu) \right.$$

$$\left. \cdot \left(\frac{\partial^2 f}{\partial x^2} \cdot \frac{\partial^2 f}{\partial y^2} - \left(\frac{\partial^2 f}{\partial x \partial y} \right)^2 \right) \right] dx \, dy \qquad (8.42)$$

This expression should be minimized with respect to the free variables in the surface equation and in view of any given constraints, which leads to a variational formulation of the surface fairing problem.

For practical purposes the expression is often considered as too complicated and is replaced by simplified approximations. Neglecting the Poisson ration ν yields

$$U = C \cdot \int_0^a \int_0^b \left[\left(\frac{\partial^2 f}{\partial x^2} \right)^2 + 2 \left(\frac{\partial^2 f}{\partial x \partial y} \right)^2 + \left(\frac{\partial^2 f}{\partial y^2} \right)^2 \right] dx \, dy \qquad (8.43)$$

This is the small deflection equivalent of the function

$$U = \iint (\kappa_1^2 + \kappa_2^2) \, d\bar{x} \, d\bar{y} \qquad (8.44)$$

i.e. the integrated sum of the squares of the principal curvatures κ_1, κ_2 with $\bar{x}$, $\bar{y}$ coordinates in the local tangential plane.

Some fairing programs based on equation (8.44) have been developed as subsystems of surface modelling.

8.6.2 Interactive fairing

Fair boundary curves do not guarantee fairness in the patch interior, which will depend on the values of the bivariate derivatives in the patch corners. Since these values of the derivatives in the patch corners are not predetermined by the boundary curves, they remain free to be chosen within reasonable limits so as to optimize the fairness of the surface. This is the basis for both interactive and rigorous methods of surface fairing.

Because the B-splines are locally-supported, i.e. non-zero over a small number of spans, calculations using B-splines are particularly convenient. The local support principle leads to an efficient design and fairing technique on the B-spline characteristic polygon. Moving vertices gives a nice direct fairing, and the use of B-spline surfaces is comparable to the traditional lofting method using a spline.

In interactive fairing, effective visualization of the shape characteristics and particularly fairness flaws on limited-size display screens is of crucial importance to solve this problem. The display of derivative and particularly Gaussian curvature maps has been developed.

The main steps when doing this interactive fairing are:

- Study the surface and decide which points to move.
- Move the points and recalculate the surface.
- Repeat until satisfied.

We have studied several approaches to curve and surface fairing based on variational principles and fairness criteria. New surface fairing methods will certainly be developed. A nice surface modelling always possesses a nice subsystem of surface fairing.

REFERENCES

[1] Douglas, R. B., The application of CAD/CAM techniques at Harland and Wolff, *Computer-aided Design,* **18**, No. 5 (1986), 280–286.

[2] Beeker, E., Smoothing of shapes designed with free-form surfaces, *Computer-aided Design,* **18**, No. 4 (1986), 224–232.

[3] Fog, N. G., Creative definition and fairing of ship hulls using a B-spline surface, *Computer-aided Design,* **16**, No. 4 (1984), 225–229.

[4] Nowacki, H. and Reese, D., Design and fairing of ship surfaces, surfaces in CAGD, North-Holland, Amsterdam, 1983.

[5] Kjellander, J., Smoothing of bicubic parametric surfaces, *Computer-aided Design,* **15**, No. 5 (1983), 288–293.

[6] Kjellander, J., Smoothing of cubic parametric splines, *Computer-aided Design,* **15**, No. 3 (1983), 175–179.

[7] Stroobant, G. and Mars, B., Ship hull form fairing, ICCAS, Amsterdam (1982).

[8] Rogers, D. F. and Dill, J. C., Colour graphics and ship hull surface curvature, ICCAS, Amsterdam (1982).

[9] Rogers, D. F. and Satterfield, S. G., Dynamic B-spline sufrace, ICCAS, Amsterdam (1982).

[10] Renz, W., Interactive smoothing of digitized point data, *Computer-aided Design,* **14**, No. 5 (1982), 267–270.

[11] Lewis, J. W., Interchanging spline curves using IGES, *Computer-aided Design,* **13**, No. 6 (1981), 359–364.

[12] Duncan, J. P. and Vickers, G. W., Simplified method for interactive adjustment of surfaces, *Computer-aided Design,* **12**, No. 6 (1980), 305–308.

[13] Yuille, J. M., Interactive Program for the design of ship hull forms, ICCAS, Amsterdam (1979).

[14] Izumida, K. & Matida, Y., Ship hull definition by surface techniques for production use, ICCAS, Amsterdam (1979).

[15] Munchmeyer, F. C., Schubert, C. and Nowacki, H., Interactive design of fair hull surfaces using B-splines, *ICCAS Conference on Computer Applications in the Automation of Shipyard Operation and Ship Design*, Strathclyde, North Holland, Amsterdam, pp. 77–86.

[16] Desimoz, J., Curve smoothing for improved feature extraction from digital pictures, *Signal Proc.,* No. 1 (1979).

[17] Mehlum, E., Curve and surface fitting based on variational criteria for smoothness, Central Inst. for Ind. Res., Oslo (1969).

9

Tool Paths for Surface Machining

9.1 INTRODUCTION

In computer-aided manufacturing we will frequenctly encounter the abbreviation NC in the literature, which is shorthand for numerical control. Machines programmed automatically to cut shaped parts from raw stock are now commonplace. Fig. 9.1 shows tool paths for surface maching. We want to machine the sculptured surface by using a milling cutter, which poses several questions, for example: Where should the cutting start? How deep should the first pass be? What path should the tool take as it cuts the shape? These imply the creation of many intermediate shapes before the final shape is produced.

To enable the shape to be machined, a manufacturing engineer or technician, called a part programmer, writes a program based on the model defined by an engineering drawing. This program includes specifying the size and shape of the raw stock of material from which the part is to be cut, type and size of cutter, tool speed for rotation, and feed rate for translation, and tool paths. After that, the engineer verifies the program by cutting a test part and/or by using a plotting device to draw the tool paths. The machine operator then loads the verified program into the appropriate NC machine tool and correctly positions the raw stock and the tool. The part is then automatically machined, perhaps with a few scheduled interruptions to reposition the part. Once a program is verified, it can produce an unlimited number of substantially identical parts.

Conventional engineering drawings of mechanical parts are rapidly being replaced by equivalent mathematical representations or geometric models constructed by a CAD/CAM system and stored in a database for subsequent retrieval. Once a part is designed and stored in the database, the engineer simply calls up the model on the display. The engineer uses the model to generate machine tool paths which can be seen graphically in either two or three dimensions.

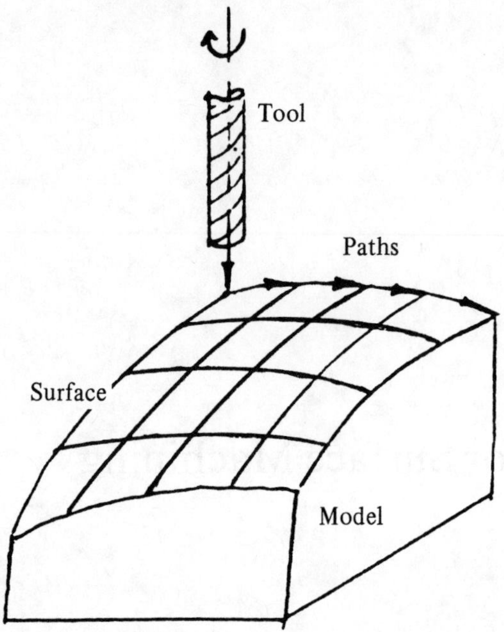

Fig. 9.1 Tool paths for surface machining

The engineer defines cutting tools, creates a tool library, and retrieves these tools later to create the tool-path information. Because a CAM package supports most cutting tool configurations, the user can describe most types of generally used cutting tools, such as flat-ended, ball-ended, tapered, mills, drills, etc. The CAM system also prompts the user to define machining characteristics such as cutting depth, feed rate and spindle speed. This is often done by a menu-driven process, which allows the engineer to generate tool paths in a controlled step-by-step procedure. As a step is defined, the tool movements are interactively displayed on the screen.

The problems of tool-path geometry become even more interesting and sophisticated when some of the physics involved is taken into consideration. This involves tool vibration, wear, cutting speed, depth of cut, and deformation under load. These factors have direct impact on the economics and profitability of manufacturing, because they determine the number of parts per hour that can be produced and still satisfy quality control requirements. At present these factors cannot fully be dealt with by CAD/CAM systems.

In this chapter, we will discuss tool-path calculations from two dimensions through two-and-a-half dimensions to three dimensions, and finally introduce tool-path simulation and verification.

9.2 TWO-DIMENSIONAL TOOL PATHS

We begin with two-dimensional tool paths for two reasons. Firstly, the concept of two-dimensional tool paths is the basis for the engineer or programmer. Secondly, the machining complex surface shapes include some plane profiles and pockets which are typical two-dimensional geometric shapes.

9.2.1 Offset curves

The programming of cutter motions is always done with a specific point of the tool in mind. For rotating cutters, this point, referred to as the tool end, is a convenient point on the axis of rotation. When a plane contour is machined, the tool centre path is offset from the contour by the tool radius R.

We will now examine the relationship between the contour of part and offset curves which represents the tool centre locus (see Fig. 9.2).

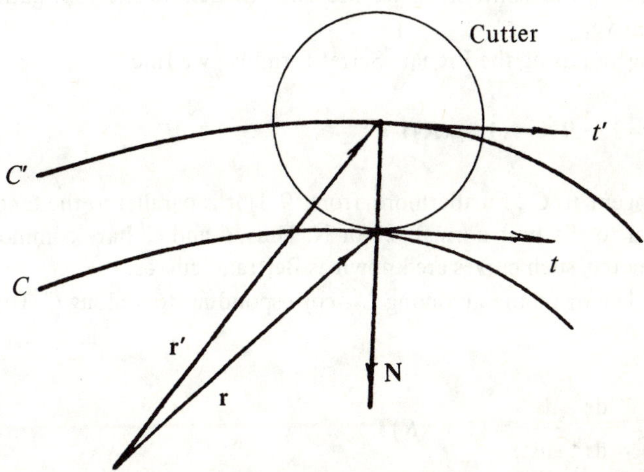

Fig. 9.2 Offset curve

Chapter 1, section 5 it was shown that a natural representation of a curve is

$$\mathbf{r} = [x(s) \quad y(s) \quad z(s)]$$

The derivative of the position vector is a unit tangent vector

$$\dot{\mathbf{r}} = d\mathbf{r}/ds = \mathbf{T}, \quad |\mathbf{T}| = 1$$

while the second derivative is a vector normal to the curve; its magnitude is equal to the curvature κ

$$\dot{\mathbf{T}} = \kappa\mathbf{N}, \quad |\mathbf{N}| = 1$$

The unit tangent and unit normal vectors, together with the unit binormal vector defined by $\mathbf{B} = \mathbf{T} \times \mathbf{N}$, satisfy the Frenet–Serret formulae

$$\dot{\mathbf{T}} = \kappa\mathbf{N}$$

$$\dot{\mathbf{N}} = -\kappa\mathbf{T} + \tau\mathbf{B}$$

$$\dot{\mathbf{B}} = -\tau\mathbf{N}$$

where τ is the torsion of the curve. Plane curves have zero torsion, and the Frenet–Serret formulae simplify in that case to

$$\dot{\mathbf{T}} = \kappa\mathbf{N}$$

$$\dot{\mathbf{N}} = -\kappa\mathbf{T} \tag{9.1}$$

Consider a rotating cutter of radius R, generating a plane contour C (see Fig. 9.2). As the point of contact travels along C, the tool centre describes a tool path C' defined by the position vector

$$\mathbf{r}'(s) = \mathbf{r}(s) - R\mathbf{N}(s) \tag{9.2}$$

Whereas $\mathbf{r}(s)$ denotes the contour C, we use $\mathbf{r}'(s)$ to denote the tool path C', which is called an offset curve.

Differentiating and using the Frenet–Serret formulae we find

$$\frac{\mathrm{d}\mathbf{r}'}{\mathrm{d}s} = \dot{\mathbf{r}} - R\dot{\mathbf{N}} = (1 + \kappa R)\mathbf{T} \tag{9.3}$$

But $\mathrm{d}\mathbf{r}'/\mathrm{d}s$ is tangent to C'. Furthermore, from (9.3) it is parallel to the tangent of C, and hence orthogonal to the unit normal vector $\mathbf{N}$. Thus, C and C' have common normals. In differential geometry, such curves are known as Bertrand curves.

Let s' be the length of the arc along C', corresponding to s along C. Then from (9.3) we see that

$$\frac{\mathrm{d}\mathbf{r}'}{\mathrm{d}s} = \frac{\mathrm{d}\mathbf{r}'}{\mathrm{d}s'}\frac{\mathrm{d}s'}{\mathrm{d}s} = (1 + \kappa R)\mathbf{T}$$

$$\frac{\mathrm{d}s'}{\mathrm{d}s} = (1 + \kappa R) \tag{9.4}$$

since $\mathbf{T}' = \mathrm{d}\mathbf{r}'/\mathrm{d}s'$ is the unit tangent vector to C', and for Bertrand curves $\mathbf{T}' = \mathbf{T}$.

In addition, differentiating $\mathbf{T}'$ with respect to s' we obtain from (9.1)

$$\dot{\mathbf{T}}' = \frac{\mathrm{d}\mathbf{T}'}{\mathrm{d}s'} = \frac{\mathrm{d}\mathbf{T}'}{\mathrm{d}s}\frac{\mathrm{d}s}{\mathrm{d}s'} = \kappa'\mathbf{N}' \tag{9.5}$$

But

$$\frac{\mathrm{d}\mathbf{T}'}{\mathrm{d}s} = \frac{\mathrm{d}\mathbf{T}}{\mathrm{d}s} = \kappa\mathbf{N}$$

Therefore, equation (9.5) gives

$$\kappa\mathbf{N}\frac{1}{1 + \kappa R} = \kappa'\mathbf{N}'$$

Since $\mathbf{N} = \mathbf{N}'$, we have

$$\kappa' = \frac{\kappa}{1 + \kappa R} \tag{9.6}$$

In terms of the radii of curvature $\rho = 1/\kappa$, $\rho' = 1/\kappa'$, equation (9.6) becomes

$$\rho' = \rho + R \tag{9.7}$$

Thus, C and C' also have common centres of curvature.

The analysis above shows that if the desired curve is composed of several segments, then the degree of continuity in C is preserved in C'. The converse is also true. So we can model the tool centre path as a spline curve. This is suitable as a theoretical basis for programming the motion.

The offset process may be summarized as follows:

- pass a spline with the desired degree of continuity through the given points $\mathbf{r}_i$ $(i = 1, \ldots, n)$;
- determine the tool centre positions $\mathbf{r}'_i$ $(i = 1, \ldots, n)$, corresponding to points $\mathbf{r}_i$;
- pass a second spline with the same degree of continuity through $\mathbf{r}'_i$;
- use the second spline to generate the necessary tool motion.

The method modelling the tool centre path as a spline can generate tool motion accurately and efficiently through interplation.

9.2.2 Linear approximation

We know that a curve, such as a polynomial or rational polynomial curve, can be approximated by a sequence of linear segments or circular arcs for draughting machines or numerically controlled machines because they use only linear interpolation or circular arc interpolation between data points.

Parabolic interpolation and spline interpolation will not be discussed, as they are used in very few numerically controlled machines.

In this subsection, we will introduce two kinds of algorithm for linear approximation, that is, the straightforward algorithm and the curvature algorithm.

Straightforward algorithm

We will calculate the maximum normal distance δ for the chord intersecting the points with parameter u and $u + \Delta u$ (see Fig. 9.3).

The choice of the step length naturally depends on the calculated tolerance δ between the true curve and the chord between successive points on the curve, measured normal to the chord whose value is about $0.0001 \sim 0.00001$ mm. We should point out again that δ is not a machined tolerance.

In general, the maximum deviation occurs at $\mathbf{r}(u + \frac{1}{2} \Delta u)$ for a subsegment from u to $u + \Delta u$. This leads to a straightforward algorithm of the maximum for general parametric curves.

We will calculate here the maximum normal distance δ for the chord joining the points at $u = 0$ and $u = 1$, because parameter transformation can be used to transform any segment $u_i \leqslant u \leqslant u_{i+1}$ into $0 \leqslant u' \leqslant 1$.

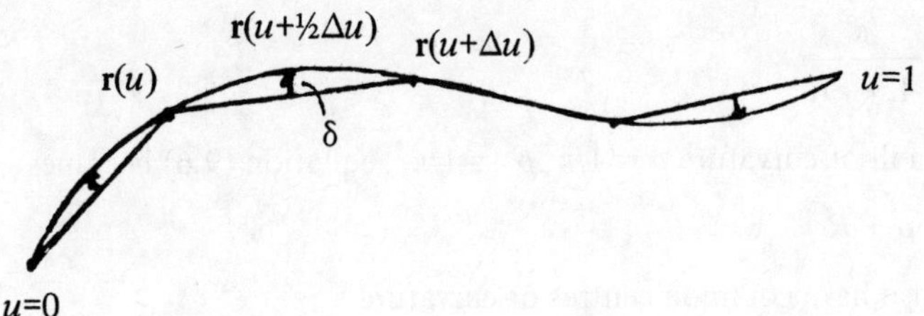

Fig. 9.3

$$u = (1 - u')u_i + u'u_{i+1} \qquad (9.8)$$

It can be seen that the parameters $u' = 0, 1$ correspond to $u = u_i, u_{i+1}$ as required. So we can apply standard results to the subsegment $u_i \leqslant u \leqslant u_{i+1}$.

According to the geometric relationship as shown in Fig. 9.4 we obtain

$$r(\tfrac{1}{2}) = r(0) + \lambda C + P$$

in which C is the chord vector joining the points $r(0)$ and $r(1)$. Then

$$P = r(\tfrac{1}{2}) - r(0) - \lambda C$$

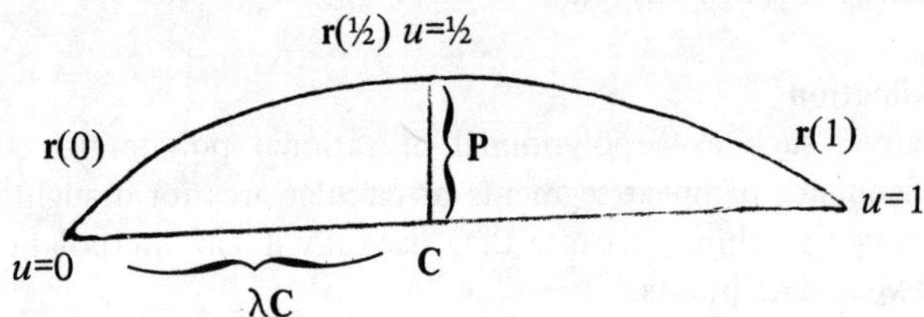

Fig. 9.4

Since

$$C \cdot P = 0$$

it follows that

$$C \cdot [r(\tfrac{1}{2}) - r(0)] = \lambda |C|^2$$

so that

$$\lambda = \frac{C \cdot [r(\tfrac{1}{2}) - r(0)]}{|C|^2}$$

Then we obtain

$$P = r(\tfrac{1}{2}) - r(0) - \frac{C \cdot [r(\tfrac{1}{2}) - r(0)]}{|C|^2} C \qquad (9.9)$$

This result leads to a rapid evaluation of the maximum deviation for general parametric curves. Furthermore, in general, $\lambda \simeq \frac{1}{2}$, and the formula (9.9) may be simplified as follows:

$$\mathbf{P} \simeq \mathbf{r}(\tfrac{1}{2}) - \tfrac{1}{2}\left[\mathbf{r}(1) + \mathbf{r}(0)\right] \qquad (9.10)$$

We may use (9.9), or even (9.10), to compute a sequence of segments of maximum length which are within the tolerance specified, that is

$$|\mathbf{P}| \leqslant \delta$$

Note that at the maximum perpendicular, the curve tangent is perpendicular to $\mathbf{P}$. Using the property, we may compute exactly the position of the point where the maximum occurs. Unfortunately, the time required to evaluate the exact position is a limitation of the method.

Curvature algorithm
The linear approximation means that the true curve is replaced by a sequence of linear segments. For small steps, it is reasonable to approximate the true curve by the circular arc of its osculating circle, so that the local curvature of the curve may be used to determine the step length (see Fig. 9.5).

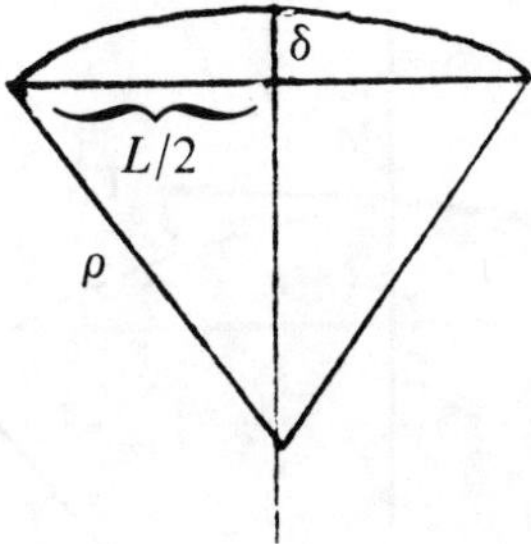

Fig. 9.5

According to the geometric relationship as shown in Fig. 9.5, the following result is

$$\rho^2 = \left(\frac{L}{2}\right)^2 + (\rho - \delta)^2$$

where L is the step length, and ρ is the radius of curvature.
  Then

$$L^2 = 4\delta(2\rho - \delta) \qquad (9.11)$$

The radius of curvature ρ can be computed directly in terms of the formulae of the true curve.

9.2.3 Circular arc approximation
The circular arc approximation means that the true curve is replaced by a sequence of circular arcs.

We now discuss a segment of the curve, that is, a segment of a spline curve. The segment will be replaced by two circular arcs (see Fig. 9.6).

There are three points P_i, M, P_{i+1} on the curve and corresponding tangent vectors T_i, T_M, T_{i+1}, which can be computed in terms of the formulae of the spline curve. Using the three points and corresponding tangent vectors, we can construct two circular arcs, their centres of circle are O_i and O_{i+1}, corresponding radii of curvature are ρ_i and ρ_{i+1}, respectively.

Then we calculate the maximum normal distance δ between the true curve segment and the circular arc (see Fig. 9.6).

If $\delta \leqslant 0.0001 \sim 0.00001$ mm, the two circular arcs will be accepted for replacing the true curve segment. Otherwise we will divide the segment.

This section has introduced linear approximation and circular arc approximation. Compare the two procedures. The former is simple to calculate, requiring a large number of straight lines, has only C^0 continuity and is suitable for cases in which the curvature of the curve segment is small. The latter is more complex to calculate, has a smaller number of circular arc sections, has C^1 continuity and is suitable for the case in which the curvature of the curve segment is large. Some CAM packages employ both methods and select the best method automatically according to the curvature of curve.

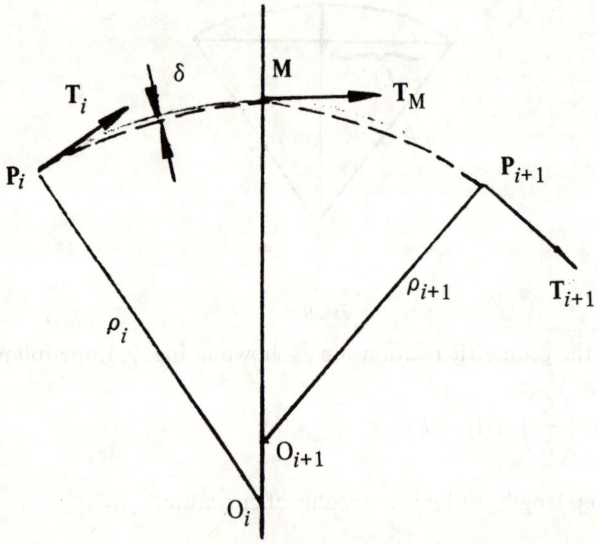

Fig. 9.6 Two circular arcs

9.3 TWO-AND-A-HALF-DIMENSIONAL TOOL PATHS

Most surface parts fall within this category. Two-and-a-half-dimensional parts require movement of either an independent or a simultaneous two-axis motion before or after the third axis is set (see Fig. 9.7).

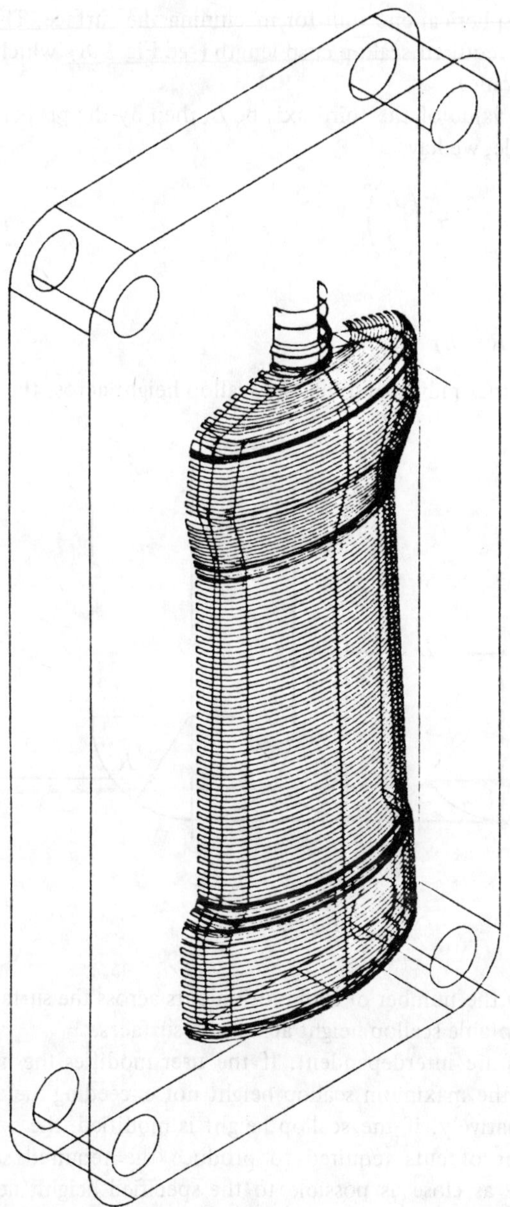

Fig. 9.7

Usually, we use a spherical end mill for machining the surface. The feed in the third axis is set to give the required scallop cusp length (see Fig. 9.8), which naturally depends on the machining tolerance.

Let the movement value of the third axis be L; then by the property of the circle and the right-angled triangle, we have

$$R^2 = (R - h)^2 + \left(\frac{L}{2}\right)^2$$

which gives

$$L^2 = 4h(2R - h) \tag{9.12}$$

where R is the tool corner radius, and h is the scallop height across the surfaces.

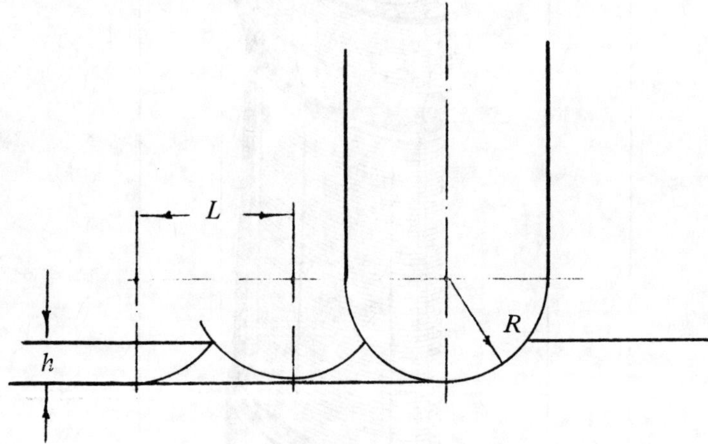

Fig. 9.8

The user can enter the number of tool motion cuts across the surfaces to be machined or the maximum acceptable scallop height across the surfaces.

These two choices are interdependent. If the user modifies the number of cuts, the system will compute the maximum scallop height not exceeding the corner radius of the specified tool. Alternatively, if the scallop height is modified, the system will calculate the minimum number of cuts required to produce the required scallop height. This scallop height will be as close as possible to the specified height, never exceeding that height. If either the number of cuts or the scallop height chosen are not acceptable, the user can repeat the procedure until he reaches the desired compromise between scallop height and number of cuts.

Two-and-a-half-dimensional machining involves the translation of three-dimensional machining into a sequence of two-dimensional machining cuts, since the simultaneous two-axis motion in two-and-a-half-dimensional machining is equivalent to two-dimensional motion.

Note that for two-and-a-half-dimensional machining the normal vectors of the cut points on the machined surface, in general, are not within the plane which is determined by the simultaneous two axes. We will analyse this in the next section.

9.4 THREE-DIMENSIONAL TOOL PATHS

9.4.1 Offset surfaces

Let S be a surface defined by the position vector

$$\mathbf{r}(u, w) = [x(u, w) \quad y(u, w) \quad z(u, w)]$$

The partial derivative vectors

$$\mathbf{r}_u = \delta\mathbf{r}/\delta u, \quad \mathbf{r}_w = \delta\mathbf{r}/\delta w$$

at a given point are tangent to the surface; these two vectors define the tangent plane.
Let

$$\mathbf{n} = \mathbf{r}_u \times \mathbf{r}_w / |\mathbf{r}_u \times \mathbf{r}_w|$$

be a unit normal vector. Then $\mathbf{n} \cdot \mathbf{n} = 1$.

Let $\mathbf{n}_u \cdot \mathbf{n} = \mathbf{n}_w \cdot \mathbf{n} = 0$, so that the vectors $\mathbf{n}_u$, $\mathbf{n}_w$ are both orthogonal to $\mathbf{n}$, and parallel to the tangent plane. Each of them can be expressed as a linear combination of $\mathbf{r}_u$ and $\mathbf{r}_w$

$$\mathbf{n}_u = a\mathbf{r}_u + b\mathbf{r}_w, \quad \mathbf{n}_w = c\mathbf{r}_u + d\mathbf{r}_w$$

Let surface S be machined by a spherical end cutter with nose radius R. Then, the centre of the spherical nose describes a surface S' with position vector

$$\mathbf{r}'(u, w) = \mathbf{r}(u, w) + R\mathbf{n}(u, w) \tag{9.13}$$

The vector $\mathbf{n}' = \mathbf{r}'_u \times \mathbf{r}'_w$ is normal to S'. Using (9.13), we obtain

$$\begin{aligned}
\mathbf{n}' &= (\mathbf{r}_u - R\mathbf{n}_u) \times (\mathbf{r}_w - R\mathbf{n}_w) \\
&= [\mathbf{r}_u - R(a\mathbf{r}_u + b\mathbf{r}_w)] \times [\mathbf{r}_w - R(c\mathbf{r}_u + d\mathbf{r}_w)] \\
&= [(1 - aR)\mathbf{r}_u - bR\mathbf{r}_w] \times [-cR\mathbf{r}_u + (1 - dR)\mathbf{r}_w] \\
&= (a'\mathbf{r}_u - b'\mathbf{r}_w) \times (c'\mathbf{r}_u + d'\mathbf{r}_w) \\
&= (a'd' - b'c')(\mathbf{r}_u \times \mathbf{r}_w) \tag{9.14}
\end{aligned}$$

The result shows that surfaces S and S' have common normal directions.

Let us analyse curves C and C' of the surfaces S and S' by a normal plane passing through the common normal direction $\overrightarrow{\mathbf{PP}'}$ (see Fig. 9.9). Since C and C' lie on the same plane and their position vectors are related by equation (9.13), they are Bertrand curves and everything stated in subsection 9.2.1 holds. In particular, their radii of curvature satisfy equation (9.7). Imagine this plane revolving around $\overrightarrow{\mathbf{PP}'}$. In differential geometry, it is shown that there exist the principal curvatures $\kappa_{n,\max}$ and $\kappa_{n,\min}$ of the surface at the given point. For the surfaces S and S' their principal curvatures are related to each other:

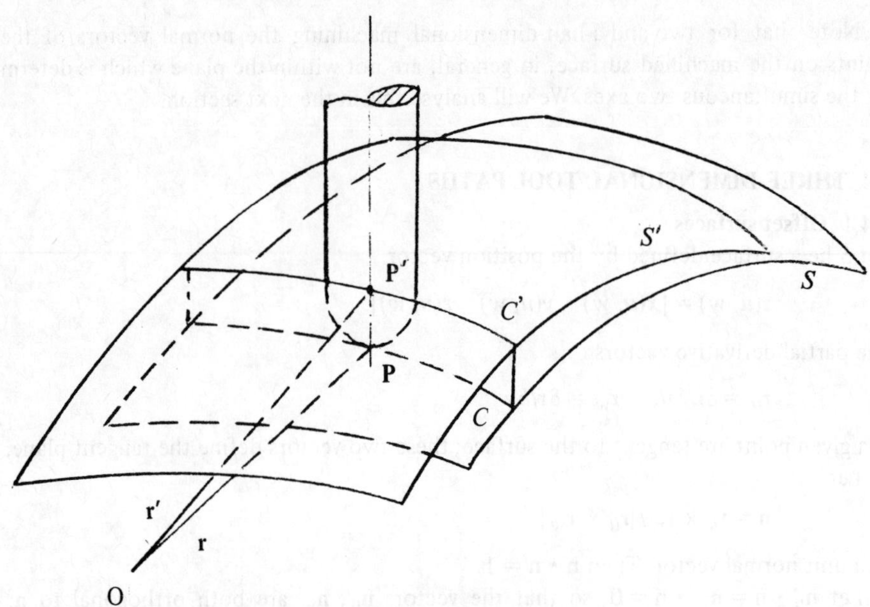

Fig. 9.9 Offset surface

$$\kappa'_{\max} = \frac{\kappa_{\max}}{1 + R\kappa_{\max}}, \quad \kappa'_{\min} = \frac{\kappa_{\min}}{1 + R\kappa_{\min}} \tag{9.15}$$

thus, we obtain

$$\rho'_{\max} = \rho_{\max} + R, \quad \rho'_{\min} = \rho_{\min} + R \tag{9.16}$$

The above analysis shows that the machined surface S and the tool centre surface S' have properties analogous to those of Bertrand curves and may properly be called Bertrand surfaces.

From the CAM standpoint, the particular value is that they possess the same degree of continuity. If S is continuous in position, slope and curvature, so is S' and vice versa. As a result, the four steps mentioned in subsection 9.2.1 for the manufacture of curves can also be used for surfaces. So we can model the tool centre path as a spline surface. This is suitable as a theoretical basis for programming the motion.

When a surface is machined using a ball end cutter, the tool centre moves on another parallel surface, offset from the original by an amount equal to the cutter radius R.

For tool setting purposes it is convenient to use the cutter tip rather than the tool centre as the reference point (see Fig. 9.10).

The tip of the ball end cutter follows the path

$$\mathbf{r}_{\text{tip}} = \mathbf{r}(u, w) + R(\mathbf{n} + \mathbf{l}) \tag{9.17}$$

where $\mathbf{n}$ is the unit normal vector of the surface at the contact point and $\mathbf{l}$ is the unit direction vector of the axis of the cutter.

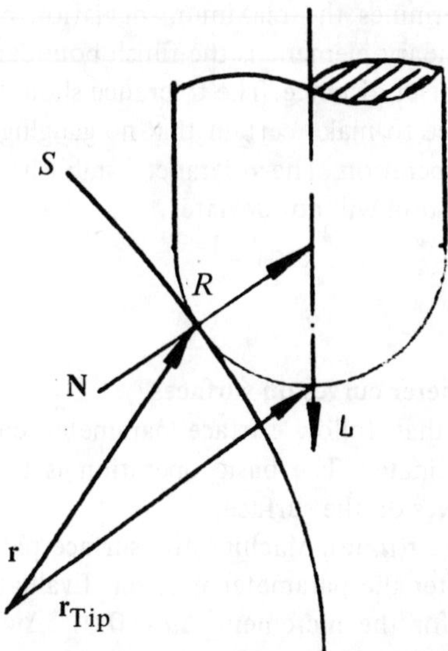

Fig. 9.10

In machining a surface, the cutter radius must obviously not exceed the minimum radius of curvature in the surface, otherwise gauging of the surface will occur. If sections of the offset surface are plotted, the danger points will appear as cusps or even loops.

The accuracy of the machining surface is a function of the cutter radius.

Finally, we will discuss some engineering applications related to offset machining.

Tool offset

We can offset the tool from the selected part surface according to the part thickness. The offset surface is normal to the part surface. The offset can also be generated along the tool axis, which is not normal to the part surface. The offset is called the rough cut offset.

The offset distance can be positive or negative, with the following restrictions: first, the distance can be greater than the tool radius only in the positive direction; second, a positive distance leaves material and a negative distance removes excess stock. The distance effectively changes the radius of the tool.

Tolerance offset

Two tolerances will be used for all finish cuts: an inside tolerance and an outside tolerance. The inside tolerance specifies the maximum excess amount of material to be removed from the part boundary. The outside tolerance specifies the maximum excess amount of material to be left after machining.

As the tool cuts along a boundary, it will not violate the boundary (undercut the part) by more than the inside tolerance value, or leave more excess material than the outside tolerance value.

The rough tolerance determines the maximum deviation of the tool side from the boundary element. This boundary element is the finish boundary plus or minus the thick offset distance and the side offset distance. The tolerance should be one-half or less of the smallest side roughing distance to make certain that no gauging of the finished boundary occurs during the roughing operation. The tolerance establishes a tolerance band around the boundary from which the tool will not deviate.

9.4.2 Tool paths along parameter curves on surfaces

Tool paths can be created that follow surface parameter curves; the output of this operation is in x, y, z coordinates. The basic operation is to calculate linear approximations to the parameter curves on the surface.

Let a patch of a surface be $\mathbf{r}(u, w)$. Machine the surface patch along the direction of the parameter u before or after the parameter w is set. Evaluate a bi-cubic surface patch for x, y and z respectively for the increment $\Delta u = 0.01$, $\Delta w = 0.01$, then the surface equations are evaluated about $30\,000$ times. Each evaluation takes many multiplications and additions; this is an unfortunate characteristic.

Horner's rule for factoring polynomials can be used to reduce the number of multiplications. For a cubic PC, the rule is

$$\mathbf{r}(u) = [(\mathbf{d}u + \mathbf{c})u + \mathbf{b}]u + \mathbf{a} \tag{9.18}$$

Here, $\mathbf{a}$, $\mathbf{b}$, $\mathbf{c}$ and $\mathbf{d}$ are vector-valued coefficients.

The rule can clearly be extended to a bi-cubic surface patch, but even so, much work is still needed.

A practical implementation of the procedure is the forward difference method, when the intervals of the parameter are constant. This method provides high calculating speed for the surface. We begin with a parameter curve on the surface patch.

The forward difference of a vector-valued function $\mathbf{r}(u)$ is

$$\Delta\mathbf{r}(u) = \mathbf{r}(u + \delta) - \mathbf{r}(u) \tag{9.19}$$

where $\delta > 0$, and represents the increment in parameter u. We can rewrite this as

$$\mathbf{r}(u + \delta) = \mathbf{r}(u) + \Delta\mathbf{r}(u)$$

This means that we can determine $\mathbf{r}(u + \delta)$ if we know $\mathbf{r}(u)$ and $\Delta\mathbf{r}(u)$. Rewriting the formula above in iterative terms, we have

$$\mathbf{r}_{n+1} = \mathbf{r}_n + \Delta\mathbf{r}_n \tag{9.20}$$

where we evaluate $\mathbf{r}$ in constant steps of increment δ, so n and u are related by $u = \delta \cdot n$, and $\mathbf{r}_n = \mathbf{r}(u_n)$.

For a cubic PC,

$$\mathbf{r}(u) = \mathbf{a} + \mathbf{b}u + \mathbf{c}u^2 + \mathbf{d}u^3 \tag{9.21}$$

so the forward difference is

$$\Delta \mathbf{r}(u) = \mathbf{a} + \mathbf{b}(u + \delta) + \mathbf{c}(u + \delta)^2 + \mathbf{d}(u + \delta)^3$$
$$- (\mathbf{a} + \mathbf{b}u + \mathbf{c}u^2 + \mathbf{d}u^3)$$
$$= (\mathbf{b}\delta + \mathbf{c}\delta^2 + \mathbf{d}\delta^3) + (2\mathbf{c}\delta + 3\mathbf{d}\delta^2)u + 3\mathbf{d}\delta u^2 \tag{9.22}$$

Thus $\Delta \mathbf{r}(u)$ is a second-order polynomial.

Similarly, considering $\Delta \mathbf{r}(u)$ itself as a function, we write

$$\Delta^2 \mathbf{r}(u) = \Delta(\Delta \mathbf{r}(u)) = \Delta \mathbf{r}(u + \delta) - \Delta \mathbf{r}(u) \tag{9.23}$$

Applying this to (9.22) gives

$$\Delta^2 \mathbf{r}(u) = 2\mathbf{c}\delta^2 + 6\mathbf{d}\delta^3 + 6\mathbf{d}\delta^2 u \tag{9.24}$$

$\Delta^2 \mathbf{r}(u)$ is a first-order equation in u. Rewriting (9.23) and using the index n, we obtain

$$\Delta^2 \mathbf{r}_n = \Delta \mathbf{r}_{n+1} - \Delta \mathbf{r}_n$$

or

$$\Delta \mathbf{r}_{n+1} = \Delta \mathbf{r}_n + \Delta^2 \mathbf{r}_n$$

Replacing index n by $(n - 1)$ yields

$$\Delta \mathbf{r}_n = \Delta \mathbf{r}_{n-1} + \Delta^2 \mathbf{r}_{n-1} \tag{9.25}$$

Furthermore, considering $\Delta^2 \mathbf{r}(u)$ as a function, repeating the process once more, we obtain

$$\Delta^3 \mathbf{r}(u) = \Delta(\Delta^2 \mathbf{r}(u)) = \Delta^2 \mathbf{r}(u + \delta) - \Delta^2 \mathbf{r}(u) \tag{9.26}$$

Applying this to (9.24) gives

$$\Delta^3 \mathbf{r}(u) = 6\mathbf{d}\delta^3 \tag{9.27}$$

We now see that this third difference is a constant, so its evaluation is very simple. Now we rewrite (9.26) using index n to obtain

$$\Delta^3 \mathbf{r}_n = \Delta^2 \mathbf{r}_{n+1} - \Delta^2 \mathbf{r}_n$$

or

$$\Delta^2 \mathbf{r}_{n+1} = \Delta^2 \mathbf{r}_n + \Delta^3 \mathbf{r}_n$$
$$= \Delta^2 \mathbf{r}_n + 6\mathbf{d}\delta^3 \tag{9.28}$$

Replacing index n by $(n - 2)$, we obtain

$$\Delta^2 \mathbf{r}_{n-1} = \Delta^2 \mathbf{r}_{n-2} + 6\mathbf{d}\delta^3 \tag{9.29}$$

Equation (9.29) can now be used in (9.25) to obtain $\Delta \mathbf{r}_n$, which is then used in (9.20) to find $\mathbf{r}_{n+1}$.

To use the forward differences in an algorithm which iterates n from $n = 0$ to $n\delta = 1$, we compute firstly the function and the first, second and third forward differences at $u = 0$, that is $n = 0$ by using (9.21), (9.22), (9.24) and (9.27):

$$\mathbf{r}_0 = \mathbf{a}$$

$$\Delta \mathbf{r}_0 = \mathbf{b}\delta + \mathbf{c}\delta^2 + \mathbf{d}\delta^3$$

$$\Delta^2 \mathbf{r}_0 = 2\mathbf{c}\delta^2 + 6\mathbf{d}\delta^3$$

$$\Delta^3 \mathbf{r}_0 = 6\mathbf{d}\delta^3 \tag{9.30}$$

We now repeat the following steps $1/\delta$ times, with n initially 0:

$$\mathbf{r}_{n+1} = \mathbf{r}_n + \Delta \mathbf{r}_n$$

$$\Delta \mathbf{r}_{n+1} = \Delta \mathbf{r}_n + \Delta^2 \mathbf{r}_n$$

$$\Delta^2 \mathbf{r}_{n+1} = \Delta^2 \mathbf{r}_n + \Delta^3 \mathbf{r}_0 \tag{9.31}$$

Fig. 9.11 shows the geometric significance for (9.30) and (9.31). Note that the calculations are performed in the order shown; no storage for intermediate results is needed. For cubic curves, $x(u)$, $y(u)$, $z(u)$ are treated separately. Equations (9.30) and (9.31) provide high calculating speed for the cubic parameter curves. After the computations to initialize the four parameters $\mathbf{r}_0$, $\Delta \mathbf{r}_0$. $\Delta^2 \mathbf{r}_0$ and $\Delta^3 \mathbf{r}_0$, only three additions are required for each point; other methods for evaluating cubic curves require several multiplications for each evaluation. A difficulty with the forward difference method is that the number of equal increments must be carefully selected to ensure appropriate tolerances. The method is widely used in NC drawing and display.

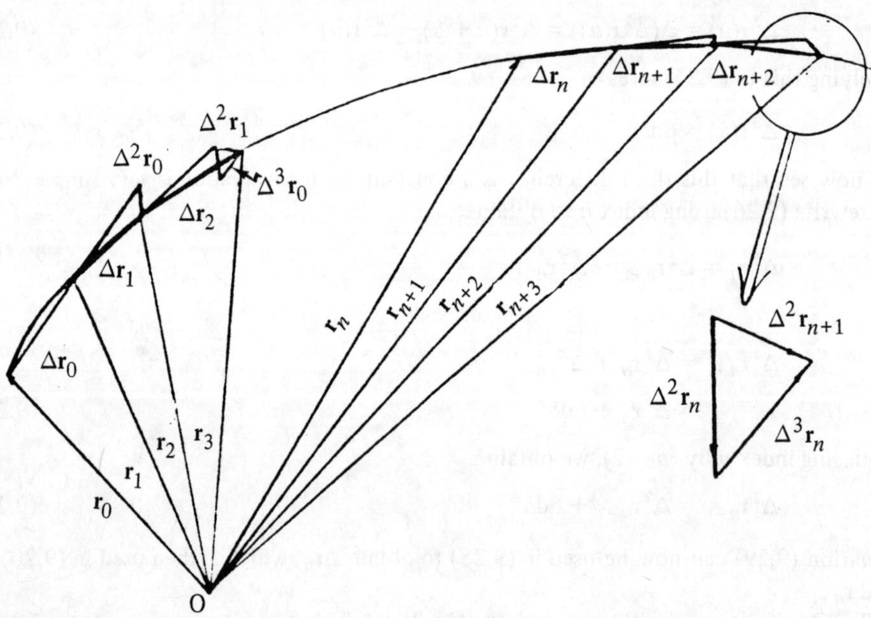

Fig. 9.11

(9.30) can be rewritten in matrix form

$$\begin{bmatrix} \mathbf{r}_0 \\ \Delta\mathbf{r}_0 \\ \Delta^2\mathbf{r}_0 \\ \Delta^3\mathbf{r}_0 \end{bmatrix} = \begin{bmatrix} 1 & 0 & 0 & 0 \\ 0 & \delta & \delta^2 & \delta^3 \\ 0 & 0 & 2\delta^2 & 6\delta^3 \\ 0 & 0 & 0 & 6\delta^3 \end{bmatrix} \begin{bmatrix} a \\ b \\ c \\ d \end{bmatrix} \tag{9.32}$$

This is more conveniently written as

$$R_0 = E(\delta)A \tag{9.33}$$

A is a 1×4 matrix of the coefficients of the curve.

It is useful to extend forward differences to surfaces.

The parametric bi-cubic is

$$\mathbf{r}(u, w) = \begin{matrix} a_{11} & + a_{12}w & + a_{13}w^2 & + a_{14}w^3 & + \\ a_{21}u & + a_{22}uw & + a_{23}uw^2 & + a_{24}uw^3 & + \\ a_{31}u^2 & + a_{32}u^2w & + a_{33}u^2w^2 & + a_{34}u^2w^3 & + \\ a_{41}u^3 & + a_{42}u^3w & + a_{43}u^3w^2 & + a_{44}u^3w^3 & \end{matrix} \tag{9.34}$$

Rewriting (9.34) in matrix form:

$$\mathbf{r}(u, w) = \begin{bmatrix} 1 & u & u^2 & u^3 \end{bmatrix} A \begin{bmatrix} 1 \\ w \\ w^2 \\ w^3 \end{bmatrix} \tag{9.35}$$

A is a 4×4 matrix of the coefficients of the surface.

The simplest form is

$$\mathbf{r}(u, w) = UAW^T \tag{9.36}$$

By analogy with the initialization for curves according to (9.33), we calculate for the surface:

$$R_{00} = E(\delta)AE(\epsilon)^T \tag{9.37}$$

where δ is the interval in parameter u, and ϵ is the interval in parameter w. The matrix R_{00} is 4×4 and the first column contains the corresponding values needed to compute $\mathbf{r}(u, 0)$, while the first row contains the corresponding values to compute $\mathbf{r}(0, w)$.

After computing $\mathbf{r}(u, 0)$ for all steps in u, the next problem is to compute $\mathbf{r}(u, \epsilon)$ (see Fig. 9.12). The iteration is very similar to that for a curve, but is performed on all columns of R_{00}:

$$\text{Column 1} = \text{Column 1} + \text{Column 2}$$

$$\text{Column 2} = \text{Column 2} + \text{Column 3}$$

$$\text{Column 3} = \text{Column 3} + \text{Column 4} \tag{9.38}$$

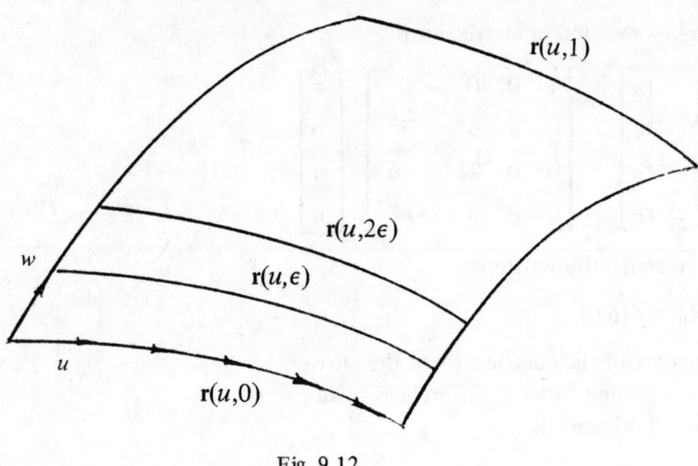

Fig. 9.12

Now Column 1 is used for $\mathbf{r}(u, \epsilon)$. The steps of (9.38) are repeated and Column 1 now defines $\mathbf{r}(u, 2\epsilon)$ etc.

The interval δ depends on the tolerance and local surface properties, but interval ϵ depends on the radius of the ball end mill, the tolerance and local surface properties.

9.4.3 Tool paths along intersection curves between a surface and a plane

Computing tool paths along the intersection between a surface and a plane is an important part of a CAM system. This important problem is often encountered when surface cross-sections are required at the manufacturing stage.

Consider the intersection between a surface $\mathbf{r}(u, w)$ and an unbounded plane, as Fig. 9.13 shows.

As we know, a plane is also defined by two parameters as

$$\mathbf{r}(s, t) = \mathbf{a} + \mathbf{b}s + \mathbf{c}t \tag{9.39}$$

The intersection equation is of the form

$$\mathbf{r}(u, w) = \mathbf{r}(s, t) \tag{9.40}$$

which means that we have three component equations having four degrees of freedom. The extra degree of freedom manifests itself as a curve of intersection.

We may now arbitrarily fix one of the variables as constant, either u, w, s or t. This furnishes an additional equation or constraint, for example, $u = u_i$, where u_i is a constant. We compute the equation

$$\mathbf{r}(u_i, w) = \mathbf{r}(s, t) \tag{9.41}$$

to obtain one point on the intersection. By incrementing u by $\Delta u = \delta$ we find a series of points sufficient to define the intersection.

In engineering, the plane may be defined by different forms, such as the normal vector form

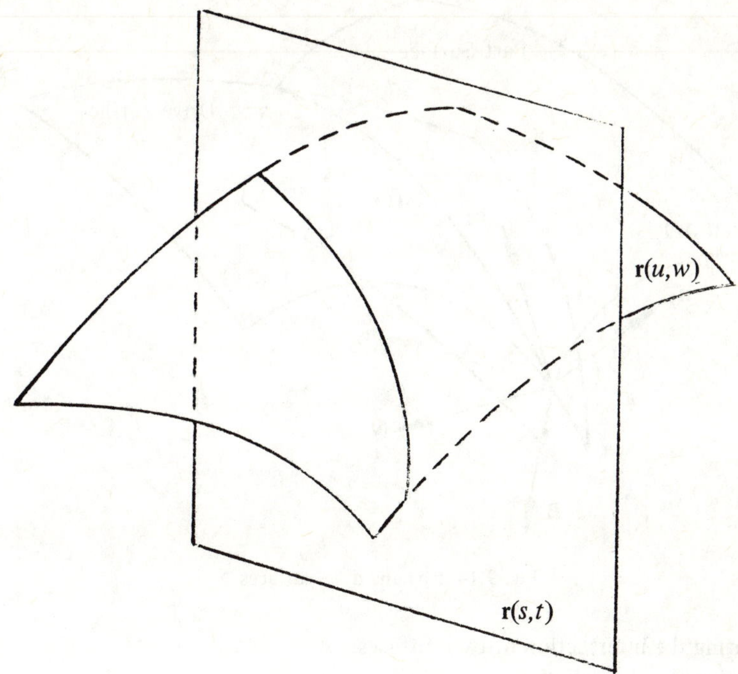

Fig. 9.13 The intersection

$$\mathbf{n} \cdot (\mathbf{r} - \mathbf{r}_0) = 0$$

or the intercept form

$$\frac{x}{a} + \frac{y}{b} + \frac{z}{c} = 1$$

or the polar coordinate form. Furthermore, the plane may be coincident or parallel with the coordinate plane. The principle of computing for an intersection is similar, but the solution may be simplified, especially for the last case. It must be remembered that the program is designed to deal with a wide variety of plane and surface definitions.

9.4.4 Tool paths along curves between two surfaces

As we know, when a surface is machined using a ball end cutter, the tool centre moves on another parallel surface, offset from the original by an amount equal to the cutter radius R. In engineering, the surfaces machined are not unbounded; a common problem is to machine a surface which is bounded on one or more sides by surfaces, which must also be accurately machined. The surface can be cut where the tool is required to maintain contact with both part and drive surfaces (see Fig. 9.14). This is similar to the concept used in APT. Because it is so difficult to define tool paths along curves between part and drive surfaces, we will decompose the procedure into three distinct phases:

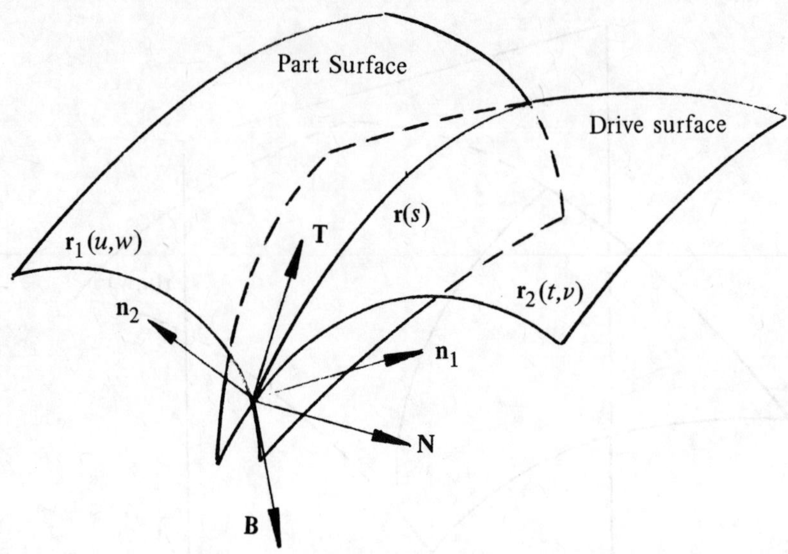

Fig. 9.14 Part and drive surfaces

- calculating the intersection of two surfaces;
- calculating the step length;
- calculating the end points of segments on the intersection.

1. Calculating the intersection of two surfaces

Consider the intersection between a surface $\mathbf{r}_1(u, w)$ and a surface $\mathbf{r}_2(t, v)$; the intersection $\mathbf{r}(s)$ can be obtained from the equation

$$\mathbf{r}_1(u, w) - \mathbf{r}_2(t, v) = 0 \tag{9.42}$$

as shown in Fig. 9.14.

We know that there are three component equations having four unknowns and that we could resolve this problem by holding one of the unknowns constant. Setting $u = u_i$, we obtain

$$\mathbf{r}_1(u_i, w) - \mathbf{r}_2(t, v) = 0 \tag{9.43}$$

Because we cannot directly resolve three component equations analytically we need an iteration procedure, which will be discussed in more detail in Chapter 10. We expect the general solution to be a space curve $\mathbf{r}(s)$ which is a function of a single new parameter, as shown in Fig. 9.14.

2. Calculating step length

We recall the curvature algorithm for the linear approximation mentioned in subsection 9.2.2. Equation (9.11) shows that the step length L depends on the local curvature of the intersection curve.

Now, consider the local curvature of the intersection curve $\mathbf{r}(s)$. Let the tangent, normal and binormanl vectors to the space curve be $\mathbf{T}$, $\mathbf{N}$ and $\mathbf{B}$ (see Fig. 9.14), and let both surfaces have the corresponding surface normals $\mathbf{n}_1$ and $\mathbf{n}_2$.

The unit tangent vector $\mathbf{T}$ is perpendicular to both surface normals so that

$$\mathbf{T} = \pm \mathbf{n}_1 \times \mathbf{n}_2 / |\mathbf{n}_1 \times \mathbf{n}_2| \tag{9.44}$$

The curvature κ of the space curve can be computed directly in terms of $\mathbf{r}(s)$, $\mathbf{r}(s + \delta s)$ and $\mathbf{T}(s)$. Consider two adjacent points on the space curve $\mathbf{r}(s)$, having arc length parameters s and $s + \delta s$, respectively.

By a Taylor expansion of $\mathbf{r}(s)$, we have

$$\mathbf{r}(s + \delta s) = \mathbf{r}(s) + \delta s \dot{\mathbf{r}}(s) + \tfrac{1}{2} \delta s^2 \ddot{\mathbf{r}}(s) + O(\delta s^3)$$

in which the dots denote differentiation with respect to s. Because

$$\dot{\mathbf{r}}(s) = \mathbf{T} \quad \text{and} \quad \ddot{\mathbf{r}}(s) = \kappa \mathbf{N}$$

we obtain

$$\mathbf{r}(s + \delta s) - \mathbf{r}(s) = \delta s \mathbf{T} + \tfrac{1}{2} \delta s^2 \kappa \mathbf{N} + O(\delta s^3)$$

thus

$$\Delta \mathbf{r} \times \mathbf{T} = \tfrac{1}{2} \delta s^2 \kappa (-\mathbf{B}) + O(\delta s^3)$$

that is

$$|\Delta \mathbf{r} \times \mathbf{T}| = \tfrac{1}{2} \delta s^2 \kappa + O(\delta s^3)$$

By approximating the arc length δs by the chord length and neglecting the remainder, we obtain

$$\kappa = \frac{2 |\Delta \mathbf{r} \times \mathbf{T}|}{|\Delta \mathbf{r}|^2} \tag{9.45}$$

From (9.44) and (9.45), we see that the curvature of the intersection of the two surfaces $\mathbf{r}_1$ and $\mathbf{r}_2$ may be expressed in terms of $\mathbf{r}(s)$, $\mathbf{r}(s + \delta s)$ and the unit normals $\mathbf{n}_1$ and $\mathbf{n}_2$ to the two surfaces.

Alternatively, the curvature κ may also be expressed in terms of the normal curvatures κ_{n1} and κ_{n2} of the curves on the two surfaces $\mathbf{r}_1$ and $\mathbf{r}_2$.

By the differential geometry theorem, we have

$$\kappa \mathbf{B} = - \kappa \mathbf{N} \times \mathbf{T} = \mp \kappa \mathbf{N} \times (\mathbf{n}_1 \times \mathbf{n}_2) / |\mathbf{n}_1 \times \mathbf{n}_2|$$

since using the triple vector product

$$\kappa \mathbf{N} \times (\mathbf{n}_1 \times \mathbf{n}_2) = \kappa (\mathbf{N} \cdot \mathbf{n}_2) \mathbf{n}_1 - \kappa (\mathbf{N} \cdot \mathbf{n}_1) \mathbf{n}_2$$

$$= \kappa_{n2} \mathbf{n}_1 - \kappa_{n1} \mathbf{n}_2$$

we obtain

$$\kappa \mathbf{B} = \frac{\pm(\kappa_{n1}\mathbf{n}_2 - \kappa_{n2}\mathbf{n}_1)}{|\mathbf{n}_1 \times \mathbf{n}_2|}$$

If the angle between the surface normals is θ the curvature is given by

$$\kappa^2 = \frac{\kappa_{n1}^2 - 2\kappa_{n1}\kappa_{n2}\cos\theta + \kappa_{n2}^2}{\sin^2\theta} \tag{9.46}$$

in which

$$\kappa_{n1} = \frac{2\mathbf{n}_1 \cdot \Delta\mathbf{r}}{|\Delta\mathbf{r}|^2}$$

$$\kappa_{n2} = \frac{2\mathbf{n}_2 \cdot \Delta\mathbf{r}}{|\Delta\mathbf{r}|^2} \tag{9.47}$$

Proving the formulae (9.47) is very similar to that of (9.45).

As equation (9.46) shows, the curvature may become very large when the angle is small, so that the step length must be very small (see Fig. 9.5 and equation (9.11). When the normals $\mathbf{n}_1$ and $\mathbf{n}_2$ are parallel or nearly parallel, we will encounter difficulty in defining the step length.

3. *Calculating end points of segments on the section*

We obtained the intersection curve $\mathbf{r}(s)$, and then we obtained the step length L by using the radius of curvature ρ. Now, we should calculate the next point on the space curve $\mathbf{r}(s)$ from the current point on $\mathbf{r}(s)$ by using the step length L.

A sphere of radius L would appear to be the obvious choice; the next point can be obtained by calculating the intersection between the equation of the sphere and the space curve $\mathbf{r}(s)$.

We would like to introduce the following method, which has been used in NC programs. A plane may be chosen to be normal to the current tangent $\mathbf{T}_i$ (see Fig. 9.15).

On the basis of the osculating circle approximation, the distance d from the plane to the current point $\mathbf{r}_i$ is taken as

$$d = L\left(1 - \frac{\delta}{\rho}\right) \tag{9.48}$$

in which L is taken from equation (9.11).

The plane can be represented as

$$(\mathbf{P} - \mathbf{r}_i) \cdot \mathbf{T}_i = d \tag{9.49}$$

where $\mathbf{r}_i$ is the current point, and $\mathbf{T}_i$ is the current tangent vector. $\mathbf{P}$ is the point on the plane.

Finally, the next point $\mathbf{r}_{i+1}$ can be obtained by calculating the intersection between the equation of the plane (9.49) and the space curve $\mathbf{r}(s)$. The equation of a plane is linear, but the equation of a sphere is quadric.

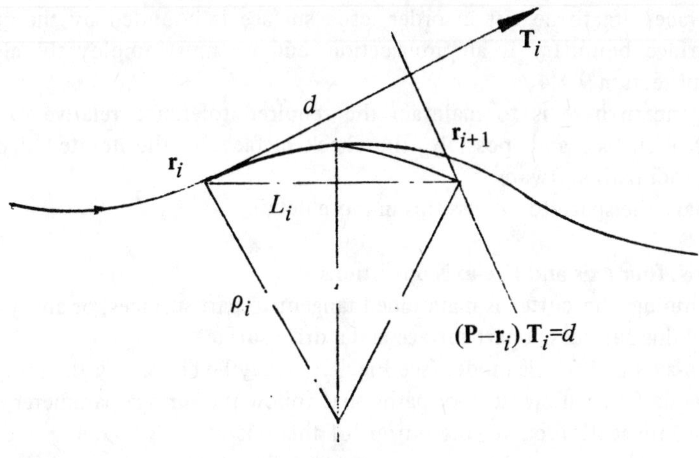

Fig. 9.15

9.4.5 Part surface, drive surface and check surface

In NC programming, it is assumed the part remains stationary and the tool moves. Three surfaces control the tool motion in contouring. The tool end moves on the surface which is called the part surface, the tool slides along the surface called the drive surface, and the motion continues until the tool meets the surface called the check surface (see Fig. 9.16).

These three surfaces control the cutter motion in contouring. Note that the terms 'part surface' and 'drive surface' are reversed when we machine r_2 with r_1 as the boundary, and that the check surface r_3 usually becomes the drive surface of the next motion statement.

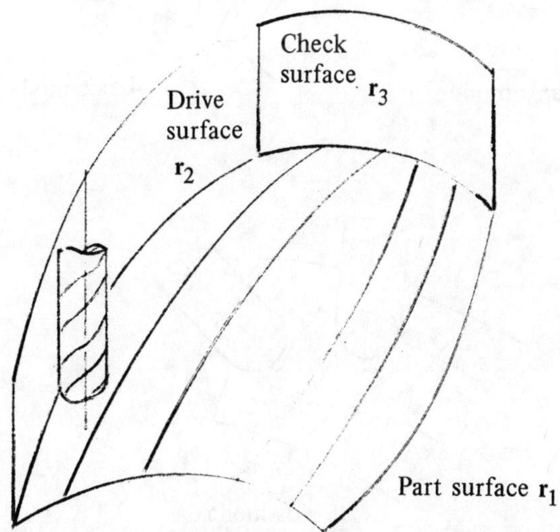

Fig. 9.16 Part, drive and check surfaces

If three surfaces are to be cut in order, each surface is bounded by the other two surfaces. A surface boundary is an intersection, and we must employ the algorithms mentioned in subsection 9.4.4.

Our main concern here is to maintain the required tolerance relative to the part surface, the drive surface and, possibly, the check surface. So the iterated algorithm is usually used in tool-path software.

We do not have the space to discuss this in more detail.

9.4.6 Three-axis, four-axis and five-axis operations

In surface machining, the cutter is maintained tangent to part surfaces, or always tangent to the two adjoining surfaces, a part surface and a drive surface.

The 3-axis, 4-axis and 5-axis modes (see Fig. 9.17) may be chosen by the programmer. In the 3-axis mode, we can create tool paths that follow the surface parameter curves or travel along the intersection curve; the output of this operation is in x, y, z coordinates. Tool paths keep the cutting tool tangent to surfaces. The tool axis is normal to the view in which the path is created and is constant throughout the path.

In 4-axis machining, the tool axis has the freedom to rotate within a given plane. Equivalently, the tool axis is restricted to being perpendicular to a given vector, which is the normal vector to the tool axis plane.

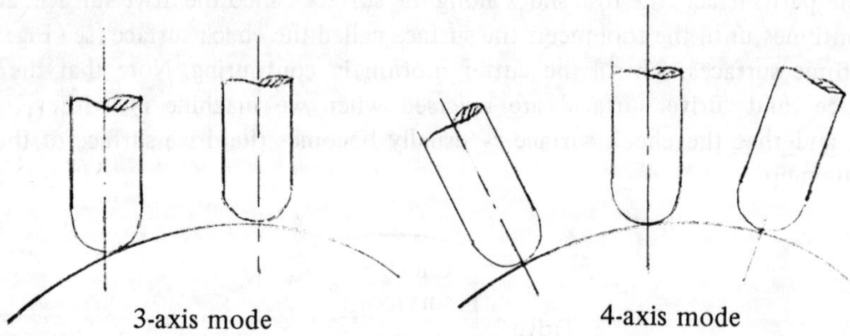

3-axis mode   4-axis mode

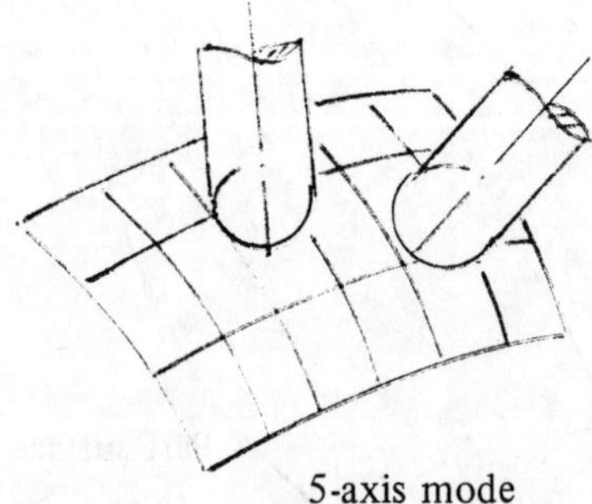

5-axis mode

Fig. 9.17 3-axis, 4-axis and 5-axis modes

The 4-axis option gives the user three methods for specifying the relation between the part and the tool axis. The first method is to enter the **i, j, k** values of a vector, which must be perpendicular to the tool axis. The second method is to digitize the vector instead of entering its **i, j, k** values. The third method is to digitize a planar surface to which the tool axis will be parallel.

In the 5-axis mode, the tool centreline is normal to the 3-D surface so that the output contains the necessary tool axis orientation, that is, the necessary **i, j, k** tool axis vectors in addition to the x, y, z coordinates. The **i, j, k** tool axis vectors can be calculated in terms of the normal vector of the surface at the cut contact point.

9.5 TOOL-PATH SIMULATION AND VERIFICATION

From the surface modeller, a CAM package will automatically generate cutter paths for finish machining and drawing on the screen. Preliminary roughing paths can also be automatically generated for initial removal of the bulk of the material.

A CAM package can provide useful assistance for the user, who can decide how he wants to machine the surface modelled by selecting the machine tool and the cutting tools, the feed rate and depth of cut for initial roughing and finish machining.

A CAM package will automatically adjust the cutter paths to achieve the required surface if the 'cusp' height is specified.

A CAM package will provide fully automatic cutter clearance checks. The cutter and surface can be drawn and displayed along any selected view to establish how they relate.

A CAM package will provide machining on 3-axis, 4-axis or 5-axis machines with simultaneous control on all axes.

The concepts and algorithms mentioned in this chapter are the bases of generating tool paths for surface machining, which is the core of any 3-D CAM package.

Although much of the tool-path generation is automatically performed by the system software, a part-programmer can design tool paths for a machine tool in the conventional way. This option is available, which allows the part-programmer to make specific choices if desired, with the advantage of flexibility. In this case the concepts and algorithms mentioned in this chapter are very useful for the part-programmer.

Most CAM packages allow for accurate and realistic verification of 2-D, $2\frac{1}{2}$-D, and 3-D toolpaths without actually cutting metal. The user can simulate and visually verify the tool path on the screen. The tool patch seen on the screen shows the tool actually moving along the part from any perspective. This allows the engineer to check for tool-path correctness and clearance of tools, components and fixtures. The tool-path data are independent of the actual machine tool control system.

Post-processor software converts the cutter path output into NC or CNC machine tool control language. The data can be transferred into the machine tool controller. The post-processor adapts the general data and converts them into the specific format required by the machine tool control system. Options include a data recorder for magnetic tape, tape punch for punched paper tape, or additional software for a direct computer link.

9.6 TOOL-PATH SOFTWARE

A number of firms now offer tool-path software; typical softwares and their suppliers are

- APT
- CADDS4   Computervision
- MEDUSA   Cambridge Interactive Systems Ltd
- NC Programming   Intergraph
- ITS   Counting House
- CAM-X   Infographics
- DUCT   Deltacam

9.6.1 APT

APT (Automatically Programmed Tools) is a programming language which allows geometrical data to be specified together with tool motion statements for any NC machine. The user of APT defines the geometry of the workpiece and the requisite tool motions using simple English-like statements.

The APT systems consist of three parts: the part-program, the program processor, the program post-processor.

The part-program is first written to specify the geometry of a component or workpiece. The program processor is a very large program normally resident on a large storage unit which is run mostly on a mainframe computer. It accepts part-programs and produces an output which is called the Cutter Location Data. These data are then normally passed on to a post-processor which produces an NC tape for a specific machine tool.

One of APT's biggest advantages is that it has become a world-wide standard for NC machines. Variations of APT have been developed outside the US.

A disadvantage is the large overhead in terms of computing capacity and power for relatively simple components.

Its post-processing activity can be considerable for older types of NC systems with limited built-in intelligence. This is necessary since the program would have to provide information on accelerations, decelerations and velocities of the tool or cutter in order to maintain the correct path. In modern systems, machine control parameters and characteristics are built into a minicomputer or microcomputer controller attached to the machine tool.

9.6.2 CADDS 4 of Computervision

Computervision's CADDS 4 Designer V System is an interactive conversational graphics system providing design, drafting and manufacturing capabilities. The Designer V System provides a graphical approach to numerical control. NC involves generating tool paths and producing machine control data for a variety of machining operations.

The CADDS 4 is based on the use of interactive graphics facilities for inputing and editing geometrical data into a 3-D database from which all output and post-processed programs compatible with the APT Cutter Location Data can be generated. The system supports a set of geometrical elements similar in their format to the APT language.

Computervision is probably the world leader as far as the number of systems installed is concerned.

9.6.3 MEDUSA of Cambridge

MEDUSA is developed in England, supported by Cambridge Interactive Systems Ltd, and marketed by the Computervision organization throughout the world.

The MEDUSA Manufacturing System carries design into production. Each module within the manufacturing system allows the user to extract design information from his MEDUSA database, to add manufacturing instructions and to generate control tapes, for a wide variety of numerically controlled machines.

The system is linked to filling systems based on IGES (International Graphics Exchange Standard). MEDUSA is one of the best known of CAD/CAM systems.

9.6.4 NC programming of Intergraph

Intergraph Corporation provides users with an extensive set of facilities for generating machine-specific output from part design geometry.

Creating tool paths

Any 3-D part design produced on an Intergraph graphics system can be used to support tool-path creation. Once the tool-path parameters have been established, Intergraph NC programming software automatically creates the tool paths from part geometry. The resulting graphics represent the centreline motion of the selected tool.

Multiple-cut milling sequences with undercut detection are developed automatically about any planar or sculptured (B-spline) surface.

Its NC programming software allows the programmer to display multiple reference files simultaneously. For example, to visually check for tool-path interference, the operator can display a design to be machined with one reference file, the graphic representation of the fixture with a second and the representation of the machine with a third.

The system's 32-bit graphics database supports generation of high-precision tool paths, maintaining one millionth of an inch accuracy of resolution on parts exceeding 100 feet in length.

Editing tool paths

The system recognizes tool paths as standard graphics elements. As such, they can be copied, modified, deleted, scaled or rotated with standard graphics manipulation commands.

Machine (post-processor) commands are associated with the tool path to indicate tool changes, speed, feed rate and other miscellaneous functions. These commands can be attached either during or after tool-path creation, and they are easily modified, deleted or resequenced.

Verification

Tool and tool-path display features allow the user to verify tool-path sequencing and to check for interferences. Graphics information, created and stored in the tool library, generates a display image of a particular tool. If tool graphics have not been defined, the system extracts the dimension from the tool library and automatically generates a tool image for display. The tool may be displayed at any given point along the tool path, at static intervals along the tool path or dynamically moving along the tool path.

In addition, the tool path can be displayed by highlighting successive segments of a tool-path sequence.

Output

Tool paths are generated individually. The operator can create them without regard to sequence. When all aspects of the machining process have been considered, the programmer may then queue the tool paths for output in the most logical order as a complete program sequence. For example, a milling sequence can be selected as the first operation, drilling as the second and tapping as the third, independent of the order in which each tool path was created.

Once the program sequence is generated, the system translates the part-program into a standard NC language for output to paper tape, magnetic tape or floopy disk media or directly to a machine control unit.

Intergraph NC software interfaces with three industry-standard processors, APT, COMPACT II and SPLIT, for source output.

Intergraph Corporation achieved rapid growth through sales of its CAD/CAM software.

Counting House became the leading supplier of graphic NC part-programming systems. Inforgraphics and Deltacam are also major suppliers of the graphic NC system.

Most integrated CAD/CAM systems use geometric contours as a link between design and manufacture. This is due to NC languages having the requirement for precise definitions of geometry in order to calculate tool paths.

REFERENCES

[1] Paraidannou, S. G. and Kiritsis, D., An application of Bertrand curves and surfaces to CADCAM, *Computer-aided Design*, **17**, No. 8 (1985), 348–352.

[2] Faux, I. D. and Pratt, M. J., *Computational Geometry for Design and Manufacture*, Ellis Horwood, Chichester, 1985.

[3] Mortenson, M. E., *Geometric Modelling*, John Wiley & Sons, New York, 1985.

[4] Besant, C. B. and Lui, C. W. K., *Computer-aided Design and Manufacture*, 3rd edn, Ellis Horwood, Chichester, 1986.

[5] Foley, J. D. and Dam, A. V., *Fundamentals of Interactive Computer Graphics*, Addison-Wesley, Reading, MA, 1982.

[6] Haigh, M. J., *An Introduction to Computer-aided Design and Manufacture*, Blackwell Scientific Publications, Oxford, 1985.

10

The Surface Intersection Problem

10.1 INTRODUCTION

The surface intersection problem is one of the most important computational tasks in surface modelling. The intersection calculations will be applied in four cases: design, drawing, display and manufacture. In the design process, we hope that we can mathematically express the surface intersection. We often encounter the surface intersection problem in drawing and display. In order to machine a surface without violating a neighbouring surface, the correct tool paths along the surface intersection are absolutely necessary.

A surface modelling system will provide a mass of data for aircraft design, drawing, display and manufacture; much of this relates to the intersection between aircraft surfaces (such as fuselage, wings, etc). (See Fig. 10.1.)

Unfortunately, the intersection curve between two surfaces is determined by the solution of non-linear equations, unless the two surfaces are planes. Except for some simpler surfaces, such as quadrics, for which analytical methods may be used, it is usually necessary to solve the problem by numerical methods. As the number of surface patches increases, the need for computational complexity increases.

The surfaces used in CAD/CAM can be classified as follows:

- planes, bi-quadrics and bi-cubics by the degrees of the surfaces, sometimes 1×3 or 2×3 degrees;
- Ferguson, Bezier and B-spline surfaces, and rational surfaces, etc. by the defining methods;
- implicit equations and parameter equations of surfaces by the defining forms.

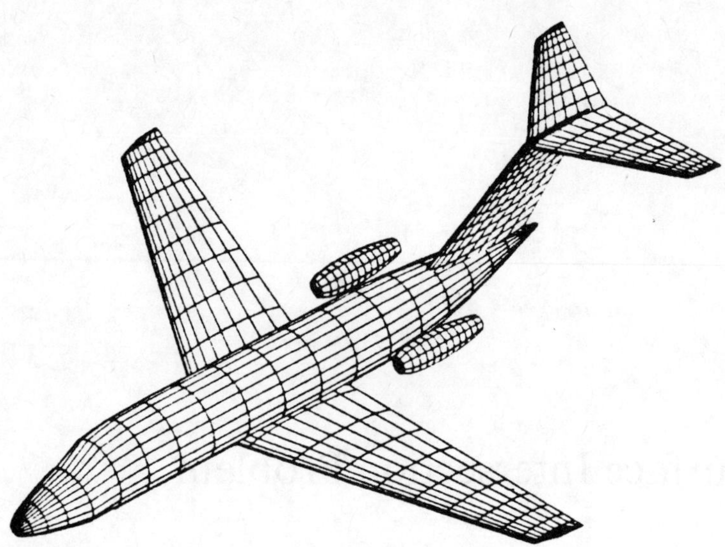

Fig. 10.1 The surface intersection

Some of the algorithms for solving surface intersection problems include: the analytical method, the iteration method and the least-squares minimization method. It must be remembered that the algorithms are designed to deal with a wide variety of surface defining methods and forms.

This chapter begins with the principle of calculation, and general algorithms; it then discusses the intersection between a surface and a plane. The surface–surface intersection will be considered in detail.

10.2 PRINCIPLE OF SOLUTION

The calculation of the intersection curve between two surfaces $\mathbf{r}_1$ and $\mathbf{r}_2$ may be regarded as a problem involving the solution of simultaneous equations.

10.2.1 Parameter equations
If the two surface equations are defined parametrically by

$$\mathbf{r}_1 = \mathbf{r}_1(u, w)$$

$$\mathbf{r}_2 = \mathbf{r}_2(s, t) \tag{10.1}$$

their intersection must be defined as

$$\mathbf{r}_1(u, w) = \mathbf{r}_2(s, t)$$

or

$$\mathbf{r}_1(u, w) - \mathbf{r}_2(s, t) = 0 \tag{10.2}$$

Most of the mathematics for the solution of the surface intersection problem involves solving three simultaneous equations, one for each of the Cartesian coordinates or vector components. The vector equation (10.2) may be expressed by three scalar equations as follows:

$$X_1(u,\,w) - X_2(s,\,t) = 0$$

$$Y_1(u,\,w) - Y_2(s,\,t) = 0$$

$$Z_1(u,\,w) - Z_2(s,\,t) = 0 \qquad (10.3)$$

in which the four variables are u, w, s and t.

We see from (10.3) that there is one more variable than there are equations, since the intersection curve possesses one degree of freedom.

If the parameter u is fixed (or any of the parameters w, s, t) in equation (10.3), the equations can be solved, and we can obtain a point on the intersection curve. Similarly, if we provide a sequence of values of the parameter u, substitute them into (10.3), solve (10.3) at each step and produce a sequence of points, these points define the intersection curve.

Alternatively, by imposing a further constraint equation

$$g(x,\,y,\,z) = 0 \qquad (10.4)$$

which is usually a plane equation, and may be translated into a parameter constraint equation

$$g_1(x(u,\,w),\quad y(u,\,w),\quad z(u,\,w)) = 0$$

we obtain

$$g_1(u,\,w) = 0 \qquad (10.5)$$

we solve equations (10.3) and (10.5) and obtain a point on the intersection curve.

Similarly, we may obtain from equation (10.4)

$$g_2(s,\,t) = 0 \qquad (10.6)$$

we can also solve equations (10.3) and (10.6).

These equivalent constraint equations may be combined as

$$\lambda g_1(u,\,w) + \mu g_2(s,\,t) = 0$$

where λ and μ may be chosen to simplify the constraint equation. Using (10.3) and the combined equation, we can thus obtain the solution of four parameters, which define a point on the intersection curve. By providing a sequence of constraint planes we obtain a sequence of points defining the intersection curve.

10.2.2 Implicit equations

Suppose two surfaces are expressed by the implicit equations

$$f_1(x, y, z) = 0$$

$$f_2(x, y, z) = 0 \qquad (10.7)$$

If the variable x is fixed (or variable y, or z) in equation (10.7), the equation can be solved. We can obtain a point on the intersection curve. Similarly, we can provide a sequence of values of the variable x, substitute them into (10.7), solve it at each step, and produce a sequence of points defining the intersection curve.

We can impose a sequence of constraint equations

$$f_3(x, y, z) = 0 \qquad (10,8)$$

solve the equations (10.7) and (10.8) at each step, and obtain a sequence of points (x_i, y_i, z_i), which describe the intersection curve. In fact, we solve a sequence of three surface intersection problems. The process is simpler than that for parameter equations.

Unfortunately, the most commonly used parametric surfaces, such as Bezier patches and B-spline patches, cannot be expressed in this way.

10.2.3 Mixed form equations

If a surface is defined by the implicit equation

$$f_1(x, y, z) = 0$$

and another surface is defined by the parameter equation

$$\mathbf{r}_2 = \mathbf{r}_2(u, w)$$

we can substitute its three components into the first surface equation, and obtain

$$f_1(x(u, w), \quad y(u, w), \quad z(u, w)) = 0$$

which is the intersection curve equation. We can see that the intersection curve equation takes the form

$$F(u, w) = 0 \qquad (10.9)$$

If the parameter u is fixed (or parameter w) in equation (10.9), then the equation can be solved, to obtain a point. Repeating the operation, we can produce the intersection curve.

We can provide an additional constraint equation

$$G(u, w) = 0 \qquad (10.10)$$

which is, in general, a plane parameter equation. We can solve the simultaneous equations (10.9) and (10.10), and obtain a point at each step.

We can now make some generalizations. First, we may solve the simultaneous equations by imposing a fixed parameter or variable at each step as a further constraint. Secondly, we can provide a plane equation as a further constraint; in general, this is convenient to solve the two-surface intersection problem.

10.3 METHODS OF SOLUTION

The Newton–Raphson iteration algorithm has been widely used for solving non-linear equations in engineering calculations, since it combines the virtues of efficiency and simplicity.

We recall how to obtain the solution of a single equation by using the Newton–Raphson iteration method. If a function $y = f(x)$ is differentiated, and $y' = f'(x) \neq 0$, using the relation of the right-angled triangle, we obtain

$$f'(x_i) = \frac{f(x_i)}{x_i - x_{i+1}}$$

which may be rewritten as

$$x_{i+1} = x_i - f(x_i)/f'(x_i) \tag{10.11}$$

This is the well-known Newton–Raphson iteration formula for a single non-linear equation. This formula has a simple geometrical interpretation. Reference to Fig. 10.2 shows that the tangent to the curve $y = f(x)$ at the point (x_i, y_i) were to cut the x-axis at a point x_{i+1} lying closer than x_i to the true solution X. The process may now be repeated with x_{i+1} as a new approximation to the true solution X, to derive a new point x_{i+2} which lies still closer to X, and so on. A reasonable starting approximation x_0 is a prerequisite for the success of the iteration.

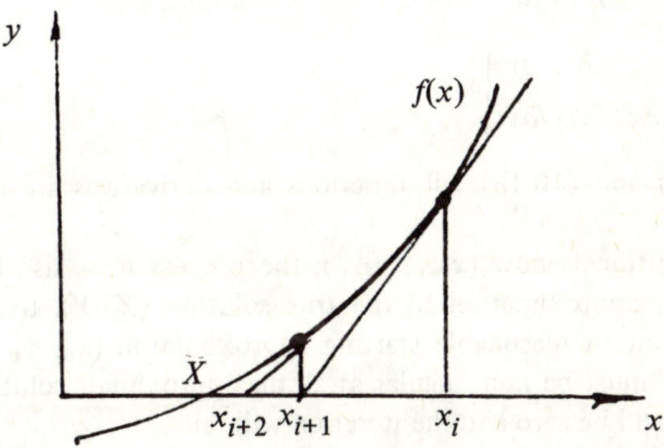

Fig. 10.2 The Newton–Raphson iteration

The Newton–Raphson method may be used for solving simultaneous non-linear equations. In the two-dimensional case, we have two non-linear equations

$$f_1(x, y) = 0$$

$$f_2(x, y) = 0 \tag{10.12}$$

which have corresponding partial derivatives $\partial f_1/\partial x$, $\partial f_1/\partial y$, $\partial f_2/\partial x$ and $\partial f_2/\partial y$. The two-dimensional Taylor expansions of $f_1(X, Y)$ and $f_2(X, Y)$ are respectively

$$f_1(X, Y) = f_1(x_i, y_i) + (X - x_i)\frac{\partial f_1}{\partial x}(x_i, y_i) + (Y - y_i)\frac{\partial f_1}{\partial y}(x_i, y_i) + \ldots$$

$$f_2(X, Y) = f_2(x_i, y_i) + (X - x_i)\frac{\partial f_2}{\partial x}(x_i, y_i) + (Y - y_i)\frac{\partial f_2}{\partial y}(x_i, y_i) + \ldots$$

If we neglect higher-order terms on the right and set $f_1(X, Y) = f_2(X, Y) = 0$ on the left, we obtain a pair of linear equations for $(x_{i+1} - x_i)$ and $(y_{i+1} - y_i)$, which are approximations to $(X - x_i)$ and $(Y - y_i)$:

$$(x_{i+1} - x_i)\frac{\partial f_1}{\partial x}(x_i, y_i) + (y_{i+1} - y_i)\frac{\partial f_1}{\partial y}(x_i, y_i) = -f_1(x_i, y_i)$$

$$(x_{i+1} - x_i)\frac{\partial f_2}{\partial x}(x_i, y_i) + (y_{i+1} - y_i)\frac{\partial f_2}{\partial y}(x_i, y_i) = -f_2(x_i, y_i) \qquad (10.13)$$

The results are

$$x_{i+1} = x_i - \begin{vmatrix} f_1 & \partial f_1/\partial y \\ f_2 & \partial f_2/\partial y \end{vmatrix} \Big/ D$$

$$y_{i+1} = y_i - \begin{vmatrix} \partial f_1/\partial x & f_1 \\ \partial f_2/\partial x & f_2 \end{vmatrix} \Big/ D \qquad (10.14)$$

where D is the determinant of the Jacobian matrix J defined by

$$J = \begin{bmatrix} \partial f_1/\partial x & \partial f_1/\partial y \\ \partial f_2/\partial x & \partial f_2/\partial y \end{bmatrix} \qquad (10.15)$$

In equations (10.14) and (10.15), all functions and derivatives are understood to be derived at (x_i, y_i).

The improved solution is now (x_{i+1}, y_{i+1}); the process may also be repeated with (x_{i+1}, y_{i+1}) as a new approximation to the true solution (X, Y), to give a new point (x_{i+2}, y_{i+2}), and so on. A reasonable starting approximation (x_0, y_0) is necessary for successful iteration. J must be non-singular at all the approximate solution points, otherwise, its determinant will be zero and the iteration will fail.

Equation (10.14) is a straightforward extension of equation (10.11). The extension of this approach to the solution of systems of more than two equations is straightforward.

In the n-dimensional case, we have n non-linear equations

$$F_1(x_1, x_2, \ldots, x_n) = 0$$

$$F_2(x_1, x_2, \ldots, x_n) = 0$$

$$\vdots$$

$$F_n(x_1, x_2, \ldots, x_n) = 0 \qquad (10.16)$$

where $x_1, x_2, \ldots, x_n$ are variables.

The solutions of the Newton–Raphson iteration method are

$$
x_{1,i+1} = x_{1,i} - \begin{vmatrix} F_1 & \partial F_1/\partial x_2 & \ldots & \partial F_1/\partial x_n \\ F_2 & \partial F_2/\partial x_2 & \ldots & \partial F_2/\partial x_n \\ \vdots & \vdots & & \vdots \\ F_n & \partial F_n/\partial x_2 & \ldots & \partial F_n/\partial x_n \end{vmatrix} \Bigg/ D
$$

$$
x_{2,i+1} = x_{2,i} - \begin{vmatrix} \partial F_1/\partial x_1 & F_1 & \ldots & \partial F_1/\partial x_n \\ \partial F_2/\partial x_1 & F_2 & \ldots & \partial F_2/\partial x_n \\ \vdots & \vdots & & \vdots \\ \partial F_n/\partial x_1 & F_n & \ldots & \partial F_n/\partial x_n \end{vmatrix} \Bigg/ D
$$

$$
x_{n,i+1} = x_{n,i} - \begin{vmatrix} \partial F_1 \partial x_1 & \partial F_1/\partial x_2 & \ldots & F_1 \\ \partial F_2/\partial x_1 & \partial F_2/\partial x_2 & \ldots & F_2 \\ \vdots & \vdots & & \vdots \\ \partial F_n/\partial x_1 & \partial F_n/\partial x_2 & \ldots & F_n \end{vmatrix} \Bigg/ D \tag{10.17}
$$

where D is the determinant of the $n \times n$ Jacobian matrix J defined by

$$
J = \begin{bmatrix} \partial F_1/\partial x_1 & \partial F_1/\partial x_2 & \ldots & \partial F_1/\partial x_n \\ \partial F_2/\partial x_1 & \partial F_2/\partial x_2 & \ldots & \partial F_2/\partial x_n \\ \vdots & \vdots & & \vdots \\ \partial F_n/\partial x_1 & \partial F_2/\partial x_2 & \ldots & \partial F_n/\partial x_n \end{bmatrix} \tag{10.18}
$$

In equations (10.17) and (10.18), all functions and derivatives are understood to be derived at $(x_{1,i}, x_{2,i}, \ldots, x_{n,i})$.

Non-linear equations of higher degree cannot, in general, be solved exactly. Fortunately, the iteration method gives the required solutions to any desired accuracy with great efficiency.

By using the iteration algorithm it is efficient to calculate the intersection of surfaces.

10.4 INTERSECTIONS BETWEEN SURFACES AND A PLANE

Computing intersections between surfaces and a plane is a key requirement for modelling in design and manufacture. Conventional cross-sections of products can be obtained by computing the appropriate intersection between surfaces of a modeller and a plane required.

We begin with the study of the intersection between surfaces and a plane which can be represented as

$$\mathbf{r}_1 = \mathbf{r}(u, w)$$

$$\mathbf{r}_2 = \mathbf{A} + \mathbf{B}s + \mathbf{C}t \qquad (10.19)$$

Since we already know that the plane $\mathbf{r}_2$ is also a two-parameter geometric element, we expect to derive three component equations having four degrees of freedom. The extra degree of freedom manifests itself as a curve of intersection (see Fig. 10.3). The intersection equation is of the form

$$\mathbf{r}(u, w) = \mathbf{A} + \mathbf{B}s + \mathbf{C}t \qquad (10.20)$$

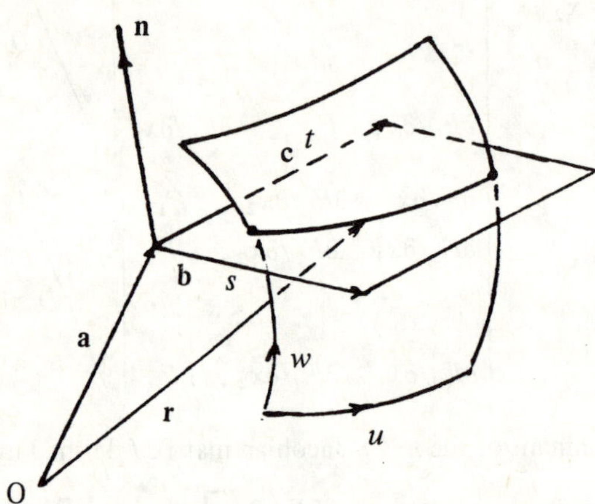

Fig. 10.3 Intersection between a surface and a plane

We may now arbitrarily fix as constant one of the variables, i.e. u, w, s, or t. This furnishes an additional constraint, for example, $u = u_i$, where u_i is a constraint. Then, we derive three component equations having three unknowns or variables. We can obtain the solution using the iteration method at each step.

If the normal vector $\mathbf{n}$ of the plane is known, we may represent the plane as (see Fig. 10.3)

$$(\mathbf{r} - \mathbf{a}) \cdot \mathbf{n} = 0 \qquad (10.21)$$

where $\mathbf{a}$ is a constant vector.

The intersection equation is

$$(\mathbf{r}(u, w) - \mathbf{a}) \cdot \mathbf{n} = 0 \qquad (10.22)$$

We may now arbitrarily set one of the variables to zero, i.e. u or w in equation (10.22). Once one end of the curve of intersection is found, by incrementing u_i by Δu (or w_j by same Δw), we can find a series of points sufficient to define the intersection curve.

A surface may be defined in several ways, such as the parameter form or the implicit form. A plane may be defined in several ways, such as the parameter form, the normal form, or the intercept form. A surface modelling system should include these most common forms for computing the intersection.

Three practical examples of the surface intersections used in surface modelling packages are now introduced in more detail. This will enable surface modelling systems to be applied more effectively and efficiently.

Example 1 Intersection between classical surfaces and a plane
Since classical surfaces possess simple and clear geometrical properties, they are widely used in mechanical engineering, e.g. shipbuilding, and aviation and aerospace. The equation for a classical surface is a function of three variables x, y and z and can be written in the implicit form as follows:

$$F(x, y, z) = 0 \tag{10.23}$$

If we consider how to form a circular arc surface of a fuselage of an aircraft, the equation of a circular arc with its centre (y_0, z_0) and radius R may be expressed in the yOz plane as

$$(y - y_0)^2 + (z - z_0)^2 - R^2 = 0$$

Every curved surface may be regarded as generated by the movement of a curve. Thus the circular arc curved surface may be generated by moving the arc along the x-axis in the Cartesian coordinate system as

$$[y - y_0(x)]^2 + [z - z_0(x)]^2 - R^2(x) = 0 \tag{10.24}$$

where $y_0(x)$, $z_0(x)$ and $R(x)$ are functions of the variable x, which is along the direction of the centroidal axis of the fuselage. The surface modeller of the fuselage consists of many strings of circular arc curved surfaces.

The general equation of a plane is of the form

$$Ax + By + Cz + D = 0 \tag{10.25}$$

This equation may assume many truncated forms, representative of special cases. For instance, according to the convention in aircraft design, a section of a fuselage may be defined by the three parameters (see Fig. 10.4):

- x_i is the intercept of the section on the x-axis;
- α_i is the angle between the positive direction of the x-axis and the intersection line between the section and the xOy plane;
- β_i is the angle between the positive direction of the x-axis and the intersection line between the section and the xOz plane.

Thus, the intercept on the y-axis is $-x_i \, \mathrm{tg}\, \alpha_i$ and on the z-axis is $-x_i \, \mathrm{tg}\, \beta_i$. The intercept equation for the section is of the form

$$\frac{x}{x_i} - \frac{y}{x_i \, \mathrm{tg}\, \alpha_i} - \frac{z}{x_i \, \mathrm{tg}\, \beta_i} = 1$$

that is

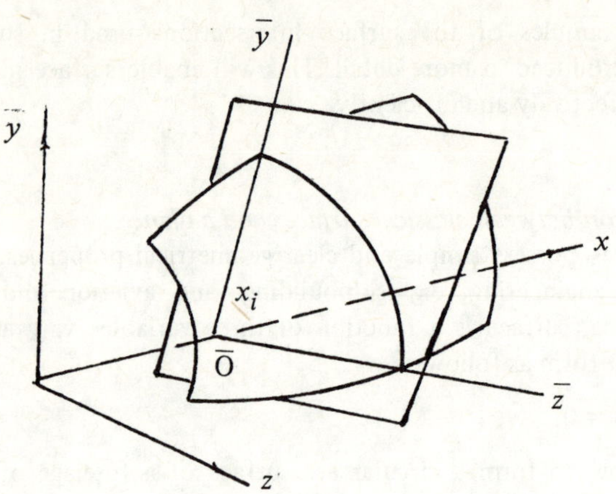

Fig. 10.4

$$x - \frac{1}{\text{tg } \alpha_i} y - \frac{1}{\text{tg } \beta_i} z - x_i = 0 \qquad (10.26)$$

We now derive two equations (10.24), (10.26) having three unknowns; the extra degree of freedom manifests itself as a curve of the intersection. We found we could resolve this problem by holding one of the unknowns constant, usually variable x. This reduces the problem to the circular arc — straight line — intersection problem. It is easy to calculate coordinates y, z of the intersection point. By providing a series of values of coordinate x, and repeating the procedure above, we find a series of points sufficient to define the intersection.

Example 2 Intersection between a composite parameter surface and a plane
The general parameter surface equation is of the form

$$\mathbf{r}(u, w) = UMVM^T W^T \qquad (10.27)$$

where

$$U = \begin{bmatrix} 1 & u & u^2 & u^3 \end{bmatrix}, \quad W = \begin{bmatrix} 1 & w & w^2 & w^3 \end{bmatrix},$$

M is a 4 × 4 coefficient matrix which depends on blending functions,

V is a 4 × 4 vector matrix; the three components are V_x, V_y, V_z.

The three components of the surface equation (10.27) are

$$x(u, w) = UMV_x M^T W^T$$

$$y(u, w) = UMV_y M^T W^T$$

$$z(u, w) = UMV_z M^T W^T \qquad (10.28)$$

Substituting (10.28) into the plane equation (10.25), we obtain

$$UM(AV_x + BV_y + CV_z)M^T W^T + D = 0 \qquad (10.29)$$

This is the intersection equation including parameters u and w, which are not independent. We can solve the equation by holding one of the parameters constant. This reduces the problem to the cubic function solution problem. By providing a series of values of parameter u (or w), and repeating the procedure above, we find a series of points sufficient to define the intersection.

The intersection obtained above is an intersection only between a surface patch and a plane. A surface is usually a rectangular mesh of bi-cubic patches. Fig. 10.5 represents a surface defined by 4×5 mesh patches.

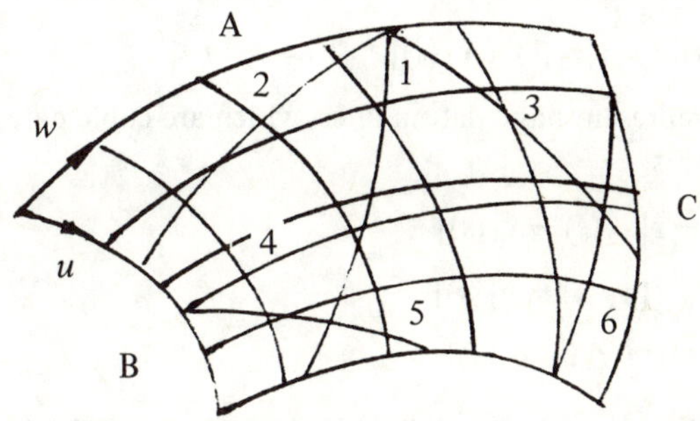

Fig. 10.5

Since the surface is bounded, as just described, we can simplify the solution by recognizing first that the curve of intersection is bounded and secondly that the end points of this curve lie on a boundary curve of the surfaces ($u = 0$, $u = 1$, $w = 0$, or $w = 1$). This gives us a clue to the method of solution.

In order to find the intersection between the composite surface and the plane, we decompose the procedure into two distinct phases: the hunting phase and the tracing phase. The hunting phase locates the starting point required for the intersection tracing operation. The tracing phase creates a series of points lying on the intersection.

In the hunting phase, we compute the possible intersection point of each boundary curve defined by $u = 0$, $u = 1$, $w = 0$ and $w = 1$ with the plane defined by (10.25). Since there are six possible cases (see Fig. 10.5), we seek only the starting point along three boundaries such as boundaries A, B, C.

In the tracing phase there are three cases of intersection between the patch and the plane (see Fig. 10.6). If the starting point is on the boundary $u = 0$, by increasing Δu at each step, we compute the intersection points sequentially. Finally, when a point lying on the curve ($u = 1$) is found, the tracing turns to surface patch $r_{i+1,j}$; the point lying on the curve ($w = 0$), the tracing turns to $r_{i,j-1}$; the point lying on the curve ($w = 1$) the tracing turns to $r_{i,j+1}$. By the procedure we can obtain the intersection between the composite surfaces and the plane.

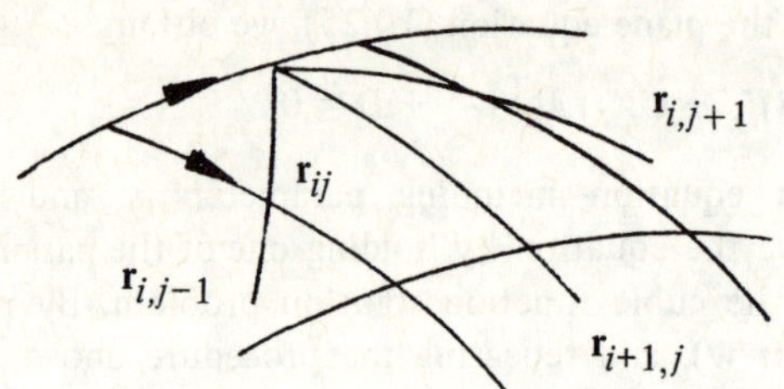

Fig. 10.6

Example 3   Intersection between a ruled surface and a plane
A ruled surface, such as a wing surface of an aircraft, may be defined as

$$\mathbf{r}(s, t) = \mathbf{r}_1(s) + t[\mathbf{r}_2(s) - \mathbf{r}_1(s)] \qquad (0 \leqslant s, \quad t \leqslant 1) \tag{10.30}$$

where $\mathbf{r}_1(s)$ and $\mathbf{r}_2(s)$ represent basic datum lines, which are cubic parameter curves.
   Its component form is

$$x = x_1(s) + t[x_2(s) - x_1(s)]$$
$$y = y_1(s) + t[y_2(s) - y_1(s)]$$
$$z = z_1(s) + t[z_2(s) - z_1(s)] \tag{10.31}$$

Substituting (10.31) into (10.25) we obtain the intersection equation

$$A\{x_1(s) + t[x_2(s) - x_1(s)]\} +$$
$$B\{y_1(s) + t[y_2(s) - y_1(s)]\} +$$
$$C\{z_1(s) + t[z_2(s) - z_1(s)]\} + D = 0$$

Solving for t, which is a function of variable s, and denoting it by $t_1(s)$, we obtain

$$t_1(s) = \frac{-[Ax_1(s) + By_1(s) + Cz_1(s) + D]}{A[x_2(s) - x_1(s)] + B[y_2(s) - y_1(s)] + C[z_2(s) - z_1(s)]} \tag{10.32}$$

then substituting (10.32) into (10.31), we obtain the parametric equations of the intersection

$$x = x_1(s) + t_1(s)[x_2(s) - x_1(s)]$$
$$y = y_1(s) + t_1(s)[y_2(s) - y_1(s)]$$
$$z = z_1(s) + t_1(s)[z_2(s) - z_1(s)] \tag{10.33}$$

Using (10.33), by increasing s by Δs at each step, we compute a series of points lying on the intersection.

10.5 INTERSECTION BETWEEN SURFACES (1)

The intersection between surfaces is very complex; there are many approaches for computing the intersection between two surfaces.

We will now consider finding the intersection between the surface $\mathbf{r}_1(u, w)$, defined by a mesh of patches, and the surface $\mathbf{r}_2(s, t)$, which is not a composite surface (see Fig. 10.7).

We decompose the solution procedure into three distinct phases: the hunting phase, the tracing phase, and the ordering phase. The hunding phase locates the discrete starting required for the curve-tracing operation. The tracing phase creates strings of points lying on the intersection. Finally, the ordering phase reorders the point strings to establish their proper connectivity.

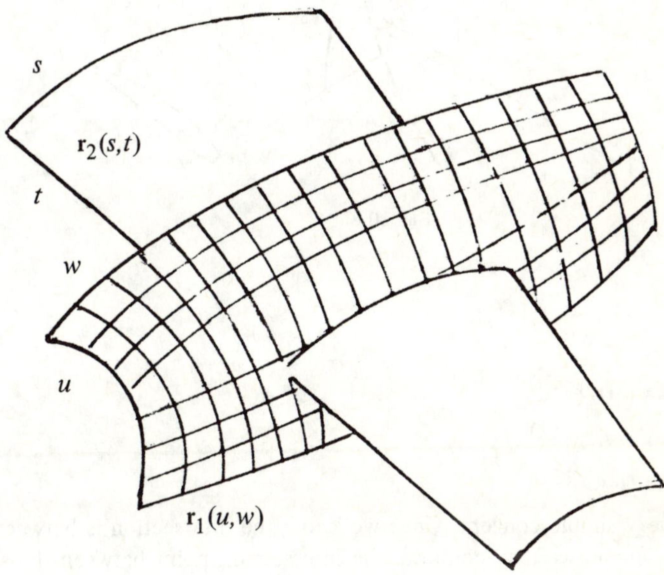

Fig. 10.7

10.5.1 The hunting phase

In the hunting phase, we compute the possible intersection of each parametric curve on the surface $\mathbf{r}_1(u, w)$ with $\mathbf{r}_2(s, t)$. By first taking u parameter curves and then w parameter curves, the intersection points are calculated sequentially. In other words, we regard the parameter curve net on the surface $\mathbf{r}_1(u, w)$ as the hunting grid.

Since each parameter curve u consists of m segments (each parameter curve w consists of n segments), we must first find which segment has an intersection point with $\mathbf{r}_2(s, t)$. We may choose a function that identifies the presence of an intersection point. Suppose $\mathbf{P}_c$ is a point on the curve, $\mathbf{P}_s$ is a point on the surface $\mathbf{r}_2(s, t)$ closest to $\mathbf{P}_c$ and $\mathbf{r} = \mathbf{P}_c - \mathbf{P}_s$ is the shortest distance between these two points (see Fig. 10.8). If an intersection occurs between nodes i and $i + 1$ on the curve, then all of the following conditions must hold:

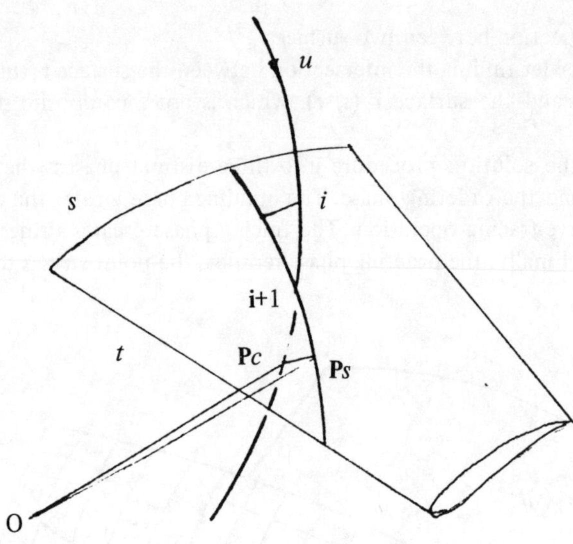

Fig. 10.8

$$r_{i,x}\, r_{i+1,x} < 0$$

$$r_{i,y}\, r_{i+1,y} < 0$$

$$r_{i,z}\, r_{i+1,z} < 0 \tag{10.34}$$

This is a very simple concept. Once we know the intersection is between node i and $(i+1)$ on the curve, we may compute the intersection point between the segment with node i and $(i+1)$ on the curve and the surface $\mathbf{r}_2(s, t)$.

Now, consider the problem of finding the intersection between the curve segment and a surface. We express the point of intersection as a fully specified system of three equations in three unknowns. Denote the curve segement by $\mathbf{r}_1(u, w_j)$ and the surface by $\mathbf{r}_2(s, t)$. Then, express the system of equations as

$$\mathbf{r} = \mathbf{r}_1(u, w_j) - \mathbf{r}_2(s, t) = \mathbf{0} \tag{10.35}$$

where $\mathbf{r}$ is the minimum distance between the surface and successive points on the curve segment.

The vector equation (10.35) may be expressed by its three component equations as

$$r_x(u, s, t) = 0$$

$$r_y(u, s, t) = 0$$

$$r_z(u, s, t) = 0 \tag{10.36}$$

Using the Newton–Raphson iteration method from (10.17), we obtain the solutions

$$u_{i+1} = u_i - \begin{vmatrix} r_x & \partial r_x/\partial s & \partial r_x/\partial t \\ r_y & \partial r_y/\partial s & \partial r_y/\partial t \\ r_z & \partial r_z/\partial s & \partial r_z/\partial t \end{vmatrix} \bigg/ \begin{vmatrix} \partial r_x/\partial u & \partial r_x/\partial s & \partial r_x/\partial t \\ \partial r_y/\partial u & \partial r_y/\partial s & \partial r_y/\partial t \\ \partial r_z/\partial u & \partial r_z/\partial s & \partial r_z/\partial t \end{vmatrix}$$

$$= u_i - \frac{\mathbf{r} \cdot (\mathbf{r}_2^s \times \mathbf{r}_2^t)}{\mathbf{r}_1^u \cdot (\mathbf{r}_2^s \times \mathbf{r}_2^t)} = u_i - \mathbf{r} \cdot (\mathbf{r}_2^s \times \mathbf{r}_2^t)/D_w \qquad (10.37.1)$$

Similarly

$$s_{i+1} = s_i + \mathbf{r} \cdot (\mathbf{r}_1^u \times \mathbf{r}_2^t)/D_w \qquad (10.37.2)$$

$$t_{i+1} = t_i + \mathbf{r} \cdot (\mathbf{r}_2^s \times \mathbf{r}_1^u)/D_w \qquad (10.37.3)$$

In equation (10.37), all functions and derivatives are understood to be calculated at (u_i, s_i, t_i).

The points of intersections between each w parameter curve and $\mathbf{r}_2(s, t)$ may be obtained in a similar way.

The hunting phase produces intersection points lying on the parameter curves of the surface $\mathbf{r}_1(u, w)$ (see Fig. 10.7).

10.5.2 The tracing phase

We see in Fig. 10.7 that the order of these intersection points lying on the parameter curves must be changed so that they can be properly interpolated to form the complete intersection curve segments across the interior regions of the parameter curve grid.

Since the intersection point-numbering scheme is related to the patch-numbering scheme, we may usually find two intersection points for each patch on the surface $\mathbf{r}_1(u, w)$.

Now consider the problem of tracing the intersection curve segment between the patch on the surface $\mathbf{r}_1(u, w)$ and the surface $\mathbf{r}_2(s, t)$.

In section 10.2, the principle of solution was discussed. The method of solution has now also been discussed. We will now provide the iteration formulae for $\mathbf{r}_1(u, w) - \mathbf{r}_2(s, t) = 0$.

We know we may solve this problem by holding one of the variables constant. This reduces the problem to the curve-surface intersection problem.

The resulting four sets of equations for $u = $ constant are

$$u_{i+1} = u_i$$

$$w_{i+1} = w_i - [\mathbf{r} \cdot (\mathbf{r}_2^s \times \mathbf{r}_2^t)]/D_u$$

$$s_{i+1} = s_i + [\mathbf{r} \cdot (\mathbf{r}_1^w \times \mathbf{r}_2^t)]/D_u$$

$$t_{i+1} = t_i + [\mathbf{r} \cdot (\mathbf{r}_2^s \times \mathbf{r}_1^w)]/D_u \qquad (10.38)$$

where

$$D = [\mathbf{r}_1^w \cdot (\mathbf{r}_2^s \times \mathbf{r}_2^t)]_u$$

For $w = $ constant, $w_{i+1} = w_i$, the equation is just (10.37). For $s = $ constant, and $t = $ constant, similar equations may be obtained from (10.17).

The criteria available to determine which variable to fix are of some interest. Perhaps the most obvious one is that the variable is fixed that produces the maximum denominator in the resulting fully specified condition. The advantage of the method is that we avoid numerical problems with a very small value in the denominator.

If the hunting point on the patch on the surface $\mathbf{r}_1(u, w)$ is only one, this implies that another hunting point should be found on the boundary of $\mathbf{r}_2(s, t)$ (see Fig. 10.7).

10.5.3 The ordering phase

The tracing phase generates many intersection curve segments (see Fig. 10.7); we now must establish their property connectivity.

For any ordering operation, only the first and last points in each string are important. Beginning with the first string, compare the beginning and end points with the remaining strings. When a match is found, save that string number in an ordering array as a signed integer. A minus sign indicates a reversal in the order of the strong points when they are joined with others.

We have described a method for computing the intersection between a composite surface $\mathbf{r}_1(u, w)$ and a surface $\mathbf{r}_2(s, t)$. The problem of the intersection between two composite surfaces is more complex and will be discussed in the next section.

10.6 INTERSECTION BETWEEN SURFACES (2)

In recent years a number of algorithms based on subdivision techniques have been suggested for hunting (detecting, estimating, finding or sounding) the intersection curves between two composite parametric surfaces. The underlying idea of these algorithms is to deal with the characteristic polyhedron (also called the Bezier net) instead of the surface description itself, that is, to subdivide both surfaces repeatedly until they can finally be approximated by planar polygons. The process of finding the intersection lines is then carried out between these planar polygons.

10.6.1 The de Casteljau subdivision algorithm

The Bezier curve point $r(u)$, for any given u, can be computed by the recursion formula mentioned in Chapter 5.

$$\mathbf{r}_i^l(u) = (1 - u)\,\mathbf{r}_i^{l-1}(u) + u\,\mathbf{r}_{i+1}^{l-1}(u) \tag{10.39}$$

The point $u = \frac{1}{2}$ subdivides a Bezier curve into two segments; each segment is again a Bezier curve of the same degree as the original one, which is defined by vertices $\mathbf{V}_0^0$, $\mathbf{V}_1^1$, $\mathbf{V}_2^2$, $\mathbf{V}_3^3$ and $\mathbf{V}_3^3$, $\mathbf{V}_3^2$, $\mathbf{V}_3^1$, $\mathbf{V}_3^0$, respectively (see Fig. 10.9). The vertices of the two segments are 'byproducts' of the de Casteljau construction for the evaluation of the point $\mathbf{r}(\frac{1}{2})$.

By reason of the tensor product definition, the properties of Bezier surfaces can easily be deduced from the properties of the underlying Bezier curve scheme. Thus, the Bezier surface point $\mathbf{r}(u, w)$ for any given u, v can be computed by the recursion formula.

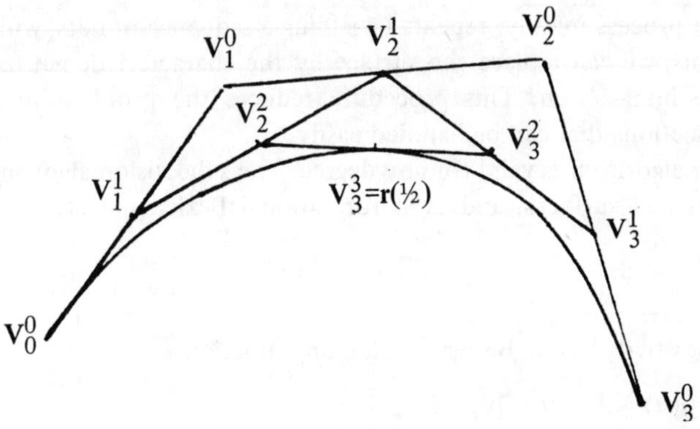

Fig. 10.9

The two curves $u = \frac{1}{2}$, $w = \frac{1}{2}$ subdivide a Bezier surface into four patches. Each patch is again a Bezier surface of the same degree as the original one. The vertices of these four patches are 'byproducts' of the de Casteljau construction for the evaluation of the point $r(\frac{1}{2}, \frac{1}{2})$. They are given by

$$V_{i,j}^{l,m}, \quad V_{3,J}^{l,m}, \quad V_{i,3}^{l,m}, \quad V_{3,3}^{l,m}$$

$$(i = 0, 1, 2, 3, \quad j = 0, 1, 2, 3, \quad l = 0, 1, 2, 3, \quad m = 0, 1, 2, 3)$$

Fig. 10.10 illustrates the order of these vertices.

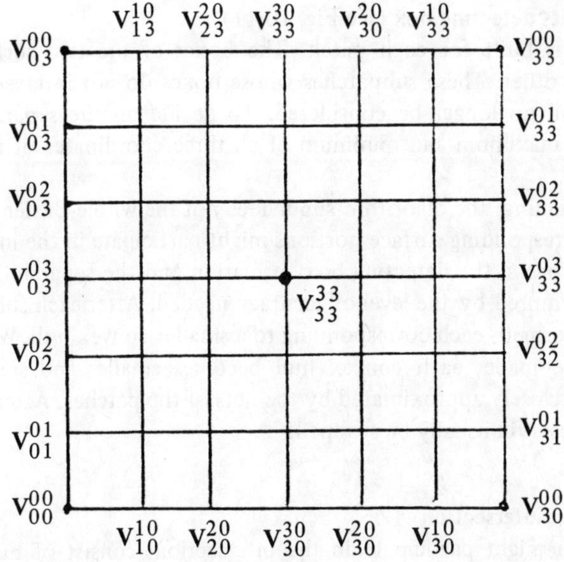

Fig. 10.10

The subdivision process may be repeated yielding a sequence of nets, which converges to the surface. Thus, we can replace the surface by the characteristic net to simplify the calculation of the intersection. This procedure reduces the problem to a number of plane–plane intersections that can be handled easily.

The subdivision algorithm is valid for any degree. The subdivision algorithm also exists for B-spline curves and surfaces, and even for rational Bezier and B-spline curves and surfaces.

10.6.2 Detecting boxes

As we know, the positivity of the Bernstein blending functions,

$$0 \leqslant J_{n,i}(u) \leqslant 1 \quad u \in [0, \quad 1]$$

guarantees the validity of the convex hull property. The Bezier surface likes completely within the convex hull of its Bezier net.

The intersection area between two composite surfaces should be detected. It is useful if we can use a coarse but very quick estimate of the possible intersection region of the two surfaces; those parts of the surfaces that do not participate in the intersection will be eliminated as early as possible in the algorithm and hence unnecessary computations will be avoided.

The convex hull seems to be a natural choice for a comparison box for Bezier surfaces. However, the convex hull is an irregular polyhedron, and the determination of two irregular polyhedrons is not an easy task.

A detecting box of a surface consists of the maximum and minimum x, y and z coordinates of the net vertices of the surface. It is clear that the surface lies completely within the convex hull (an irregular polyhedron) of its Bezier net whilst the convex hull is totally enclosed in its detecting box (see Fig. 10.11).

A detecting box is built for each patch. The boxes of the two surfaces are then compared with each other. These subpatches whose boxes do not intersect any box on the other surface will no longer be considered. To decide on the separability of two detecting boxes, the maximum and minimum of all three coordinates of the two boxes have to be compared.

Except at the beginning, the algorithm subdivides not the whole Bezier nets, but only those parts whose corresponding surface portions might participate in the intersection.

The subdivision process, the detecting box formation and the separability test will be done as often as is required by the level of accuracy needed. After each subdivision, four new subpatches are formed, each corresponding to a smaller convex hull. When more and more subdivisions are made, each convex hull becomes smaller and smaller, and the surface is reasonably closely approximated by the nets of the patches. After three or four subdivisions the process will usually be stopped.

10.6.3 Computing the intersection

The few nets, which might participate in the intersection, consist of many segments, which contain four points. In general, the four points of a segment are not situated in one plane. The 'four-point segment' may be replaced by two 'three-point segments', each one defining a planar triangle patch. After this, a plane–plane intersection is carried for every two planar triangle patches of different surfaces. Once all the lines of the intersection are computed, we obtain the intersection curves (see Fig. 10.12) for any manufacturing process involving the intersection or for hidden-surface removal. This will be discussed in the next chapter.

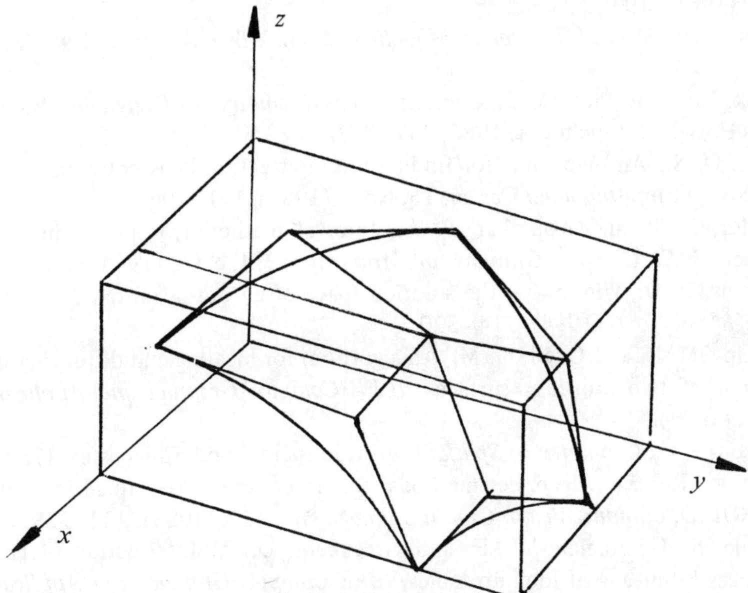

Fig. 10.11 The detecting box

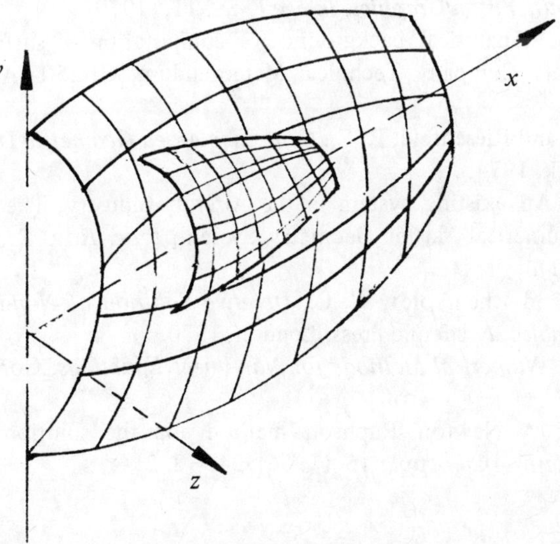

Fig. 10.12

REFERENCES

[1] Lasser, D., Intersection of parametric surfaces in the Bernstein–Bezier representation, *Computer-aided Design*, **18**, No. 4, May (1986), 186–192.

[2] Koparkar, P. A. and Mudur, S. P., Generation of continuous smooth surves resulting from operations on parametric surface patches, *Computer-aided Design,* **18**, No. 4, May (1986), 193–206.

[3] Mortenson, M. E., *Geometric Modeling*, John Wiley & Sons, New York, 1985, pp. 319–344.

[4] Faux, I. D. and Pratt, M. J., *Computational Geometry for Design and Manufacture*, Ellis Horwood, Chichester, 1985, 257–277.

[5] Peng, Q. S., An algorithm for finding the intersection lines between two B-spline surfaces, *Computer-aided Design,* **16**, No. 4 (1984), 191–196.

[6] Mudur, S. P. and Koparkar, P. A., Interval methods for processing geometric objects, *IEEE Comput. Graphics and Applications,* **4**, No. 2 (1984), 1–2.

[7] Martins, P. D., Windowing the solution space of an optimization, *Computer-aided Design,* **16**, No. 6 (1984), 314–320.

[8] Phillips, M. B. and Odell, G. M., An algorithm for locating and displaying the intersection of two arbitrary surfaces, *IEEE Comput. Graphics and Applications,* **4**, Sept. (1984).

[9] Gasson, P. C., *Geometry of Spatial Forms*, Ellis Horwood, Chichester, 1983.

[10] Sarraga, R. F., Algebraic methods for intersections of quadric surfaces in GMSOLID, *Comput. Vision Graphics, Image Proc.,* **22**, (1983), 222–238.

[11] Hanna, S. L., Abeland, J. F. and Greenberg, D. P., Intersection of parametric surfaces by means of look-up tables, *IEEE Comput. Graphics and Applications,* **3**, Oct. (1983), 39–48.

[12] Levin, J. Z., Mathematical models for determining the intersections of quadric surfaces, *Comput. Vision Graphics, Image Proc.,* **11**, (1979).

[13] Timmer, H. G., Analytical background for computation of surface intersection, Douglas Aircraft Company Technical Memorandum, C1-250-CAT-77-036, April (1977).

[14] Barnhill, R. E. and Riesenfeld, R. F., *Computer Aided Geometric Design*, Academic Press, New York, 1974.

[15] Sabin, M. A., An existing system in the Aircraft Industry, The British Aircraft Corporation Numerical Master Geometry System, *Proc. Roy. Soc. Lond.,* **A321**, 197–205 (1971).

[16] Ortega, J. M. and Rheinboldt, W. C., *Iterative Solution of Non-linear Equations in Several Variables*, Academic Press, London, 1970.

[17] Rabinowitz, P., *Numerical Methods for Non-linear Equations*, Gordon and Breach, London, 1970.

[18] Ben-Israel, A., A Newton–Raphson method for the solution of systems of equations, *J. Math. Anal. Appl.,* **15**, (1966), 243–252.

11

Hidden Surface Removal

11.1 INTRODUCTION

To produce an unambiguous drawing or a realistic display on the screen for objects composed of sculptured surfaces, we need the following initial information:

- the centre of projection for perspective projections or the direction of projection for orthogonal projections;
- the position of each grid point of each surface, or the position of vertices defining each surface;
- the view plane.

We must then determine which surfaces or curves can be seen and which cannot, so that we can draw or display only the visible curves or surfaces. This process is called hidden surface removal.

The hidden surface problem is often regarded as being difficult. J. G. Griffiths, a specialist on hidden curve and surface removal, states that the hidden surface problem is essentially a simple one, and that an elegant and robust solution should be possible. The authors believe that the principle, or fundamental idea, of hidden surface removal is simple but its implementation is a large sorting and depth comparison process which requires a large amount of computer time.

The hidden surface problem obtained a solid theoretical foundation in the work of I. E. Sutherland, R. F. Sproull and R. A. Schumacker in 1974 [1]; they studied and compared ten hidden line and surface algorithms. All of the algorithms described are for objects with planar polygonal faces. A rich literature exists on this aspect. Good textbooks introducing this subject include those by J. D. Foley and A. Van Dam [2], M. E. Mortensen [3] and W. M. Newman and R. F. Sproull [4]. J. D. Foley and A. Van Dam describe four of the ten algorithms as well as additional algorithms developed from 1972 to 1982. Algorithms for displaying objects defined by curved surfaces are also briefly described in these textbooks. However, literature on hidden line and surface elimination methods for curve surfaces is very scarce. To the authors' knowledge, there are only six papers on the subject, by E. Catmull [5], J. G. Griffiths [6], A. Appel [7], J. G. Griffiths [8], Y. Ohno [9], and J. G. Griffiths [10].

In this chapter, the geometric principles of hidden surface removal are introduced, such as depth comparisons, geometric coherence and sorting. Later sections describe basic algorithms for removing hidden surfaces from the display of 3-D objects defined with curved surfaces.

11.2 DEPTH COMPARISONS

We see that a projection system consists of three aspects: the centre of projection or the direction of projection, objects projected (points, lines, curves, planar polygons, surface patches, and so on), and the plane of projection.

Let us discuss the visibility of objects in this environment. In this section we focus on point visibility because it is the basis of object visibility. Depth comparison determines visible priority.

11.2.1 Visibility between two points

Let xOy be the plane of projection, and let the z-axis be the direction of projection; then given points $P_1(x_1, y_1, z_1)$ and $P_2(x_2, y_2, z_2)$, does either point obscure the other in the parallel projection system? (See Fig. 11.1.)

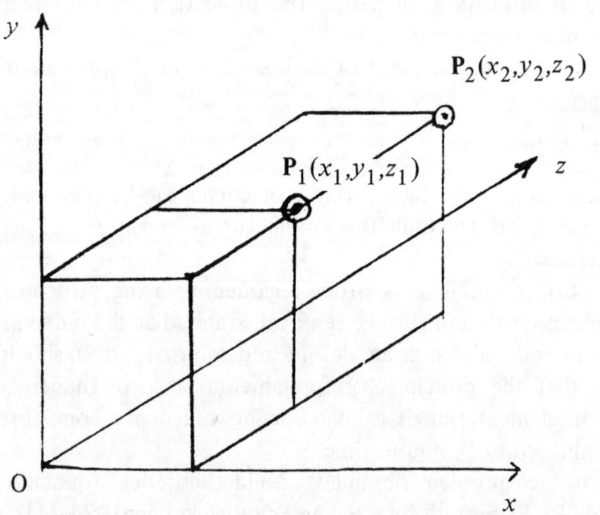

Fig. 11.1 Depth comparisons between two points in a parallel projection system

The points are on the same projection line (called projector) if

$$x_1 = x_2$$
$$y_1 = y_2 \qquad (11.1)$$

then a comparison

$$z_1 < \text{ or } > z_2$$

determines which point is closer to the viewer.

The points P_1 and P_2 are not on the same projector if $x_1 \neq x_2$, or $y_1 \neq y_2$; then neither point can obscure the other.

For a perspective projection, the points are on the same projector if

$$x_1/z_1 = x_2/z_2$$
$$y_1/z_1 = y_2/z_2 \qquad (11.2)$$

then a comparison

$$z_1 < \text{ or } > z_2$$

will determine which point is closer to the viewer. If the two points are not on the same projector, then neither point can obscure the other (see Fig. 11.2).

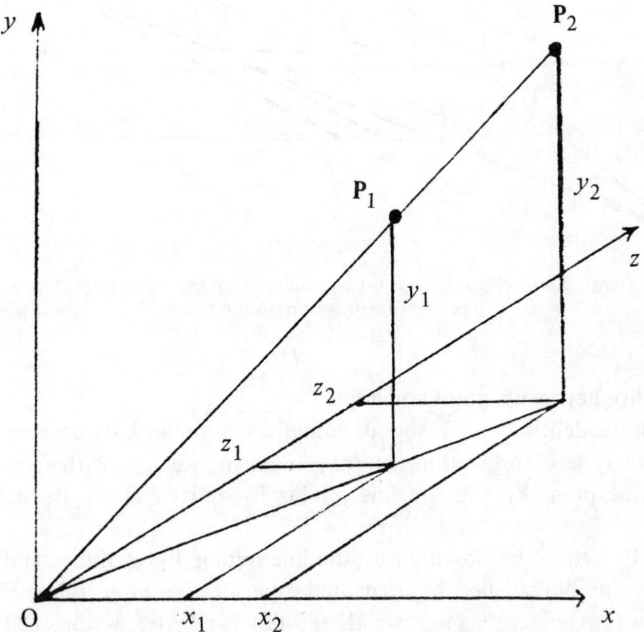

Fig. 11.2 Depth comparisons between two points in a perspective projection system

For a perspective projection with the centre of the projection on the z-axis, the points are on the same projector if

$$x_1/(d + z_1) = x_2/(d + z_2)$$

$$y_1/(d + z_1) = y_2/(d + z_2) \tag{11.3}$$

then a comparison

$$z_1 < \text{ or } > z_2$$

can determine which point is closer to the viewer (see Fig. 11.3). If the two points are not on the same projector, then neither point can obscure the other.

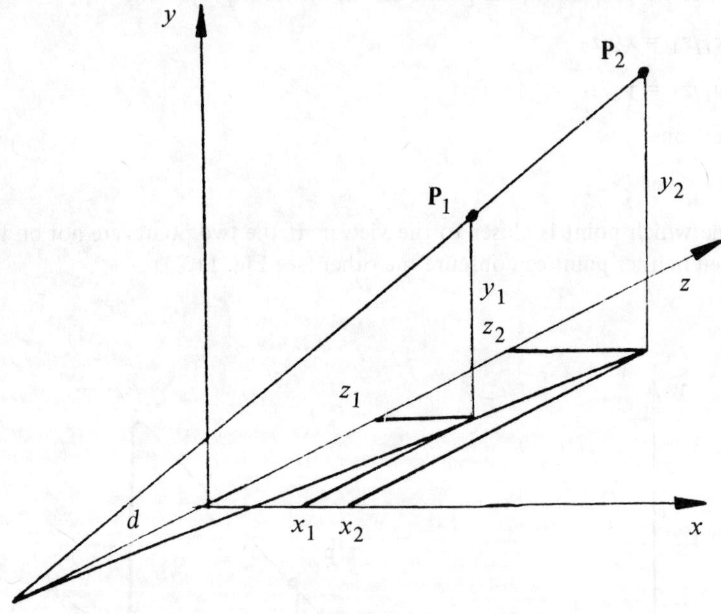

Fig. 11.3 Depth comparisons between two points in a perspective projection system with a centre of projection on the z-axis

11.2.2 Visibility between a point and a line

The problem of depth comparison is complicated somewhat, because computations depend on the type of projection. For the moment, we ignore the x component and assume that the point $\mathbf{P}_1$ and the line joining $\mathbf{P}_2$ and $\mathbf{P}_3$ are in the $x = 0$ plane (see Fig. 11.4).

The point $\mathbf{P}_1$ cannot be obscured by the line joining $\mathbf{P}_2\mathbf{P}_3$ in the parallel projections, whereas the point $\mathbf{P}_1$ can be obscured in the perspective projections. For the parallel projection, we test only $y_1 \in [y_2, y_3]$. If the test is positive, we proceed to check the z coordinates to determine depth priority. For the perspective projection, we must test $y_1^* \in [y_2^*, y_3^*]$.

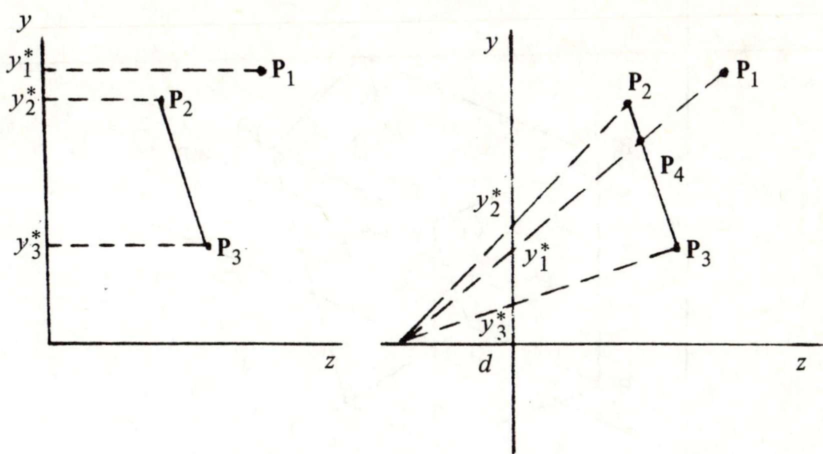

Fig. 11.4 Depth comparisons between a point and a line

$$y_1^* = dy_1/(d + z_1)$$

$$y_2^* = dy_2/(d + z_2)$$

$$y_3^* = dy_3/(d + z_3) \tag{11.4}$$

If the point P_1 and the line joining P_2 and P_3 overlap in their perspective projections, we compare the z values of P_1 and P_4 lying on the line joining P_2 and P_3; the point with the lowest z value is visible.

11.2.3 Visibility between a point and a planar polygon

Given a space point P and a planar polygon $P_1P_2P_3P_4$, consider their parallel projection onto the $z = 0$ plane (see Fig. 11.5). We will use a left-hand coordinate system and view the projection from the negative z side of the projection plane.

P^* is the projection of the point P; then $x^* = x$, $y^* = y$, and $z^* = 0$.

If P^* lies inside the boundary of the polygon on the projection plane, they overlap. We must determine on which side of the unprojected polygon plane the space point P lies.

The equation of the polygon plane is

$$Ax + By + Cz + D = 0$$

Substitute the x, y coordinates for P into the above equation, and solve for z_P, where z_P is the z coordinate of the point P^0 on the plane on the intersection with the parallel projector through P (see Fig. 11.5).

$$z_P = -(Ax + By + D)/C \tag{11.5}$$

then if

$$z \leqslant z_P \tag{11.6}$$

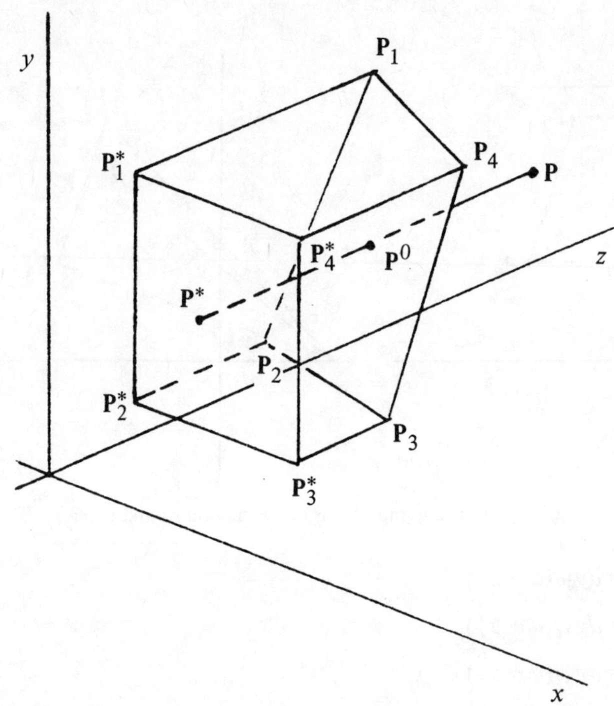

Fig. 11.5 Depth comparisons between a point and a planar polygon

P is visible, or if

$$z > z_{\mathbf{P}} \tag{11.7}$$

P is hidden by the plane of the polygon.

If $\mathbf{P}^*$ lies outside the boundary of the projected polygon, they do not overlap and the polygon does not obscure the point from view.

How can we determine if $\mathbf{P}^*$ is inside or outside the projection of the polygon? An odd–even intersection criterion can be used (see Fig. 11.6). If $\mathbf{P}^*$ is outside the boundary of the polygon, then a straight line drawn from $\mathbf{P}^*$ in any direction to infinity intersects the boundary of the polygon an even number of times or not at all. Conversely, if $\mathbf{P}^*$ lies inside the boundary of the polygon, then a straight line drawn from $\mathbf{P}^*$ in any direction to infinity will intersect the boundary of the projected polygon an odd number of times. Note that if the semi-infinite test line intersected a vertex, then another line must be chosen.

This odd–even instruction criterion is suitable for both the convex polygon and the concave polygon and even the polygons including holes.

11.2.4 Visibility between a point and a surface patch
In a similar way to subsection 11.2.3, if the point projection $\mathbf{P}^*$ and the surface patch

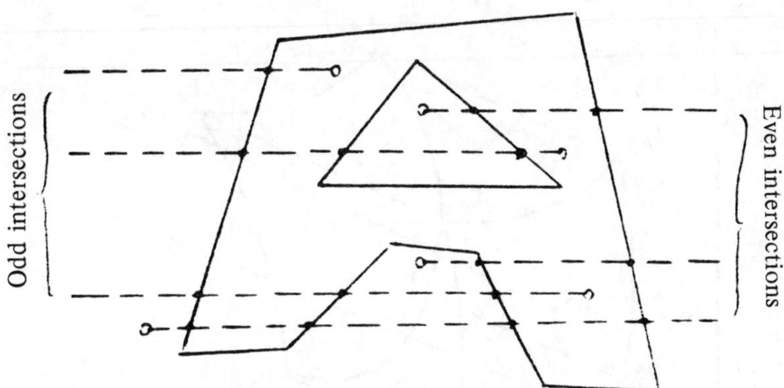

Fig. 11.6 Odd–even intersection criterion

projection overlap, we must determine on which side of the unprojected surface patch the space point **P** lies.

The surface patch can be described as

$$x = y(u, w)$$

$$y = y(u, w)$$

$$z = z(u, w)$$

Fig. 11.7 shows $x_i = x$, $y_i = y$. Substituting the coordinates x_i, y_i into the first two equations above, we obtain

$$x_i = x(u, w)$$

$$y_i = y(u, w)$$

Solving the simultaneous equations by iterating the method, we obtain u_i, w_i. Then substituting u_i, w_i into $z_i = z(u_i, w_i)$, we finally obtain z_i, where z_i is the z coordinate of the point $\mathbf{P}^0$ on the surface patch on the intersection with the parallel projector through **P** (see Fig. 11.7).

If $z \leqslant z_i$, the point **P** is visible; but if $z > z_i$, **P** is hidden by the surface patch.

We must then test the visibility of the point **P** against every surface patch in the display. If the point is visible with respect to every patch, then it is visible. Otherwise, it is hidden.

Note that depth comparisons are usually carried out after the normalizing transformation has been applied, so that parallel-projection projectors are parallel to the z-axis and perspective-projection projectors emanate from the origin.

We now see that visibility depends basically on depth comparisons. It is essential to simplify depth comparisons for an efficient hidden line or hidden surface algorithm.

J. D. Foley and A. Van Dam [2] suggest using a matrix transform to transform a normalized-perspective-view volume into a rectangular parallelepiped, distorting the object and moving the centre of projection to infinity on the negative z-axis, that is,

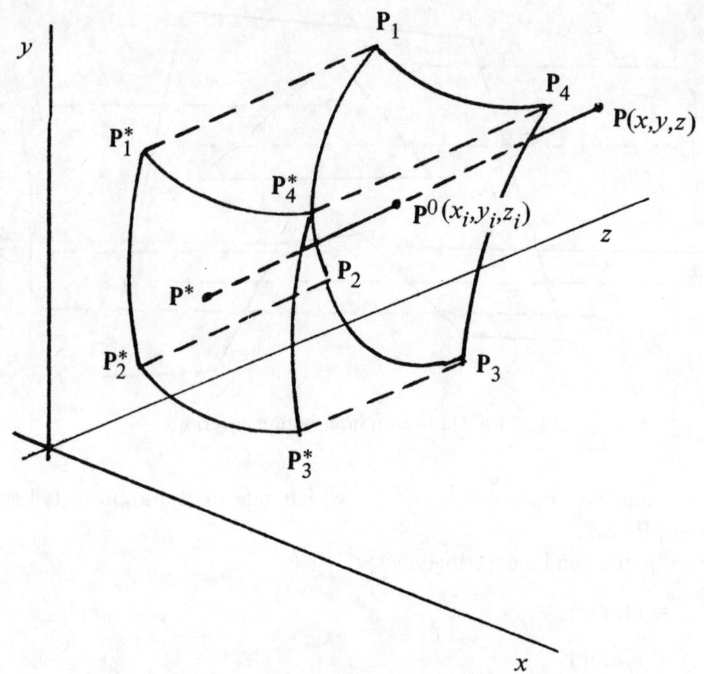

Fig. 11.7 Depth comparisons between a point and a surface patch

making the projectors parallel. This leads to the fact that the parallel projection of the transformed object is the same as the perspective projection of the untransformed object. The advantage is that the test for one point obscuring another is the same as for parallel projections, reducing the number of divisions required in formulae (11.2) and (11.3) for depth comparisons.

11.3 COHERENCE PRINCIPLES

Calculations for hidden surface removal are very time-consuming. Many techniques have been applied for simplifying and avoiding unnecessary depth comparisons and reducing the problem size. One technique is the coherence technique.

Coherence means the element interrelationships and is present in many forms, in object space and image space, i.e. the frame of reference of the geometric computations. There are several coherences, which make hidden surface algorithms more effective:

- point coherence
- line (edge) coherence
- polygon coherence
- surface coherence
- object coherence
- angle coherence
- area coherence
- depth coherence

Point coherence: if two points are not on the same projector, then neither point can obscure the other. Only if the two points are on the same projector, then depth comparison is necessary, this using the point coherence principle.

Fig. 11.8 shows that P_1 and P_2 are coherent but that P_3 and P_1 (or P_2) are not coherent.

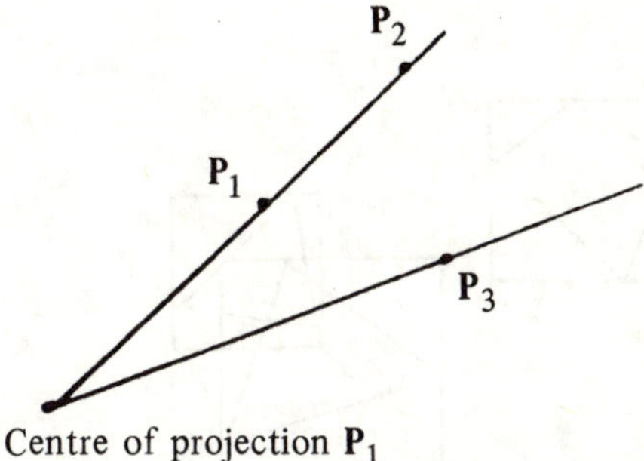

Fig. 11.8 Point coherence

Line (edge) coherence: depth comparisons are necessary only when the projections of the lines overlap. The line joining $P_1 P_2$ and line $P_3 P_4$ are not coherent in parallel projection, but are coherent in perspective projection (see Fig. 11.9).

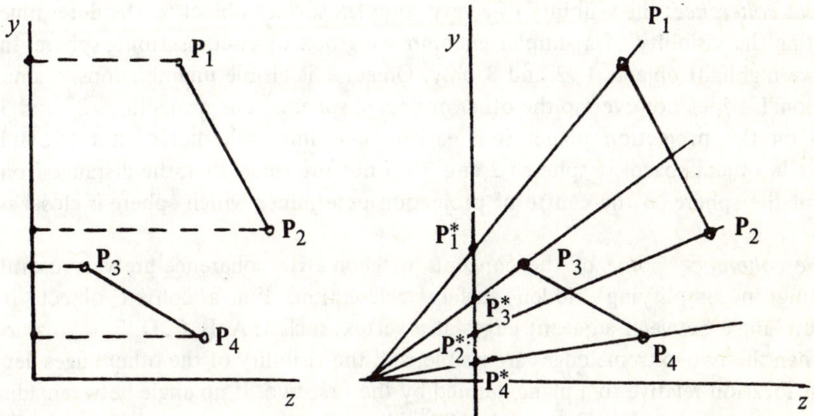

Fig. 11.9 Line (edge) coherence

Polygon (face) coherence: a minimum-sized rectangle can be constructed for each polygon in the projection plane. Using these rectangles, we can rapidly find the relationship between them. Overlapping rectangles require additional calculation, but the isolated rectangles require no further analysis.

Note that if the rectangles overlap, one of two cases occurs: either the polygon projections also overlap, or they do not (see Fig. 11.10). However, these 'false alarms' do not significantly alter the efficiency obtained by eliminating some polygons from further calculations.

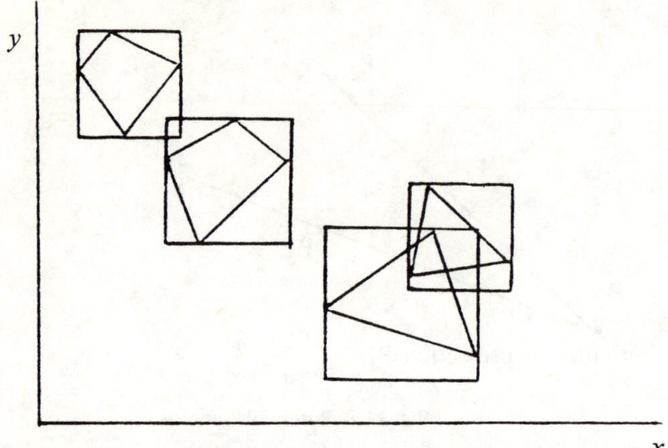

Fig. 11.10 Polygon (face) coherence

Surface coherence: we use the subdivision technique and detecting boxes mentioned in subsection 10.6.2, and when complete, all hidden surfaces will be found and deleted.

Object coherence: the visibility of a very complex surface object can be determined by computing the visibility of a simpler encompassing box or circumscribing sphere. In Fig. 11.11 we highlight objects 1, 2 and 3 only. Object 1 is visible unambiguously, since the projection 1^* does not overlap the other projected spheres. The projections 2^* and 3^* do overlap on the projection plane. It is easy to determine whether or not two spheres intersect in object space. If spheres 2 and 3 do not intersect, then the distance from the centre of the sphere to the centre of projection determines which sphere is closer to the viewer.

Angle coherence: some of the concepts of geometric coherence are very useful and interesting in simplifying hidden surface calculation. For a convex object, if the maximum angle between adjacent edges at a vertex, such as A, B, C, D, E, is greater than $180°$, then the two extreme edges are visible, and the visibility of the other edges depends on their location relative to a plane defined by the first two. If no angle between adjacent edges at a vertex, such as F, exceeds $180°$, then all the edges have the same visibility. Note that these angles are measured in the projection plane (see Fig. 11.12).

Area coherence: a projection of a polygon has one of four relationships to an area element of a display screen: surrounding polygon, intersecting polygon, contained polygon and disjoint polygon (see Fig. 11.13). Some hidden surface algorithms employ the principle of area coherence. This is clearly an image space approach.

Depth coherence: Some of the hidden surface algorithms exploit the depth relationships, that is, the principle of depth coherence.

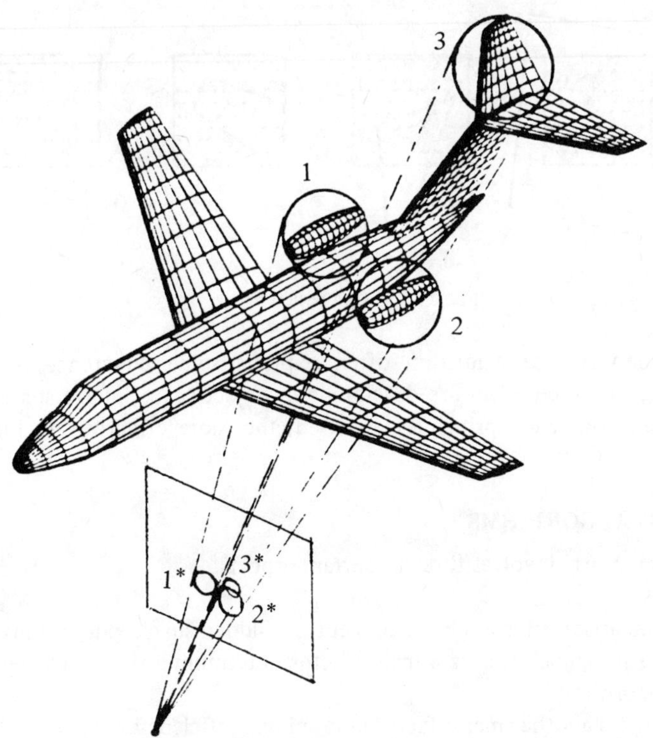

Fig. 11.11 Object coherence

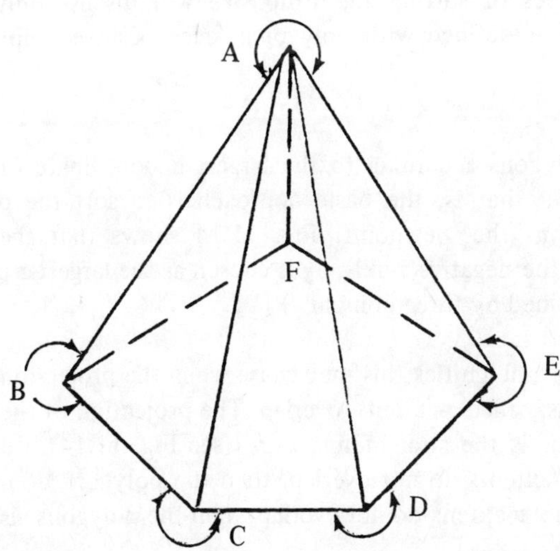

Fig. 11.12 Angle coherence

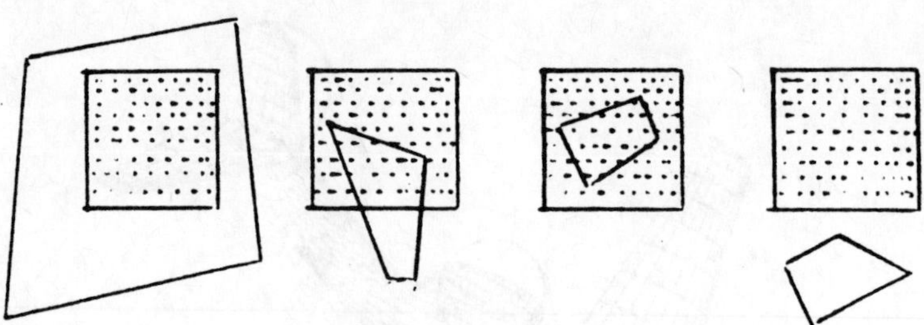

Fig. 11.13 Area coherence

A new hidden surface algorithm often exploits some coherence principles. The coherence principles themselves are developing in object space, image space, or some of both. The more coherence principles are used, the more effective are hidden surface algorithms.

11.4 SORTING ALGORITHMS

Hidden surface removal involves three important aspects:

- depth comparison: this is a basic concept for hidden surface algorithms;
- coherence principle: this is a major factor determining the efficiency of a hidden surface algorithm;
- sorting: this is another major factor determining efficiency.

Hidden surface removal can be considered as a large sorting process. An excellent sorting algorithm is a crucial requirement for hidden surface removal.

There are many types of sorting algorithm. We will discuss only the depth sort algorithm for 3-D objects defined with polygonal faces as an example. The algorithm consists of three steps:

Step 1:   Sort all polygons according to the largest z coordinate of each polygon in object space; that is, the basic approach is to sort the polygons by their distance from the viewpoint. Fig. 11.14 shows that the viewpoint is at infinity on the negative z-axis; z_2 is chosen as the largest z coordinate for the polygon defined by three points $\mathbf{P_1 P_2 P_3}$.

Step 2:   Resolve any ambiguities this may cause when the projections of the polygons on the z-axis, called z-extents, overlap. The projection of the polygon $\mathbf{P_1 P_2 P_3}$ on the z-axis is the straight line $z_1 z_2$ (see Fig. 11.14). For example, if the polygon's x-extents do not overlap, then the polygons do not overlap; and if the polygon's y-extens do not overlap, then the polygons also do not overlap.

Step 3:   Scan-convert each polygon onto the screen according to the descending order of the largest z coordinate. This places these polygons into the refresher

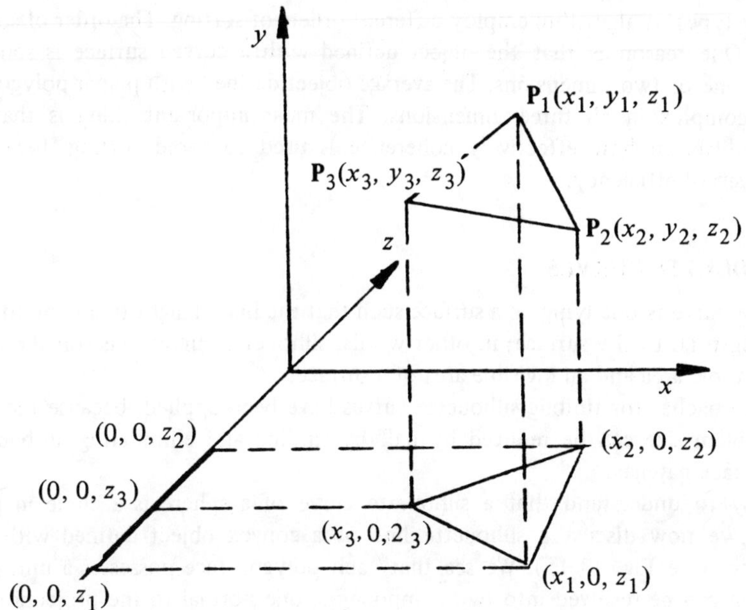

Fig. 11.14 z-extent

buffer in order of decreasing distance from the viewpoint. Because the nearest polygons are scan-converted last, they obscure polygons which are farther away by writing over them in the refresh buffer.

The basic idea of the depth sort algorithm is to sort the polygons by their distance from the viewpoint and to move these polygons into the refresh buffer in order of decreasing distance. Some steps are performed in object space, others in image space. So the algorithm is a hybrid between an object space and image space algorithm.

J. D. Foley and A. Van Dam [2] introduced the following four basic algorithms:

- the depth sort algorithm;
- the z-buffer algorithm;
- scan-line algorithm;
- area subdivision algorithm.

The depth sort algorithm sorts on the z coordinate, then on the x and y by using extents; it is thus called a zxy algorithm.

The scan-line algorithm sorts on y by using a bucket sort and then on x, and finally searches in z for the polygon nearest the viewpoint; it is thus called a yxz algorithm.

The area subdivision algorithm does a parallel sort on x and y, and then searches in z, and so is called an $(xy)z$ algorithm.

The z-buffer algorithm searches only in z by xy, and so is called an (xyz) algorithm.

The four types of algorithm employ different orders of sorting. The order of sorting is important. One reason is that the object defined with a curved surface is sometimes complex in one or two dimensions. The average object defined with planar polygon faces is equally complex in all three dimensions. The most important thing is that these algorithms differ in how effectively coherence is used to avoid sorting, hence their different levels of efficiency.

11.5 SILHOUETTE CURVES

A silhouette curve is one lying on a surface such that the line of sight to any point on the curve is tangential to the surface; in other words, silhouette curves exist on the borders between a visible area and an invisible area of a surface.

Many approaches for finding silhouette curves have been applied, because the hidden surface problem size can be reduced by half by finding and eliminating all backward-pointing surface patches.

It is easy to understand that a silhouette curve of a sphere is a circle in parallel projection. We now discuss a silhouette line of a convex object defined with planar polygon faces (see Fig. 11.15). We see that each polygon face possesses a unit normal vector which can be resolved into two components, one normal to the projection plane xOy, and one parallel to it. Those polygon faces are visible, whose normal vector has a component in the $-z$ direction, which is pointing toward the viewpoint, e.g. $\triangle ABE$, $\triangle BCE$, $\triangle ABF$ and $\triangle BCF$. Those polygon faces whose normal vector has a component in the $+z$ direction, which is pointing away from viewpoint, are not visible, such as $\triangle ADE$, $\triangle CDE$, $\triangle ADF$ and $\triangle CDF$. Those polygon faces whose normal vector has a z component equal to zero, are their bounding edges.

Fig. 11.15 shows that only four of the eight visible edges define the silhouette line, such as AE, EC, CF and FA. The other edges are not involved in the silhoueete line. How can the two types of visible edge be recognized mathematically? If an edge has a visible adjacent face and one not visible, the edge will contribute to the silhouette line. If an edge has two visible adjacent faces, the edge will not contribute to the silhouette line. We may design an algorithm according to the above rule and determine the silhouette line.

The above results can be developed to form a silhouette curve on a convex surface. When the surface has some undulations, we may employ the subdivision technique.

Fig. 11.16 shows that the visible part of a surface has a negative normal component on the z-axis direction, but the non-visible part of the surface has a positive normal component on the z-axis direction. Then the silhouette curve of a convex surface is that curve along which the z components of surface normals are zero. The condition of the silhouette curve may be represented as

$$\left(\frac{\partial \mathbf{r}(u, w)}{\partial u} \times \frac{\partial \mathbf{r}(u, w)}{\partial w} \right)_z = 0 \tag{11.8}$$

There are many approaches to calculating the silhouette curve. One of them is that by providing a series of values of parameter u (or w), and using iteration, we find a series of

w (or u) from (11.8), thereby substituting them into the surface equation $\mathbf{r}(u, w)$, we obtain a series of points defining the silhouette curve.

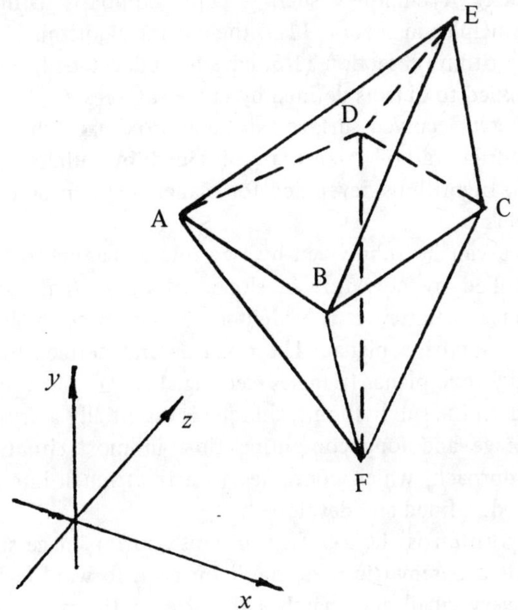

Fig. 11.15 Silhouette line of a polyhedron

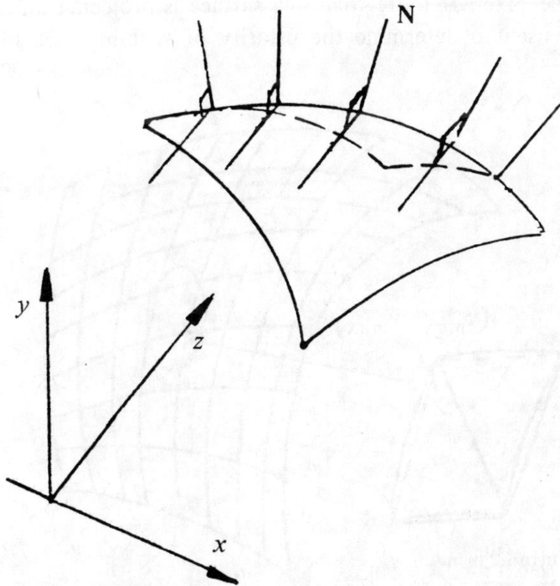

Fig. 11.16 Silhouette curve of a surface

11.6 HIDDEN SURFACE REMOVAL

There is an abundance of literature on hidden surface removal; most is for objects defined by planar polygonal faces. Techniques, such as depth comparisons discussed in section 11.2, the coherence principles in section 11.3, the sorting algorithms in section 11.4 and the silhouette curve algorithms in section 11.5, have been developed.

They can also be applied to objects defined by curve surfaces.

The basic idea is that the curved surface can be approximated by many small planar polygons, usually quadrilateral or triangular, obtained by subdivision of the curved surface. Then all of the algorithms developed for planar polygon objects can be applied for curved surface objects.

A parametric surface can be subdivided by two sets of parametric curves. The mesh spacing may be controlled by curvature or slope criteria so that the mesh spacing is greater where the surface is flatter. It is evident that four space mesh points defining a quadrilateral will often not be coplanar. The quadrilateral defined by four space mesh points can be expressed as two planar triangles (see Fig. 11.17).

The algorithm based on the subdivision technique is essentially a brute force approach, and requires large storage and long computing time in most situations, but it is an important and basic approach, which continues to attract much intellectual effort and continues to be improved, refined and developed.

Another popular algorithm is the z-buffer or depth-buffer image space algorithm. It requires the creation of a paremetric u, w mesh on each forward-facing surface in the display. The mesh is very small and matches the size of the pixel, which is a screen element defining the resolution of the display (there are more than a million pixels on a 1280×1024 screen). In other words, subdivision is repeated until a surface patch covers no more than a single pixel. If more than one surface is projected into a pixel, then a depth comparison is used to determine the priority of visibility (see Fig. 11.18). This

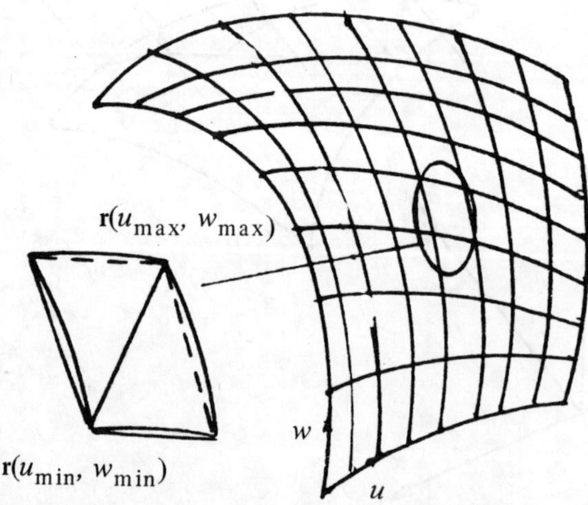

Fig. 11.17 Approximation of a surface by planar polygons

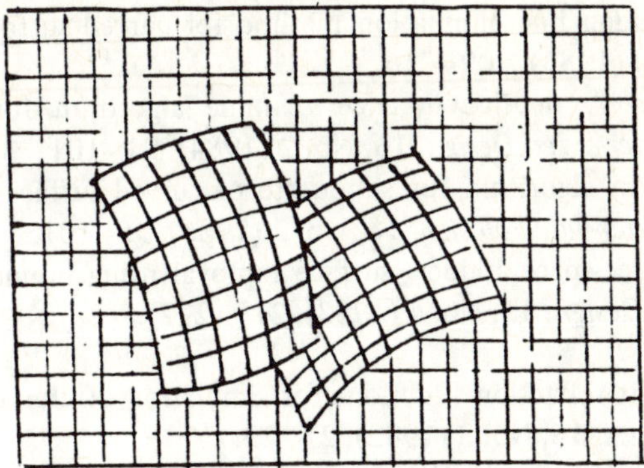

Fig. 11.18 z-buffer algorithm for a curved surface

method has the disadvantage of requiring a large amount of space for the z-buffer but is simple to implement.

There are other methods to solve the hidden surface removal problem for objects with curved surfaces, but they are not discussed here. In this area the most important steps are: to explore the new subdivision approach; to apply the principles discussed in sub-sections 11.2–11.5; and to use the new image display hardware.

To create realistic images of surface objects, two very effective approaches are shading and colouring of visible surfaces after the hidden surface removal. Shading and colouring can be displayed in computer graphics.

We now can define surface objects in 3-D geometric space, project them onto a 2-D plane, and eliminate hidden surfaces to obtain an unambiguous drawing. Then shading and colouring techniques can produce lifelike images.

REFERENCES

[1] Sutherland, I. E., Sproull, R. F. and Schumacker, R. A., A characterisation of ten hidden-surface algorithms, *Computing Surveys,* **6**, Mar. (1974), 1–56.

[2] Foley, J. D. and Van Dam, A., *Fundamentals of Interactive Computer Graphics*, Addison-Wesley, Reading, MA, 1982.

[3] Mortenson, M. E., *Geometric Modelling*, John Wiley and Sons, New York, 1985.

[4] Newman, W. M. and Sproull, R. F., *Principles of Interactive Computer Graphics*, McGraw-Hill, New York, 1979.

[5] Catmull, E. E., A subdivision algorithm for computer display of curved surfaces, *Tech. Report UTEC CSc-74-133*, University of Utah, UT, USA, December (1974).

[6] Griffiths, J. G., A data structure for the elimination of hidden surfaces by patch subdivision, *Computer-aided Design,* **7**, No. 3, July (1975), 171–178.

[7] Appel, A., Hidden line elimination for complex surfaces, *IBM Technical Disclosure Bulletin,* **18**, No. 11, April (1976), 3873–3876.

[8] Griffiths, J. G., Bibliography of hidden-line and hidden-surface algorithms, *Computer-aided Design,* **10**, No. 3 (1978), 203–206.

[9] Ohno, Y., A hidden line elmination method for curved surfaces, *Computer-aided Design*, **15**, No. 4 (1983), 209–216.

[10] Griffiths, J. G., A depth-coherence scanline algorithm for displaying curved surfaces, *Computer-aided Design*, **16**, No. 2 (1984), 91–101.

[11] Bonfiglioli, L., An algorithm for silhouette of curved surfaces based on graphical relations, *Computer-aided Design*, **18**, No. 2 (1986), 95–101.

[12] Duncan, R., Three-space hidden surface removal using boundary traversal logic, *Computer-aided Design*, **15**, No. 4 (1983), 217–222.

[13] Blinn, J. F., Light reflection functions for simulation of clouds and dirty surfaces, *Computer Graphics*, **16**, No. 3 (1982), 21–29.

[14] Crow, F. C., A more flexible image generation environment, *Computer Graphics*, **16**, No. 3 (1982), 9–18.

[15] Schweitzer, D. and Cobb, E. S., Scanline rendering of parametric surfaces, *Computer Graphics*, **16**, No. 3 (1982), 265–271.

[16] Hedgely, D. R., A general solution to the hidden-line problem, *NASA Reference Publication 1085*, March (1982).

[17] Griffiths, J. G., Tape-oriented hidden-line algorithm, *Computer-aided Design*, **13**, No. 1 (1981), 19–26.

[18] Wittram, M., Hidden-line algorithm for scenes of high complexity, *Computer-aided Design*, **13**, No. 4 (1981), 187–192.

[19] Pavlidis, T., Algorithms for graphics and image processing: computer graphics and pictorial information processing, *Computer Science* (1981).

[20] Whitted, J. T., An improved illumination model for shaded display, *Commun.*, ACM **23**, No. 6 (1980), 343–349.

[21] Lane, J. M., Carpenter, L. C., Whitted, J. T. and Blinn, J. F., Scanline methods for displaying parametrically defined surfaces, *Commun.*, ACM **23**, (1980), 23–34.

[22] Griffiths, J. G., A surface display algorithm, *Computer-aided Design*, **10**, No. 1, January (1978), 65–73.

[23] Gouraud, H., Continuous shading of curved surfaces, *IEEE Trans. Comput.*, **C-20**, (1971), 623–629.

[24] Watkins, G. S., A real time visible surface algorithm, *PhD thesis*, Dept of Electrical Engineering, University of Utah (1970).

12

Implementation of Surface Modelling

12.1 CHOOSING A SURFACE MODELLING SYSTEM

There are three methods of geometric modelling, which are wireframe modelling, surface modelling, and solid modelling. The importance of these methods is rapidly increasing in engineering. A key question is how to choose a suitable modelling system for a specific application. This depends mainly on the shape of the product being designed and machined. For example, surface modelling systems are always chosen in the aircraft industry, in ship design and production, and in the motor industry, for the complex surface contours required; wireframe modelling systems are usually chosen in machine design for simple machined parts, tools and fixtures and structures; solid modelling systems are beginning to be used in mechanical design, e.g. robot design, as this integrates best with CAM.

Wireframe modelling is the oldest 3-D geometric modelling technology and is the simplest. Surface models permit the designer to use a collection of mathematically defined curves and surface patches to define the contour of the model surface. Modelling can be used to generate surfaces from, on the one hand, simple planes, cones, spheres, to, on the other, highly complex and irregular sculptured surfaces.

Sculptured surface systems have been developed in conjunction with customers for a wide range of applications including:

aircraft fuselage and wing design;
automobile body and windshield design;
ship design;
casting and forging (die) design;

mould design;
model design;
container design such as wine bottles or flower vases;
product shape design, e.g. clocks and watches;
shoe mould and last design;
costume design;
cloth pattern design;
etc.

These design applications are very well suited to surface modelling. Sculptured surfaces are used heavily where product design requires an aerodynamic surface or visually acceptable contour with radical changes in shape from one area to another.

These products may be designed and defined efficiently using a surface modelling system, whereas manual design and calculation can be very time-consuming, and difficult, and even impossible in certain cases.

For numerically controlled machining, wireframes are sufficient in only two-axis and two-and-a-half-axis cases. For three-axis, four-axis or five-axis machining, well-defined surfaces are essential. A wireframe model defines a product by points, lines, arcs and spline curves. The resulting model does not 'know' whether a plane bounded by visible lines represents solid material within or outside the lines; the designer has to supply this information at the CAM stage. A surface modelling system can calculate the normal vector at any point on the surface which is needed to define the tool path.

Surfaces may be used for defining complex finite element models. To design an optimal structure or to determine the cause of failure after manufacture, designers commonly use the finite element method, which is a versatile engineering tool that provides a mathematical simulation of the behaviour of a complex structure. Using this method, engineers can determine the amount and location of stress in a structural design, without building a prototype. Mesh generation is made much easier when the initial model is defined by surfaces in a CAD system.

Surface models are represented by meshes. The mesh may be of variable density, as specified by the user. In advance surface modelling systems, the surfaces may be displayed as shaded, full-colour images that provide the user with a more complete visualization. This shaded, full-colour image often gives the false visual impression that a solid model has been used, but the surface model represents only the 'shell' of a geometric object, and not its volume.

Solid modelling is the ideal geometric modelling tool. It is the complete mathematical description of a physical object. Today, however, solid modelling is computationally intensive and requires a high processing capacity for an interactive response. The database storage requirements are greater for a solid model than for wireframe or surface models of the same part. Currently most solid modelling systems can define only simple goemetric entities such as cubes, spheres, cylinders and cones, etc. Certain advanced solid modelling systems include arbitrary second-degree surface patches as the boundaries of building-blocks. Solid modelling software continues to develop.

Recently, surface modelling software has developed rapidly in three areas:

The capabilities of surface modelling have become more and more powerful. More intelligence is added to surface modelling systems (i.e. the so-called expert system approach).

Surface modelling is now run in a microcomputer environment. Until recently, all surface modelling required mainframe computers, because only mainframes were powerful enough to drive surface modelling software. Now things are rapidly changing and microcomputers have become powerful enough to run 3-D surface software.

Surface modelling and solid modelling software are becoming unified.

12.2 IMPLEMENTING A SURFACE MODELLING SYSTEM

Let us first review some of the problems of working with classical design and manual drawings. Many complex objects are difficult to describe and often require a large number of views. When drawing a new view, the draughtsman has continually to refer to the views already detailed to ensure accuracy, compatibility and continuity. Classical surface definition can only be represented on a drawing by lines drawn across the intended surface. At best this is only a partial definition because the surface between the lines is only implicit.

When extracting information and data from a conventional drawing, reference has often to be made to many or all of the views. When outfitting a structure such as arranging piping for engineering systems, the draughtsman has to route the pipes through the structure, between the various items of equipment, ensuring that they do not clash with each other, with the equipment and with its maintenance envelope and the structure. To do this with a drawing composed of sets of 2-D views is a time-consuming and difficult operation requiring much experience.

In order to implement a surface modelling efficiently a CAD/CAM system should provide the following capabilities.

Model mode

To produce a drawing, a designer thinks in three dimensions, but with paper and pencil he is compelled to work in two dimensions. A CAD/CAM system allows the designer to 'build' a 3-D geometric model. Visual inspection of the 3-D is made possible by a variety of features, including dynamic display, which allows the model to be rotated and scaled up or down, by sectioning through any portion of the model, and by temporarily blanking off any part of the model not currently required. Large complex models can therefore be constructed on the screen with only that position of the model visible which is required. The building of the model is referred to as operating a system in the 'model mode'.

Drawing mode

With the 3-D model either fully or partially complete, the designer can use 'drawing mode' to produce a notated, clearly-laid-out, finished drawing displaying selected views of the model. The designer defines different views, i.e. ways of looking at the model, and places one or more of these on a single drawing.

Layers
A facility of the CAD/CAM system which assists in differentiating between parts of a large complex 3-D model is the ability to place different geometric entities, i.e. lines, arcs, circles, etc., on different layers. The designer can then decide whether to display all or any combination of layers. This assists in visualizing and working with complex 3-D models on the screen.

A further important aid to handling large complex models is to adopt a hierarchy of sub-models referred to as nodal figures. These can be designed and detailed separately and then inserted into the main model as required. When not in position, their location is defined by a circumscribing envelope, to avoid clashing. The size and content of these sub-models can be selected to be a unit. The main model therefore fulfils the role of an arrangement definition showing the interconnections and supporting structure.

Documentation
The CAD/CAM system can assist the designer to produce technical publications and manufacturing documentation. The system allows the designer to produce technial illustrations, including perspective views, exploded views, and assembly drawings, which may be used in customer documentation, training and maintenance manuals, or for sales proposals. The illustrations might also be used for generating presentation slides or computer output microfilm records. Appropriate illustrations used in the manufacturing sequence can also be produced. This is a valuable tool on the shop-floor for creating visual process planning or product assembly documentation. Non-graphic capabilities are also available to the designer, for example, reports such as bills of materials and part lists can be automatically generated for specification manuals.

Common database
A CAD/CAM system uses a common database to support all the activities associated with the design and manufacturing cycle. First, the designer creates a model of the part geometry which forms the original database. The analytical engineer can use this model for calculation of mass properties and construction of finite element models. Next, the draughtsman uses this database to produce the required detail drawings. The manufacturing engineer uses the same database representing the design geometry of the model to generate tool paths for numerically controlled machines. Once these tool paths are verified, the system is used to produce numerical control tapes. Any tools, fixtures or moulds required for production of the part can also be designed and NC tapes can be generated for them.

In CAD/CAM systems, all the views of a model are related to the model in the common database. This means that if some aspect of the model is changed, all drawings containing views of that part of the model are regenerated by the system. Apart from the benefit of alleviating the designer of a great deal of additional work, this ensures that the consequences of a change are carried through automatically to all associated drawings, thus avoiding the error of forgetting to modify a particular drawing. Dimensions and appearance graphics, e.g. cross-hatching, are also updated automatically to be compatible with the change.

Using one database greatly reduces redundant procedures and consequently reduces a major source of errors. The chance of misinterpreting information is lessened since all groups — designers, draughtsmen and manufacturing engineers — work from the same information contained in the common database.

Easy-to-use tablet
When using surface modelling software, the designer uses a tablet menu to enter commands quickly. A single menu square can execute part of a command, an entire command, or a series of commands. The designer can use the tablet menu included with the software or can create his own menu to reflect a personal design approach and optimize productivity.

On-line query
The on-line query feature provides instant access to information. The query feature quickly lists available options for any command, and briefly explains each command and available modifiers on the display screen.

Designers and engineers can thus use the surface modelling system as a professional tool to enhance productivity. Because the user designs interactively, he can change his design at any time to experiment with or to implement engineering changes. This extends the design capabilities and speeds up the design process.

12.3 USING A SURFACE MODELLING SYSTEM

This section has been produced with the aim of introducing the typical instructions and commands used to define and manipulate curves and surfaces in surface modelling systems.

The following examples will help us to understand the command structure of surface modelling and are based on the Computervision CDS 4000 system.

Instruction:

> > INSERT RSURFACE MU 6 MW 4 : entity d1 d2 < CR >

The instruction means inserting a ruled surface which is defined by two existing curves and displayed by a mesh which consists of isoparametric lines in the U direction and the W direction (see Fig. 12.1).

Instruction:

> > INSERT TCYLINDER MU 5 MW 5 : entity WIN d1 d2,
> digit from Z0 to Z10 < CR >

The instruction means generating a tabulated cylinder created by projecting a profile for a specified distance along a specified axis (see Fig. 12.2).

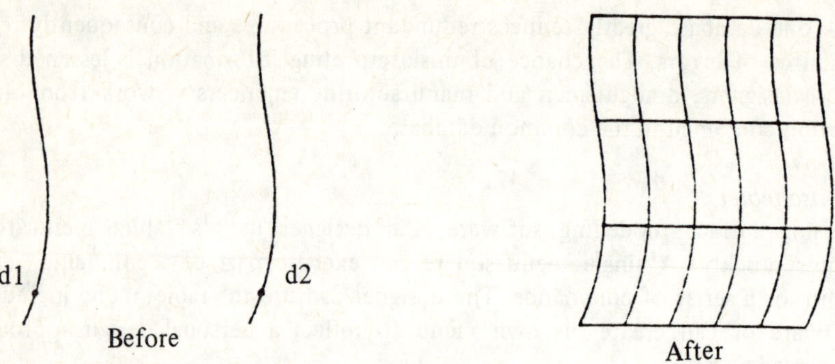

Fig. 12.1 Ruled surface

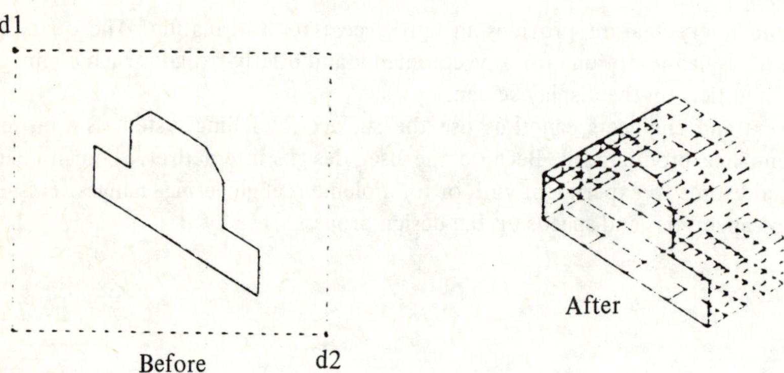

Fig. 12.2 Tabulated cylinder

Instruction:

> ≫ INSERT SREVOLUTION MU 4 MW 4 : axis digit d1 d2
> ent WIN d3 d4, origin POI d5 from d6 to d7 < CR >

The instruction creates a surface by sweeping a profile through a specified angle around a specified axis (see Fig. 12.3).

Instruction:

> ≫ INSERT CPOLE LAY 4 : digit d1 d2 d3 d4 d5 d6 d7 < CR >

The instruction specifies a Bezier curve defined by 7 vertices called 'poles' on layer 4 (see Fig. 12.4).

Instruction:

> ≫ INSERT SPOLE MU7 MW7 : digit d1 d2 d3 d4; d5 d6 d7 d8;
> d9 d10 d11 d12 < CR >

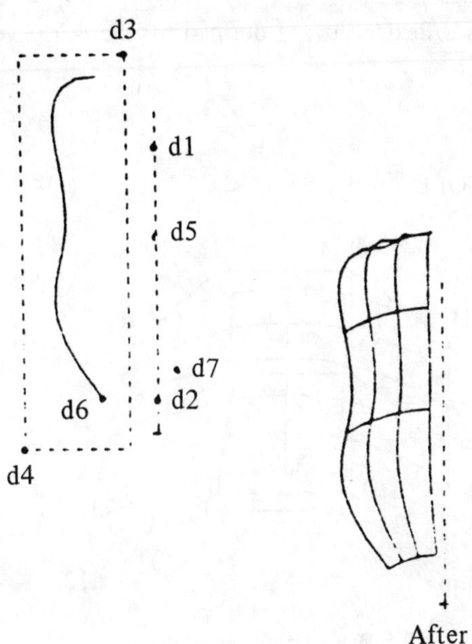

After

Fig. 12.3 A surface of revolution

Fig. 12.4 A Bezier curve of degree 6

This instruction forms a Bezier surface defined by the 4 × 3 vertices of a polyhedron (see Fig. 12.5).

Instruction:

> BLEND CPOLE : entity d1 d2 < CR >

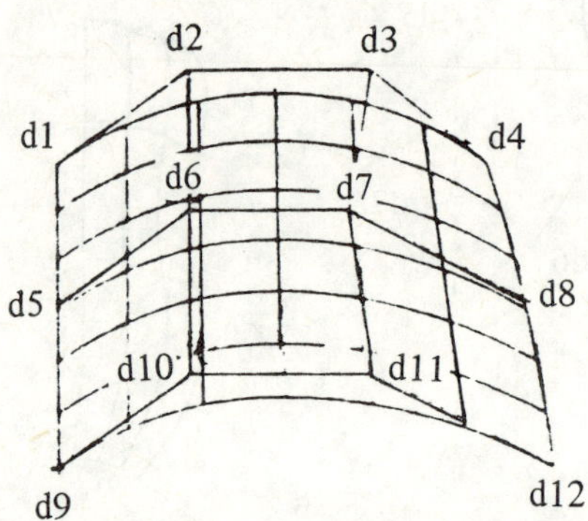

Fig. 12.5 A Bezier surface of degree 3 × 2

The instruction creates a Bezier curve blending two existing Bezier curves smoothly and filling the gap between them (see Fig. 12.6).

Instruction:

> BLEND SPOLE : entity d1 d2 d3 < CR >

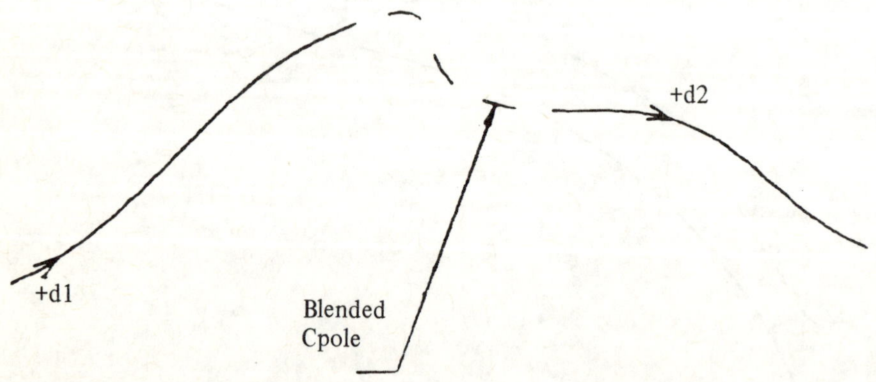

Fig. 12.6 Blending of Bezier curves

This creates a blending surface between, two, three or four existing Bezier surfaces. The blending Bezier surfaces are matched in tangency along their edges (see Fig. 12.7).

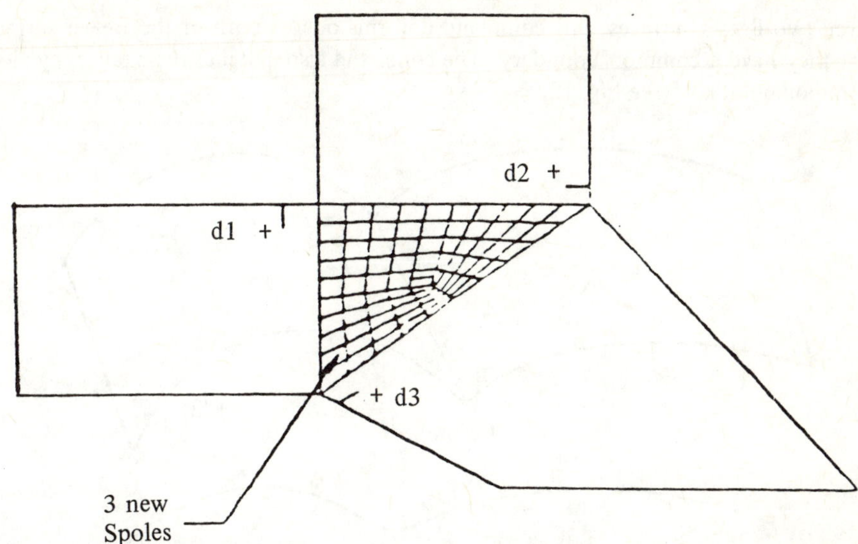

Fig. 12.7 Blending of Bezier surfaces

Instruction:

>> MATCH CPOLE : entity d1 d2 < CR >

Given two Bezier curves, this facility deforms one or both the Bezier curves so that they are matched in tangency at the common end point. To a certain extent, depending on the size of the Bezier curves, Bezier curves with gaps can be matched (see Fig. 12.8).

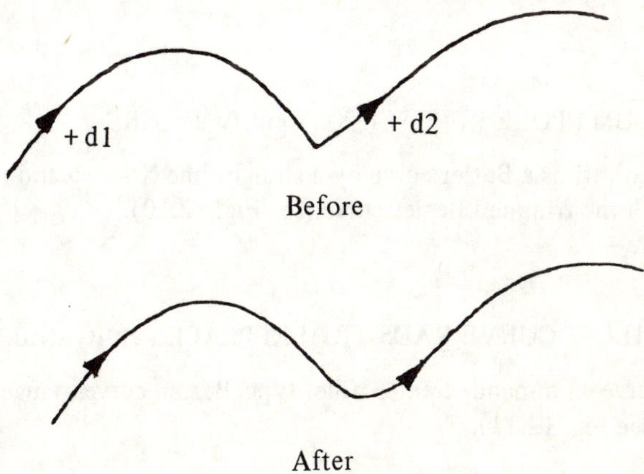

Fig. 12.8 Matching of Bezier curves

Instruction:

>> MATCH SPOLE : entity d1 d2 < CR >

Given two Bezier surfaces, this command deforms one or both of the Bezier surfaces so that they have a common boundary. The command also matches their tangency along the common boundary (see Fig. 12.9).

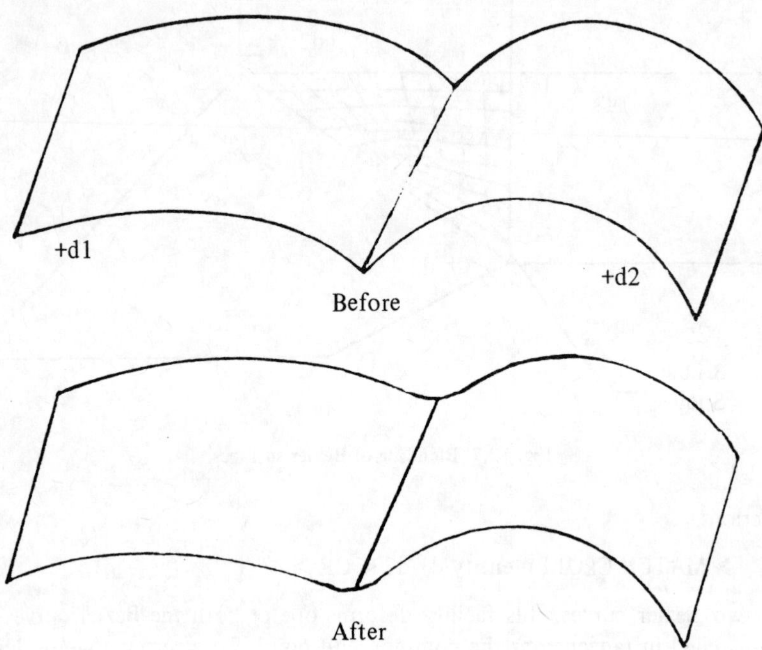

Fig. 12.9 Matching of Bezier surfaces

Instruction:

> TRIM CPOLE REPLACE X-5 : entity d < CR >

This instruction trims a Bezier curve by a straight line $X = -5$ and replaces the original Bezier curve with the trimmed Bezier curve (see Fig. 12.10).

Instruction:

> FILLET CURVE RAD5 TRIM REPLACE : entity d1 d2 < CR >

The fillet curve command creates fillet-type Bezier curves tangential to two intersecting curves (see Fig. 12.11).

Instruction:

> FILLET SURFACE RAD6 TRIM REPLACE : entity
  d1 d2 d3 d4 d5 < CR >

This command is used for the filleting of Bezier surfaces (see Fig. 12.12).

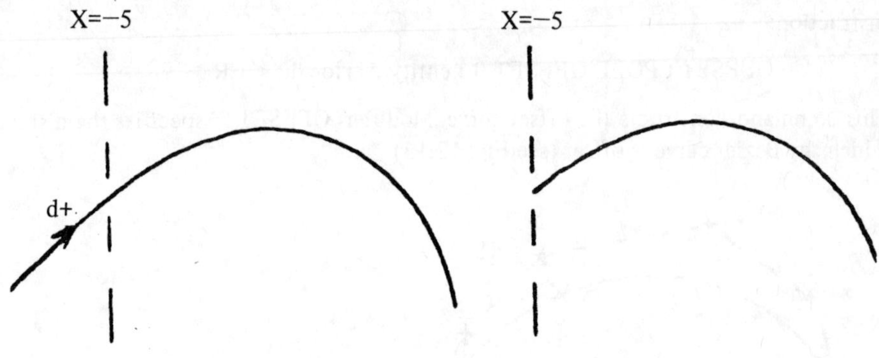

Fig. 12.10 Trimming of a Bezier curve

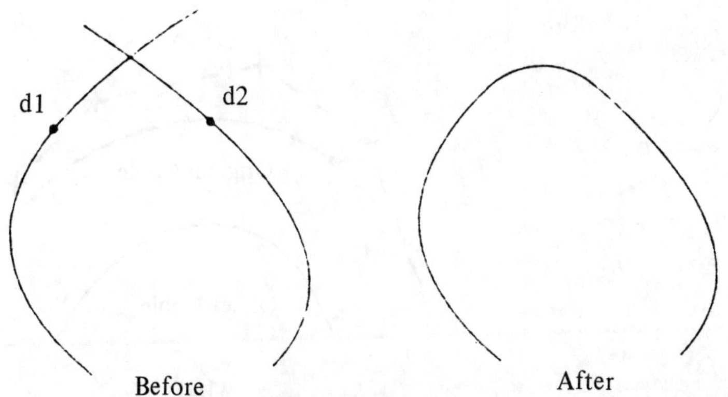

Fig. 12.11 Filleting of curves

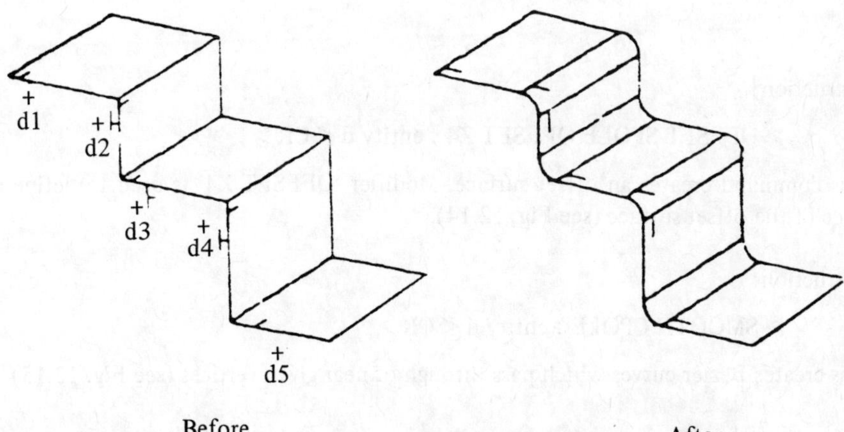

Fig. 12.12 Filleting of surfaces

Instruction:

> ≫ OFFSET CPOLE OFFSET 3 : entity d1; loc d2 < CR >

This command constructs the offset curve. Modifier 'OFFSET 3' specifies the distance by which the Bezier curve is offset (see Fig. 12.13).

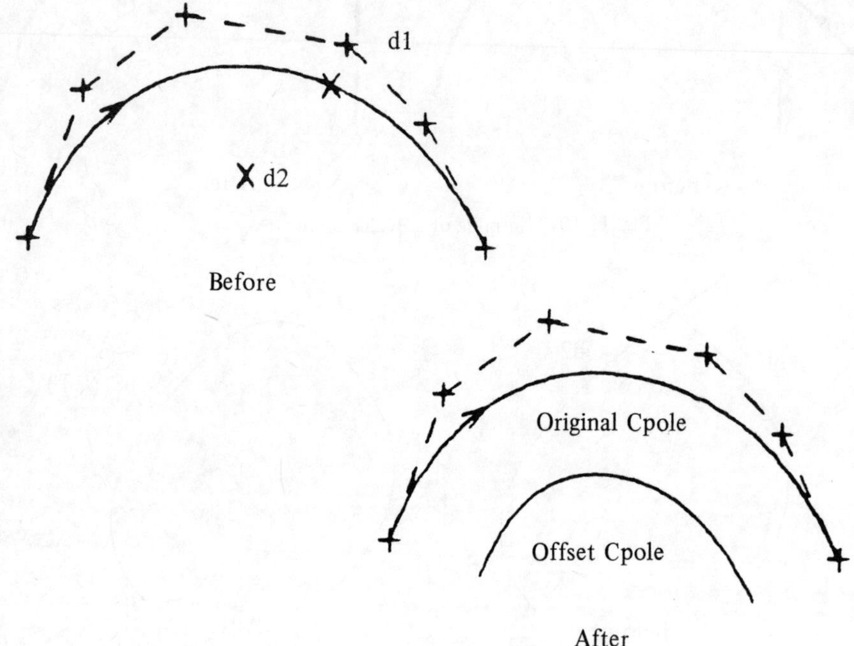

Fig. 12.13 Offsetting of a curve

Instruction:

> ≫ OFFSET SPOLE OFFSET Z4 : entity d < CR >

This command creates an offset surface. Modifier 'OFFSET Z4' is used to define the distance of the offset surface (see Fig. 12.14).

Instruction:

> ≫ SMOOTH CPOLE : entity d < CR >

This creates Bezier curves which pass through or near given vertices (see Fig. 12.15).

Instruction:

> ≫ SMOOTH SPOLE FLAT : entity d1 d2 d3 d4 < CR >

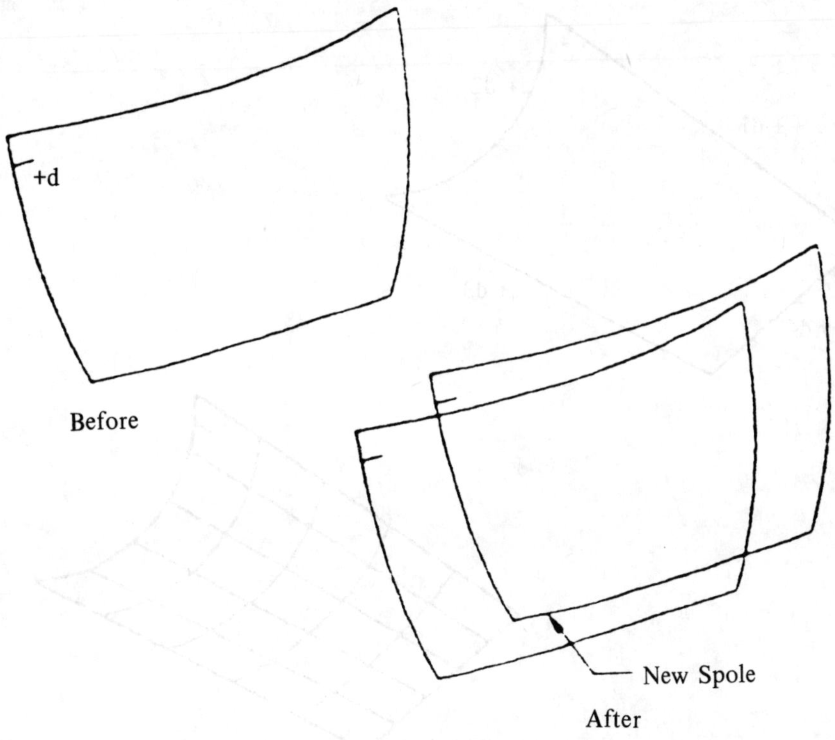

Fig. 12.14 Offsetting of a surface

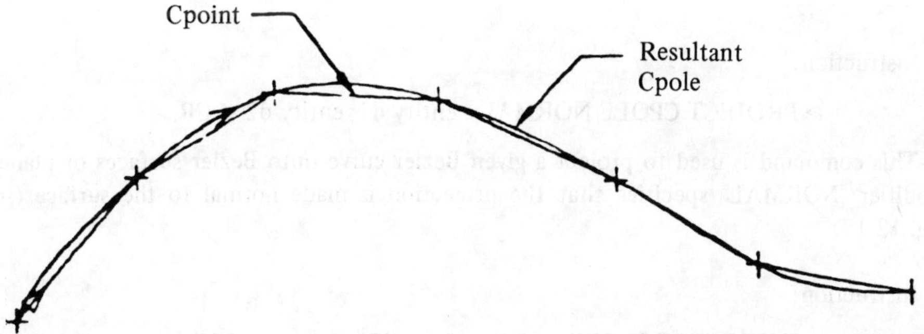

Fig. 12.15 Smoothing Bezier curves

With this command, the user can create a Bezier surface. Modifier 'FLAT' specifies that a blending function is required to create a Bezier surface from four Bezier curves. This creates the flattest possible blend (see Fig. 12.16).

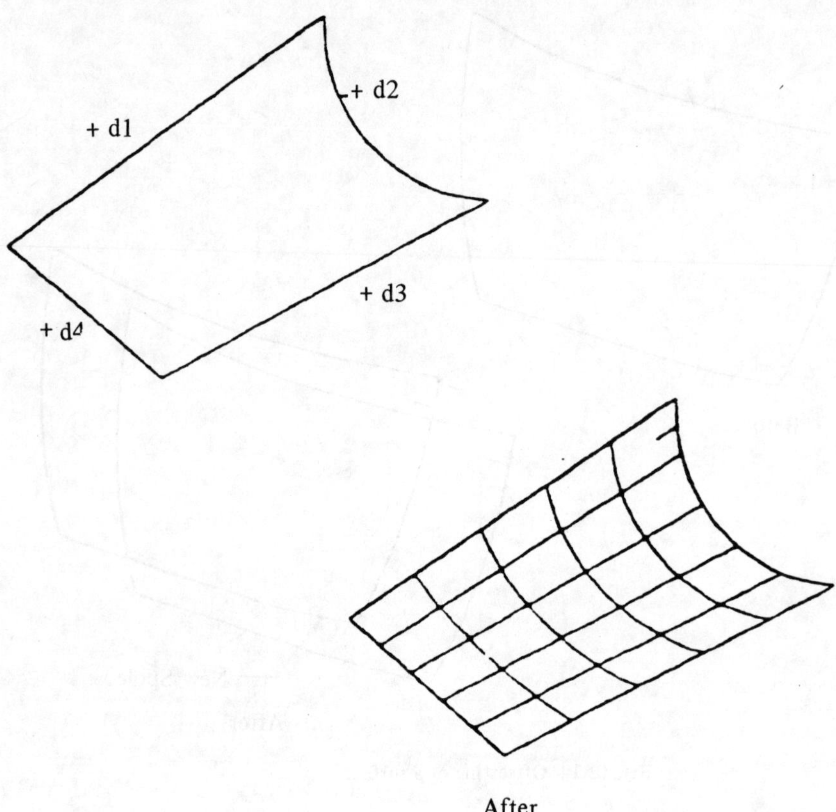

Fig. 12.16 Smoothing a Bezier surface

Instruction:

> ≫ PROJECT CPOLE NORMAL : entity d1; entity d2 < CR >

This command is used to project a given Bezier curve onto Bezier surfaces or planes. Modifier 'NORMAL' specifies that the projection is made normal to the surface (see Fig. 12.17).

Instruction:

> ≫ INTERSECT CPOLE : entity d1 . . . d7; entity d8 < CR >

The intersection command is used to generate curves of intersection between two series of Bezier surfaces (see Fig. 12.18).

The instructions and commands described in this chapter are essential for describing surfaces. These instructions and commands are all similarly structure, i.e.

> ≫ VERB NAME [modifiers] : date input < CR >

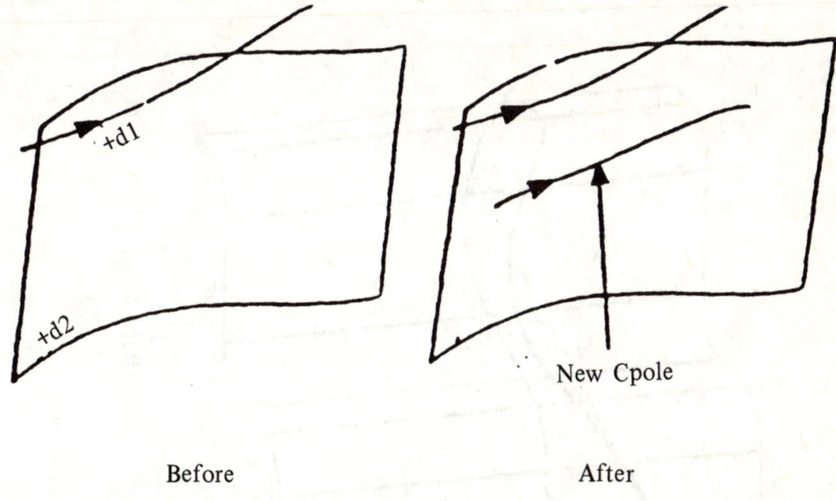

Fig. 12.17 Projecting a curve

Some complex commands provide several ways of choosing input data by interactive Yes–No answers to questions.

These instructions and commands are being developed by both the software companies and the users. The advanced and complex instructions may be designed by software companies, but the instructions for special requirements can be developed by the user.

REFERENCES

[1] Besant, C. B. and Lui, C. W. K., *Computer-Aided Design and Manufacture*, Ellis Horwood, Chichester, 1986.

[2] Smith, W. A., *et al.*, Computervision CADDS 4X Surface Modelling Course, *Computer Aided Engineering*, UMIST UK, 1986.

[3] Smith, W. A., *et al.*, Computervision Micro CADDS Surface Modelling Course, *Computer Aided Engineering*, UMIST UK, 1986.

[4] Haigh, M. J., *An Introduction to Computer-Aided Design and Manufacture*, Blackwell Scientific Publications, Oxford, 1985.

[5] Emmerson, W. C., CAD in the motor industry, *Computer-aided Design,* **8**, No. 3 (1976), 193–197.

[6] Walter, H., Computer-aided design in the aircraft industry, in *Computer-Aided Design*, North Holland, Amsterdam, 1973.

[7] Walker, L. F., Curved surfaces in shipbuilding design and production, in *Computer-Aided Design*, IPC Science & Technology Press, Cambridge, U.K., 1972.

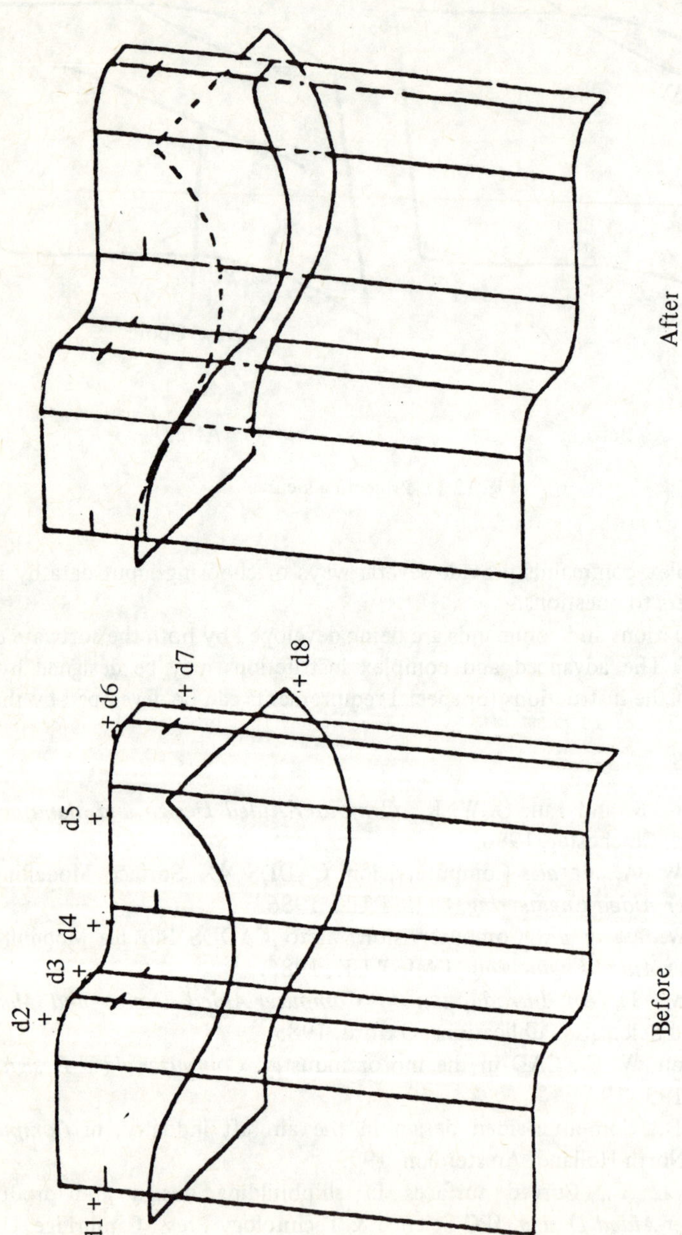

Fig. 12.18 Intersection between two series of Bezier surfaces

13

Environment of Surface Modelling
(B.J. Davies)

13.1 INTRODUCTION

Computer-aided design and computer-aided manufacture (CAD/CAM) are techniques by which the designer and computer are combined into a design and manufacturing team, sharing tasks according to their abilities. CAD/CAM is probably the most significant advance in engineering design and manufacture this century. It will have a major effect on manufactured products by the 1990s and will radically change the economies of the manufacturing nations in the next century.

CAD/CAM systems can be classified as follows:

First Generation: Mainframe systems.

Second Generation: Minicomputer systems.

Third Generation: Microcomputer systems.

In this chapter we will discuss mainly the microcomputer environment of surface modelling.

13.2 THE THREE GENERATIONS OF CAD/CAM SYSTEMS

13.2.1 The First-generation CAD/CAM systems

The first generation of systems was expensive beacause the systems were complex, making heavy demands on the power of a mainfram computer. They were adopted in general only in major industries such as the aircraft industry, where their use in design and manufacture justified the high capital costs.

13.2.2 Second-generation CAD/CAM systems

Second-generation CAD/CAM systems have resulted from the increased power and reduced cost of minicomputers, and in developments in graphic display hardware and software. The cost of such systems has reduced to the point where they can be economically applied in design and manufacture in a wide range of industries.

1

Computervision (CV) is probably the world leader in the number of minicomputer CAD/CAM systems installed.

2

Intergraph computer graphics systems are based on the DEC VAX range of 32-bit computers, enhanced by special Intergraph-designed hardware accelerators to provide the speed of response required for interactive graphics.

3

The Applicon company's BRAVO family of turnkey systems is based upon DEX VAX 32-bit computers and Applicon workstations run under the DEC VAX VMS operating system.

4

The McDonnel Douglas Automation Company provides a complete turnkey system for mechanical design, and can provide either a complete stand-alone workstation system, or a multi-workstation system complete with a full range of peripheral devices such as plotter, listing printer and paper tape punch/reader.

Computervision, Intergraph, Applicon and McAuto are currently probably the major international minicomputer CAD/CAM system suppliers. They provide powerful software packages which run on minicomputers, including 2-D draughting, 3-D draughting, 3-D modelling, FEA (Finite Element Analysis), NC programming, robotics, simulation, etc. These companies offer turnkey CAD/CAM systems. A turnkey system is a package of compatible hardware and software (that may or may not be from the same manufacturer) which is sold as a complete ready-to-use system.

This minicomputer CAD/CAM system is still relatively expensive but has some facilities that the small company does not need. This has led to the development of the third-generation CAD/CAM system, running on microcomputers, providing an integrated inexpensive CAD/CAM system, suitable for many large- middle- and small-sized firms.

13.2.3 Third-generation CAD/CAM systems

IBM PC and micro VAX-based systems are leading products in this field, with many other host computers, e.g. SUN, Apollo, IBM 'look-alike', etc., rapidly developing the market. These systems have floppy or hard disk stores, memories from a quarter to several megabytes and generating speeds of up to about 2 MIPS (million instructions per second). They are capable of running simulation applications, high-resolution graphics, the Unix operating system, and interface with a mouse and joystick, and provide windows, icons and pop-up menus, all at a relatively modest price.

13.3 THE TYPICAL WORKSTATION FOR A THIRD-GENERATION CAD/CAM SYSTEM

Fig. 13.1 shows a typical microcomputer-based CAD/CAM system. It includes a 16- or 32-bit processor with floppy and fixed disks, plus the normal input and output peripherals. Such systems can be linked by a local area network which allows them to share printers, plotters and fixed disks and to communicate with other systems.

13.4 MICRO CAD/CAM HARDWARE

13.4.1 The microprocessor

A microprocessor is the CPU (Central Processing Unit) of a microcomputer, and its processing power is vital for CAD/CAM applications. An important factor is word length, which determines the accuracy with which computations can be carried out. Double-word-length working is possible but at slower computing speed. Microprocessors started as 8-bit machines, then 16-bit, and now the latest generation of microprocessors provides a 32-bit word length.

1 8-bit microprocessors

Performance: Standard 8-bit microprocessor instructions are normally executed within $1\,\mu$s, depending on the clock frequency of the microprocessor. These instructions include a comprehensive set of program control codes for conditional branch, subroutine jumps and interrupts with priority. A workstation not requiring to perform excessive data manipulation or arithmetic functions could use 8-bit microprocessors. The performance of the standard 8-bit microprocessors can, in some cases, be enhanced by the addition of arithmetic LSI chips. It is unusual for standard 8-bit microprocessors to have multiplication and division in their instruction sets, and so these processes must be carried out in many steps, and are slow.

Limitations: 8-bit microprocessors have limitations when applied to CAD/CAM tasks, such as the lack of processing power for the arithmetical operations required and the lack of high-level scientific programming languages such as Fortran and Pascal, and the limited size of primary memory addressable by a standard 8-bit microprocessor (typically 64 K bytes).

Application: However, there are many instances where an 8-bit microprocessor system would suffice, such as 2-D design and draughting, and this would result in a minimum cost system. The possibility of using these low-cost systems in CAD/CAM is attractive to small companies.

2 16-bit microprocessors

16-bit microprocessors are now readily available. They provide greater capability than 8-bit machines in performing the arithmetic operations crucial to CAD/CAM applications.

The Intel 8086 was the first standard 16-bit microprocessor with processing power comparable to a standard minicomputer's CPU. The Intel 8086 has eight standard general registers. The first four are general-purpose 16-bit arithmetic registers which are used for arithmetic or logic operations. In addition there is a set of four pointers and index registers used for program control. The Intel 8086 has a comprehensive instruction set

Monitor
Local area network
Plotter
Microcomputer
RAM
ROM
16- or 32-bit microcomputer
Floppy disk unit
Fixed disc
Magnetic tape unit
Other workstation
Keyboard
Digitizer
Printer

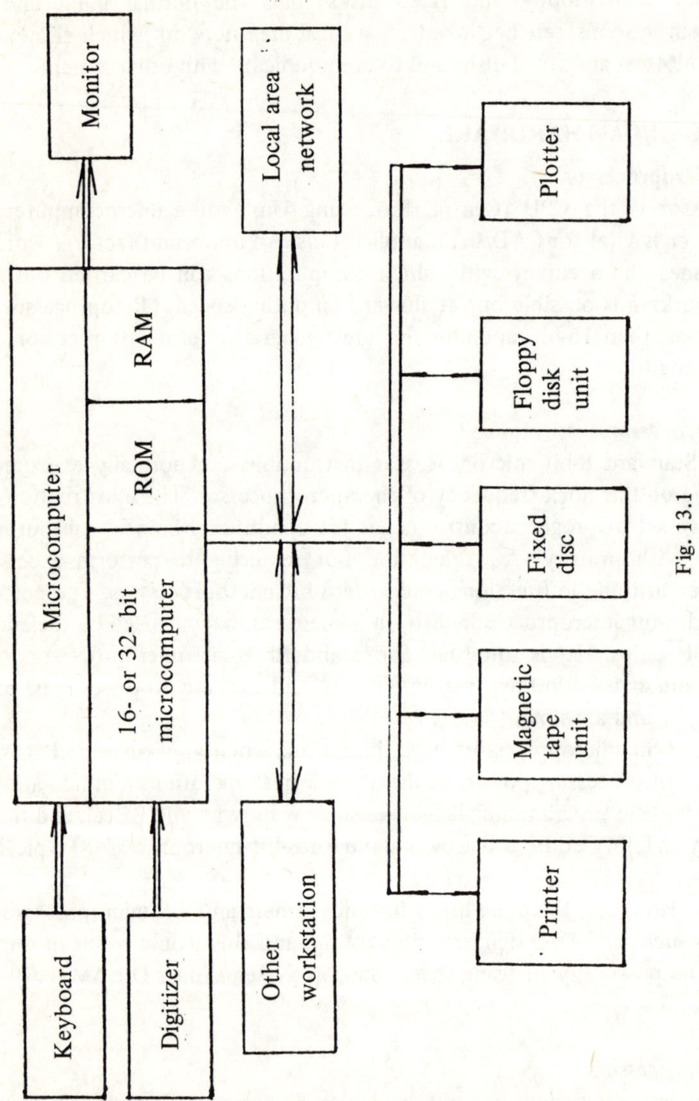

Fig. 13.1

and addressing modes, including indirect addressing, which is useful for implementing high-level language compilers. The Intel 8086 can address up to 1 M byte of memory in 64 K byte memory segments. This is a clear advantage over the standard 16-bit mini-computer's CPUs which can only address 128 K bytes of memory without extra support in the form of memory management hardware. The Intel 80286 is the latest Intel 16-bit microprocessor.

Other 16-bit microprocessors are the Zylog 8001 and the Motorola 68000.

3 32-bit microprocessor

The main thrust in microprocessor development is in the new 32-bit microcomputers. IBM's 32-bit personal computer was launched in 1986; the IBM 16-bit microcomputer presently dominates the market. The DEC Micro VAX with a 32-bit microprocessor is the new-generation microcomputer. Applicon's stand-alone workstation is Aria-II is based on the Micro VAX II with 5 M bytes of main memory and a 160 M byte disk. It runs all Applicon–MDSI software, including 2-D layout, 3-D wireframe, surface modelling, solid modelling and finite element analysis, NC programming and documentation. A competitor of the Micro VAX is Daisy with Logician VX.

The SUN-3 family from the Ascot-based Sun Microsystems is built around the 32-bit 68020 processor, and is claimed to be twice the speed of a DEC VAX 11/780 and 0.7 the speed of DEC's top-end 8600 supermini.

13.4.2 Main memory and mass storage

1 Definition

All computer systems must have facilities for storing information. The main memory (working memory or immediate access store) is where all or part of the programs and data are held whilst in use. The main memory needed in CAD/CAM systems is mostly Random-Access Memory (RAM) and partly Read-Only Memory (ROM). Mass storage (or secondary, backing, back-up storage) is necessary for almost all CAD/CAM systems.

2 Sizes

The capacity for memory and storage of microcomputer CAD/CAM systems varies, but typical sizes are as follows:

	Main memory		Mass storage		
	ROM	RAM	Magnetic tape	Floppy disk	Hard disk
8-bit microcomputer	< 16 K	64 K	~ 3 M	125 K–1.5 M	4–20 M
16-bit microcomputer	64–128 K	256–512 K	~ 40 M	125 K–1.5 M	20–70 M
32-bit microcomputer	< 0.5 M	1–5 M	~ 145 M	125 K–1.5 M	70–160 M

3 Costs

The cost of semiconductor memories is falling each year. This is due to the ability of semiconductor manufacturers to pack more memory onto one chip. Memory costs used to be a significant factor in a computer system, but with the increasing size of memory on a single chip and the consequent reduction in unit memory cost, memory is no longer a major cost consideration. The cost of magnetic tape and disk is also falling each year.

4 Speeds

RAM is used for the temporary storage of programs and data which can be randomly accessed by the microprocessor at speeds limited only by the access time of memory chips. This access time can be as short as 125 μs for some memory devices. In CAD/CAM applications, a large and fast main memory is desirable since programs can be accessed without overlaying, thus reducing the processing time for large programs. Furthermore, large amounts of data can be processed quickly, which is particularly useful in many CAD areas such as in 3-D data transformations. Some microcomputers are capable of processing at 2–35 MIPS.

5 Winchester disk and floppy disk

Winchester disks are non-removable disks and capable of storing up to 160 M bytes of programs and data with transfer rates of up to 8 m byte/s and an average access time of 30 μs. The common type of mass storage found on microcomputers is the floppy disk. The biggest disadvantage of the floppy disk is the maximum storage capacity being limited to 1.5 M, which is not adequate for some CAD/CAM applications. Floppy disks are removable and are suitable for permanent storage of programs or data files. The most suitable medium for permanent records is the magnetic tape of 3 M bytes capacity. A drive unit for the magnetic tape cassette is inexpensive. Hard disks based on Winchester technology are generally thought to be the best solution for mass storage, although it has a more expensive drive than that for a floppy disk. The Winchester disk units are approximately two to three times the cost of a floppy disk, but their performance is at least an order of magnitude better and therefore represents a much more cost-effective and practical disk system for CAD/CAM application.

13.4.3 Input devices

The digitizer is a common method of input in a CAD/CAM system, although the keyboard has been a traditional, but not very ergonomic, method of input. Sometimes a joystick, a tracking ball or a tracking mouse are used instead of a digitizer. A light pen can only be used with refresh display devices, which are now seldom found because of the high cost.

1 Digitizer

A high-resolution digitizing board with either a cursor or a pen allows direct input, to a computer, of data from an outline drawing in the form of digital coordinates. The digitizer board looks similar to a traditional drawing board and is underlayed by a fine measurement grid. The positions on the board are indicated either by a pen or by a cursor. The pen or cursor contains a switch which enables the user to register x, y coordinates at any desired position identified on the digitizing tablet. A low-resolution digitizing board is often used in conjunction with a graphic terminal. The face of the board corresponds to the face of the display terminal. The user may point to areas on the face of the board with a pen, and the position of the selected area may be transmitted to the computer and displayed on the screen. Part of the digitizing board is often divided into areas which are called function blocks, or menus. The use of a menu eliminates the need for typing and greatly speeds up data input. Menus can be called up in a hierarchical fashion. The digitizer is particularly suitable for interactive design because it allows the designer to work naturally with a pen in hand.

2 *Joystick, tracking ball and mouse*
A joystick is an analogue, lever-operated, two-axis control device, similar to an aircraft control column. Motions of the joystick may be considered as an x, y coordinate reference frame. The cursor of the display screen can be moved directly by the joystick. A trigger switch can be incorporated in the joystick for inputting on/off commands. The joystick is popular for computer games.

A tracking ball is an alternative to the joystick. It comprises a sphere mounted on rollers. The ball can be rolled with the palm of the hand, causing potentionmeters attached to the roller to turn. Thus, it is possible to roll the cursor around the screen.

A mouse has a ball or two sets of wheels on its underside which rotate when the mouse is moved along a surface, and which determine the cursor position on the display screen.

A command menu instructs the computer what to do, but it does not always specify where on the display to execute the instruction. To specify the position, a joystick, tracking ball or mouse can be used instead of a digitizer to move a cursor to any position on the face of the display screen.

3 *Keyboard*
The traditional input device for a computer has been the keyboard. Graphics can be input from a keyboard by using a range of primitives to build up complex shapes. A primitive can be called from memory via a keyboard instruction and then given a precise dimension. This method of inputting data is more satisfactory for CAD/CAM applications than using a digitizer because the keyboard gives the high precision required for many geometrical data. This method of inputting data is basic for 3-D geometric design.

Some digitizer boards have areas allocated to 'keyboard' use which are identified by the pen, mouse or puck.

4 *Light pen*
A light pen can be used as an input device for drawing or moving items on a display screen. The tip of the pen is connected to a photo-cell by a fibre optic bundle and then to the computer. Once the computer has detected the spot at which the pen is pointing, it generates a cross on the screen to inform the designer that this point has been detected.

The keyboard is the basic device for inputting data and instructions, and a digitizer is a popular device for CAD/CAM systems.

13.4.4 Output devices

1 Video terminals (monitors)
The main output device is the monitor. In recent years there has been a move towards the refreshed graphics display, which uses a cathode ray tube (CRT) similar to that of a television set, because these devices provide colour and are now of low cost and are improving in resolution. In these devices the computer now takes over the picture refreshing, and local primitive editing can be carried out. The standard resolution is 640 × 400, but a resolution of 1024 × 1448 on a 20-inch tube is now available.

2 Printers
Hard copy output for alphanumeric output is normally provided by a serial printer. Some of the modern printers can also give a graphics output, providing a useful combined alphanumeric/graphics hard copy unit. This type of device is low in cost and can satisfy many of the CAD graphics requirements.

3 Plotters
There are five basic types of plotter available.

The *drum plotter*, which is one of the most common, in which the paper is wrapped round a drum which rotates. The pen moves in an axial direction along the drum surface.

The *flatbed plotter*, which is used when increased drawing accuracy is desirable. In some cases it can be tilted so that it assumes the position of a conventional drawing board.

The *photoplotter* includes a light source for producing an image on photosensitive media and is suitable for the production of printed circuit masters.

The *electrostatic plotter* consists of an electronic dot matrix, which can print dots onto charge-sensitive paper in a similar way to an electrostatic duplicator

The *ink jet plotter* is a raster device which can product full-colour, chaded pictures, by squirting fine controlled ink jets onto the paper.

Drum and flatbed plotters are common for CAD/CAM applications.

13.4.5 Communcations interfaces
The communications capability of each of the microsystems can be expanded. There are now a number of international standards for communication bus systems. These bus systems fall into two categories. The serial bus (asynchronous and synchronous) and the paralle bus (real time). The main difference between these two bus systems is that in a serial bus discrete bits, constituting a character, are sent serially, while in parallel transfers these items of information are sent simultaneously.

1 The serial bus

The most common serial bus standard is the EIA-RS 232, asynchronous communcation standard. The bus uses plus and minus 12 volt pulses to perform information transfers. The maximum rate of data transfer is 2×10^4 bits/s over a wire length of 30 m. Most microcomputer manufacturers produce a variety of special-purpose programmable chips for communication interfaces using this standard.

The RS 232 standard is an adequate choice for relatively low-speed data communication between local workstations in a CAD/CAM applications area. The RS 422 standard is another serial bus interfacing standard.

2 The parallel bus

The parallel communications system is much more specialized than serial systems, but its use is becoming significant as multi-microcomputer systems develop in CAD/CAM systems. The most widely adopted parallel bus standard for communcation between microcomputers is the IEEE 488 system.

Many manufacturers provide modem units to enable the microsystems to communicate with remote terminals and systems over standard telephone lines.

13.5 THE SOFTWARE

13.5.1 Operating systems

The task of an operating system is to supervise the computer, software, and peripherals. It is most important and probably the most complex program on the computer system.

PC DOS (the Disk Operating System) is the most popular operating system for the IBM Personal computer.

The Micro VMS operating system is a general-purpose virtual-memory operating system for the Micro VAX.

In order that CAD/CAM has the widest possible expansion capabilities for the future, an operating system should enjoy wide support among software development companies.

The UNIX operating system is proprietary to Bell Laboratories Inc., and was developed independently of any particular manufacturer. At present it is the strongest hope for a standard operating system for CAD/CAM. Many software companies are porting UNIX onto their machines which already include microcomputers based on the Motorola 68000 and the Zilog 8001 microprocessors, DEC's VAX range, the IBM 370, and others. Once the impetus towards UNIX gets under way, in the engineering sphere, the problem of CAD/CAM software being associated with particular hardware will hopefully tend to disappear. Many years ago, system developers had some reservations about UNIX as a standard operating system, but this resistance is quickly breaking down. The other most popular operating systems are MS-DOS and CP/M-86.

13.5.2 High-level languages

High-level languages take the words and symbols entered by the programmer and translate them into a series of binary codes that the computer can understand. When the computer is ready to output information in high-level language it translates the internal binary codes into a language which is programmer-readable. Different applications may require different methods of programming. This accounts for the growth of many different programming languages.

At the present time, most CAD/CAM programs are written in FORTRAN, although there are other languages now which would be better for the task. FORTRAN is the standard language for CAD/CAM in industry because of the wealth of existing engineering software already written in FORTRAN. FORTRAN IV is a fast, one-pass, optimizing compiler that implements an extended superset of the 1966 ANSI standard for FORTRAN. FORTRAN IV works efficiently on small-memory environments and is capable of producing absolute binary code for loading into ROM memory. FORTRAN-77 is built on an ANSI subset of the ANSI FORTRAN 1978 standard. FORTRAN is the most widely used programming language for developing programs dealing with scientific applications. There are several other languages which should be supported by a CAD/CAM engineering workstation, e.g. C, Logo, and Basic.

Various CAD/CAM system suppliers provide their own general-purpose programming languages (macro languages) for graphics, producing user-specific graphics software, e.g. Computervision's CV MAP.

13.5.3 Database management software

Information management software provides an integrated system of data management for CAD/CAM. Computer Aided Design and Manufacturing activities, which include draughting, 3-D milling, finite element analysis, machine tool programming, production planning, etc., should share a common data base. Many companies now store details of products on computer files. The graphical data can be stored along with the alphanumeric data to provide a very powerful database system for products.

The success of a database depends on the method of structuring the data and in the speed at which information can be entered and retrieved. There are now many methods of storing data. A tree-like structure is popular; it contains pointers so that a user can quickly trace a path through the database to the required information. A graphics display can be used to great advantage because large amounts of information can be quickly displayed, so making use of mass visual sensing to assist in decision-making. A sequential organization of a database is not suitable for CAD application.

Computer disk filing systems
There are three types of disk data file:

Work file	High speed	Random access	Image format
Semi-permanent file	Medium speed	Sequential access	Binary format
Permanent file	Low speed	Sequential access	ASC II format

Work files are ideal for the temporary storage of volumes of data too large to be held in core. Semi-permanent files can be deleted. It is intended that these should be used for the storage of work files over periods of days or weeks. Permanent files are for archival data, and are usually on magnetic tape.

13.5.4 Micro CAD application software

There are several different types of microcomputer-aided design software, falling into the following categories:

Period	Microcomputer	CAD application software		Typical package
1970–80	8–16-bit	2-D drawing software		Auto-CAD
1981–85	16-bit or 32-bit	3-D modelling	Wireframe	Personal designer
			Surface	Personal designer
			Solid	Applicon MDSI
1986–	32-bit	FEM simulation and robotics		Applicon MDSI

1 Two-dimensional draughting software

The most simple 2-D draughting software can offer 2-D draughting and plotting facilities. Most draughting software can be used interactively.

The more sophisticated 2-D draughting software allows parametric symbol creation, and some software includes powerful facilities for manipulating drawing data and interfacing them with other software such as CAM, stress analysis, etc.

2 Three-dimensional modelling software

Geometric modelling is now assuming a major importance in manufacturing industries which require a precise geometrical description of the product. Mechanical products are 3-D objects and are sometimes complex in form. It is difficult to represent a 3-D shape adequately in a 2-D graphics screen, and the software to perform this task is necessarily very complex. 3-D modelling software is a very useful tool, as it gives the user a real-life visualization of the product. 3-D software can be classified into three categories: wireframe modelling, surface modelling, and solid modelling.

Wireframe modelling software can run on 16-bit microcomputers. Simple surface modelling software can also run on 16-bit microcomputers. Complex surface modelling software requires a 32-bit microcomputer, and solid modelling is computationally-intensive and requires a 32-bit processing capacity for interactive response.

3 Finite element software

The Finite Element Method (FEM) is now widely used for the analysis of engineering problems, as accurate structural analysis is an important part of the engineering design process in many engineering industries, including civil, mechanical, aerospace, automative, ships, petrochemical and offshore structure design.

With the development of computational geometry, especially surface modelling techniques used to express complex forms of products, and with the arrival of high-speed digital computers, it has become possible to produce accurate solutions to a wide range of previously insoluble problems. FEM has now been widely used and intensively developed. Many CAD/CAM system suppliers provide FEM software which is widely used in the aerospace, defence, and civil and mechanical engineering industries, in both large- and medium-sized companies.

More recently, with the development of the microcomputer and the removal of the mystique which once surrounded this method, the applications of FEM have become available to small-sized companies.

13.5.5 Microcomputer CAM application software

1 Three generations of programming languages

First generation of NC programming language

APT (Automatically Programmed Tools) is a programming language which allows geometrical data to be specified together with tool motion statements for any NC machine. One of APT's biggest advantages is that it has become a worldwide standard for NC machines. Several variations of APT have been developed.

APT is a very large program, normally resident on a large storage unit, and runs mainly on mainframe computers. APT is a typical first-generation programming language. When APT was developed, the use of computers in design and manufacture was considered as two separate activities with no apparent link between them.

Second generation of NC programming language

Over the past ten years many manufacturing companies have become increasingly aware of the importance of linking design and manufacture. The availability of powerful mini-computers and associated graphics facilities has resulted in a number of relatively low-cost CAD/CAM systems which use a common database for design and manufacture. A number of firms now offer such CAD/CAM systems, e.g. Computervision. The CV (Computervision) system CADDS (Computer Aided Design and Drafting System) is based on the use of interactive graphics facilities for inputting and editing geometrical data into a 3-D database from which all outputs and part-programs compatible with the APT cutter location data can be generated. The system supports a set of geometrical elements similar in their format to the APT language.

Most of the other available CAM system software works on a similar principle to that of Computervision.

At this stage, CV system hardware is based on a 16-bit minicomputer.

Third generation of NC programming language
Microcomputers have provided NC tape for many years, and this is a relatively simple task. Many 2-D draughting systems can now be linked to CAM software to provide NC tape. A widely applied and typical software linked CAM is Auto CAD.

CAD/CAM system manufacturers now provide integrated CAD/CAM software systems running on microcomputers. Recently, the Computervision company has introduced CAM software running on IBM PC XT, or AT, which covers most of the functions which were originally performed by the CV minicomputer system.

Some powerful integrated CAD/CAM software systems will run on the new micro VAX computers.

The third-generation integrated microcomputer CAD/CAM systems are getting cheaper and more powerful.

2 Processor and post-processor
An NC programming language system consists of two parts: the processor and the post-processor. The processor produces NC output called the cutter location data (CLDATA), which specify the location of the cutter tip centre point. These data are then normally passed to a post-processor which converts generalized CLDATA into a specific numerical code for a specific machine tool/NC controller combination. The NC processor is usually a large program whereas the post-processor is usually small.

3 Software for specific applications
There are now a large number of microcomputer CAD/CAM software packages designed for specific applications, produced both by software suppliers and by users.

13.6 A TYPICAL TURNKEY MICROCOMPUTER CAD/CAM SYSTEM

13.6.1 Computervision's Personal Designer
Computervision's (CV) Personal Designer is a typical microcomputer CAD/CAM system.

1 Hardware
   IBM PC XT or AT.
   16-bit processor.
   Long-persistence colour monitor.
   High-resolution display driver (640 X 400 pixels).
   Serial communications part.
   12″ X 12″ digitizing tablet.
   Additional graphics hardware.
   Hewlett-Packard (HP) plotter size E.

2 Software
   PC DOS operation system.
   BASIC language.
   Micro CADDS Geometric Construction and Detailing (GCD).

Micro CADDS Surface Modelling.
MSC/Pal Finite Element Analysis.
NC programming.

3 *Features and functions*

The Personal Designer combines the benefits of Computervision's software with the IBM XT or AT Personal Computer and allows various third-party software packages to be run. Personal Designer is based on many of the concepts used in the larger Computervision system's CADDS application software, which has been developed and perfected over 15 years in more than 2000 installations world-wide.

All standard IBM and third-party software packages, including word processing, spread sheet, and engineering analysis, will run on the Personal Designer.

The Personal Designer software offers geometric construction and editing tools, including points, lines, arcs, circles, fillets and strings (continuous line segments). Other design elements include text dimensions (point, linear, angular, radial), cross-hitching, properties (non-graphic information associated with specific geometric elements), labels, line fents and 16 colours.

Libraries of frequently used objects can be created and the display can be manipulated. To view 3-D geometry more easily, the user can specify multiple views and can size pre-defined orthogonal views. Users interact with the system via a tablet with a defined menu square that can eliminate the need to enter commands from the keyboard. The English-like commands are very powerful but simple to use.

The Personal Designer supports the MSC/Pal Finite Element Analysis, which is a full 3-D implementation of the finite element method for mechanical design. Its users can accurately and swiftly analyse relatively simple mechanical systems. MSC/Pal also enables users to analyse variable cross-sectional rectangular beams and plates.

Personal Designer is suitable for the desk of very engineering professional.

Users can also network together Personal Designer systems and interconnect them with Computervison's Designer and the large CDS series, as well as other common computers such as IBM and DEC VAX. Personal Designer makes the benefits of CAD available in areas that were previously limited by cost.

13.6.2 Intergraph's Micro II system

Intergraph has announced its Micro II system based on DEC's Micro VAX II, which is one of the powerful 32-bit microcomputers used in the CAD/CAM environment.

1 *Hardware*

32-bit processor on a chip.
64 K byte ROM.
1-M byte, 2-M byte, or 4-M byte additional memory.
31-M byte or 71-M byte fixed 5.25″ Winchester disk subsystem.
2 × 400-K byte diskette subsystem.
95 M Cartridge streaming tape.
Q-bus interface.
Asynchronous and synchronous communications.

2 Software

Operating system: DEC offers users a choice of Operative Systems (OS) to help users address different classes of problem.

Micro VMS is the general-purpose OS for multi-user, real time, and time sharing. It can be used in both the general-purpose multi-function and the multi-user environments. It is a fully compatible modular version of the VAX/VMS operating system.

Micro VAX ULTRIX-32 M is a stand-alone operating system based on the UNIX operating system for the multi-user development environment.

3 Features and functions

The Micro VAX II microcomputer is the newest member of DEC's 32-bit VAX family of computer systems. Its virtual memory allows users to write programs without concern for the specific location of data in physical memory. Overlaps are a thing of the past; programs can be larger than the physical memory allocated to each user. Applications with high-level floating-point demands can obtain faster execution speed with the addition of the Micro VAX II floating-point unit.

The micro VAX is a powerful workstation for mechanical design in CAD/CAM environments and gives users software compatibility with larger VAX systems.

13.6.3 List of microcomputer CAD/CAM systems

Software	Supplier	Hardware	Supplier
Personal Designer	Computervision	IBM PC AT	IBM
Micro II system	Intergraph	Micro VAX II	DEC
Interpro 32 (workstation)	Intergraph	Micro VAX II	DEC
Micro-Cadam	IBM	IBM-PC	IBM
Aria-II (workstation)	Applicon	Micro VAX II	DEC
Graftec	Calma	Micro VAX or Apollo	DEC

The CAD market is still dominated by a few large US turnkey suppliers, principally Computervision, IBM, Intergraph, Calma, and Applicon. These five suppliers between them probably have some 81 per cent of the total market, but some significant changes are taking place. One of the most important things has been the rapid growth of a number of start-up companies offering microcomputer CAD/CAM systems.

13.7 CHOOSING A MICROCOMPUTER CAD/CAM SYSTEM

A company should consider the following aspects when selecting a microcomputer CAD/CAM system.

13.7.1 Turnkey systems

A turnkey CAD/CAM system is a package of compatible hardware and software (which may or may not be from the same manufacturer) which is sold as a complete ready-to-use system.

Maintenance and support are usually provided by the turnkey system vendor. If the user buys hardware and software separately, the maintenance and support may be shared between hardware and software suppliers, which can cause problems.

The stability of the vendor company is absolutely essential for the future support of a CAD/CAM system. The vendor company must have a sound financial backing and an established customer base.

Some vendor's literature and product specifications are very informative, but users have to remember that they were written as an aid to marketing the product and not specifically to give the information users need. Vendor's literature will always avoid the discussion of the areas in which the product is weak and will concentrate on the more obvious features, or where the company feels safe in stretching its claims for a system.

The user's requirements are often a complex mix of wants and needs. Needs are what is required to make the CAD/CAM system perform to the user's objective requirement specification, whereas wants are very much tied up with emotions and are what the user would like to have. Any vendor will tell you that it is the wants that are concentrated upon, because if sales were targeted at needs there would be a very significant drop in the rate of sales success. When specifying what is needed in a CAD/CAM system, customers have to make a conscious effort to separate their needs from their wants.

13.7.2 Key facilities

When choosing a micro CAD/CAM system, there are eleven key items about which the user should ask the prospective supplier.

The microprocessor: 16-bit or 32-bit.
Main memory: size of ROM and RAM.
Mass storage: size of fixed disk; size of floppy disk.
Digitizer: functions and resolution.
Monitor: size and resolution.
Plotter: type, size and precision.
Communications interfaces.
Operating system: micro UNIX.
High-level language.
Database management software.
Micro CAD/CAM software.

13.7.3 Key capabilities

When choosing a micro CAD/CAM system there are four key capabilities that the user should ask the prospective supplier about. They are:

    Maintenance capabilities.
    Expansion capabilities.
    Compatibility capabilities.
    Network capabilities.

Microcomputer CAD/CAM systems are getting cheaper yet more powerful. They are designed to work in ordinary offices and do not need the clear-air environment demanded by many mainframe and minicomputer installations. A 'Computer Room' becomes a thing of the past. They have opened up need sectors of the CAD/CAM market. The microcomputer CAD/CAM systems are probably the most significant advance in engineering design and manufacture in modern times. They will have a major effect on design and manufacture for larger, medium and small companies.

13.8 THE FUTURE OF MICROCOMPUTER CAD/CAM SYSTEMS

13.8.1 Future hardware development

32-bit microprocessors
Many years ago, the lack of processing power of the 8-bit microprocessor caused deficiencies in executing arithmetic operations required for the effective manipulation of design and manufacturing data. Microcomputers have more recently employed 16-bit microprocessors which make the processing power comparable with some minicomputers. Modern microcomputers now employ 32-bit microprocessors which make the processing power better than some minicomputers. New powerful 32-bit systems will be increasingly used over the next few years.

Mass storage
In the past, the mass storage capability of microcomputers was based on floppy disk systems, which have a physical limit on storage capacity. Microcomputer systems have now taken advantage of hard-disk systems like the Winchester. The density of information which can be stored on a magnetic disk is increasing at a rapid rate. Other mass storage media look set to play a part in CAD/CAM systems, such as laser disks or bubble memories.

Monitoring
In recent years there has been a move towards the refreshed graphics display. Modern monitors now provide a high resolution of 1024 × 1448. Flat-screen solid state displays will replace the CRT in the next 10 years.

Input and output devices
All of the different types of input and output devices which are used on minicomputer systems can equally well be used on microcomputer systems. In recent years there has

been a trend towards using microcomputers more effectively so that peripherals could be simplified and therefore reduced in cost. Voice input is coming soon and will replace the keyboard for many input operations.

13.8.2 Future software development
1. Communications interfaces standardization.
2. UNIX operating system: this is now one of the best operating systems for micro-computers and the strongest hope for a standard operating system for CAD/CAM.
3. High-level languages: in the past, the absence of high-level scientific languages on microcomputers made it difficult for engineers to develop application software, but now high-level languages such as FORTRAN and PASCAL can be compiled and run on a microcomputer.
4. The 'C' language will be the future language in CAD/CAM. Languages will become more natural, i.e. more like English.
5. Database management software standardization.

Application software: artificial intelligence will be used to create Expert Systems, which will greatly assist the engineer with different design tasks. It is now possible to allow the designer to visualize design concepts before starting detailed work and produce a complete and unambiguous description of a design with geometric precision.

CAD/CAM system manufacturers are marketing products which are no longer designed to be stand-alone. The majority of the newly developed systems have the ability to link with other aspects of design or manufacture. As this trend continues there will be a gradual swing away from the traditional separation of design and manufacturing activities and a move towards total systems integration.

REFERENCES

[1] Besant, C. B. and Lui, C. W. K., *Computer-Aided Design and Manufacture,* Ellis Horwood, Chichester, 1986.

[2] Haigh, M. J., *An Introduction to Computer-Aided Design and Manufacture,* Blackwell Scientific Publications, Oxford, 1985.

[3] Newman, W. M. and Sproull, R. F., *Principles of Interactive Computer Graphics,* McGraw-Hill, Maidenhead, 1979.

[4] Mini—micro systems, *Special Report: Technology,* Cahners Publication, Dec. (1982).

[5] Osland, C. and Hopgood, B., *Standard Progress,* Systems International, Jan. (1985).

[6] Fellows, J. W., *All About CAD/CAM,* Sigma Technical Press Wilmslow, Cheshire, 1983.

14

Recent Developments of Surface Modelling (B.J. Davies)

14.1 THE CAPABILITIES OF ADVANCED SURFACE MODELLING

Advanced surface modelling should offer a complete capability for defining, analysing and manipulating complex surfaces. There are some general criteria or characteristics to consider when choosing a surface modeller as follows:

- surface definition model
- surface definition procedure
- surface generation
- surface editing
- surface data extraction
- surface display
- surface software compatibility

14.1.1 Surface definition model

The choice of mathematical method greatly influences the overall capabilities of the surface modelling system, together with its data structure and algorithms. In recent years the number of available methods has continued to grow. However, in practice most CAD systems have concentrated on implementing one or other of the specialized surface methods. The most important thing is that the surface method must provide shape flexibility. We often see that a new surface modeller usually employs a newly developed surface method so that CAD/CAM users have a choice of surface methods.

14.1.2 Surface definition procedure

A surface can be defined either by using free-form design techniques (i.e. design mode) or by directly entering data points describing an existing product (i.e. fitting mode).

In the design mode, the designer sketches a set of vertices of the characteristic polygon for curves, or a net of vertices of characteristic polyhedra for surfaces. From the coordinates of these vertices, the surface modeller automatically interpolates a curve or a surface. The system should provide great freedom in modelling to achieve smooth and aesthetic surfaces. In the fitting mode, the designer uses a 3-D digitizing technique to measure data coordinates from an existing model or an actual product. Generally, a 3-D coordinate measuring machine is used to identify points on the model, and these data are transferred to the system. Sometimes, the designer uses drawings of a product to read the coordinate data of sections of the product. Recently, coordinate data have been generated by using industrial photogrammetric equipment. Once the data are input, the system should perform interpolation calculations and automatically generate the complex surface. This mode of data input is especially useful for modifying existing products, for testing products, or for preparing data for tool-path programming. The least-squares fitting algorithm calculates a 'low energy curve' which smoothes the surface between data points taken from a rough model or product.

14.1.3 Surface generation

The system should provide multiple choice methods to generate a surface, i.e.

- Generating a surface over multiple cross-sections. This is the most usual method.
- Four-boundary definition — surface bordered by four curves or lines, according to the 'flattest' principle.
- Three-boundary definition — surface bordered by three boundaries.
- Two -boundary definition — ruled surfaces created between two curves.
- Surface of revolution — rotating the curve about an axis of revolution.
- Tabulated cylinder — projecting the curve along a vector.
- Sweep surface — the surfaces can be defined by the edges of some given surfaces, profiles or a series of guide curves.

Complex sculptured surface models often include many surface faces pieced together in a curved composition. The system capabilities for joining and analysing surfaces are:

- Blend or transition area between two sections. The system automatically blends a perfectly fitted curved surface between two existing surfaces — connecting two end boundaries or two internal curves.
- Fillet between two surfaces. The operator can specify the fillet radius. The system generates fillets between planar or curved surfaces.
- Matching adjoining surfaces. The two surfaces can be matched at the same tangency along the common boundary.
- Comparison of two adjoining surfaces. The information about the tangency of the two surfaces along the common boundary can be obtained.

- Intersection between a surface and a curve, plane or another surface can be calculated.
- Offset surface. A surface can be offset from another surface representing the entire surface area or a discrete portion at a constant or varying distance.
- Shrink surface. A shrunken surface can be obtained by offsetting the boundary lines of existing surfaces.

14.1.4 Surface editing

Surface modelling should provide a full complement of editing features including:

- Moving a vertex or changing coordinate data. The system should automatically regenerate the new surface.
- Trimming. The system should trim a surface to a user-specified boundary.
- Imposing internal boundaries. This is useful for defining holes or cut-outs on a surface.

14.1.5 Surface data extraction

Surface data are stored in the database, allowing the operator to make a variety of enquiries. The operator can select any information developed by surface models, including:

- Any point coordinates X, Y, Z and parameters U, W.
- Normal and tangent vectors.
- Area of a surface.
- Volume (given thickness).
- Area of a cross-section.
- Arc length of a curve.
- Centroid of a surface.

14.1.6 Surface display

There are four types of visiual checking of the design on the terminal screen:

- Wireframe. Surface models are sometimes included in wireframe systems where a wireframe can reflect the shape of the surface.
- Mesh. Changing the density of the surface mesh allows the operator to re-paint the model to see more detail with a finer mesh.
- Shading. The system enables the designer to specify the viewing angle and light source.
- Colour. Systems can provide many colours on high-resolution screens.

Usually, a system can perform all the display generation functions, including zoom and rotate and other graphics operations. All of these capabilities enhance visual checking of the design and provide a realistic representation of a product.

14.1.7 Surface software compatibility

As part of a CAD/CAM system, surface modelling software should be fully compatible with other software, for example:

- Finite element analysis software automatically generates nodes on the surface, eliminating redundant data input and ensuring model accuracy.
- NC programming software automatically generates tool paths for surface machining.
- Technical documentation publication software can extract surface information.
- Other surface modelling can exchange surface information with the surface modelling.

All these facilities should be provided by an advanced surface modeller.

Computervision's Advanced Surface Design package is used as an example of the creation of a complex surface model. Two types of product are considered. The intake of an engine is shown in Fig. 14.1. It contains two parts, the top port and bottom port. The short segments in the figure are the signs of each surface patch. The fitting mode was used for this example.

A cream cleanser bottle is shown in Fig. 14.2. The shape is defined by the boundaries. The design mode was used for this example.

14.2 RECENT DEVELOPMENTS OF ADVANCED SURFACE MODELLING

14.2.1 Method development

The problem of selection of the mathematical method is undoubtedly a key one for any surface modelling system. In recent years the number of available methods has continued to grow. The application of the B-spline continues to grow and is very popular in CAGD, but the use of the B-spline has its limitations:

- Too much work is involved in calculating the intersection between two curves, between two surfaces and between a curve and a surface, and the process is slow.
- The finished designs cannot be treated conveniently in a systematic way, because of the heterogeneity of the models in the different stages of design, displaying and plotting.

The development of the discrete B-spline offers a satisfactory solution to these two problems. Moreover, it makes piecewise treatments and local adjustments much easier. Since the discrete B-spline expresses and treats the continuous B-spline by the discrete form method, it is especially suitable for the interactive design by computer. While the discrete B-spline is mainly concerned with the application of the B-spline in engineering by discrete treatment, the multivariate B-spline offers the possibility of further development.

Based on a solid theoretical foundation, the B-spline method is developing further both in theory and in application. It is a very promising geometrical tool for designing. It

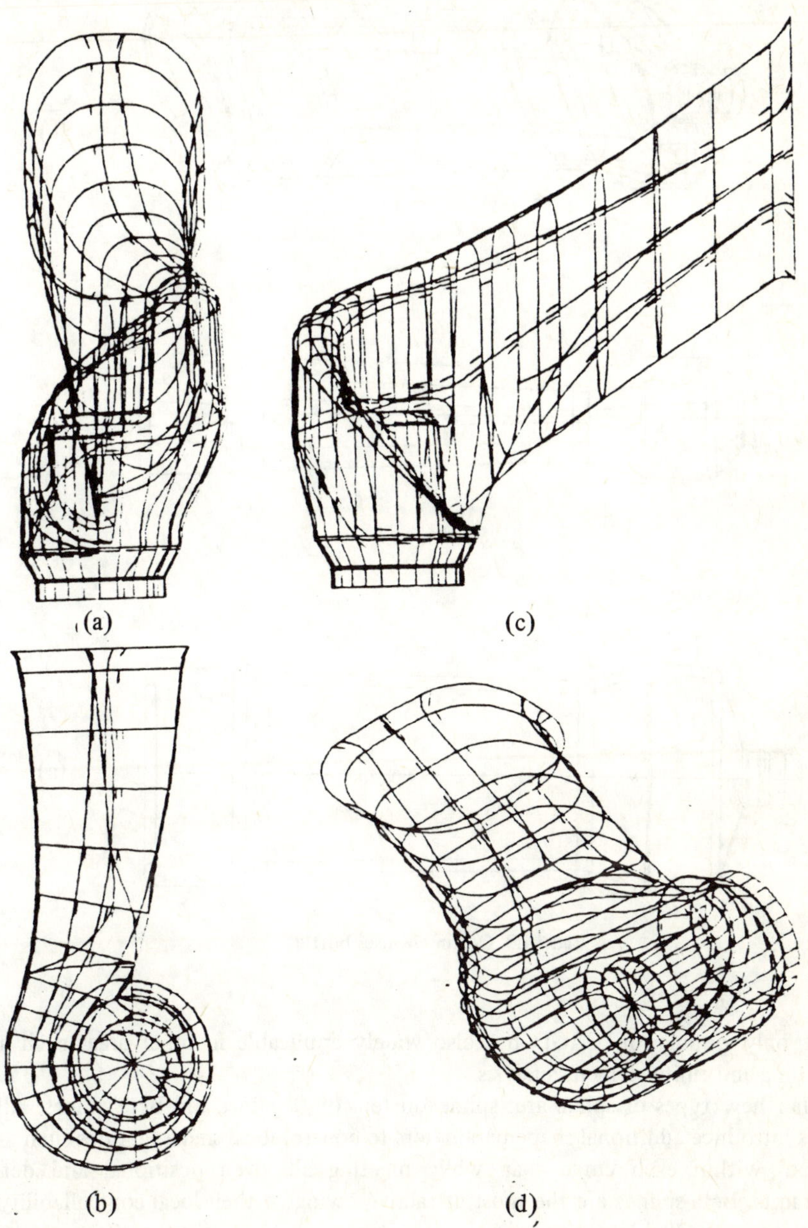

Fig. 14.1 Intake of an engine

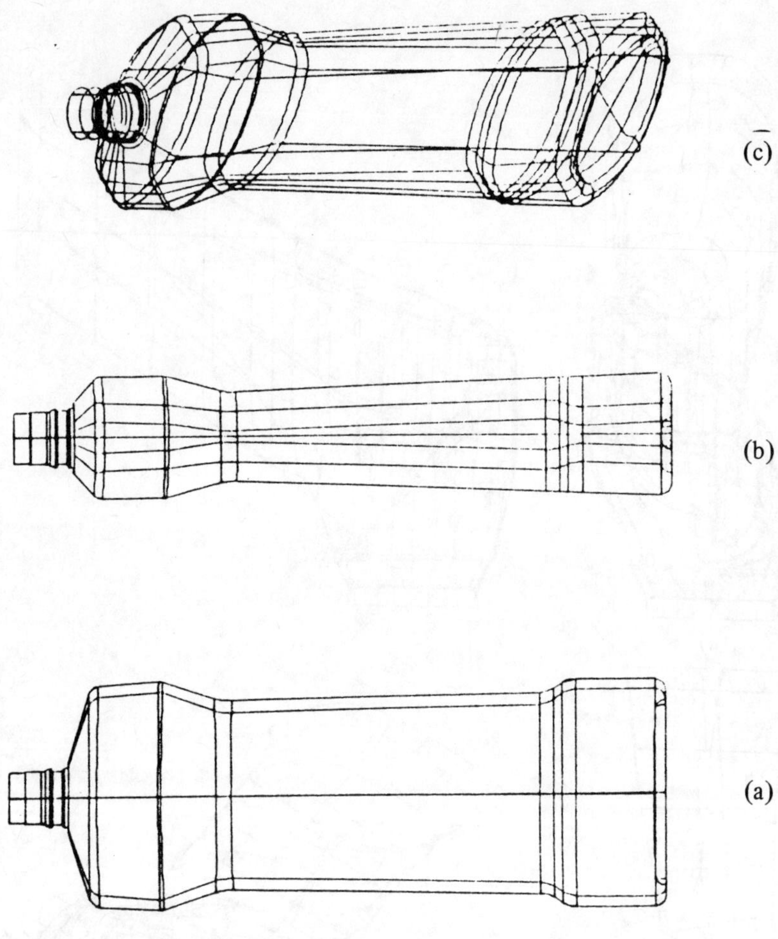

Fig. 14.2 Cream cleanser bottle

is not only popular in CAGD but also widely applicable in other areas such as data processing and finite element analysis.

Other new types of spline are: splines in tension, ν-plines and Beta-splines. All these splines introduce additional shape parameters to control local shape features such as curve 'tension' within each curve span while meeting all given positional and derivative constraints. Beta-splines are the most attractive owing to their local controllability; their shapes are controlled in each span by two parameters. Note that the different modelling approaches have a large common basis so that transition from one scheme to another appears feasible. This will facilitate exploiting the advantages of several modelling schemes in different stages of the same modelling system. Using some forms of fuzzy geometry we may be able to provide a logical mathematical framework for handling the most complex of shapes.

The surface patches described have all been topologically rectangular, i.e. defined in terms of four boundary curves. Sometimes there is a need for using a topologically triangular patch. In this case, a three-sided patch may be obtained by allowing the length of one boundary curve to tend to zero. Such a patch is said to be degnerate. Note that composite surfaces based entirely on triangular elements are in common use for the numerical solution of certain variational problems by the finite element method. The triangular patch mesh is increasingly used in CAD systems supporting finite element analysis (FEA).

14.2.2 Unified surface and solid modelling

A major trend that is beginning to make an impact on future system development is the emergence of a new generation of very powerful unified surface and solid modellers which promise to become the basic building blocks for a future CAD system. Until recently an engineer in mechanical engineering has had to decide on the level of CAD/CAM system which will suit his requirements, which could be a 2-D drafting, 3-D wireframe, sculptured surfaces or a solid modelling system. This situation is now changing. New sytems are being offered which have been designed around a complete and unambiguous single mathematical representation, such as the rational B-spline.

The B-spline form is defined by straight polynomials, but a generalization of the straight polynomial produces the rational B-spline form.

The rational B-spline form has the following advantages:

- It contains a greater supply of shapes than straight polynomials.
- Conic sections can be represented exactly by the rational cubic B-spline.
- Simple matrix representations exist in homogeneous coordinates.

The rational B-spline in modelling provides greater flexibility of shapes for all geometric entities from ruled surfaces through sculptured surfaces to solid modelling.

Great care has been taken with the associated geometric database and with the intelligent user interfaces for driving the systems. The advantages of this sort of system are interactiveness, robustness, unlimited size and integration of graphics with a single data base for complex surface and solid modelling.

Many of these new software systems are being promoted by small start-up companies, but the established vendors also recognize the importance of this new trend. These new systems can overcome current limitations, and meet the functional and accuracy requirements of industry.

14.2.3 Adding artificial intelligence in surface modelling systems

Adding artificial intelligence to surface modelling systems means that the system itself should be able to perform new and more complicated design operations without requiring instructions from a designer on how to do so. The application of the artificial intelligence technique is possible in several directions:

- Development of languages which are as close as possible to natural ones.
- Development of expert systems that allow planning and evaluation of the solution on the basis of a given general problem description, and then choosing automatically the optimal way of achieving the solution.

A prospective geometric modelling system as an important component of CAD should possess a number of functional subsystems with their specific informational resources:

- object formation
- geometric analysis of objects
- modifying and editing of geometric objects
- location of geometric objects on the surface
- optimization of formulation and solution of geometric problems.

Advanced surface modelling incorporating artificial intelligence should include a knowledge base of geometry and a methodology of applicable solutions.

14.2.4 Surface modelling in a microcomputer environment

About ten years ago, surface modelling systems were expensive because they were sophisticated and made heavy demands on the power and resources of a mainframe computer. They were adopted only in the aircraft industries where their use in design and manufacture justifies the high capital costs. IBM's CAD/CAM system developed by Lockheed includes such surface modelling. The user base for CAD/CAM is now very large. Customers for CAD/CAM systems were traditionally the larger organizations requiring fast access to large management information databases and with many sites running hundreds of CAD terminals. Great progress has recently been made in the field of minicomputers and visual display units in computer graphics. Computervision, Intergraph, Applicon and McAuto are, for example, major international minicomputer-based CAD/CAM system suppliers. They provide powerful surface modelling software packages which run on minicomputers. Unfortunately the minicomputer CAD/CAM systems are high-cost systems but have many facilities that the small company can design simple products without.

In the past, microcomputer systems had only poor graphics, slow response, and limited software. Most engineers may be familiar with the conventional microcomputer systems which are used for developing programs and running them. Such systems commonly consist of an 8-bit microprocessor together with ROM and RAM to form the basic computer unit. Mass storage is usually in the form of dual floppy disk units and cassette magnetic tape. The input/output unit is normally a keyboard with an alphanumeric display. Hard-copy output is in the form of a low-cost serial printer. These microcomputers are typically home computers and have limitations when applied to surface modelling tasks.

New microcomputers have modelling capabilities. IBM's Personal Computer system and the micro VAX system are probably the leader products providing 2 MIPS (million instructions per second) of computing power for running surface modelling systems, high-resolution graphics, the Unix operating system, large memory and a user-friendly interface with mouse-controlled windows and multiple windows, mouse-operated icons and pop-up menus, all at a relatively modest price.

Surface modelling systems running on microcomputers are now inexpensive systems, suitable for large-, middle- and small-sized firms. In future the microcomputer system's function will become more and more powerful.

REFERENCES

[1] Kochan, D., *CAM Developments in Computer-integrated Manufacturing*, Springer-Verlag, Berlin, Heidelberg, 1986.

[2] Mortenson, M. E., *Geometric Modelling*, John Wiley & Sons, New York, 1985.

[3] Barnhill, R. E. and Boehm, W., *Surfaces in Computer Aided Geometric Design*, North-Holland, Amsterdam, 1983.

[4] Haigh, M. J., *An Introduction to Computer-aided Design and Manufacture*, Blackwell Scientific Publications, Oxford, 1985.

[5] Schrefler, B. A. and Lewis, R. W., *Microcomputers in Engineering*, Pineridge Press, Swansea, UK, 1986.

[6] Ding, Q.-L., Li, Z. R. and Davis, B. J., Theoretical and experimental investigation of advanced surface modelling, 26 International MTDR Proc., Macmillan, London, 1986, pp. 65–72.

Index

A

accumulated chord length, 91
anti-clockwise, 216
APT, 322
arc length, 225
artificial intelligence, 335

B

Ball, A. A., 176
    Ball curves, 176
    Ball surfaces, 199
    rational Ball curves, 178
    rational Ball surfaces, 199
bending energy, 218
blending function, 82
blending surface, 302
Bernstein polynomials, 112
Bernstein functions, 114
Bertrand curve, 232
Bertrand surface, 240
Bezier, P., 112
    Bezier curve, 113
    Bezier point, 113
    Bezier polygon, 113
    Bezier surface, 135
    Bezier's UNISURF system, 135
    rational Bezier curve, 182
    rational Bezier surface, 198

B-spline, 141
    B-spline curve, 141
    B-spline surface, 168
    rational B-spline curve, 184
    rational B-spline surface, 198
    non-uniform B-spline curve, 158
    non-uniform B-spline surface, 174
bus
    serial bus, 319
    parallel bus, 319

C

CAD/CAM, 49
CAGD, 26, 141
Cartesian coordinates, 259
characteristic polygon, 113
characteristic polyhedron, 133
circle rate, 216
coherence principle, 284
concave segment, 212
convex segment, 212
coons, 134
constraint equation, 259
continuity, 80
CPU, 313
curve, 19
    parametric curve, 21
    polynomial curve, 112
    spline curve, 80, 108

curvature, 29
    normal curvature, 43
    principal curvature, 45
    Gaussian curvature, 46
coefficient matrix, 223

D

database, 298
de Boor, 151
de Casteljau, 112, 272
deformation, 230
degenerate rational curve, 186
distribution, 218
digitizer, 316
directrix, 71
disk
    floppy disk, 315
    hard disk, 315
    Winchester disk, 316
depth comparison, 277
detecting box, 274
determinant, 262
duck, 78

E

elastic beam, 218
elastic plate, 226
energy method, 218
Euler formula, 79

F

Faux, I. D., 89
fairing criteria, 211
fairness, 227
FEM, 322
Ferguson, J. C., 113
    Ferguson patch, 102
    Ferguson–Coons approach, 134
fillet, 330
finish fairing, 212
flexure, 226
Forrest, R., 112
forward difference, 242
Frenet–Serret formulae, 29

G

generalized conic segment, 191
Gordon, W. J., 112, 141, 161

H

Hermite interpolation, 80
Hermite patch, 102
hidden curve, 277
hidden surface, 277
homogeneous coordinate, 179
Horner's rule, 242

I

indicator, 213
inflexion, 215
interactive, 227
interface, 328
interruption, 229
implicit equations, 259
irregular boundaries, 104

J

Jacobian matrix, 262, 263
joystick, 316

K

knot, 151

L

layer, 298
Li Jianxin, 203
linear parameter segment, 192

M

mesh, 225
    rectangular mesh, 267
microprocessor, 313
mode
    3-axis mode, 252
    4-axis mode, 252
    5-axis mode, 252
    drawing mode, 297
    model mode, 297
mouse, 317

N

Newton–Raphson iteration, 260
numerical control, 229

O

odd–even intersection, 282
offset curve, 231
offset surface, 239
on-line query, 299
oscillation, 89
osculating circle, 250

P

parameter, 20
    nature parameter, 26
    polar angle parameter, 96
PC, 176
physical spline, 78

phase
    hunting phase, 269
    tracing phase, 271
    ordering phase, 272
piecewise, 80
pixel, 292
polar coordinate, 97
post processor, 253, 323
Pratt, M. J., 89
projections, 64, 65, 67
    orthogonal projection, 64, 277
    perspective projection, 65, 277
projector, 279

R

RAM, 315
rational curve, 176
rational polynomials, 179
rational surface, 193
rational spline, 193
remainder, 249
Riesenfeld, R. F., 112
ROM, 315
rough fairing, 212

S

Sabin, 108
Schoenberg, I. J., 151
shear force, 213
shading, 331
silhouette curve, 290
simulation, 230
solid modelling, 335
sorting algorithm, 288
spring-back method, 211
strip, 218
subdivision algorithm, 272
support, 218
surface, 36
    bi-cubic surface, 97
    check surface, 251
    composite surface, 108
    developable surface, 72
    drive surface, 251
    part surface, 251
    ruled surface, 69

sculptured surface, 229
surface of revolution, 74
sweep surface, 330

T

tablet, 299
Taylor expansion, 249
tool library, 230
tool offset, 241
tool path, 229
tool vibration, 230
tool wear, 230
tolerance offset, 241
torsion, 31, 34, 226
tracking ball, 316
transformation, 49–64
    concatenated transformation, 63
turnkey system, 312

U

UNIX, 319

V

vector
    curve vector equation, 19
    normal vector, 29
    partial derivative vector, 40
    surface vector equation, 36
    tangent vector, 23
    twist vector, 98
    vector algebra, 19
    vector function, 19
verification, 230
vextex, 113
viewpoint, 65
visibility, 278

W

weight, 197
wireframe, 295, 331
worst data point, 213

Z

Z-buffer, 289